THE
INTERIOR LIFE

SIMPLIFIED AND REDUCED TO ITS FUNDAMENTAL PRINCIPLE

EDITED BY THE

VERY REV. FATHER JOSEPH TISSOT

SUPERIOR-GENERAL OF THE MISSIONARIES OF ST. FRANCIS OF SALES

TRANSLATED BY

W. H. MITCHELL, M.A.

𝕹ihil Obstat.
> HENRICUS S. BOWDEN,
>> Censor Deputatus.

Imprimatur.
> EDM. CAN. SURMONT,
>> Vicarius Generalis.

Westmonasterii,
Die 28 *Maii,* 1913.

TO THE READER

THE pages of this invaluable book are not from my pen; and yet they are mine so far as a religious may venture to say so. Their writer gave them me in manuscript with full liberty to do what I liked with them. Contrary to his expectation, but not without his authority, I decided to have them published as soon as I had pondered them. They had procured me inward enjoyment, and (thank God), I venture to hope, true spiritual profit. I should have blamed myself had I kept them to myself, and I remembered the words of the Wise Man: "I have learned without guile and communicate wisdom without envy; and her riches I hide not."[1]

What, then, did this manuscript contain? Substantially, nothing new; for, starting from the well-known *Fundamental Principle* of St. Ignatius, admirably commented on, it reaches conclusions that the simplest of logic suffices to deduce. But it is just the simplicity and unanswerable logic of the argument, and the astonishing richness of the Scriptural texts wherewith it is corroborated, which have delighted me.

In these latter days, indeed, there is a great dearth of spiritual treatises primarily arresting the intelligence, persuading it by means of reason and faith, and compelling it to set the will towards duty and perfection. How different is the solidity of such a foundation from that of sentimentalism, so much exploited in these days in the service, or rather, to the prejudice, of piety!

Is feeling, then, excluded from these pages? One would think so, on opening them and seeing the author's efforts to reduce it to a secondary rôle. Nevertheless, soon, in the light of his clear and irrefutable teaching, arises a warmth that wins the heart. The great law of love, *Diliges Dominum*, sets free the soul from the returns of selfishness, and pene-

[1] *Wisdom*, vii. 13.

TO THE READER

trates it with a beneficent and ardent activity, free from all admixture, and rich in consolation and unction.

It is thus that, apparently all unconsciously, but really in a way which is eminently logical, this book ascends from the regions of asceticism to those of the freest and surest mysticism. In this way—and herein it seems to me to gain a truly Salesian charm—its doctrine is linked and identified with that of St. Francis of Sales and his best interpreters.[1] We shall find many quotations from the sweet Doctor, and he seems to have inspired the plan and practical deductions of this work in his counsel to the Lady-president Brulart: " We must not judge of things according to our own liking, but according to God's; this is the great thing. If we are holy according to our own will, we shall never be really so; we must be holy according to the will of God."[2]

These few words will explain my humble part in the publication of this book. I beg the reader not to skip a single line of it, beginning with the Preface. This is necessary if he is to get a good grasp of what it teaches, and to appreciate and practise its teaching.

The author, in giving me his work, ingenuously said he was entrusting me with a foundling, and begged me to adopt it. I do so with only one regret—that I have not the honour of being its father. I have baptized it by giving it a name which appears to me appropriate; and I have had the good fortune to find it an eminent god-father in my Bishop, whose approbation, with God's help, will assure the work success.

Annecy, Feast of Our Lady of Good Counsel.

JOSEPH TISSOT,
Missionary of St. Francis of Sales.

[1] Here I am pleased to be able to mention one of St. Francis of Sales' daughters who has best understood their holy Father, the venerated Mère Marie de Sales Chappuis, whose teaching and life are wonderfully in accord with the theories laid down in this book.
[2] Letter, dated, June 8th, 1606.

APPROBATIONS

The Bishop of Annecy

... THIS higher life ... is called the interior life by mystical writers. In it there are two factors, the grace of God and the action of the soul: an action which is subject to great varieties of form and manner, according to character, disposition, habit of mind or impulse of heart, in each individual. The direction of the soul, in this union of its own activity with the graces it receives from God, is therefore a science, and an art. That is why so many books have been written on this subject: the safest and readiest means of procuring for the soul the inexpressible happiness of living inwardly with God, and of beginning the life of heaven by the inner life. Simplicity of procedure, such is the aim of the unknown, but surely thoroughly competent, author of this work, presented to us by the Reverend Father Superior of the Missionaries of St. Francis of Sales, and for which he solicits our approbation: *The Interior Life simplified and reduced to its Fundamental Principle.*

The desire to make the interior life more accessible, by curtailing the often very complicated apparatus wherewith it is surrounded by so many masters of the spiritual life, is certainly an excellent thing: how many souls are kept at a distance by the number of acts which they are asked to perform to live in union with God, by the multiplicity of distinctions and minutiæ of detail! This idea, which was good in itself, has been happily set forth and carried out. We advise and recommend the attentive and repeated reading of this book to priests and people. Priests will find in it much profit to their own progress in the interior life, and clear light for the guidance of souls whose direction is entrusted to them.

Given at Annecy, April 23rd, 1894.

✝ LOUIS,
Bishop of Annecy.

APROBATIONS

His Eminence Cardinal Bourret, Bishop of Rodez

DEAR REVEREND FATHER,

The book you have just published, entitled: *The Interior Life simplified and reduced to its Fundamental Principle*, combats an evil which disfigures piety in many souls; *i.e.*, vague and sentimental religiosity, encumbered with petty practices.

This book concentrates upon one point, the fulfilment of God's will, so much light as to illuminate and inundate it.

The Preface gives a clear outline of its plan. But when, after a very substantial commentary on the *Fundamental Principle* of St. Ignatius, the author rises, by inference, to an analysis of the different degrees of piety, and especially when he speaks of God's good pleasure and of its acceptance, he appears to me to be really new and suggestive.

Filled as it is with Scriptural quotations admirably commented on, and passages from the Fathers and from St. Thomas, this book leaves far behind it all the host of little treatises which are destitute of theology, depth, or unction.

If well digested, it is capable of transforming and sanctifying any aspiring soul who is ready to follow the teachings of logic and of faith.

I believe I am doing a good work in recommending it. . . .

✝ JOSEPH CARD. BOURRET,
Bishop of Rodez.

RODEZ,
June 25th. 1894.

TRANSLATOR'S NOTE

WHILE this translation was in the printer's hands, the late Mr. H. G. Worth, who kindly helped in preparing the manuscript for the Press, was taken from his many sorrowing friends. Some of them may be interested to hear that he was so impressed with the value of the work that he intended, had he been spared, to distribute it as widely as possible, as he agreed with the translator in thinking that such a masterly exposition of typical Catholic asceticism is better calculated to win appreciation for Catholicism from other Christians than brilliant controversial writing. May his wishes for its success be fulfilled !

W. H. M.

ALL SAINTS' DAY, 1912.

PREFACE

1. **Souls are ailing.**—I have no wish to speak of our unhappy society at large, moribund afar from God, bandied about and pulled hither and thither between the two opposite extremes of materialism and occultism. Its bewilderment and agitation and anguish grow keener from day to day, and show how deep the evil is. What now claims my attention is not this society in its reversion from Christianity to paganism, but rather the society which calls and believes itself Christian, and which, as a matter of fact, still adheres to the appearances and practices of a Christian life. Again, in this society, I am rather considering those who are professedly devout, and who, by their position or taste or vocation, are more devoted to the exercises of religion. As I look on these, I see so many whose life is languishing in mediocrity! Anæmia seems to threaten the soul more than the body. Poor staggering souls, they lean for support on a host of petty practices, and never succeed in being able to stand upright! They are like consumptives, afraid of the open air: they know it no longer, and are stifling in the muggy atmosphere of an enervating sentimentalism. Their eyes are blurred by being fastened upon the dimness of books lacking in doctrine and phrases without reality! Of a truth, if they are condemned to such a *régime* as this, it must be because their constitution has been singularly impaired. Many think of improving the *régime*: those who are wise believe that the improvement must be made in the constitution. This, too, is my opinion, and to the best of my limited ability, I would fain try to find some light that may help towards the discovery of the real remedy.

Such is the aim of this little essay. If any soul find therein some ray of light, let him attribute it to Him alone who is all

PREFACE

light and no darkness.[1] Man in himself is always darkness; he is only light in the Lord.[2]

2. Want of substance.—The piety of to-day suffers from a general[3] malady: it is wanting in substance and depth, and is deficient in solidity. In some souls everything is superficial —and it is the same with some books. Must we say that piety has followed the downward progress of the times, or that the decadence of our days is due to the weakening of piety?—I cannot tell. Both are doubtless true. But would it not be equally true to say that the insipidity of the salt has let the world become corrupt? You are the salt of the earth:[4] these words, addressed to the Apostles and to all those who participate in their ministry, also apply to higher souls who, by the bitter strength concealed in piety, are called upon to purify the world and to keep it from corruption. And if the salt has become unsavoury, wherewith shall it be seasoned?

3. Sentimentalism.—However this may be, the evil is the same in both directions. From the region of ideas and principles we have come down to the right earth of the senses and emotions. In public as in private life, in intellectual as in moral life, we are too often in search of emotions, we live too readily according to the senses. Life tends to become animal, and to be merely a succession of sensations. The deep ways of the mind and heart are more and more unknown; romanticism penetrates everything, even piety.

How, indeed, has sentimentalism perverted piety! It has become attached to the mawkish externals which it adorns with the brightest flowers of pseudo-mysticism, feeding on the disturbing illusions of the senses and hiding from many souls, under deceptive appearances, the absolute emptiness that it conceals! so that they often hardly know that they have nothing left but a show of piety, and that they have lost its

---

[1] Quoniam Deus lux est, et tenebræ in eo non sunt ullæ (1 Joan. i. 5).
[2] Eratis enim aliquando tenebræ, nunc autem lux in Domino (Eph. v. 8).
[3] By "general," I mean that it affects both the constitution of piety, and a vast number of souls.
[4] Vos estis sal terræ; quod si sal evanuerit, in quo salietur? (Matt. v. 13).

PREFACE

power.[1] The fascination of trifles has made them lose sight of the deeper good,[2] because they see nothing but seductive superficiality.

4. **Superficiality of life.**—Living by the senses, our life becomes outward, on the surface; we no longer penetrate into the inner depths of the soul. The soul has infinite deeps. "God," it is said, "speaks in the depths of every soul. To listen in these deeps, where truth makes herself heard, and where ideas are gathered, to go by way of piety to the Master within"[3]—how many are there who can do this, or who think of doing it? How many are there who understand the intellectual way whereby God comes to us, and who, in order to find Him, know how to explore the innermost chambers of their own house and the unspotted profundity of their own heart?[4] Unfortunately, we know so little of our inmost being and of how to enter therein! Sometimes we care so little about doing it! And are we not too often afraid to try?

We are satisfied with a cursory and superficial glance, which is enough to maintain a fair amount of outward propriety; but the profound purification of the soul, the progressive transformation of the human life into the divine, the putting off of the old man and the putting on of the new, all this work done deep down we are scarcely acquainted with. We allow these depths to be invaded by all sorts of wretchedness. Self-seeking, which is the abstract of all man's vices and the source of all his sins, very easily comes to terms with this superficial sentimentalism. It is so agreeable to be pleased with oneself—and with God!—And when all goes so well with us on our Thabor, why should we not pitch three tents there?[5] Yes,—only in them will dwell neither Jesus Christ, nor Moses, nor Elias; there, along with our piety of the senses, will abide second-rate virtue, if not sensualism and pride.

---

[1] Speciem quidem pietatis habentes, virtutem autem ejus abnegantes (2 Tim. iii. 5).
[2] Fascinatio nugacitatis obscurat bona (Sap. iv. 12).
[3] Gratry, *Perreyve*.
[4] Intelligam in via immaculata, quando venies ad me. Perambulabam in innocentia cordis mei in medio domus meæ (Ps. c. 2).
[5] Bonum est nos hic esse, faciamus hic tria tabernacula (Matt. xvii. 4).

PREFACE

5. **Ignorance of the depths.**—This is not the place that God has chosen for the uplifting of the heart : the heart takes its rise from deeper down, from the vale of tears.[1] Down there in the depths is the place for the combat and the toil. We must tear out and uproot this self-seeking and self-love which have such a living hold upon the heart, and which have struck such deep root in all directions. It means hard labour and few joys, at any rate for the senses. Yet here, too, there are joys, joys which are more real and in greater fulness. God Himself takes part in the work, and communicates to the worker the gladness of His presence, and this is why he is happy, says the sacred text.

But the senses are unacquainted with these joys ; they perceive the tears and the toil, the pains and the uphill character of the struggle : this is why we instinctively dread the depths in which the work has to be done. It is easy to delude oneself, when, on the one hand, one has no difficulty in finding joys that seem quite pure, and, on the other, one sees a strife which scarcely appears quite necessary !—Moreover, pretexts abound for preferring immediate and easy surface pleasures to the toil and combat of the depths.

And thus occurs what is spoken of by St. John of the Cross. " Many," says he, " from want of knowledge use spiritual goods for the sole satisfaction of the senses, and their spirit therefore remains void. The soul is in great measure corrupted by sensible sweetness, and draws off all the life-giving waters of grace before they reach the spirit, which is left dry and barren. Scarcely one can be found who is not subject to this tyranny of the senses."[2]

6. **External piety.**—Living on the surface of the soul, we come to live on the surface in everything ; for he who knows not how to penetrate within the soul has forgotten how to penetrate into the depths of anything else. He is taken up with externals, and matters of detail become chiefly important to him. Thus in duties and obligations, he sees the letter rather than the spirit, the bark rather than the sap, the body

---

[1] Beatus vir cujus est auxilium abs te, ascensiones in corde suo disposuit in valle lacrymarum, in loco quem posuit (Ps. lxxxiii. 6, 7).
[2] *The Ascent of Mount Carmel* (Book III 32).

rather than the soul. He knows that such and such details are prescribed, and certain others forbidden. He sees the external side of the law, the material fact of the prescription, and this is the only thing to which he attaches a certain amount of importance. He does not see the inward side, the reason and end of the prescription, the spirit of the law; and thus he brings an external and mechanical fidelity to the material observance of the letter which he sees and which killeth, without drawing any inspiration from the spirit which quickeneth,[1] and which he does not see.

We so rarely ask ourselves to what deep needs correspond the observances imposed by the law or introduced by custom! We are no longer acquainted with needs which are deep. Above all we want external agitation and surface sensations; and as these are not to be found in the law, we go on to seek for them in factitious practices which are calculated to produce emotions. In the meantime, so far as what is of obligation is concerned, we are satisfied with keeping a watch upon externals; for this, indeed, costs us less. "The mind dwells in the elementary, in the word only, and does not really enter into the region of thought. For want of piety, the mind neither goes from the word to the idea, nor from the idea to the soul, and still less from the soul to God."[2] And in this way, a soul whose fidelity to external practices leaves nothing to be desired does not make any progress, because it does not enter within where it would draw the water of life; it is like an automaton, the movement of which is regulated throughout, but remains ever the same. This is materialism in piety.

7. **The lessening of souls.**—Being attached to external practices, the soul cannot soar. It is imprisoned, chained, stuck fast. Seeing things in their littleness, it becomes small and cramped. Petty practices make petty souls; for the soul always takes its proportions from the things to which it becomes attached. I become little if I am attached to little things, or rather, to the petty side of things; for even little things have a great side, as great things have a petty

---

[1] Littera occidit, spiritus autem vivificat (2 Cor. iii. 6).
[2] Gratry, *loc. cit.*

side. There are souls who only know how to get attached to the smaller side of things, whether the things be great or small; and hence they become mean and narrow. Others, on the contrary, have ever in view the greater aspects to which they become attached, and which constantly help to make them expand.

In piety, as, indeed, in all other matters, the external is the smaller side. As soon as I give it importance, everything within me begins to get wasted and mean; my spiritual horizon grows narrow, I become the slave of trifles, which check my expansion. I suppose that a few infidelities in things external kill piety, and this is unfortunately true of mine, which is altogether outward. Thus I am faithful to my petty practices and become imprisoned in them: if I neglect them, I have nothing left. This is common experience; and this is why we find unhappy souls constantly playing fast and loose, resuming their practices, forsaking them by degrees, and then coming back to them only to give them up again.

8. **Division.**—Hence spring dissection and division. Our piety drags us through a crowd of incoherent and meaningless details. There is no unity in the soul; its forces are frittered away amidst a host of practices which have no common centre and no higher aim. Nothing is more deplorable than this lack of co-ordination in ideas, of continuity in the will, and of consistency in action. Piety is no longer a living body; it is a series of attempts, fumblings, and hesitations. One would think that there was no compass, so incoherent is the steering of the ship. As a matter of fact, it is wanting: this body is without a soul.

9. **Weakness.**—And what weakness there is! There is no life; it is merely a matter of dragging on. And this, too, in spite of a fair amount of good-will. "I cannot make it out," once said an old veteran in sacerdotal struggles, "the more I go forward, the more I slide back. I think I am making efforts, and that I have already made a great many, and yet, in spite of them all, I feel that I am making less and less progress." I admit these words concealed a certain amount of unconscious humility; yet they contained a good deal of the sad truth which is experienced by many.

PREFACE

" Martha, Martha, thou art careful, and art troubled about many things " (Luke x. 41). Was not multiplicity Martha's misfortune, and yet Jesus loved her, and loved her devotion? But she had too many irons in the fire! Multiplicity distracted her; and by distracting, disturbed her; and by disturbing, troubled her; and by troubling, weakened her; so that she was unequal to her work and was obliged to come and ask for her sister's help. Thus, too, is it with ourselves. The manifold occupations of life and thousands of anxieties about personal matters distract the soul; and the incoherent multiplicity of our devotional exercises, instead of bringing unity, strength, and peace to the soul, add to its evils by scattering, troubling, and weakening it still further. How can we wonder at the languor of souls, when what ought to be their healing and their life only increases the evils from which they suffer?

10. **Building without foundations.**—If we only knew the one thing necessary![1]—If we only thought of building the one house upon the one foundation!—But what can we expect? We build upon the sand.[2] Is it any wonder that the house will not stand? Such winds blow! such floods come down! And when the dilapidated building has almost tumbled to the ground, we go into a retreat to try to prop it up. And like a child, who sees his house of cards collapse and wishes to put it up again, we think about making fresh resolutions and new practices, as external and shallow and incoherent as those which have preceded them, and therefore, as frail, and our building is bound to come to the ground once more when smitten by the winds and the floods. And we do not think of trying to find the rock, we do not endeavour to build upon a solid and deep foundation. Do we even know that our building must have such a foundation?

11. **The enlightening of good-will.**—Is it necessary to say that these remarks are not of universal application and that they do not suit everyone? They indicate defects and do not refer to virtues. It were foolish to attempt to strike a balance

[1] Porro unum est necessarium (Luc. x. 42).
[2] Aedificavit domum suam super arenam, et descendit pluvia, et venerunt flumina, et flaverunt venti, et irruerunt in domum illam, et cecidit, et fuit ruina illius magna (Matt. vii. 26, 27).

between the two. There are many very excellent souls who walk in the true ways of God and who have no need of my poor reflections to find their way to Him. Their own light is far greater than any that they will find here. Yet the work of the ministry proves to me daily that there are souls who deceive themselves and are in ignorance. Such, indeed, are full of good-will, but are exposed to the dangers here indicated, and they inhale the morbid atmosphere of a crowd of false notions which render their piety unhealthy.

If only some small ray of light from this little work might enlighten one of them to some extent !—if it were only to be in some degree remedial and healing !—Then, indeed, would not my work have won too ample a reward ?—But Thou alone, O God, Thou alone canst heal. If there be here anything of Thine, that it is which will give light and healing. Thou alone knowest if there be any such thing in these reflections.—Oh, how consoling would it be, if they really bore some ray of Thy light and love ! This, O my God, is all that they fain would bear ! May they bring it to souls of good-will, souls who err because they are in ignorance.[1] It is to such, above all, that these considerations are addressed ; for, generally speaking, the counsels here given have in view rather those who know not than those who will not ; they tend to the enlightening of good-will rather than to the arousing of evil will.

12. **The foundation of the spiritual life.**—All these evils : sentimentalism, depression, incoherence, division, weakness, have one common source and depend upon the same cause,— a want of foundation. No cure will be effected as long as the attention is not brought to bear upon this essential point, and it is this that I would wish to illumine.

In order to erect a solid building, one must first of all pay attention to the foundations ; for the solidity of the construction will depend upon the foundations. Without foundations, there is nothing solid, nothing strong, and nothing lasting. The important thing, therefore, is to know the foundations of the spiritual life, and to lay them down strongly, and to set the building of perfection solidly on the one basis,

---

[1] —iis qui ignorant et errant (Heb. v. 2).

PREFACE

apart from which nothing living can be erected; for no one can lay any other foundation than that which has been already laid.[1]

It is this one foundation that I desire to point out and bring fully into the light, if I can. I should like to be able to say to souls: Look, there is the one foundation. I should only be too happy if I could add with St. Paul: According to the grace of God, that is given to me, as a wise architect, I have laid the foundation. It is for each one to build thereon; but let him take heed how he buildeth thereupon.[2]

13. This book is only a preface.—But again, I never thought of trying to throw light upon the whole of the foundation of which St. Paul speaks, namely, Jesus Christ: my book would then have grown into a large treatise. The person, indeed, of Jesus Christ, the head and model of all the predestinate, will hardly be directly dealt with in these considerations. This book is only a preface; it is a preparation, which has become necessary, for the return of Jesus Christ to the soul. Our artificial and superficial Christianity leaves Jesus Christ outside and on the surface. And He Himself declares that He wishes to dwell within the soul, and the soul to dwell within Himself.[3] Is not this the point to which souls must be brought back to-day, when so many of them have forgotten the paths of the interior life? When the wood is green, it must first of all be dried; otherwise you get from it nought but choking smoke instead of comforting flame. This book does not in any way pretend to set the fire alight; it only endeavours to prepare a little green wood.

Hence, here will be found elementary reflections, and they will be focussed on only one of the corners of the great building, that which St. Ignatius calls, in his *Exercises*, the *Fundamental Principle*. Everything will be confined to this *unique* and truly *fundamental* idea; all will converge upon this *unity* and this *foundation;* and nothing will be said that is

---

[1] Fundamentum enim aliud nemo potest ponere præter id, quod positum est (1 Cor. iii. 11).
[2] Secundum gratiam Dei quæ data est mihi, ut sapiens architectus fundamentum posui: alius autem superædificat. Unusquisque autem videat quomodo superædificet (1 Cor. iii. 10).
[3] Manete in me: et ego in vobis (Joan. xv. 4)

PREFACE

not directly and immediately relevant thereto. This is why the little work is called—*The Interior Life simplified and reduced to its Fundamental Principle.*

14. **The rod, the root, and the flower.**—Here it will be well to indicate our mode of procedure. From the root of David will rise a rod, and on this rod, a flower, and on this flower will rest the Spirit of God.[1] Under this image Isaias announces Jesus Christ. Now, Jesus Christ is the head and the model of all Christians, and He is the archetype of the spiritual life; what is fitting for Him is fitting, in due proportion, for all that springs from Him.

Moreover, piety is well represented by this same image. It has a root, which is reason; a rod, which is faith; and a flower, which is the spiritual life. Without the root, there will be no rod; without the rod, no flower. The flower rises from the rod, and the rod from the root. The mysterious sap fructifying the root, rises in the rod, and bursts into bloom in the flower. Thus, under the mysterious action of the divine sap which is called grace, reason, which is the root, is fructified; on it rises the rod of faith;[2] and on this rod of faith expands the wonderful flower of the spiritual life. Thus the spiritual life is the flower of faith and reason, it rises as a whole from reason and faith; and all spiritual life which has not this rod and this root, or to speak plainly, all spiritual life which, in its foundations, is not theological and rational, is not the flower upon which rests the Spirit of God.

15. **The importance of the reason in piety.**—This is why we here address the reason in the first place, and very little will be found herein for the feelings To-day so many books exaggerate in the matter of sentiment, that we may here be excused for giving it a very small place. Besides, wishing to

---

[1] Egredietur virga de radice Jesse, et flos de radice ejus ascendet, et requiescet super eum Spiritus Domini (Is. xi. 1, 2).

[2] I say: Faith rises from reason; not, Faith springs from reason. Although faith, being composed of a twofold element, like all that belongs to and comes from the Man-God, springs in reality, so far as it is human, from reason; yet its divine element, which is the chief thing and which springs from grace and revelation, does not allow us to say that faith springs from reason, as we say that Jesus was born of Mary. This assimilation has, at least, never been used in Catholic writings, in order to avoid Pelagianism

PREFACE

go to the foundation and the root, we must go to the reason. In this way a simple syllogism, founded on a rational idea, will suffice to lead us to the ultimate conclusions of the most perfect holiness.

Reason, no doubt, will be enlightened by faith, the root will not be separated from the rod in producing its flower; but it is no less true that this flower of piety appears as the full and perfect blossom of the reason by means of faith. We shall see this in the explanations which follow; we shall see that, in order to be a saint in the strict sense of the term, it would suffice, by God's grace, I do not say, to possess right reason, but to act in accordance with reason; so that, if man has been defined as a rational animal, it must be added that he spends his life irrationally. Piety is the exquisite power of faith and reason; neither reason nor faith find their full bloom except in piety.

16. **Reason and sentimentalism.**—No one, I think, will misunderstand the bearing of the demands here set forth in favour of reason; it is easy to be convinced that they are in no way detrimental to faith or grace, but only to sentimentalism (I was about to say, to animalism, for the two are so nearly related). Sentiment has taken an importance in the guidance of life which does not belong to it either by nature or by grace, and in this way it diminishes both nature and grace.

The intellect is the master-faculty in man, it is this that ought to direct us. It is the intellect which prepares the paths of faith, and it is in the former faculty that dwells this great virtue.[1] When the directive functions of the intellect have been supplanted, not only nature, but faith suffers from it, and the spiritual life is vitiated. This is just what is happening to-day. Sensibiity, which holds the second rank in man's faculties, takes the first place; it even aspires to direct our piety. Thus it is that life becomes a matter of feeling, and faith an impression. Everything becomes animal and material; everything, even the highest of all, declines and sinks; everything tends to become external and empty; everything totters and falls, stagnates and wastes away.

[1] *Cf.* S. Thomas, 2a, 2ae, q. 4, a. 2.

PREFACE

Why?—Because the tree no longer has any roots, the building has no foundation, the mountain has moved from its basis, the body no longer has a soul.

This disorder must be remedied, and we must overthrow the usurpation of sensibility, and restore to the reason its rôle of being the first handmaid of faith. Hence, what we so energetically call for on behalf of the reason is still more called for in the interest of faith and piety. We aim at restoring to both their basis and root, so that they may grow in strength and truth.

17. *How this book is divided.*—Three great ideas sum up this little work: the end, the way, and the means. What is the end of every supernatural life? what is the way? and what are the means? the end towards which it must tend; the way it has to go; the means it should use. To show the one unique and highest end, the way that leads to this end, and the means of walking in this way: such is the threefold object of this work, which is thus divided into three parts.

This is a fundamental division. Most people's interest to-day is concentrated too much upon questions of means. Our ears are incessantly dinned with a multitude of considerations, recommendations, and exhortations, which would lead us to suppose that external practices were the fundamental part of religion. Devotions, confraternities, and sacraments; soon we shall hear nothing else spoken of so far as religion is concerned. All these things are good and, indeed, very good; they are holy and, indeed, very holy; but in their rôle and place. All these things are means, and means are of use only in the way, and the way is useful only towards the end. Questions of means are only questions of the third order in true religion. Questions as to the way come before them and explain them; and questions of the end come first and explain all else, both the way and the means. Without this end, we can understand nothing about the way; and without the way, nothing about the means. The means will pass away, the way will pass away, the end alone will abide.

It is well to put things in their proper place and to restore a little substance and order to our ideas. That is why the

PREFACE

first and most important part is here given to the end, the second deals with the way, and the third treats of the means. This is the logical order of things.

18. **Here we give only the framework of piety.**—These questions will only be dealt with on their great main lines : we shall only give our attention to the most fundamental principles, not going into detail or into their application ; for this would be endless, and would not correspond with the object we have set before us. Here will be found only the broad canvas, or rather, the skeleton and framework of piety. What would a piece of embroidery be without any canvas, a body with no skeleton, a building without a framework ? The piety of to-day is too much like that ; we must come back, then, to the canvas, the skeleton, the timber-work.

For this reason we shall only point out the chief parts and their connexion.

Thus, in the first part, we shall not look, in particular, at any habit, virtue or disposition, that constitutes the interior life. There will be no detailed consideration of acts or virtues, but we shall alone consider the one disposition which focusses and reunites all the rest, in which, therefore, the interior life is summed up and concentrated.

In the same way, in the second part, we shall not study in detail either the commandments or the operations of God ; but we shall concentrate our thoughts upon the divine will, which is the primary rule and the one source of all His commandments and operations.

Lastly, in the third part, will be found no rule or special practice for spiritual exercises, but we shall exclusively give our attention to the conditions of their vital unity.

Any reflecting person will see that nothing seems to be finished ; everywhere he will seem to see toothing-stones ; a great thought is no sooner sketched than we pass on to another. This is done on purpose, so that each one may be forced to build for himself, and to complete in all its parts the great work of which the first outline is here put into his hands. Once more, it is a skeleton which has to be covered with flesh, veins, nerves, muscles and skin, so as to become a complete body.

PREFACE

Jesus Christ is He who is the perfect form[1] and life of this body; He, too, is its clothing[2] and fulfilment. He, indeed, is the real blood that flows in these veins, carrying with it everywhere, even to the utmost extremities, the most perfect forms of life. The perfect form of life is given by Him alone. But His sacred person and His life-giving rôle, as I have said, are here very little touched upon. In a word, there is a canvas, but no embroidery: a skeleton, but not a perfect body: a framework, but not a finished building. Nothing is completed, but everything is in readiness. Only may the preparation be solid enough and strong enough for the erection of a building of the highest value and for the growth of a body of the greatest beauty!

19. **The connexion of the ideas.**—The principles and ideas are here so connected that the reader can only be fully satisfied after having gone right through the whole book in all seriousness. Perhaps, in the beginning, some difficulties may occur to him; I venture to think that they will be cleared up as he reads on. He need only have patience and not allow himself to become systematically confused, but permit the many questions which are raised to arrange themselves at the proper moment in their right order. This is not a book in which one can take a bit here and a bit there at will, and cut it out; all is interdependent and linked together and reciprocal. If you break the chain, you lose the best of the work and will no longer understand it.

20. **Get to the bottom of the fundamental principle.**—Here is a remark of some importance. The fundamental idea may at first sight seem so well known that one may be tempted to pass it over hastily. I beg, however, the reader to weigh it well, and to get as deep a knowledge as possible of it; because it is just from this that the reason will deduce conclusions that are strictly logical and practically important, and which one would be far from suspecting at the outset. It is like some small box of mean appearance, which conceals treasures within. As long as it is unopened, nothing is

---

[1] —quos prædestinavit conformes fieri imaginis Filii sui (Rom. viii. 29).
[2] Induimini Dominum Jesum Christum (Rom. xiii. 14).

PREFACE

known, and it is the same as if nothing were possessed. But, to open it, much searching is needed to discover the secret. Look for this secret, dear reader, and reflect. And, if inside my little box you find some pearl of price, pray to the Giver of every perfect gift, to the Father of lights,[1] not to leave in too great penury the soul of him who tells you of these things.

21. Shut out any notion of methods.—I add a final word. Some, at the outset, may think that they have here a new devotional method. Nothing can be farther from the author's mind. His one aim is to remind people of principles, and he conjures the reader not to look for anything but principles herein, and to shake himself free from anything that appears to him like a method. Principles alone are the foundation, method is merely an accessory. Whoever takes away from this book the least notion of a method will not have obtained any real view of the idea which inspired and governed the work.

I insist on this recommendation, since experience proves every day how many illusions arise from the mania for finding expedients where there are nothing but principles. Souls in the elementary stage of Christian life, and therefore still more those who are superficial, only require expedients; I beg them not to open this book, which is not in any way intended for them; they would not understand it. Deeper souls, whose piety is sincere, feed upon principles; I venture to believe that this book may be of some benefit to them and that they will understand it; in any case, it was written for them.

[1] Omne datum optimum et omne donum perfectum desursum est, descendens a Patre luminum (Jac. i. 17).

CONTENTS

PART I

THE END

	PAGES
TO THE READER	v—vi
APPROBATIONS	vii—viii
PREFACE	xi—xxv
PRELIMINARY—LIFE	3—6

1. Perfect and imperfect life, p. 3.—2. Natural and supernatural life, p. 4.—3. "Increase," p. 4.—4. Christian life, p. 5.—5. Subject of Part I, p. 5.—6. Its divisions, p. 6.

BOOK I. THE ELEMENTS

CHAPTER

I. THE PURPOSE OF CREATION - 8—10

1. God created everything, p. 8.—2. For Himself, p. 8.—3. He is the first principle and the end, p. 9.—4. God's glory is the essential good of His creatures, p. 9.

II. MY END - 10—14

5. God made me, p. 10.—6. For His glory, p. 11.—7. This is all man, p. 11.—8. On earth, p. 12.—9. In heaven, p. 12.—10. For my happiness, p. 13.—11. Union of both ends, p 13.

III. UNION - 14—17

12. The Incarnation, p. 14.—13. The Church eternal, p. 15.—14. Glory by union, p. 15.—15. The difference between glory and union, p. 16.—16. The Saviour's prayer, p. 16.—17. My prayer, p. 17.

IV. THE ORDER OF MY RELATIONS WITH GOD - 17—20

18. The intelligible essence of things, p. 17.—19. Their real essence, p. 18.—20. Is my satisfaction in the essence of things? p. 19.—21. I can lose it, p. 19.

CONTENTS

CHAPTER	PAGES
V. THE DEPENDENCE OF MY SATISFACTION	20—22

22. The joy of heaven, p. 20.—23. My joy in this world, p. 20.—24. Subordinate to God's glory, p. 21.—25. And springs from it, p. 21.—26. The Lord's joy, p. 22.

VI. THE USE OF CREATURES — 22—26

27. Creatures, p. 22.—28. Use, p. 23.—29. Instruments, p. 24.—30. The way to use them, p. 24.—31. For God, p. 25.—32. For myself, p. 25.—33. Here and hereafter, p. 26.

VII. SATISFACTIONS IN CREATURES — 27—29

34. The variety of pleasures in things created, p. 27.—35. The drop of oil, p. 27.—36. Before and after sin, p. 28.—37. Pleasure is merely instrumental, p. 29.

VIII. THE ORDER OF MY RELATIONS WITH CREATURES — 30—33

38. Pleasure, p. 30.—39. Human utility, p. 30.—40. Corporal utility, p. 31.—41. Intellectual and moral utility, p. 31.—42. Divine utility, p. 32.—43. The complete order of the instruments, p. 32.

IX. THE ESSENTIAL ORDER OF CREATION — 33—35

44. Summing up, p. 33.—45. *Quærite primum regnum Dei*, p. 34.—46. My greatness: all things are mine, p. 35.—47. I am God's, p. 35.

X. AN EXPLANATION OF THE PATER NOSTER — 36—40

48. The greatness of this prayer, p. 36.—49. *Hallowed be Thy name*, p. 37.—50. *Thy kingdom come*, p. 37.—51. *Thy will be done*, p. 37.—52. *Give us our bread*, p. 38.—53. The three last petitions, p. 38.—54. All is here, p. 39.

BOOK II. ORGANIZATION

I. MY OBLIGATIONS — 42—46

1. Knowing, willing, acting, p. 42.—2. My mind must know God, p. 42.—3. Truth, p. 43.—4. My heart must love God, p. 43.—5. Charity, p. 44.—6. My action must serve God, p. 45.—7. Liberty, p. 46.

II. THE ESSENCE OF PIETY — 46—50

8. Seeing, loving, and seeking God, p. 46.—9. *Veritatem facientes in charitate*, p. 47.—10. The union of these three operations in piety, p. 48.—11. Other texts, p. 48.—12. The great commandment, p. 49.—13. The definition of the Catechism, p. 49.

CONTENTS

CHAPTER	PAGES
III. The Virtue of Piety	50—54

14. The living unity of my being in piety, p. 50.—15. Facility and readiness, p. 51.—16. Piety is the great disposition, p. 51.—17. The body and the soul of piety, p. 52.—18. It is a matter of the mind, p. 53.—19. The function of sentiment, p. 53.—20. The loss of sensible impressions, p. 54.

IV. God's Glory	55—58

21. What glorifying God means, p. 55.—22. The material and formal elements of glory, p. 55.—23. Intrinsic glory, p. 56.—24. Extrinsic glory, p. 56.—25. The fulness of the word " glory," p. 57.—26. *Crescamus*, p. 57.

V. Zeal	58—61

27. *Multiplicamini*, p. 58.—28. Divine honour, p. 59.—29. The human bond, p. 59.—30. The eternal bond, p. 60.—31. Zeal in one's vocation, p. 61.

VI. Disorder—Adherence to Creatures	61—63

32. The journey far from God, p. 61.—33. Stopping, p. 62.—34. Adherence, p. 62.—35. Rest, p. 63.

VII. Disorder—Attachment to Self	64—66

36. Appropriation, p. 64.—37. Self-seeking, p. 64.—38. The evil is not in satisfaction, but in subversion, p. 65.—39. *Gloria mea nihil est*, p. 65.

VIII. Disorder—Its Effects	66—71

40. Perversion, p. 66.—41. Evil, p. 67.—42. Lies, p. 67.—43. Vanity, p. 68.—44. Slavery, p. 68.—45. Universal groaning, p. 69.—46. Death, p. 70.

IX. Disorder—Its Degrees	71—74

47. The descent, p. 71.—48. Division, p. 71.—49. Domination, p. 72.—50. Exclusion, p. 72.—51. The three stages of evil, p. 73.—52. The three stages of life, p. 73.

X. Avoiding Mortal Sin—The First Degree of Piety	74—78

53. Sin, p. 74.—54. Restoration, p. 75.—55. Habit, p. 75.—56. The multiplicity of actions and the oneness of disposition, p. 76.—57. Eagerness to be avoided, p. 77.—58. The height of this first step, p. 78.

CONTENTS

BOOK III. GROWTH

I. AVOIDING VENIAL SIN — THE SECOND DEGREE OF PIETY — 80–82
1. Sin, p. 80.—2. Its gravity, p. 80.—3. Restoration, p. 81.—4. The height of this step, p. 81.

II. IMPERFECTION—THE DOMINATION OF THE HUMAN — 82–85
5. Its definition, p. 82.—6. The domination of human pleasure, p. 83.—7. What is the harm of it? p. 84.—8. The source of the evil, p. 84.

III. IMPERFECTION—THE ABSENCE OF FORMAL OFFENCE — 85–88
9. The second characteristic of imperfection, p. 85.—10. The transgression of a counsel, p. 86.—11. The non-culpable transgression of a precept, p. 86.—12. "Go behind Me, Satan," p. 86.—13. The Saviour's reasons, p. 87.

IV. IMPERFECTION—ITS EVIL — 88–90
14. Why is not imperfection a sin? p. 88.—15. Its connexion therewith, p. 89.—16. Its frequency, p. 89.—17. Its evil, p. 90.

V. PERFECTION—THE THIRD DEGREE OF PIETY — 90–92
18. Its proper object, p. 90.—19. The scope of the word, p. 91.—20. *Ex toto*, p. 91.—21. Perfection according to St. Francis of Sales, p. 92.

VI. THE STATE OF PERFECTION — 93–95
22. The external state, p. 93.—23. The internal state, p. 93.—24. Religious perfection, p. 94.—25. Episcopal and sacerdotal perfection, p. 94.

VII. PERFECTION AND SACRIFICE — 95–99
26. Perfection is not sacrifice, p. 95.—27. Aberration p. 96.—28. Failure, p. 96.—29. Would not sacrifice be more perfect? p. 97.—30. Sacrifices necessary, p. 97.—31. To what extent? p. 97.—32. The fear of sacrifice, p. 98.

VIII. THE STATE OF MY SOUL — 99–103
33. Where am I? p. 99.—34. Human utility, p. 100.—35. In ordinary life, p. 100.—36. God's interest and mine are not incompatible, p. 101.—37. In the spiritual life, p. 101.—38. If I would only go down deep! p. 102.

CONTENTS

CHAPTER	PAGES
IX. THE GENERAL STATE	103—105

39. The state of society, p. 103.—40. Bible ideas, p. 104.—41. The ages of faith, p. 104.—42. Ideas of to-day, p. 105.

X. THE STATE OF THIS EVIL — 106—108

43. The centre of the evil, p. 106.—44. We do not see or see amiss, p. 106.—45. The worth of sentimental books, p. 107.—46. Dogmas make nations, p. 107.

XI. RESTORATION — 108—112

47. Knowing and seeing, p. 108.—48. The influence of habit on actions, p. 109.—49. The morning intention: its value, p. 109.—50. Actual and habitual intention, p. 110.—51. Complete subversion, p. 111.

BOOK IV. THE SUMMITS

I. HOLINESS—THE FOURTH DEGREE OF PIETY — 114—117

1. Work done and work to do, p. 114.—2. The acts of holiness, p. 115.—3. The state of holiness, p. 115.—4. The greatest glory of God, p. 116.—5. Indifference, p. 116.

II. MYSTICAL DEATH — 117—120

6. The mystery of life and death, p. 117.—7. The human, p. 118.—8. It must die, p. 118.—9. *Seminatur . . . surget*, p. 119.—10. Passing away, p. 119.

III. TRANSFORMATION — 120—122

11. *Quotidie morior*, p. 120.—12. Renewal, p. 120.—13. Rising by degrees, p. 121.—14. The vow of the most perfect and trifles, p. 122.

IV CONSUMMATION—THE FIFTH DEGREE OF PIETY — 123—127

15. The two crowns, p. 123.—16. Immolation, p. 124.—17. The supreme conclusion, p. 124.—18. *Beati mortui*, p. 125.—19. The rational man, p. 126.—20. St. Francis of Sales's wish, p. 127.

V. PURGATORY — 127—130

21. Nothing defiled enters into heaven, p. 127.—22. The duration of purgatory, p. 128.—23. Purification and glorification, p. 128.—24. Glorification stopped, p. 129.—25. Purification continued, p. 129.

CONTENTS

CHAPTER   PAGES

VI. A GENERAL VIEW—UNITY   -   ·   ·   ·   130—134

26. Unity, p. 130.—27. Simplicity, p. 131.—28. Strength, p. 131.—29. Division, p. 132.—30. The three struggles, p. 132.—31. Nothing to give unity, p. 133.

VII. A GENERAL VIEW—PEACE -   ·   ·   ·   134—136

32. Liberty, p. 134.—33. Equanimity, p. 135.—34. Peace, p. 135.—35. Glory and peace, p. 136.

VIII. FOR PRIESTS   ·   -   -   -   -   137—141

36. The duel between the ministry and spiritual exercises, p. 137.—37. The priest seeks self, p. 137.—38. He also seeks the good of others, p. 138.—39. Destroy the common enemy, p. 139.—40. Centre and circumference, p. 140.—41. Exhortation, p. 141.

CONCLUSION   ·   ·   ·   ·   ·   ·   142

PART II

THE WAY

PRELIMINARY—THE WILL OF GOD   ·   ·   145—150

1. Who must mark out the way? p. 145.—2. The kingdom of heaven, p. 145.—3. The two entrances, p. 146.—4. The two wills of God, p. 147.—5. The two dwellings of the Holy Ghost, p. 147.—6. Their union, p. 148.—7. The division of this Part, p. 149.

BOOK I. THE WILL SIGNIFIED

I. COMMANDMENTS AND COUNSELS   -   -   -   152—154

1. Divine manifestations, p. 152.—2. The commandments of God, p. 152.—3. The commandments of the Church, p. 153.—The counsels, p. 153.

II. THE DUTIES OF ONE'S STATE OF LIFE   -   -   154—157

5. Twofold object, p. 154.—6. The application of the commandments, p. 155. — 7. The choice of counsels, p. 155.—8. For priests, p. 156.—9. For religious, p. 156.—10. For laymen, p. 157.

CONTENTS

CHAPTER   PAGES

III. THE KNOWLEDGE OF DUTY—THE GENERAL OBLIGATION - - - - - - 158—160

11. Practical piety, p. 158.—12. Knowing, loving, executing, p. 158.—13. The necessity of knowing one's duty, p. 159.—14. Ignorance, p. 159.—15. Illusion, p. 160.

IV. THE KNOWLEDGE OF DUTY—SPECIAL OBLIGATIONS - 161—164

16. Knowing the commandments, p. 161.—17. The spirit of the commandments, p. 161.—18. Knowing the commandments of the Church, p. 162.—19. Knowing the counsels, p. 162.—20. Knowing the duties of one's state, p. 163.—21. The necessity of direction, p. 164.

V. LOVE AND PRACTICE - - - - 164—167

22. Loving duty, p. 164.—23. The divine yoke, p. 165.—24. Human appearances, p. 165.—25. Fidelity in practice, p. 166.—26. Breadth in fidelity, p. 166.

VI. THE PIETY OF THE PRIEST - - - 167—170

27. Vocations, p. 167.—28. The forms of vocation, p. 168.—29. Liturgy and canon law, the form of sacerdotal piety, p. 168.—30. The good priest knows this, p. 169.—31. The liturgical and canonical spirit, p. 169.

VII. THE PIETY OF THE RELIGIOUS - - - 170—173

32. The piety of the religious has its form in his Rule, p. 170.—33. The religious does not overstep his Rule, p. 171.—34. The rind is hard, p. 172.—35. The book to be eaten, p. 172.

VIII. THE SPIRIT OF PIETY - - - - 173—176

36. The divine encounter, p. 173.—37. Knowing how to pierce the veil, p. 174.—38. Making no distinction between things ordered, p. 174.—39. Leaving my own practices for God's, p. 175.—40. The children of God are born of God, p. 175.

BOOK II. THE WILL OF GOOD PLEASURE

I. DIVINE ACTION - - - - - 178—181

1. In God's arms, and my own little steps, p. 178.—2. God's care for me, p. 178.—3. The fresco, p. 179.—4. All works together for the good of the elect, p. 180.—5. The wonderful appropriateness of God's work, p. 181.

CONTENTS

CHAPTER	PAGES
II. THE PURPOSE OF THE DIVINE OPERATIONS	182—184

    6. God's action, p. 182.—7. His idea, p. 183.—8. His desire, p. 183.—9. *Ipse faciet*, p. 184.

  III. THE TWO MODES OF GOD'S OPERATION   185—188

    10. Putting off and putting on, p. 185.—11. Consolations and trials, p. 186.—12. God's intention, p. 186.—13. The divine effects of joy and sorrow, p. 187.—14. The divine witness of love, p. 187.

  IV. THE PROGRESS OF THE DIVINE WORK   188—192

    15. The needle and the thread, p. 188.—16. The threefold outward denudation, p. 189.—17. The threefold inward denudation, p. 190.—18. Its correspondence with the five degrees of piety, p. 191.—19. God's gifts becoming hindrances, p. 192.

  V. PASSIVE PIETY   193—197

    20. Keeping open, p. 193.—21. Acceptance, p. 194.—22. Recognizing, welcoming, submitting, p. 194.—23. Simple acceptance, p. 195.—24. Peace in acceptance, p. 195.—25. Rest in God, p. 196.—26. The definition of passive piety, p. 197.

  VI. WAITING FOR GOD   197—201

    27. The state of expectation, p. 197.—28. Returning to calmness, p. 198.—29. When God's work is to be known, p. 199.—30. Avoid curiosity, p. 200.—31. Attention and submission, p. 201.—32. The spiritual director, p. 201.

  VII. JOYS AND SUFFERINGS   202—205

    33. The difficulty of accepting consolation well, p. 202.—34. St. John of the Cross advises its rejection, p. 203.—35. The difficulty of accepting suffering well, p. 203.—36. Ask for nothing: refuse nothing, p. 204.

  VIII. "I THANK THEE"   205—208

    37. How to say "I thank Thee," p. 205.—38. The torrent of joy, p. 206.—39. Pain extinguished, p. 207.—40. A wonderful power for progress, p. 207.

  IX. THE ALOES   208—212

    41. Look trial in the face, p. 208.—42. Chew the aloe, p. 209.—43. Shun imaginary suppositions, p. 210.—44. One's eyes on God, and one's feet on the ground, p. 211.—45. Cast all care upon God, p. 211.

CONTENTS

BOOK III. THE CONCURRENCE OF THE TWO WILLS

CHAPTER PAGES

I. THE NECESSITY OF CONCURRENCE — 214—217
  1. Harmony is necessary, p. 214.—2. It is God who worketh, p. 214.—3. By His will of good pleasure, p. 215.—4. In us, p. 215.—5. Both to will, p. 216.—6. And to do, p. 216.

II. THE NATURE OF THE CONCURRENCE — 217—222
  7. The origin and the measure of my action, p. 217.—8. The meeting, p. 218.—9. Union, p. 219.—10. Electricity, p. 220.—11. The divine contact, p. 221.

III. THE DIVINE ALLIANCE — 222—226
  12. Solicitation and union, p. 222.—13. Union grows and becomes complete, p. 222.—14. *Nisi Dominus*, p. 223.—15. *Surgite postquam sederitis*, p. 224.—16. Naturalism, Quietism, Christianity, p. 225.—17. Acceptance, p. 226.

IV. GOD'S ACTION AND MAN'S ACTION — 227—229
  18. God's action is just and eternal, p. 227.—19. Man's action is false and mortal, p. 227.—20. *Nonne homines estis?* p. 228.—21. Christian action, p. 228.

V. DIVINE GUIDANCE — 229—233
  22. God requires duty, p. 229.—23. The whole of duty, p. 230.—24. Nothing but duty, p. 231.—25. Extraordinary ways, p. 231.—26. God performs all our works, p. 232.—27. Not a fatalist nor a quietist, p. 232.

VI. HUMAN RESOLUTIONS: THEIR STERILITY — 233—235
  28. Broken resolutions, p. 233.—29. Human activity, p. 234.—30. Practices of my own choosing, p. 234.—31. Ruins, p. 235.

VII. HUMAN RESOLUTIONS: THEIR FOLLY — 236—238
  32. The example of St. Peter, p. 236.—33. God so well knows my needs, p. 236.—34. I know so little, p. 237.—35. Negligence, p. 237.

VIII. CHRISTIAN RESOLUTIONS — 238—241
  36. The ease of the Christian's walk, p. 238.—37. God's yoke, p. 239.—38. Hope in God, p. 240.—39. Sobriety in resolutions, p. 240.—40. Unity, p. 241.—41 Fitness, p. 241.

CONTENTS

CHAPTER   PAGES

IX. THE FUNDAMENTAL RESOLUTION   •   -   - 242—244

    42. The one primary and governing resolution, p. 242.—
43. No uneasiness as to the present, p. 243.—44. Nor as to the future, p. 243.—45. Prayer for confidence, p. 244.

X. CONCURRENCE RESTORED   -   -   -   - 245—249

    46. Deviation, p. 245.—47. The consequences, p. 245.—48. To be accepted, p. 246.—49. Human contrition, p. 246.—50. Divine detestation, p. 247.—51. Divine reparation, p. 247.—52. Thank Thee, O God! p. 248.

PART III

THE MEANS

PRELIMINARY   -   -   -   -   - 251—254

    1. The necessity of means, p. 251.—2. God's instruments, p. 251.—3. My instruments, p. 252.—4. In Him we live and move and be, p. 253.—5. What is essential and what changes, p. 253.—6. Division, p. 254.

BOOK I. THE PRACTICES OF PENANCE

I. PENANCE   -   -   -   •   - 256—259

    1. Justice, p. 256.—2. Penalties, p. 256.—3. Mercy p. 257.—4. Their union, p. 257.—5. Redemption, p. 258.—6. *Adimpleo quæ desunt . . .*, p. 259.

II. MORTIFICATION AND ITS FUNCTION   -   • 259—264

    7. Lost ease and vigour, p. 259.—8. Expiation and reparation, p. 260.—9. Mortification, p. 260.—10. True and false mortification, p. 261.—11. The hand of Satan and the hand of God, p. 262.—12. The mind of the Church, p. 262.—13. The mind of the saints, p. 263.

III. GENERAL RULES FOR MORTIFICATION   •   - 264—267

    14. Love that destroys and hatred that preserves, p. 264.—15. No cowardly sentimentalism, p. 264.—16. The liberating agent, p. 265.—17. No degrading cruelty, p. 265.—18. Necessary cruelty, p. 266.—19. The remedy, p. 266.—20. The will to be healed, p. 267.

CONTENTS

CHAPTER	PAGES
IV. Special Rules for Mortification	268—271

21. Three kinds of mortification, p. 268.—22. The mortifications of duty, p. 268.—23. Penances occasioned by duty, p. 269.—24. Providential penances, p. 269.—25. The acceptance of death, p. 270.—26. Voluntary penances, p. 270.—27. Penance for others, p. 271.

V. The Function of Self-denial — 272—274

28. Its necessity, p. 272.—29. The evil to be avoided, p. 272.—30. Limits to be observed, p. 273.—31. The good to be gained, p. 274.

VI. The Practice of Self-denial — 274—276

32. Duty, p. 274.—33. The Rule, p. 275.—34. Personal regulations, p. 275.—35. Detachment, p. 276.

VII. The Practice of Humility — 276—279

36. Nothing through self, p. 276.—37. All through God, p. 277.—38. Nothing for self, p. 278.—39. All for God, p. 279.

VIII. The Greatness of Humility — 279—282

40. All and nothing, p. 279.—41. True greatness, p. 280.—42. The humility of the saints, p. 280.—43. Humility, holiness, unity, p. 281.

BOOK II. THE EXERCISES OF PIETY

I. The Purpose of Exercises of Piety — 285—288

1. Their twofold purpose, p. 285.—2. Means of formation, p. 285.—3. If badly used, they are means of deformation, p. 286.—4. The appetite for God, p. 287.—5. Exercises of the mind, the heart, and the senses, p. 288.

II. Pharisaic Regularity — 288—291

6. Outward regularity, p. 288.—7. The flowers of the Church's garden, p. 289.—8. My bouquet, p. 289.—9. Obligatory practices, p. 290.—10. Practices which are of counsel, p. 291.—11. Optional practices, p. 291.

III. Isolation—General Effects — 291—294

12. Definition, p. 291.—13. The drawers, p. 292.—14. Distaste, p. 293.—15. Sterility, p. 293.

CONTENTS

CHAPTER   PAGES

IV. ISOLATION—PARTICULAR EFFECTS   -   -   294—298

16. Meditation partitioned off, p. 294.—17. The mental prayer of the ancients, p. 295.—18. Living meditation, p. 296.—19. Distractions, p. 296.—20. Unity of work and prayer, p. 297.—21. The Psalms, p. 297.

V. INCONSTANCY   -   -   -   -   -   298—301

22. The inconstancy of my fancies, p. 298.—23. And of my too external procedure, p. 299.—24. And of my weakness, p. 300.—25. The remedy: sincerity and confidence, p. 301.

VI. EXAMINATION OF CONSCIENCE   •   •   -   302—306

26. Exercises must possess unity, p. 302.—27. Examination of conscience is the guiding bond of unity, p. 302.—28. The means of unity, p. 303.—29. The witness of the saints, p. 304.—30. Acts are transitory, p. 304.—31. Habits are the strings to strike, p. 305.

VII. THE GLANCE   -   -   -   -   307—309

32. Its easiness, p. 307.—33. Its object, p. 307.—34. It is the substance of self-examination, p. 308.—35. The tap, p. 309.

VIII. THE EXAMINATION INTO DETAILS   -   -   -   310—313

36. The examination into secondary dispositions, p. 310.—37. The process of fructification, p. 310.—38. Self-examination follows and aids the soul's progress, p. 311.—39. It is not a matter of statistics, p. 312.—40. Hunting up details, p. 313.

IX. CONTRITION AND FIRM PURPOSE   -   -   -   314—317

41. Their necessity, p. 314.—42. Perfect contrition, p. 314.—43. Imperfect contrition, p. 315.—44. Rising from one to the other, p. 315.—45. Firm purpose, p. 316.—46. Union of the three elements of the examination of conscience, p. 316.

X. THE DIFFERENT KINDS OF SELF-EXAMINATION   -   317—321

47. The habitual self-examination, p. 317.—48. The general self-examination, its centre and two circumferences, p. 318.—49. The two fundamental questions, p. 319.—50. The particular examen, p. 319.—51. The preliminary examination, p. 320.—52. The facilitation of confession, p. 320

CONTENTS

CHAPTER	PAGES
XI. THE UNITY OF THE EXERCISES	321—326

53. Singleness of eye, p. 321.—54. Self-examination is the eye of the exercises, p. 322.—55. It is the obligatory prolude to meditation, p. 233.—56. And of all the other exercises, p. 323.—57. The presence of God, p. 323.—58. The great means of piety, p. 324.—59. Consult spiritual writers for details of methods, p. 325.

BOOK III. GRACE

I. THE NATURE OF GRACE — 328—331

1. The necessity of a bond, p. 328.—2. Its nature, p. 328.—3. Actual grace, p. 329.—4. Habitual grace, p. 329.—5. The effects of sanctifying grace, p. 330.—6. The two kinds of grace combined, p. 330.

II. THE SOURCE OF GRACE — 332—333

7. The Saviour's merits, p. 332.—8. God's action, p. 332.—9. The reservoirs, p. 333.—10. My action, p. 333.

III. THE NECESSITY OF GRACE — 334—337

11. In general, p. 334.—12. To see, p. 334.—13. To will, p. 335.—14. To act, p. 335.—15. We are not sufficient, p. 336.—16. The new life, p. 337.

IV MY WEAKNESS — 338—340

17. Relying on myself, p. 338.—18. In my knowledge, p. 338.—19. In my will, p. 339.—20. In my activity, p. 339.

V. REMEDIES FOR WEAKNESS — 340—343

21. St. Peter's example, p. 340.—22. Do not wonder, p. 341.—23. Hope, p. 342.—24. Relapses, p. 342.

VI. PRAYER — 343—346

25. All exercises are productive of grace, p. 343.—26. The soul's aspiration and respiration, p. 344.—27. We must pray always, p. 344.—28. Ask in the name of Jesus, p. 345.—29. Why God makes us pray to Him, p. 346.—30. The function of prayer in piety, p. 346.

VII. THE SACRAMENTS — 347—350

31. Sensible signs, p. 347.—32. The seven sacraments, p. 347.—53. The seeds implanted, p. 348.—34. The rights conferred, p. 349.—35. The treasures accumulated, p. 350.

CONTENTS

CHAPTER	PAGES
VIII. THE BLESSED VIRGIN	350—354

36. The Mother of piety, p. 350.—37. *Hail, Mary!* p. 351.—38. *Full of grace*, p. 352.—39. *The Lord is with thee*, p. 352.—40. *Blessed art thou among women*, p. 353.

IX. JESUS CHRIST	354—358

41. Invocation, p. 354.—42. God and man: their union in Jesus Christ, p. 355.—43. In myself, p. 355.—44. In this book, p. 356.—45. Which is only a Preface, p. 357.

X. GENERAL RÉSUMÉ	358—360

46. Unity, p. 358.—47. Life, p. 359.—48. A commandment which lies very close to me, p. 359.—49. An easy way, p. 359.—50. Prayer, p. 360.

SUMMARY OF THE INTERIOR LIFE SIMPLIFIED

PREFACE	363
PART I. THE END	365
BOOK I. THE ELEMENTS	366
BOOK II. ORGANIZATION	369
BOOK III. GROWTH	373
BOOK IV. THE SUMMITS	376
PART II. THE WAY	379
BOOK I. THE WILL SIGNIFIED	380
BOOK II. THE WILL OF GOOD PLEASURE	382
BOOK III. THE CONCURRENCE OF THE TWO WILLS	385
PART III. THE MEANS	387
BOOK I. THE PRACTICES OF PENANCE	388
BOOK II. EXERCISES OF PIETY	390
BOOK III. GRACE	394

PART I
THE END

PRELIMINARY

Life

1. Perfect and imperfect life.—2. Natural and supernatural life.—3. "Increase."—4. Christian life.—5. Subject of Part I.—6. Its divisions.

1. Perfect and imperfect life.—This first part is entitled—THE END; and the end is living, for man was made to live.[1] And it is because I am made to live and this is my end, that it is useful to put at the head of this first part a preliminary section, entitled—*Life*.

And what is living?—It is having within one an activity of one's own, arising from an inward principle, which is capable of developing itself by its own action and of possessing its own development.[2]

There are two kinds of life, perfect and imperfect. The perfect life is that which belongs to a being which is self-possessed and finds its exercise in the fulness of a movement which leaves nothing to be achieved. The absolute fulness of such life is to be found in God alone. The divine act whereby God possesses, knows, and loves Himself in the Trinity of the divine Persons, is an infinite act, and this act is the life of God in Himself.

In heaven, I shall have the fulness of life of which my being has become capable, and I shall possess eternally and changelessly, in one act wherein my whole vital powers will find their exercise, the development which I have acquired. This will be, in my own measure and degree, perfect life.

Here below life is imperfect. And what is imperfect life?—It is the movement of acquisition whereby a being is developed. The internal principle of activity goes on increasing and expanding by its own action. It is a life which forms and builds and organizes itself. The characteristic signs of this

---
[1] Factus est homo in animam viventem (Gen. ii. 7).
[2] *Cf.* S Thomas, *De Potentia*, § 10, a., i., c.

life are acquisition and growth. The growth of an imperfect being is an essential manifestation of its life. And such is the condition of my present life.

2. **Natural and supernatural life.**—I am made to live. What does this mean ?—It means that I am called to develop in myself the fruits of holiness in this world, in order to gain in heaven, as an end, and without end, eternal life.[1] The life of this world is growth, the life of heaven is possession, and both are the proper activity of my being.

I have my soul and my body ; and my soul is itself living a life imparted to it by God ; and my body is living by my soul, which imparts animation thereto. My soul can act, and it acts by means of the faculties which appertain to it. My body can act, and it acts by means of the powers which belong to it, and which are animated and controlled by the soul. The soul has a complete organization of knowing, willing, and acting faculties, and the body has a whole series of organs attached to the faculties of the soul and acting by them. And it is in the action of these faculties and powers that my natural life consists.

By God's grace I have another life, *i.e.*, another capacity for action, which no longer depends upon me, but upon God. This is the supernatural life, whereby God, uniting ineffably with my nature, raises me above myself and imparts to my faculties the power of doing divine acts. Thus He Himself becomes the life of my life, the soul of my soul: a mystery of love ! And this life is supernatural life, *i.e.*, eternal life ;[2] for it is the development on earth of the life I shall enjoy in heaven.

3. "**Increase.**"[3]—I am made to live, and I am made for nothing else. What shall I do in heaven ?—I shall live endlessly in the one act of eternal praise, which is eternally beatifying. What have I to do here below ?—I have to live, *i.e.*, to develop myself, since imperfect life, which is all I now have, consists in self-development. " Increase," said our Lord to man, in giving him the power to develop and com-

---

[1] Habetis fructum vestrum in sanctificationem, finem vero vitam æternam (Rom. vi. 22).
[2] Gratia autem Dei vita æterna in Christo Jesu Domino nostro Rom vi 23).   [3] Crescite (Gen. i. 28).

municate his life. And this is the primal word addressed to man by the Creator. And the plenitude and the majesty of this word contain and express the law of life in its totality. All my obligations, without a single exception, have their basis and explanation in this primary obligation. It is this that gives the meaning and measure of all my duties towards God and creatures and myself. I must increase, I must develop the physical life of my body, the moral life of my heart, the intellectual life of my mind. And this is the reason for taking care and precautions for the maintenance of the body, the education of the heart, and the instruction of the mind. Everyone is bound to work for the acquisition and preservation of the full development of his faculties.

4. **Christian life.**—And this natural development must be ordered by God. The increased faculties must be used as instruments for the supernatural life. " Yield not your members as instruments of iniquity unto sin," says St. Paul, " but present yourselves to God as those that are alive from the dead, and your members as instruments of justice unto God."[1] The supernatural life thus grows in proportion to the development of the natural life and of the perfection of the union of the human with the divine.

It is even its privilege to increase further amidst the inevitable diminutions forced upon nature by the law of death. St. Paul, in the fourth chapter of his second Epistle to the Corinthians, speaks magnificently of this triumph of life even in death. " For which cause," says he, " we faint not: for though our outward man is corrupted: yet the inward man is renewed day by day."[2]

5. **Subject of Part I.**—It is this life, with its increase and results, that I mean to study here. I must live: why? how? whereunto? Life—such is the main, central, synthetic, one idea, in which all others and all our inquiries will end. Life,—but by no means in its little external details or in some

---

[1] Sed neque exhibeatis membra vestra arma iniquitatis peccato; sed exhibete vos Deo, tanquam ex mortis viventes, et membra vestra arma justitiæ Deo (Rom. vi. 13).
[2] Propter quod non deficimus; sed licet is qui foris est noster homo corrumpatur, tamen is qui intus est renovatur de die in diem (2 Cor. iv. 16).

isolated and particular instance, no: life in its highest fulness, in its unity; the interior life, the very title of this book; life supernatural and divine: in a word, my end in its totality and finality, in the great lines of its construction and completion.

The proper subject of this Part I is exclusively life in itself, *i.e.*, that which builds and acquires itself, that which, having once finished its acquisition, will eternally abide: for that is life in its proper sense, and that is the end.

As to the work whereby life is built up, as to its progress and its rules; as to the means, and as to the mode and conditions of their use, although they help towards the building and are indispensable thereto, nevertheless they are not the building itself. The work and its rules pass away; the means and their mode of use pass: the building abides. And here, in this Part I, I intend to consider alone that which abides, that which is the end; the work and the means, as I said in the Preface (§ 17), will be the subjects of the Second and Third Parts.

6. Its divisions.—In what is really the eternal building of my being in God, I shall consider four things:

    1. The elements of the building:
    2. The organization of the elements:
    3. The first developments of the building:
    4. Its higher developments.

Thus this first part will be subdivided into four books:

        I.—The Elements.
        II.—Organization.
        III.—Growth.
        IV.—The Summits.

BOOK I

THE ELEMENTS

In his Epistles, wherein he treats so divinely of the divine life, St. Paul compares it to the building of a house, to the growth of a plant, to the increase of a body. The enlargement of the building, the plant, the body, presupposes principles of organization, and materials for organization.

What are the organic principles, the fundamental principles, that ought to help in the building up of our being? This is what I must know, and mean to know, in the first place. And as I am placed between God and His creatures, having with Him and them relationships which are necessary for my life, the first and fundamental principles of my divine increase are the fundamental relationships which exist between Him, them, and me. And these primary relationships are what I am about to study in this First Book.

isolated and particular instance, no: life in its highest fulness, in its unity; the interior life, the very title of this book; life supernatural and divine: in a word, my end in its totality and finality, in the great lines of its construction and completion.

The proper subject of this Part I is exclusively life in itself, *i.e.*, that which builds and acquires itself, that which, having once finished its acquisition, will eternally abide: for that is life in its proper sense, and that is the end.

As to the work whereby life is built up, as to its progress and its rules; as to the means, and as to the mode and conditions of their use, although they help towards the building and are indispensable thereto, nevertheless they are not the building itself. The work and its rules pass away; the means and their mode of use pass: the building abides. And here, in this Part I, I intend to consider alone that which abides, that which is the end; the work and the means, as I said in the Preface (§ 17), will be the subjects of the Second and Third Parts.

6. Its divisions.—In what is really the eternal building of my being in God, I shall consider four things:

1. The elements of the building:
2. The organization of the elements:
3. The first developments of the building:
4. Its higher developments.

Thus this first part will be subdivided into four books:

I.—The Elements.
II.—Organization.
III.—Growth.
IV.—The Summits.

BOOK I

THE ELEMENTS

In his Epistles, wherein he treats so divinely of the divine life, St. Paul compares it to the building of a house, to the growth of a plant, to the increase of a body. The enlargement of the building, the plant, the body, presupposes principles of organization, and materials for organization.

What are the organic principles, the fundamental principles, that ought to help in the building up of our being ? This is what I must know, and mean to know, in the first place. And as I am placed between God and His creatures, having with Him and them relationships which are necessary for my life, the first and fundamental principles of my divine increase are the fundamental relationships which exist between Him, them, and me. And these primary relationships are what I am about to study in this First Book.

CHAPTER I

The Purpose of Creation

1. God created everything.—2. For Himself.—3. He is the first principle and the end.—4. God's glory is the essential good of His creatures.

1. **God created everything.**—God created all things. All things were made by Him : and without Him was made nothing that was made (John i. 3). For He spoke, and they were made : He commanded, and they were created (Ps. clxviii. 5). It is He who giveth to all life, and breath, and all things (Acts xvii. 25) ; for in Him we live and move, and be (*ibid.* 28).

This is a truth proved to me by reason, and which faith teaches me to adore Yes, O God, Thou hast made all things with Thy word (Wisd. ix. 1), and that alone has been done which Thou hast willed.[1] Thine is the day, and Thine is the night : Thou hast made the morning light and the sun. Thou hast made all the borders of the earth (Ps. lxviii. 16). Thou hast made heaven and earth, and all things that are under the cope of heaven (Esther xiii. 10).

2. **For Himself.**—God Himself that formed the earth, and made it, the very Maker thereof ; He did not create it in vain (Isa. xlv. 18). For the Lord by wisdom hath founded the earth ; He hath established the heavens by prudence (Prov. iii. 19). Yea, Lord, Thou hast made all things in wisdom (Ps. ciii. 24), and Thou hast ordered all things in measure, and number, and weight (Wisd. xi. 21). But it is the property of wisdom to attain all her ends mightily, and to order all things sweetly thereto.[2] God, who is infinite wisdom, has, then, set before Himself an end in the work of creation ; and to this end He has adapted His creatures.

Creatures have an end, they exist for an end. And what

---

[1] Et hoc factum est quod ipse voluisti (Judith ix. 4).
[2] Attingit a fine usque ad finem fortiter et disponit omnia suaviter (Sap. viii. 1).

is this end ?—It can be no other than God Himself. For, if God had created things for any other end than Himself, He would have referred and subordinated His action to that end ; He would have subordinated Himself thereto, since His action is Himself. Thus the end would have been above God Himself, in other words, God would not be God. Hence, God could only create things for Himself ; creatures can only exist for Him and for His glory.

3. **He is the first principle and the end.**—It is I, saith He, I am He that created the heavens, and stretched them out : that established the earth. and the things that spring out of it : that giveth bread to the people upon it, and breath to them that tread thereon. It is I, the Lord, this is My name : I will not give My glory to another.[1] For My own sake, for My own sake will I do it, and I will not give My glory to another. Hearken to Me, O Jacob, and thou, O Israel: I am He ; I am the first, and I am the last.[2] I am the beginning and the end, the Alpha and the Omega, the first and the last (Apoc. i. 8).

Hence it is, therefore, for Himself that the Lord hath made all things (Prov. xvi. 4). All things were made by Him, and all things were made for Him. Nothing exists without Him, nothing exists except for Him. All things come from Him, all things go to Him. He is their one beginning, He is their total end. He is alone their first principle, He is alone their end. He is the first, He is the last. It is impossible for anything to exist without His power, it is impossible for anything to exist otherwise than for His glory. His power is the one *raison d'être* of things, considered as their first principle ; His glory is their one *raison d'être*, considered as their end.

4. **God's glory is the essential good of His creatures.**—If God's glory is the one *raison d'être*, the one end of things, it is also their one good ; for a being cannot have any other

---

[1] Hæc dicit Dominus Deus, creans cœlos et extendens eos, firmans terram et quæ germinant ex ea, dans flatum populo quæ est super eam, et spiritum calcantibus eam. . . . Ego Dominus, hoc est nomen meum ; gloriam meam alteri non dabo (Is. xlii. 5, 8).

[2] Propter me, propter me faciam, ut non blasphemer, et gloriam meam alteri non dabo. Audi me Jacob, et Israel quem ego voco ; ego ipse, ego primus, et ego novissimus (Is. xlviii. 11, 12).

essential good than its one end. The good is what every creature desires and tries to find; but what every creature thus desires and tries to find is its end. Its end is, therefore, for every creature its own true good.[1] And, since God's glory is the one essential end of His creatures, it is also their one true good. " The one and sovereign good is called the end," says St. Augustine, " just because for the sake of this we wish for all other things, but we wish for itself, only for its own sake."[2] The means for reaching the end are only good so far as they help towards this end. In the means, there is no true good except that which leads on to the end.

N.B.—The word " essential " is here always used in its most absolute philosophical sense. It will never be used except to denote that which is of the very essence of things, *i.e.*, that which, in creatures and in their relations, is of such necessity, that without it, the creatures and their relations would not exist.

CHAPTER II

My End

5. God made me.—6. For His glory.—7. This is all man.—8. On earth.—9. In heaven.—10. For my happiness.—11. Union of both ends.

5. God made me.—All things were made by God, therefore I, too, was made by Him. It is He who has made me, not I who have made myself.[3] Thy hands have made me, and fashioned me wholly round about (Job x. 8). Concerning the creation of the first man, God said: Let us make man to our image and likeness: and let him have dominion over the fishes of the sea, and the fowls of the air, and the beasts, and the whole earth, and every creeping creature that moveth upon the earth. And God created man to His own image

---

[1] Cum bonum sit quod omnia appetunt, hoc autem habeat rationem finis, manifestum est quod bonum rationem finis importat (S. Thomas I. q. 5, a. 4, c).

[2] Ideo quippe et finis dictus est summum bonum, quia propter hunc cætera volumus, ipsum autem nonnisi propter ipsum (S. Aug., *De Civit. Dei*, viii. 8).

[3] Ipse fecit nos, et non ipsi nos (Ps. xcix. 3).

(Gen. i. 26, 27). And the Lord God formed man of the slime of the earth: and breathed into his face the breath of life, and man became a living soul (Gen. xxxiii. 7).

The masterpiece of visible creation, the image of God, man is the last and the supreme link in the chain of terrestrial beings, the term of the work of creation. Possessing a material body and a spiritual soul, he touches both the visible and the invisible world. Bearing in his body the likeness of inferior beings, bearing in his soul the likeness of God Himself, he is placed between creation and the Creator as the meeting-place of matter and spirit, the link between heaven and earth.

6. **For His glory.**—But why has God created me?—All things were made for God, therefore I, too, am made for Him, solely for Him. He is alone my essential end, my total end; He is the entire reason of my existence, the sole purpose of my life. I have no other *raison d'être* than His glory. I only exist to procure this one good for Him. It is for Him, for Him alone that I live, it is for Him that I die, it is for Him that I shall live world without end. It is not for myself that I live, it is not for myself that I die; for none of us liveth for himself. For whether we live, we live unto the Lord; or whether we die, we die unto the Lord. Therefore whether we live or whether we die, we are the Lord's (Rom. xiv. 7, 8).

And every one that calleth upon My name, saith the Lord, I have created Him for My glory, and it is for this that I have formed him and made him.[1]

7. **This is all man.**—God's glory is the whole purpose of my life, it is my all, the whole of me; for if I do not procure it, I have no more *raison d'être*, I am good for nothing, and am nothing. Let us hear together the conclusion of the discourse. Fear God, and keep His commandments: for this is all man (Eccles. xii. 13). This is all man! How, asks St. Augustine, can we put a more wholesome truth into fewer words? Fear God, and keep His commandments: this is all man. All man, indeed, is there: this is true of everyone: he is a *keeper* of God's commandments; if he is not that, he is nothing. The

---

[1] Et omnem qui invocat nomen meum, in gloriam meam creavi eum, formavi eum et feci eum (Is. xliii. 7).

image of the truth cannot be refashioned in him in whom dwells the likeness of vanity.[1]

This is all man, whether on earth or in heaven, all his mortal life, and all his eternal life. For I have this twofold destiny in time and in eternity; or rather, my one destiny is made up of two periods, for time prepares for eternity. I am made to live for a time in this world and to grow up in it, in order to live afterwards in the mansions of eternity, possessing in immutable fulness the complete growth to which I shall have attained.

8. On earth.—Then, why must I grow on earth?—For God and His glory. All the powers and capacities I have received, all the obligations and laws that are binding on me, all the means and helps given me, all these have in view this final, high, absolute, infinite goal — the glorification of God's sovereign Majesty. My soul and my body, my mind, my heart and my senses, my days and my nights, my activities and my repose, my life and my death, all these must praise God. This is all man, the whole of his life, the plenitude of his existence. Further on, I shall see still better the immense scope and the profound meaning of this expression—this is ALL man. It is thereby that he is something: it is thereby that he *is*. Apart from that, he is nothing, he has no being. It is thereby that he attains full growth: and apart from that, his life becomes void, and wastes away.

9. In heaven.—This is all man in heaven. For what are the saints doing in the splendour of glory?—One thing only, even that which they had begun in their life of transition— they praise God. Heaven resounds with nothing but the chants of sacred praise, which re-echoes on every side. This is the chant that suffices both angels and men; and of itself it fills all eternity. In the unity of Jesus Christ's body, all the elect unite to extol in endless concert the name of the thrice holy Trinity. Each one has his part in the universal concert, according to the qualities of his life and vocation;

---

[1] Quid brevius, verius, salubrius dici potuit? Deum time, inquit, et mandata ejus serva, hoc est enim omnis homo. Quicumque enim est, hoc est, custos utique mandatorum Dei; quoniam qui hoc non est, nihil est, Non enim ad veritatis imaginem reformatur remanens in similitudine vanitatis (S. Aug., *De Civit. Dei*, xx. 3).

each one has his place assigned to him in the great body. And all together, harmoniously ordered, correspond with one another in the marvellous *entente* which composes the eternal communion of saints, and gather up their life in the supreme hymn which delights the divine heart.—This is eternal life! Oh, how shall we then find in all its fulness the whole meaning of the expression of the sacred text—this is all man!

10. For my happiness.—In creating me for Himself, God manifests to me the essential love which He has for Himself. God is love (1 John iv. 8), and He has created everything by love: by love for Himself before all, and thus it is that He has made all for His glory. But His work of creation was also for the love of me, and thus it is that He has made all things for my happiness. My happiness—this is the secondary end of my creation. I am made for happiness, this, too, is an end of my being; all that is within me aspires to happiness; desires, demands, seeks happiness; it is my nature's irresistible need. Whether I will or no, whether deliberately or instinctively, I am always seeking my own satisfaction, because God has thus ordered my being. Satisfaction in this world, satisfaction in eternity, this need is so deep that infinity alone can fill it to the full. My senses, my soul, my heart, my mind, everything within me, is made for happiness. God intends me to find, even in this world, a host of satisfactions in my life's progress towards Him, in my acquisition of the being which constitutes my temporal existence; and finally, in eternity, the one, infinite, ultimate, complete repose of my whole being, which is called salvation. Happiness in this world, happiness in the next, this, too, is my end.

11. The union of both ends. — Have I, then, two ends assigned to my existence?—Yes, and No. Yes, for in my life there are God's part and my part, His rights and my hopes. No, for these two ends must, according to the divine idea, be so blended into one that the supreme and final term of my existence is my consummation in the unity which is in God.[1]

God has done what He intended to do; and He intended to

---

[1] Ut sint consummati in unum (Joan. xvii. 23).

unite my happiness to His own honour; He intended to beatify me in glorifying Himself; thus He has united His interest with mine, my life with His, my being with His own. I have thus two purposes of my existence; and these two purposes are but one; for God has so joined them that my felicity is finally found solely in Him. What He puts forward as the final end of His work is my eternal union with Himself, my consummation in unity with Him for His glory and for my happiness. He wishes Himself to be the life of my life, the soul of my soul, the all of my being: He wishes to glorify Himself in me and to beatify me in Himself. The wonders of this unity and the means for realizing it are what I here desire to meditate upon.

CHAPTER III

Union

12 The Incarnation.—13. The Church eternal.—14. Glory by union.—15. The difference between glory and union.—16. The Saviour's prayer.—17. My prayer.

12. The Incarnation.—" God knew from all eternity," says St. Francis of Sales, " that He could make an innumerable quantity of creatures of different perfections and qualities, and that He could communicate Himself to them. And, considering that amidst all the various ways of communicating Himself, there was none so excellent as to unite with some created being in such wise that its nature should be, as it were, made one entity with, and subsisting in the Divinity so as to make therewith one single person; His infinite goodness . . . resolved and determined to make one in this manner."[1]

" Now, among all the creatures which this sovereign power could bring forth, He thought good to choose the same human nature that afterwards was, in fact, united to the person of God the Son, designing to give it the incomparable honour of personal union with His divine Majesty, in order that it might

[1] St. Francis of Sales, *Traité de l'Amour de Dieu*. Book II 4.

eternally enjoy in the most excellent way the treasures of His infinite glory."

" Then, having thus preferred the sacred humanity of our Saviour to this happiness, supreme Providence ordained not to confine His loving-kindness to the single person of His well-beloved Son, but to spread it on His behalf amidst many other creatures. And amongst the mass of this innumerable quantity of things which He could have brought forth, He chose to create men and angels, as it were to keep His Son company, to participate in His graces and in His glory, and to adore and praise Him everlastingly."

13. **The Church eternal.**—What is first in the intention is that which is realized in the last term of the execution. Now, that which will be the terminal result of the whole work of creation, its final crown, will be the Church eternal. The Church eternal, *i.e.*, the society of angels and saints, joined together in the unity of the great body of Jesus Christ : He, God and man, being their head ; they, angels or men only, but participating in Him and by Him in the divine life. This is the body of the elect, which will sing the great praises intended and desired by God the Creator. Each of the elect, whether angel or man, there has his place and function according to his vocation. And since each one will perform in the universal concert the part assigned to him, the resultant harmony will be the delight of all eternity and the bliss of heaven.

It is of this society that I am already now an associate by grace, and I shall be eventually incorporated in it by glory. I shall have my own part in the eternal song. Here I am getting ready, I am practising, I am acquiring an aptitude for this beatific praise. I shall sing of God with all the more plenitude and perfection, the better I have worked down here on the development of my life for God and according to God.

14. **Glory by union.**—It is, then, by Jesus Christ, with Him and in Him, that all honour and glory must be given to God the Father in the unity of the Holy Ghost.[1] Thus, presiding over the work of creation, there are, as it were, two divine ideas. One general, absolute, anterior to everything else,

---

[1] Per ipsum, et cum ipso, et in ipso, est tibi Deo Patri omnipotenti, in unitate Spiritus Sancti, omnis honor et gloria (*Canon Missæ*).

expressed in these words—God's glory. The other special, free, putting the former into concrete and particular shape, expressed in the word—union. It is through the special mode of union with God in Jesus Christ that I am called to praise God. And in this union will be my felicity.

In absolute principle, no potential creature can be of any use finally except to proclaim God's glory. As a matter of fact, every creature actually called into being must help to procure God's honour by the special mode of union. Hence, God's glory by union in Jesus Christ, such is the last word of the idea of creation.

15. The difference between glory and union.—Nevertheless, the two terms of this idea in its totality remain distinct : glory remains the aim essentially laid down ; union, the mode freely proposed for the attainment of this aim. And, in the reality of things, these two parts of the one creative idea will emphasize the fact that they are eternally distinct. For there will be beings called to divine union who will never attain to it. Will they not glorify God ?—Yes, they will certainly glorify Him, but in a different mode from that to which they have refused to rise. They will have lost the honour and happiness of beatific union, but God will lose none of His glory. He will be glorified in the damned ; but He will be glorified by their subjection to avenging punishment, instead of being glorified by their union with His beatitude. The mode which was freely and mercifully offered for eternal praise will be found to be changed, and the praise itself will be ultimately rediscovered in its absolutely and fundamentally imperishable character.

16. The Saviour's prayer.—Glory through union in Him, this is, indeed, what is asked for in the final prayer of Him who is the first-born of every creature, and who came into this world to speak the last word on everything, and revealed to us His Father's secrets. " And not for them [My Apostles] only do I pray, but for them also who through their word shall believe in Me : that they all may be one. As Thou, Father, in Me, and I in Thee, that they also may be one in Us ; and that the world may believe that Thou hast sent Me. And the glory which Thou hast given Me, I have given to

them : that they may be one, as We also are one. I in them, and Thou in Me : that they may be made perfect in one " (John xvii. 20-23).[1]

17. **My prayer.**—O my God, I adore Thy greatness and Thy goodness :—Thy greatness which imposeth Thy glory upon all creatures, so that none can withdraw therefrom :—Thy goodness, which calleth Thine elect to the honour of the divine banquet. O my God, I am one of those whom Thou hast called, grant that I be not one of the unworthy. Many are called, but few chosen (Matt. xx. 16) ! And, for the sake of Thy glory, I so long to be one of the chosen ! I desire to take my place at Thine eternal feast, not only or principally to enjoy Thee, but above all to give Thee the perfect praise which will come from union with Thee. Oh, let my praise be perfect, my God ! Let my life expand to increase Thy glory ! The full blessedness of this praise is all my desire and hope and petition. Wherefore, O Lord, for the glory of Thy name, deliver me from all that hinders me from union with Thee.[2]

CHAPTER IV

The Order of my Relations with God

18. The intelligible essence of things.—19. Their real essence.—20. Is my satisfaction in the essence of things ?—21. I can lose it.

18. **The intelligible essence of things.**—I am therefore called to the dignity of being a child of God, living by His life ; He has intended my union with Himself. In this union, there is the part of His glory, and the part of my satisfaction. But in this union of my satisfaction with His glorification, what order is to be observed ? I cannot separate them, how are they to be united ? Have these two parts the same importance ? In this union, are the two interests on the same footing ?—Certainly not. God's part is the supreme aim, the

---

[1] This passage corresponds verbatim with the English Catholic version : the punctuation is the French author's, where it differs from the English.

[2] Propter gloriam nominis tui, Domine, libera nos (Ps. lxxviii. 9).

absolute end, the essential good. It is the one thing necessary,[1] the one thing absolute. So necessary, so absolute, that before any beings began to exist, it was true, eternally and invariably true, that no potential being could come into existence except for the glory of its Author.

The mode of glorification, the measure of honour to be paid, may vary infinitely, according to the nature and action of the creature. And in fact, this mode and measure vary endlessly according to the capacity and the conduct of creatures. I can personally render more or less glory to my Creator according as I advance more or less in union with Him. I can also fail to rise to this supreme mode of glorification which consists in my union with God, and only procure Him the glory of submission to a deserved punishment, and of the avenging of His justice by this punishment. The particular modes of glorification are not in the absolute essence, in the pre-existing necessity which comes before everything, and which is called the intelligible essence of things.

What is in this essence is the obligation that binds every being, in the whole measure of its being, to be referred in some way or other to the honour of its Creator. And it is this final absolute reference which is the external, and essentially necessary, glory.

19. **The real essence.**—This divine glory, independently of the mode and measure in which it is procured, also belongs to the real essence of things. This real essence, as it is called, is that which so enters into the proper constitution of a being that without it, it would cease to have any being. And God's glory enters so fully into the real constitution of a creature that without it, it would cease to exist. It penetrates so deeply into man's nature, it dominates his life so fully, that even the damned, suffering the penalties of divine justice, are obliged to yield God the glory they were unwilling to render Him freely at the solicitation of His mercy. God has made all things for Himself, all things, even the wicked reserved for the day of eternal evil.[2] And St. Augustine affirms that

---

[1] Porro unum est necessarium (Luc. x. 42).
[2] Universa propter semetipsum operatus est Dominus, et impium ad diem malum (Prov. xvi. 4).

the goodness of God could not permit evil unless His omnipotence were able to bring good out of evil.[1]

20. **Is my satisfaction in the essence of things?**—To begin with, God might not have created me; nothing in the essence of things called for my existence. Therefore, He created me freely by the gratuitous decree of His goodness. And, from the moment of my creation, the absolute essence of His nature demanded that it should be for His glory. But when He created me, what bound Him to choose for His glory the pre-eminent mode of supernatural union in which I become a participator in His very life? He willed to raise me to the honour of participating in His own felicity, and He has given my faculties the special mode of action whereby they unite with their object, they feed upon it, they assimilate it, or rather, they are assimilated thereto and live thereby. The initial aptitude and the need of beatific union are implanted in all my powers, and these are entirely gratuitous gifts, they are the splendours of God's free good pleasure. My creation is, then, a free gift which the essence of things did not demand, and my adaptation to union with God is a still freer gift, which my nature in itself did not in any way call for.

21. **I can lose it.**—As a matter of fact, I may suffer in this world and be damned in eternity without destroying my nature and the essential order of things. If my pleasure here below and my eternal salvation were of the intelligible essence of things, it would be absolutely impossible for me to lose them; for what is of the essence of things is invariably necessary and cannot be otherwise. If they were merely of the real essence of my nature, I could not lose them without losing my nature. As soon as I am able to lose them, they are not altogether essential things. There is only one thing altogether essential, God's glory procured somehow or other; my satisfaction, my salvation itself, so far as it is a matter of my satisfaction, is a relative thing, or rather, a thing correlative to God's glory.

Therefore, I may and must honour my Creator with the supreme honour which consists in my union with Him, and

---

[1] Nec sineret bonus fieri male, nisi omnipotens et de malo facere posset bene (*Enchir.* 26).

it is to this mode of glorification that my happiness is annexed. But I also may, by the abuse of my free-will, deny my Saviour this glory, and then His justice will avenge on me the order I have violated ; He will derive His glory from me in another manner, and I, for my part, shall not derive my happiness from Him.

CHAPTER V

The Dependence of my Satisfaction

22. The joy of heaven.—23. My joy in this world.—24. Subordinate to God's glory.—25. And springs from it.—26. The Lord's joy.

22. The joy of heaven.—Not only is my satisfaction by no means essentially necessary, but this satisfaction, given me gratuitously by God, is necessarily dependent upon His glory. My eternal satisfaction, which is my salvation, depends absolutely upon the glory of God ; for I am only able to obtain it by working in this world for God's honour ; and in heaven I shall be happy because I shall sing the divine praises. It is the singing of God's praises which is the source of the blessedness of the saints. " Blessed, O Lord, are they that dwell in Thy house " (Ps. lxxxiii. 5).—Why blessed ?—Because " they shall praise Thee for ever and ever " (*ibid.*).

23. My joy in this world.—It is true that I may seek the satisfaction of my increasing growth in this world while forgetting God's glory ; but it is a false and deceptive satisfaction, short and incomplete, mingled and disturbed, and it is finally cruelly expiated.

I no more think of my true satisfaction, even in this world, before or apart from God's glory, than I think of wages apart from work, reward apart from merit, the value of a thing apart from the thing itself. The wages depend on the work, and are measured by it, the reward by the merit, the value by the thing. Such is the order. Thus my satisfaction depends on God's glory and is measured thereby. Our Lord says to His Apostles : " These things I have spoken to you, that My joy may be in you, and that your joy may be filled "

(John xv. 11). The things He had spoken to them were, to abide in His love by keeping His commandments, *i.e.*, by procuring God's glory. And this Jesus calls His joy. Jesus' joy, which is God's glory, must be in them in order that their joy, *i.e.*, their satisfaction, may be filled and fully real.

24. **It is subordinate to God's glory.**—My satisfaction depends on God's glory in two ways. First, in that it is secondary, and God's glory is the chief thing. Therefore, my satisfaction cannot take precedence nor dominate. In all things, God's honour must come first, and my happiness come to me afterwards; in all things, God's glory must be the rule; God's interest is the supreme interest, man's interest is absolutely subordinate thereto. The disciple is not above the master, nor the servant above his lord (Matt. x. 24). God's glory and man's happiness are the two pages of one leaflet which follow one another, and which cannot be separated nor reversed without spoiling the sense of the book of creation. Hence, subordination of the human interest to the divine interest, and co-ordination of the two. God first, myself second; God's glory before everything, my satisfaction after it, subject to it, in conformity with it; such is the first part of the divine plan.

25. **It springs therefrom.**—But further: not only must my joy never outstrip, dominate, or contravene God's glory, but it must spring and come therefrom, or rather, exist therein. The just shall rejoice in the Lord (Ps. lxiii. 11). Be glad in the Lord, and rejoice, ye just (Ps. xxxi. 11). Rejoice in the Lord always; again, I say rejoice (Phil. iv. 4). Holy Scripture is full of passages which repeat this profound thought.— What is meant by the joy of the just?—The joy which is proper to the just man, his own joy; for there is a joy which is the joy of the just, and a joy which is not the joy of the just. I give you peace, My peace, and not that which is of of the world, says our Lord.[1] Where is this joy of the just, which is his own, which is true joy, the only true joy, because it is the only joy which is in conformity with the divine order? whence can it be drawn? whence comes it? whither goes it?

---

[1] Pacem relinquo vobis, pacem meam do vobis; non quomodo mundus dat, ego do vobis (Joan. xiv. 27).

where does it dwell ?—*In Domino*, in the Lord ; it is in God, it is to be drawn from God, it comes from God, it dwells in God.

26. The Lord's joy.—He wills to be, Himself, Himself alone, the full and infinite source of my happiness. In Himself, Himself alone, does He intend to beatify me. To what extent ! In what way !—He intends to consummate my life in the unity of His own life, to give me the eternal delights of the beatific vision, to inebriate me with the plenty of His house, to make me drink of the torrent of His pleasure.[1] The happiness will be so full that it will not only enter into me, but that I shall enter into it, because it will overflow on all sides, and I shall not attain to any of its borders. " Enter thou into the joy of thy Lord " (Matt. xxv. 21) : such will be the ineffable word that will bid the servant to the eternal feast. The joy is so immense as to be supernatural, so supernatural as to overflow the capacity possessed by any possible creature. God has by no means willed to be satisfied with receiving from me a glory which is purely natural, but He has willed to give my nature, in its union with Himself, a supernatural capacity for glorifying Him. In the same way, He is not satisfied with giving me a natural capacity for a limited happiness, but He has created in me a supernatural capacity for an infinite happiness. O my God! grant that my being may expand in all its supernatural capacity for the glory and happiness which Thou hast created for it.

CHAPTER VI

The Use of Creatures

27. Creatures.—28. Use.—29. Instruments.—30. The way to use them.—31. For God.—32. For myself.—33. Here and hereafter.

27. Creatures.—I have just seen my relations with God in their primary and fundamental notions. His glory, as the essential end ; my happiness in Him, as an end attached to

---

[1] Inebriabuntur ab ubertate domus tuæ et torrente voluptatis tuæ potabis eos (Ps. xxxv. 9).

THE END: ELEMENTS

the former; my union with Him, as the highest and perfect mode of glorifying Him; the subordination of my happiness to His honour, as the order of union. We must now look at my essential relations with other creatures in their general principles.

I cannot of myself maintain the existence which God has given me. Come from nothingness, I revert to it of my own accord. God alone hath life in Himself;[1] I have not life in myself; neither my body nor my soul have in themselves the means of their own subsistence, they must seek them beyond themselves, and they must look to other creatures for them: for this reason these are placed at my disposal.

By creatures, I mean universally all that is not God, all created things. Consequently, things spiritual as well as things material: grace, virtues, sacraments, the Church, etc.: food, the vegetable world, the animal world, and all material creation; in a word, all that has been made in the world of spirit or of things corporal. And not only everything that has been made, but all that happens day by day, all passing events: physical events in the progress of the world, moral events in the conduct of mankind, divine events in the intervention of grace, all these are comprised in the generic term—creatures.

28. Use.—When I speak of the use of creatures, I speak of the manner in which I must make use of existing things, spiritual and corporal, and of events which follow one another. The word "creatures" has, then, an absolutely universal sense, and denotes all that is not God, all that is between God and me, all that is, and all that takes place and happens around me, in me, for me or against me. The word will never be employed here in the restricted sense popularly attributed to it, and which makes use of it to denote solely material beings. In this broad and absolute sense, it is very useful for explaining the great principles of my life; alone of itself it sums up all that is for my use.

Consequently, I do not need to descend into particulars,

---

[1] Qui solus habet immortalitatem (1 Tim. vi. 16). Sicut enim Pater habet vitam in semetipso, sic dedit et Filio habere vitam in semetipso (Joan. v. 26).

and I am not obliged to mention one after the other, for instance, grace, sacraments, food, events, and so forth ; no, all that is designated by the words—use of creatures : and in these words I sum up all that is, and all that can be, of use to my soul and body. It is most important to grasp this deep meaning attributed to the word " creatures," and to understand its scope, because this word will be frequently employed.

29. Instruments.—Creatures are for my use, God has given them me. Why ? Is it ultimately for myself that God has placed them at my disposal ?—He has created them for Himself before all things ; if He gives me the use of them, it cannot be for myself in the main, but essentially for Himself. They are for my use for the sole end of all things, God's glory. He has given them me, as He gave Israel the lands of the nations, as He gave him the labours of the peoples, that they might observe His commandments and seek after His law.[1]

What, then, are creatures to me in reality ?—Means to procure God's glory—means and instruments proper for this work, made, ordered, and given primarily for this purpose. Means and instruments !—essentially, so far as I am concerned, creatures are solely intended for this. Means and instruments for giving glory to God !—They are given me, in the last resort, neither for themselves, nor for myself, but for God's glory. This is what I must diligently and deeply meditate upon, to comprehend it clearly.

30. The way to use them.—Means and instruments : therefore I must only use them as instruments are used. And how are instruments used ?—They are used for the work for which they were made. Thus, I make use of a knife to cut, of glasses to see, of a carriage for conveyance. Who ever thought of trying to see with a knife, or to cut with a carriage, or to be conveyed anywhere by means of glasses ?

Only madmen and infants who are ignorant of the meaning of an instrument, put it to some ridiculous use. No man of sense employs any instrument for any other use than that

[1] Et dedit illis regiones gentium, et labores populorum possederunt, ut custodiant justificationes ejus et legem ejus requirant (Ps. civ. 44. 45).

for which it is intended. And not only is an instrument not used for other purposes, but it is used in the measure—neither more nor less—in which it is useful for its purpose. This is the nature of an instrument, and this is the way to use it.

31. **For God.**—Creatures, all creatures, so far as 1 am concerned, are essentially and solely instruments—instruments ordered for the sanctification of God's name, this is their essential destination. Nothing can come into contact with my life except for this higher purpose. The relations which are dependent upon my free-will, like those which events independent of my will impose upon me, everything coming into contact with my soul and my body, with my mind, my heart, and my senses, through angels and men, animals and the vegetable world, inanimate elements and the stars, all these encounters, voluntary or passive, internal or external, what should their direction be ? what result should they bring about ?—They should develop my life according to God and for God, and increase in me His holy glory. This is the higher and divinely intended purpose of all these contacts with creatures. My life ought to be like a lyre pitched to echo a hymn to its Creator's praise. The contacts with creatures strike the various strings one after the other to make them resound according to the designs and desires of their Author. The contacts which I choose, like those which I undergo, must produce this harmony.

32. **For myself.**—Along with this primary service for His glory, God has ordered in creatures another service for my happiness. He did not will to enjoy His glory alone ; His love has willed to make me enter into participation in His goods, and has made Him reveal this marvellous ordinance of loving affection, whereby creatures, the instruments of His glory, become at the same time the instruments of my satisfaction. Every creature says first of all : Glory to God ; and then, Peace to His servant.[1] And thus I become an associate of God, I share in the benefits of the vast work of creation.

[1] Et dicant semper : Magnificetur Dominus, qui volunt pacem servi ejus (Ps. xxxiv. 27).

What am I saying ? that I share in the benefits ? But I have all the benefits: "for," says St. Francis of Sales,[1] "this is how He shares His divine loving-kindness with us; He gives us the fruits of His benefits, and reserves the honour and praise of them for Himself." "He does not need our service," says St. Augustine,[2] "but we require His governance, to operate in us and to guard us. And this is why He is our sole and true Lord, since we serve Him without His gaining anything by it, all the gain being for us and for our salvation. If He had any need of us, He would not be wholly our Lord, since He would Himself be subject to the necessity of finding help in us." Here is the wonder of His love for me. He has made all things for His glory and for my service.

33. **Here and hereafter.**—God intends me to grow in this world, to increase my capacity for glorifying Him in eternity; and creatures are ordered to bring me this increase. But each increment brings me enjoyment; for a being enjoys according to the measure of its completion. Every creature, by completing my being for God and according to God, brings, therefore, with it a proportional amount of happiness; it gives my aspirations more or less satisfaction and repose. Yes, in the expansion of my being for God by means of creatures, I get joys, true, deep, and substantial joys. No doubt, they are but partial, because my divine growth takes place by degrees. But ultimately will come the great joy, the eternal felicity, the immensity of happiness, for which the work done in me by God's instruments is preparing me. Hence, creatures bring me some amount of true happiness in this world, and prepare me for the infinite satisfaction of eternal salvation. O divine Goodness! if I only knew Thee! O Love! if I only loved Thee!

---

[1] *Théotime*, Book IV, ch. vi.
[2] Deus servitute nostra non indiget, nos vero dominatione illius indigemus, ut operetur et custodiat nos. Et ideo verus et solus Dominus, quia non illi ad suam sed ad nostram utilitatem salutemque servimus. Nam si nobis indigeret, eo ipso non verus Dominus esset, cum per nos ejus adjuvaretur necessitas, sub qua et ipse serviret (*De Doctrina Christ.*, I, viii. 24).

CHAPTER VII

Satisfactions in Creatures

34. The variety of pleasures in things created.—35. The drop of oil.—36. Before and after sin.—37. Pleasure is merely instrumental.

34. The variety of pleasures in things created.—I willingly make use of the term " satisfaction " as better indicating the nature of the need which I feel in searching and of the contentment I experience in possession. I require satisfaction, and this is why I seek ; I am at rest, when I am satisfied.

But God has not only given me this essentially reposeful satisfaction, which is in my growth for Him, in my union with Him. This enjoyment is final, it is part of the very purpose of my life. His goodness has contrived other satisfactions for me, and these are also encouraging, but they have quite a different place and *rôle* in my existence. These are satisfactions in creatures.

There are, indeed, for me in creatures, placed there by the hand of their Author, infinitely varied pleasures :—material pleasures, of sight, hearing, smell, taste, and touch ; beauties of nature and of art, the charm of music, the perfume of flowers, the flavour of food, and so forth : moral pleasures, of the family, of friendship, of appreciation, of practised virtue, and the like : intellectual pleasures, of literature and science, of discovering or of contemplating truth : supernatural pleasures, in prayer, in religious practices, and in the divine touches of grace. What a quantity of pleasures ! how great is their variety and extent ! What are they in the mind of God who made them, and what is their function ?

35. The drop of oil.—To know what they are, I have only to look where they are.—Where are they ?—In the creature —And what is the creature ?—An instrument, nothing but an instrument. Consequently, the pleasure which is therein is no more than it ; it is, then, an instrumental pleasure, a quality given by God to the instruments placed at my service. Why does this quality exist ?—To facilitate the use of the instruments.

A cutting tool will not always cut, it gets dull; and when it has lost its edge, it must be sharpened on the grindstone. The rapidly revolving wheel would soon become worn but for the drop of oil to ease the friction and prevent heating. Thus my faculties are soon wearied and worn out: they, too, must have their lubricating drop of oil, their refreshing drop of water, their sharpening on the grindstone. They need dash and vigour, fire and force, ease and liveliness. When the wheels of my spirit are smooth-running and well-oiled, then my lips chant God's praises with wonderful readiness.[1] Such is the function of this drop of the oil of gladness which God has implanted in His creatures for the benefit of those who love justice and hate iniquity.[2]

36. **Before and after sin.**—This is pleasure in things created in the mind of God, such is its function; this is why His infinitely foreseeing loving-kindness has provided it in all instruments. In God's original purpose every creature was merely an instrument, not one was a hindrance; and every creature was furnished with its little drop of oil, its joy, which facilitated its use for God. To-day sin has upset this beautiful order; I find hindrances at every step and troubles at every turn. God did not make either the hindrances or the troubles; they are the penalty of sin. In restoring this impaired order, Jesus Christ neither removed the hindrances nor the troubles; but He provided both with a utility which I shall study later on.

In spite of sin, there remain a multitude of pleasures; the oil of joy is still not wanting to my faculties. Everywhere, if there is a duty to be done, I find instruments for its performance; and in these instruments there is often a pleasure which facilitates my use of them. Thus, why are there family pleasures?—To make the great duty of education easier for parents and children.—Why the pleasures of friendship?—To provide souls thus drawn together with an impetus towards the good.—Why are there the pleasures of feeding?—They correspond to the fundamental duties of the

---

[1] Sicut adipe et pinguedine repleatur anima mea, et labiis exultationis laudabit os meum (Ps. lxii. 6).
[2] Dilexisti justitiam et odisti iniquitatem, propterea unxit te Deus, Deus tuus, oleo lætitiæ (Ps. xliv. 8).

conservation of life.—Why, the pleasures of prayer, of the sacraments, of meditation, and of all spiritual favours ?— They correspond with the great and very sacred duties of the divine relations they assist. Thus pleasure always corresponds with duty, to help on its accomplishment. The pleasure will be all the more intense in proportion to the importance of the duty.

37. Pleasure is merely instrumental.—This pleasure is, then, really a satisfaction, since it corresponds with a need of my faculties and satisfies this need. But it is only an instrumental satisfaction which I must make use of ; and not a final satisfaction in which I may find my repose. It is a means and not an end. When I say that I am made for happiness and that happiness is the secondary end of my existence, there is no question of the happiness which is in created things. For me there is no trace of any end in these ; my end is in God, my final happiness is in Him ; they only contain means.

It is a terrible reversal of God's plan to misunderstand pleasure in created things and to live for the sake of enjoying it. Unfortunately, this reversal frequently occurs ! This, indeed, is just where I make mistakes whenever I leave the established order. Further on,[1] I shall see that this is the sole disorder. I seek to put myself to sleep in enjoyment instead of making use of it for the facilitation of duty. To leave God, I make use of the very thing which should render me more alert in giving Him glory.

Yes, pleasure is, indeed, a good thing, but only when it is well employed. If I abuse it, it becomes the worst of all evils and the source of all my aberrations. When well used, it makes saints ; badly used, it brings damnation. Happy is the man who knows how to make use of it ! unhappy is he who misuses it ! May I learn never to pervert what is in the divine mind ! No pleasure is bad in itself ; its misuse alone can make it evil. Every pleasure that helps to facilitate duty is wholesome, fortifying, uplifting. If it runs counter to duty, it becomes pernicious, deleterious, lowering. On the one hand, how it brutalizes ! on the other, what virtues it sustains ! It is for me to see how I mean to use it.

[1] See Book II, ch. vi. *ff.*

CHAPTER VIII

The Order of my Relations with Creatures

38. Pleasure.—39. Human utility.—40. Corporal utility —41. Intellectual and moral utility.—42. Divine utility.—43. The complete order of the instruments.

38. Pleasure.—For me there are two things in creatures: utility and pleasure: their utility, as instruments for developing my life; their pleasure, as facilitating this development. We must then consider the order of their utility, and the order of their pleasure.

First of all, it is fairly clear that as pleasure only exists to facilitate the function of the instrument, it must be subordinate to this function. Oil is only used in a machine according to the nature of its construction and the necessities of the work to be done. A watch does not require the same quantity nor the same quality of oil as a steam-engine. Every instrument and every work has its own measure. It is by utility and necessity that the distribution and economy of the lubrication are governed. But it is thus that the economy and distribution of pleasure must be governed in human life. It must be subordinate not only to the end, but to the instrument and to the work of the instrument. The pleasure of food and drink, for instance, must be subordinate to our need of nourishment; the pleasure of sleep, subordinate to our need of rest; the pleasure of recreation, subordinate to our need of renewal of strength. And thus it is with the whole scale of pleasure, from the lowest to the highest, from the most material to the most spiritual. The absolute rule is to take satisfaction in created things in the measure, and on the conditions, necessary for the proper performance of duty. They must facilitate, and not encumber; and, above *all*, they must never stop.

39. Human utility.—This, then, is the first subordination, that of pleasure to utility. But how is utility itself to be governed?—For me creatures contain a twofold utility: that which works for my natural human utility, which is human utility; next, that which co-operates towards my supernatural divine development, which is divine utility. What is the order of the relation of these two utilities? They must unquestionably be so interwoven and united as not to impede one another. How is this interweaving and union to be established?

Human utility is that which belongs to my natural being: the material development of my physical life, the virtuous development of my moral life, the rational development of my intellectual life. How many are the beings and influences destined by the omnipotent wisdom of Love to concur in the threefold growth of my life as man!

And all these beings and influences preserve order in their utility, if they work towards my vital expansion, according to the rule of their subordination. For, even in human utility, there is a necessary subordination of material interest to intellectual interest, and of both to moral interest. My health is important, but less so than my knowledge; my knowledge is necessary, but less so than my virtues.

40. Corporal utility.—Hence, questions dealing with the protection, the maintenance, and the development of our material life have their importance, and they comprise obligations. The manifold economic cares of work, business, industry, hygiene, and so forth, are praiseworthy in themselves; for they concur towards a necessary end. Material interest, however, if it is the first in the order of vital necessities, is only last in the order of importance and of dignity. It must be, consequently, subordinate and referred to the interests which are superior to itself. I must attend to my body, and, according to the conditions of my calling, not neglect such cares of a material order as are incumbent upon me. This is a duty; and if it is less in dignity, it nevertheless involves a number of grave obligations.

41. Intellectual and moral utility.—The growth of the mind is of a far higher order, for we are far more human by the mind than by the body; but moral growth is that which best fulfils and completes our human dignity, for we are still more human by the heart than by the mind. Hence, the means that work for our physical development are subordinate

to, and co-ordinate with, those that work for our intellectual development; and these, again, to and with those that concur in our moral development. Health is for knowledge, and knowledge for virtue: this is the natural order. And thus is it that I must measure the use of my instruments. My bodily strength must subserve my intellectual vigour, my intellectual vigour my moral energy; and all three, united in concord, must attain to the fulness of their development. They must be united and in concord in their gradations of dignity, without the inferior encroaching upon the superior, and without excluding one another. All developments are not normal. A wen or a hump is a growth, but they are, above all, excrescences; and this is what must be avoided.

42. Divine utility.—Divine utility is that which belongs to the supernatural development of the divine life, to the increase of God's glory. Beings and their influences upon me possess a special power of leading me to this height. The natural growth of my life cannot stop at myself, since I am made for God. Consequently, the natural efficacy of created means must be subordinate to their divine efficacy.

In fact, if it is the mission of creatures to develop me, it is with God in view. If I make a selfish use of them, stopping short at myself, I deprive them of their essential function. In using them, I must therefore not put aside, or relegate to the second place, that which is their primary object. God's supreme glory must be the practically dominant and effectively determinant motive of my use of them. I may, and I ought, to look upon them as instruments of my growth, but with God in view. I may, and I ought, to like them for the advantage they bring to my life, but according to God. I may, and I ought, to go in search of them for the work of expansion which they produce in my existence, but for God. It matters little whether the intention of His glory be actual or virtual; the essential thing is that this should be in some way its highest, and the final, term; the essential thing is that my human growth should end in God, since man is made for God.

43. The complete order of the instruments.—This, then, is the order to be kept in the use of the instruments of my life.

Pleasure, subject to utility; human utility, ordered according to the dignity of its interests and referred to divine utility.—I must take things, and the enjoyment of them, to increase myself, and to raise me up to God. Creatures and the pleasure connected with them must produce in me an upward movement unto God, and not any need of resting in myself, or in them. St. Augustine observes that God, after the work of creation, took His joy and rest, not in His work, but in Himself.[1] Thus, creatures and enjoyment in them are solely intended to make me increase and rest in God. I use them, and rest in Him: this the law of justice, and this is God's plan.

And the order of creation only exists in its plentitude, God's plan is only realized in its integrity, I only attain my end in its totality, when God is all in all to me,[2] when I look for nothing beyond Him, when all things lead me to Him, and finally, when His glory has dominated and absorbed my satisfaction, and has become alone my end, my joy and my repose.

CHAPTER IX

The essential Order of Creation

44. Summing up.—45. *Quærite primum regnum Dei.*—46. My greatness: all things are mine.—47. I am God's.

44. Summing up.—This, then, is the essential order of creation.

Firstly, God's glory, the sole essential good, the supreme end of all things, which must be sought for its own sake, before all things, in all things.

Secondly, my satisfaction in heaven and on earth, a secondary good, subordinate to and united to the fundamental good, which I ought to seek only in the second place, in conformity with God's glory, in it, and by it.

Thirdly, other created goods, with their twofold utility,

---

[1] Ab ipsis in seipso requievit (*De Gen. ad litt.* iv. 26).
[2] Ut sit Deus omnia in omnibus (1 Cor. xv. 28).

human and divine, means and instruments of the two first goods, and which I ought to use finally and before everything for God's glory, and in the measure, neither more nor less, in which they procure it.

Fourthly, satisfaction in things created, a purely instrumental property, but an exquisite refinement of the Creator's, who wills thereby to make my journey through creatures to Himself easy and expeditious.

Such is the essential order of my creation, such the supreme rule of my life.

45. Quærite primum regnum Dei.—" Seek ye therefore first the kingdom of God, and His justice, and all these things shall be added unto you " (Matt. vi. 33). What are the kingdom of God and the justice of God ?—They mean God's glory, and my happiness therein. This is the end, twofold yet one, towards which my life should be directed, whereto it should be devoted. I am obliged to tend towards it, for our Lord formally commands me to seek it. And He commands me to seek it before all things, and in the first place. He does not separate God's kingdom from His justice, for my felicity is united with its immensity.

Other things are means, they are the manifold and the contingent, they must serve to the end. " Therefore," says St. Augustine,[1] " God's kingdom and justice are our good, it is these we must desire, it is these that must be our end, this is why we must do everything which we do. But this life is the battle through which we have to fight our way to that kingdom, and this life is subject to necessities. But, as to these necessities, says the Lord, all things shall be given you in abundance. As for yourselves, seek ye first the kingdom of God and His justice. When He says : that first, this afterwards : afterwards, not in order of time, but in order of

[1] Regnum ergo et justitia Dei bonum nostrum est, et hoc appetendum, et ibi finis constituendus, propter quod omnia faciamus quæcumque facimus. Sed quia in hac vita militamus, ut ad illud regnum pervenire possimus, quæ vita sine his necessariis agi non potest : Apponentur vobis hæc, inquit ; sed vos regnum Dei et justitiam ejus primum quærite. Cum enim dixit illud primum, significavit quia hoc posterius quærendum est, non tempore sed dignitate ; illud tanquam bonum nostrum, hoc tanquam necessarium nostrum, necessarium autem propter illud bonum (*De Serm. Dei in monte.* ii. 53).

dignity : that, means my good ; this, my necessity ; and this is my necessity in view of that which is my good."

46. My greatness : all things are mine.—And in this order I see my greatness. " All things are yours," says St. Paul, " whether it be Paul, or Apollo, or Cephas, or the world, or life, or death, or things present, or things to come : all are yours : and you are Christ's : and Christ is God's " (1 Cor. iii. 22, 23). All things are mine, all things in this world, in life or in death, in time or in eternity, all things are mine, all is for me. I am master of all things, above all things. Lord, what, then, is man ?—Why hast Thou set him over the works of Thy hands ? What glory and honour ! Thou hast subjected all things under His feet, all sheep and oxen : moreover the beasts also of the field, the birds of the air and the fishes of the sea.[1] Here is my dignity : I am set over all things, the owner of all things, the master of all. God has created all things for me, He has placed all things at my disposal.

47. I am God's.—Yet this is only the smaller side of my greatness. I am God's, and I am for God : here is my true greatness. God wills to raise me to Himself, to unite me to Himself, to make me participate in His glory. Apart from God, nothing is great enough to be my end. He Himself is infinitely above me, and He wishes me to rise to Him in the measure in which it is given me to attain unto Him. There is the whole object of my life : to go to God, while making use of His creatures. My God, how wonderful Thou art !—How great is man in Thy thoughts ! But how little is he in his own ! For man, enriched with all these honours, has never understood them ; he has lowered himself to the level of creatures without reason, and has become like unto them.[2] And when at last I get to understand my dignity, shall I appreciate it enough never to lower it ?—Called to rise to God, how can I descend towards the level of the brute ?

---

[1] Quid est homo quod memor es ejus ? . . . gloria et honore coronasti eum et constituisti eum super opera manuum tuarum. Omnia subjecisti sub pedibus ejus, oves et boves universas, insuper et pecora campi, volucres cœli et pisces maris (Ps. viii. 5-9).

[2] Et homo, cum in honore esset, non intellexit, comparatus est jumentis insipientibus et similis factus est illis (Ps. xlviii. 13)

CHAPTER X

An Explanation of the Pater noster

48. The greatness of this prayer. — 49. Hallowed be Thy name. — 50. Thy kingdom come.—51. Thy will be done.—52. Give us our bread.—53. The three last petitions. 54. All is here.

48. The greatness of this prayer.—I find a luminous confirmation of this teaching in the *Pater noster*. This is the perfect prayer; therein are contained all goods, the only true goods, and these in the order in which I ought to ask for them. Now, these goods and their order of dignity are just those which I have been considering. It is, therefore, useful to stop a few minutes to meditate upon it, in order to enter more profoundly into the essential order of my life.

Everything in the *Pater noster* is so divine! Of a truth, it is the summing up of all prayer, and not only of all prayer, but of all faith and of all religion. He who meditates upon it meets with the depths of the infinite on every side; his meditation will suffice to make him enter into the deep things of God.[1] It is, indeed, the short word which the Lord made upon the earth;[2] and therein our Lord has set all the treasures of wisdom and knowledge which were hidden in His heart. How consoling would it be, were charity to instruct my heart and pour therein all the riches of fulness of understanding to know the mystery of God the Father and of Jesus Christ![3]

In the *Pater noster*, I find explained not only what is my end, but also the way and the means, *i.e.*, the three ideas which sum up all that I want to meditate upon in this little work; and I find them in their order and in their mutual interdependence. The *Pater noster* is, then, for me a light and a support, and I have every interest in meditating upon

---
[1] Spiritus omnia scrutatur etiam profunda Dei (1 Cor. ii. 10).
[2] Verbum breviatum faciet Dominus super terram (Rom. ix. 28).
[3] Ut consolentur corda ipsorum, instructi in charitate et in omnes divitias plenitudinis intellectus, in cognitionem mysterii Dei Patris et Christi Jesu, in quo sunt omnes thesauri sapientiæ et scientiæ absconditi (Col. ii. 2, 3).

it after St. Thomas,[1] whose short but sublime exposition of it will be my guide.

49. **Hallowed be Thy name.**—What is the subject of this first petition ? What is the first good that I ask for before all the rest ?—The hallowing of God's name. But is that anything else than His glory ? God's name expresses God and all that is in Him. Hallowing expresses all that man can do for the honour of His name. Consequently, the hallowing of God's name is God's glory for His own sake, the praise which all creatures owe to Him, the first, essential, fundamental, unique, necessary good ; this is what I desire and ask for before all. This first good dominates and contains all other goods, the goods I afterwards ask for depend thereupon, and are correlative thereto. Moreover, this first petition of the *Pater noster* dominates and contains the other petitions, in the same way as the first of God's commandments contains and dominates the other commandments.

50. **Thy kingdom come.**—What is the reign or kingdom of God, if it be not the riches, the goods He communicates to those whom He wishes to participate in that kingdom ? Here, then, is my secondary good, my own good, my participation in God's goods, my final satisfaction in this world and in the next. This is why I ask that this kingdom of God, wherein are comprised all the increments that God communicates to His creatures, may come : and to whom ?—To myself. What I ask for is to participate in God's goods, here and hereafter. And this I only ask for in the second place ; it could not be the first petition, because my utility, even my eternal utility, only comes after God's glory. This is why the petition, " Thy kingdom come," follows the petition, " Hallowed be Thy name," which necessarily comes first.

51. **Thy will be done.**—To procure God's glory, a way has to be followed. How shall I procure it, if I know not the way thither ? God's will marks out the way for me · His will shows me the road I have to go, what I ought to avoid, what I must do, to procure His glory and to find my own advantage. This it is that gives me guidance to procure God the sanctification of His name, and for myself the coming of

---

2 a, 2 ae, q. 83, a. 9, c.

His kingdom. After the two first petitions naturally comes the third, " Thy will be done on earth as it is in heaven."

52. Give us our bread.—It is not enough to know the road ; we must also have the means to walk in it. In vain do I know the road, if I faint from inanition by the way ; I shall be no further forward. My soul as well as my body requires nourishment, that is to say, what maintains life and strength. This is what is called my daily bread ; and thereby I designate all that must help me as a means to walk in the way of God's will to the end, which is God's glory. It is, therefore, in order for this petition for my daily bread to come immediately after that for God's will.

53. The three last petitions.—The fifth petition, " forgive us our trespasses as we forgive them that trespass against us."

I know the end, the way, the means ; what remains for me to ask for ?—The removal of hindrances. Now, there are three hindrances, one of which is opposed to each of these three things : the end, the way, and the means.

The first hindrance, the essential, radical hindrance, is sin. Sin is the hindrance that turns us away from the end. I therefore ask for its removal before everything, it is the subject of the fifth petition.

The sixth petition, " lead us not into temptation."

After sin, the most serious hindrance is what leads to sin, temptation. Temptation is the hindrance that turns us aside from the way of God's will. I beg God to guarantee me against it and to keep me from falling into it, because it is a hindrance by nature, and always a danger.

The seventh petition, " deliver us from evil."

A final hindrance, apart from sin and temptation, is to be found in the other evils of soul and body which deprive me of the means that are necessary for my progress. They may therefore be a hindrance to my end, and I beg for their removal in that measure only in which they may diminish God's glory and my own true happiness.

Such is the *Pater noster*, the perfect pattern of prayer, and also the perfect pattern of duty. Our Lord therein drew for us the foundations of all prayer and of all spiritual life in a few bold strokes.

54. All is there.—What a beautiful frame would the *Pater noster* make for a complete treatise on the Christian life! All is there: both good and evil, the good to be done, and the evil to be avoided. All is there, ranked according to its importance, and co-ordinated in its interdependence: the order of good to be done, the order of evil to be avoided. All is there, for me and for others: what I ought to do, and what I can do, for myself, and what I ought to do, and what I can do, for others.

For myself, if I would have the full pattern of my life, I have only to meditate upon the *Pater noster*. It will tell me what is the good, and what is my good; the order, the dignity, and the connection of goods; the way to follow, the means to use. It will tell me what is evil; why, how, and in what measure it is evil, and in what order it must be avoided. I therefore have the entire pattern of my development.

I have also an entire scheme of service. Should I desire to know what good is to be done around me, the *Pater noster* says to me: Give God's bread to further God's will in the hope of God's kingdom in view of God's name. Should I desire to know the evil to be avoided by my neighbour: Deliver him, it says, from physical, moral, and intellectual evils, set him free from temptation, help him to quit sin. Such is the ascending scheme of service. What a programme for life!—If only I knew how to meditate upon it!—If only I knew how to put it into practice!

BOOK II

ORGANIZATION

I know the elementary principles of the organization of my life. I must now set them together. Life consists in unity; and organic life consists in the unity of manifold elements brought into action and interwoven in and by the activity of a single principle. Every being lives in the measure in which it attains to unity, says St. Augustine.[1] In this book I mean to consider the unity of my life. And as my life is a compound of movements, acts, and manifold habits, what I require and intend to examine is not the multiplicity of the elements, but their living unity.

To live, I have many acts to perform, manifold habits to acquire, various kinds of knowledge and virtue to cultivate. To give a character to my nature, the necessity, and even the place, of each of these habits and forms of knowledge and virtue, is, indeed, of the highest importance for my interior life; but that does not enter into the more simple and fundamental purpose that I have in view. I must be one, all the dispositions of my being must be focussed into one. It is the one disposition, the universal resultant of partial dispositions that I am anxious to cultivate. What I am trying to find is the secret of the unity in which life consists.

In what is the total and living unity of my being constituted, and in what does it consist? On the other hand, how is the disorganization of this unity and life brought about, and in what does it consist? This is a twofold question which sums up the whole of the contents of this second Book.

---

[1] Nihil est autem esse quam unum esse. Itaque in quantum quidque adipiscitur unitatem, in tantum est (*De moribus Manich.* ii. 8)

CHAPTER I

My Obligations

1. Knowing, willing, acting.—2. My mind must know God.—3. Truth.—4. My heart must love God.—5. Charity.—6. My action must serve God.—7 Liberty.

1. Knowing, willing, acting.—For me, what duties flow from the great principles according to which it has pleased God to organize my life?—For it is evident that they must be my rule of conduct; my life must conform to them and carry them into practice. To act, I must know, will, and do: to know, to will, to do, are the three elements of a complete human action. I have, then, an obligation which is at once threefold and one: threefold, since it touches my intelligence, my will, and my actions one, since these three things must not be separated.

2. My mind must know God.—The intelligence is the first principle of human acts. The mind sees and judges. It sees what has to be done, and it judges whether the means are proportioned to the end. I am made for God's glory; creatures are the instruments put into my hands to procure this glory; that is the great principle. What practical obligation does this fundamental truth bind upon my mind?—It binds upon my mind the obligation of seeing God as the one essential purpose of my life; of seeing Him, I say, of having Him before my eyes, of knowing and remembering that His glory is the great end which must dominate, inspire, and direct my whole conduct.

It binds upon my mind the obligation of considering creatures as being what in reality they are, means for glorifying God. Consequently, my mind must be applied to know in each creature what may serve God's glory, and how far each one is useful or hurtful to this end. Creatures are instruments: is this or that creature a good instrument? how can I make use of it ? This, before all else, is what I must get to know about the creatures I have to make use of. (Remember the broad sense I have given to the word "creatures," p. 23.)

To see God in all things, to see all things according to God and for God, this is my mind's absolute duty. In all my ways I must have this view of God present to my mind, and this view will direct my steps in uprightness ;[1] and I shall be in the truth, which is the summing up of the obligations and of the life of my intelligence.

3. **Truth.**—It is God who is the substantial truth, and ideas make the truth of things ; for things are only true so far as they are in conformity with the divine ideas. To have the truth is, then, to see God and God's ideas ; to see God in Himself, and to see Him in things.

Let me see Him in Himself. Let me see Him here on earth in the misty brightness of faith, for the veils that impede direct vision are not lifted in this world. Let me see Him in heaven in the splendours of His glory. Let me apply my mind to knowing Him, let me feed my intelligence on the substance of His ideas. Truth grows in me in the measure in which my mind enters into the view of God.

Let me see Him in things. When I see in things that which leads to God, I see the truth. For this true, this entirely true, side of creatures is that which glorifies God, since that is its essential destiny and the fundamental reason of its existence. The whole constitution and properties of beings are ordained and disposed to procure the glory of their Author. The great and full truth of things is their aptitude for revealing the greatness of God. When I see them in this light, I have the truth, which is the law and the life of my mind.

4. **My heart must love God.**—The will is determined by the intelligence, according to the old adage of philosophy : " We cannot will unless we know."[2] But it is not forcibly determined ; for I may know and not will. Hence, there is also a duty for my will.

---

[1] In omnibus viis tuis cogita illum, et ipse diriget gressus tuos (Prov. iii. 6).
[2] Nihil volitum nisi prius cognitum.

The will esteems, appreciates, loves.[1] With my will, therefore, I must esteem, appreciate, and love God's glory as my one essential good, love nothing above it, nothing contrary to it, nothing apart from it ; feel that therein is my all, and that without this, all is nothing to me. I must esteem, appreciate, and love in creatures, above all, that in them which is essential, *i.e.*, the means of obtaining my all. That is what I must supremely love and esteem in them. I must not love them at all for their own sake, nor for my sake, but for God before all else. The measure of my love, the cause of my preference, must be just the measure in which they help me to glorify God. If, before all else, my will is attached to that in creatures which leads me to God, it is in the fulness of its duty ; and this fulness of the duty of my will is entirely expressed in the great word used by St. John to denote God Himself : charity.

5. **Charity.**—God is charity, and he who abideth in charity abideth in God, and God abideth in him.[2] Charity, then, is God loved, loved in Himself, and loved in all things.

God loved in Himself. Love is the desire for the good, the will for the good. And the good is God. He is the sovereign Good, the first principle of all good ; the supreme Goodness, the first cause of all that is good ; the essential Love, the source of all that is really love. Let me love God in Himself and for Himself, apply to loving Him all the will-power of my being, nourish my heart on the substance of His love. Charity grows in me in the measure in which my heart enters into the love of God.

Charity is also God loved in His creatures. If, in all things, my heart tries to find and embrace that which contributes to the honour of holy goodness, I have and I know the charity of Christ which surpasseth all knowledge, and thereby I am filled unto all the fulness of God.[3] Charity enables me to

---

[1] Appreciation and esteem may seem to be but a judgement of the intellect, but they are only completed by the adhesion of the will, that appreciative love which gives them their true character ; and this is why I attribute them to the will.

[2] Deus charitas est, et qui manet in charitate, in Deo manet et Deus in eo (1 Joan. iv 16).

[3] Scire etiam supereminentem scientiæ charitatem Christi, ut impleamini in omnem plenitudinem Dei (Eph. iii. 19).

enter into the fulness of God and of all things. Things only have their fulness in God's glory ; for what gives them their reality, essence, and individuality, is that in them which leads to God. The earth has its fulness in the possession of God,[1] it is full of the praise of God.[2] This fulness is embraced by charity, which loves in all things only that which leads to divine glory, and thus it grasps the reality of all things. This is why love is the fulfilling of the law.[3]

6. My action must serve God.—In action, I am seeking, choosing, using. I must then seek before all else, and in all things, God's glory. I must serve God, and make use of all things for God.

To serve God means to apply and refer to His honour and worship my powers of action ; to devote and consecrate my efforts and movements to them ; to direct my occupations and my work towards Him, so that there may be in me nothing that is not employed in His service, so far as the character and measure of my calling are concerned.

Let me make use of all things for God, and for this purpose, let me seek, choose, and make use of creatures so far as they help me to glorify Him—neither more—nor less.—I have no other essential reason for seeking after creatures, no other essential reason for putting them aside. No doubt I may seek for those that bring me satisfaction, and avoid those that are a source of trouble to me : must not the machine have its oil ? must not a little gladness lubricate the mechanism of my faculties ? But I ought to do this only in a secondary way, and always in conformity with and in view of the great business. My satisfaction must never be the principal and primary rule of my actions.

To act according to the will of God, to prefer what most contributes thereto, to put in the background what is less useful for the purpose, and to get rid of anything that is a hindrance, such is my rule of action. If I follow it, my works are perfect, my ways are right; consequently I am just, since it is the just whom God conducts through the right ways.[4]

[1] Impleta est terra possessione tua (Ps. ciii. 24).
[2] Laudis ejus plena est terra (Habac. iii. 3).
[3] Plenitudo ergo legis est dilectio (Rom. xiii. 10).
[4] Justum deduxit per vias rectas (Sap. x. 10).

7. Liberty.—When I see in each instrument that which helps me to go to God, when my love is attached to that, I succeed in making use of everything in the measure in which it helps me towards God's glory, which I solely consider and love in a sovereign manner. If, indeed, I consider and esteem nothing so much as this divine utility in my instruments, I use them according to their utility, *neither more—nor less.—* But to reach this point means great freedom.

These words " neither more nor less " well indicate, indeed, the degree of liberty my action has to attain. I must sufficiently master my instruments to be able to take, use, and lay them aside freely, according to their utility. To utilize each thing just as far as it is or may be profitable towards God's glory, without allowing my likings to make me outstrip the measure, or my dislikes to prevent me from attaining thereto; to employ what is useful so far as it is useful; to lay aside what is the opposite so far as it is contrary; not to permit my action to be modified, in reality, by any preference or repugnance of nature, this means having the great, sovereign and royal liberty of the children of God. And it is to this liberty of action that I am called.[1] If my mind be in truth, my heart in charity, my actions in liberty, then I shall fulfil all the obligations of my life.

CHAPTER II

The Essence of Piety

8. Seeing, loving, and seeking God.—9. *Veritatem facientes in charitate.*—10. The union of these three operations in piety.—11. Other texts.—12. The great commandment.—13. The definition in the Catechism.

8. Seeing, loving, and seeking God.—Always to see, love, and seek God's glory; to consider, esteem and utilize all things in view of God, is to accomplish the essential duty which is called piety. To have in the mind truth, in the heart charity,

[1] Vos enim in libertatem vocati estis, fratres (Gal. v. 13).

in action liberty, is having piety. Piety is unity. Piety, then, is nothing else than seeing, loving, and seeking God's glory in all and above all; it is the seeing, loving, and seeking God alone for His own sake, and all things for God.

Sight, love, search, piety is all of these together; for these three acts, joined together, concentrated upon God and applying to all creatures, constitute piety; it is one universal disposition which is profitable to all things,[1] as St. Paul says. But it is to this profound master of the spiritual life, to this first of all theologians, that we must go for the definition of piety. He gives it in terms which de Maistre declares to be untranslatable. I am about to endeavour to penetrate into their meaning, as far as my weakness permits.

9. Veritatem facientes in charitate.—" Let us do the truth in charity, in order that we may in all things grow up in Him who is the head, the Christ."[2] These words of the great Apostle point out, with a profundity of meaning and a brevity of expression which are all his own, all that constitutes piety: its end, its means, and its operations.

Its end: to grow up in God by Jesus Christ: or rather, to grow up in Jesus Christ for God's glory. For Jesus Christ is the head of the body of which I must be a member, and in which I must grow up, if I mean to procure God the glory I ought to give Him. Later on, I shall see the degrees of this increase, which St. Paul calls the increase of God.[3]

Its means: these are all things, all creatures, *per omnia*. All creatures, in God's plan, as I have seen,[4] are instruments. But these instruments are in the hands of piety; piety it is that has to handle them and to make use of them for the great work. And these instruments are only well handled and effectively used thereby. It is piety that utilizes everything.

---

[1] Pietas ad omnia utilis est (1 Tim. iv. 8).

[2] Ἀληθεύοντες δὲ ἐν ἀγάπῃ, αὐξήσωμεν εἰς αὐτὸν τὰ πάντα, ὅς ἐστιν ἡ κεφαλὴ, ὁ χριστός. The approved Douai version gives: " But doing the truth in charity, we may in all things grow up in him who is the head, *even* Christ."

Veritatem autem facientes in charitate, crescamus in illo per omnia, qui est caput Christus (Eph. iv. 15).

[3] Crescit in augmentum Dei (Col. ii. 19).

[4] See Book I. § 29.

Its operations : these are seeing, loving, and seeking God in all things ; this is what is expressed by the three terms : doing the truth in charity.

10. **The union of these three operations in piety.**—And these three operations must not in any way be separated ; for piety, in its complete essence, is at once sight, love, search : truth, charity, liberty. From this intimate union, from the mutual interpenetration of these three elements, springs the one and great disposition which is piety. This union is expressed by the words of St. Paul with remarkable energy. Of the three terms used to denote the three elements of piety, he takes the third, that of action, and joins it with the first, truth, in such a manner that he combines them into a single verb, $ἀληθεύοντες$, which is really untranslatable, and which, for want of anything better, we translate by " doing the truth." And he adds to this verb, in which the two extreme terms of piety are now concentrated, the middle term as an object, so that all is now combined *in charitate*, in charity. Thus, charity is the centre of piety, the bond of perfection.[1] I see to love, and I act by loving : the development of the body of piety thus proceeds in charity.[2]

11. **Other texts.**—This union of all the human faculties acting in charity is shown in numerous passages of Holy Scripture. The same St. Paul says elsewhere : That in the Christian religion which has any worth, is neither circumcision, nor uncircumcision ; what is of worth, is faith that worketh by charity.[3] Faith doing its works in charity, is not this again the whole of piety, in the full synthesis of the three terms ? And the Apostle of love, in the appeal in which he appears to sum up all the desires of that heart on which he had rested, speaks like the Apostle who had returned from the third heaven. " My little children," he says, " let us not love in word, nor in tongue, but in deed, and in truth " (1 John iii. 18). To St. John love is not real, if it is merely

---

[1] Super omnia autem hæc charitatem habete, quod est vinculum perfectionis (Col. iii. 14).
[2] Augmentum corporis facit in ædificationem sui in charitate (Eph. iv. 16).
[3] Nam in Christo Jesu neque circumcisio aliquid valet neque præputium, sed fides quæ per charitatem operatur (Gal. v. 6).

an affair of words and an operation of the tongue. He commends love, it is the recommendation of all his life and the summing up of all his teaching. But the love which he commends must be preceded by the truth and followed by works, love must be in deed and in truth. Thus it is that the beloved disciple also exhorts to piety.

12. **The great commandment.**—Here it is well to recall, in order to meditate upon its infinite depth, the commandment which is the greatest and first commandment (Matt. xxii. 38). "Thou shalt love the Lord thy God with thy whole heart, and with thy whole soul, and with thy whole mind, and with thy whole strength" (Mark xii. 30).

Thou shalt love—this is the central act of life. Love is the highest expression, the last word of my possibilities. When I love, I concentrate and sum up my whole being in my love, I give myself wholly to the service of him whom I love.

Whom shalt thou love?—The Lord thy God; thou shalt love Him alone. Why?—Because He is thy Saviour and thy God, which means thy Master and thy all. Thou shalt love Him for His own sake, because He is Himself.

How shalt thou love Him?—*ex toto*, with thy whole self. Thou shalt gather up, thou shalt unite the whole of thy being in love. Thou shalt love with thy whole self, says the Lord; and when God says "all," He means all. It is the totality of my faculties and of their acts, that is to say, of my life, unified in love. With thy whole mind: there is knowledge, sight, truth; with thy whole heart: there is love and charity, in the proper sense of the words; with thy whole soul and with thy whole strength: there is action, seeking, liberty.

And the commandment does not attribute love to all the powers, for only the heart loves; but all the powers to love; for all acts must meet and be bound together in love to compose the one disposition, the general and living resultant, which is piety. Thus it is that in the commandment "thou shalt love" is the great law which sums up all laws, the great duty which sums up all duties.

13. **The definition of the Catechism.**—More humble in appearance, but with a meaning no less deep, the Catechism

teaches the little child all the doctrine of St. Paul and of St. John. Why did God make man? asks the Catechism·—God made man to know Him, love Him, and serve Him, and thus to merit eternal happiness. To know, love, and serve: the three constituent terms of piety, the three words that sum up all religion. There is the whole of life, the whole of man, the one *why* of our existence. St. Paul affirms it, St. John proclaims it, the Catechism repeats it.

To know, to love, to serve; intelligence, will, action; sight, love, search; truth, charity, liberty: always the same three terms joined in the same order. To know in order to love, to love in order to serve; to serve in loving, to love in knowing: this is the whole of Christian life, according to the Catechism; and it is the whole of piety, according to St. Paul.

And this knowledge, love, and service, which are piety, and God's glory, merit the infinite recompense which is eternal salvation. God's glory in the sight, love, and service of His majesty; the happiness of man in the possession of His goodness: there is the whole of religion, and the whole of piety on earth and in heaven. What wonderful things in one little answer of the Catechism !

CHAPTER III

The Virtue of Piety

14. The living unity of my being in piety.—15. Facility and readiness.—16. Piety is the great disposition.—17. The body and the soul of piety.—18. It is a matter of the mind.—19. The function of sentiment.—20. The loss of sensible impressions.

14. **The living unity of my being in piety.**—Such is piety. If I break this bundle, if I take away one of its elements, I shall have left nothing but a mutilated and false piety. If I introduce into it a strange element, my piety will be mingled and impure. If one of its elements weakens or deteriorates, it becomes languishing and sickly. If the union of the elements gets relaxed, if their bond is broken, it becomes divided, crumbles, and falls to pieces.

It must, then, be true, full, and strong; and for this, each of the elements must be pure. It must be one; and for this, the union of the elements must be close and firm. It must also increase until it has reached its consummation; and for this, each element must go on expanding, becoming complete, extending, and their union must become constantly closer, and finally, that state must be constituted in me which forms the virtue of piety.

15. Facility and readiness.—For it is not at all the act of seeing, loving, and seeking God, that constitutes piety. Piety is a habit; and, like every habit, it is a facility, a readiness to do the acts belonging to it. It is the facility, the readiness to see, to love, and to seek God in all things, that constitutes piety. The virtue of devotion, as St. Francis of Sales calls it, does not consist in keeping the commandments, but in keeping them readily and willingly;[1] devotion being no other than a general virtue opposed to spiritual idleness, a virtue which makes us prompt in God's service.[2]

Hence, I have not acquired the virtue of piety, until I have acquired this readiness in seeing, loving, and seeking God in all things. My God, where is this readiness in myself?—How long shall I, poor son of man, be so heavy of heart? how long shall I love vanity, and seek after lying?[3] When wilt Thou enlarge my heart to run the way of Thy commandments, the way of piety?[4] Who will give me wings like a dove, that I may fly and be at rest in God?[5]

16. Piety is the great disposition.—Thus understood, piety is the great duty which sums up all duties; it is the great virtue, whence flow and whither tend all virtues. I understand St. Paul, when he says that it is profitable to all things, and that it has the promises of the life that now is, and of that which is to come.[6] I understand his saying, that when I

---

[1] St. Francis of Sales, *Letters*.
[2] St. Francis of Sales, *The Canticle of Canticles, Preface*.
[3] Filii hominum usquequo gravi corde? ut quid diligitis vanitatem et quæritis mendacium? (Ps. iv. 3).
[4] Viam mandatorum tuorum cucurri, cum dilitasti cor meum (Ps. cxviii. 32).
[5] Quis dabit mihi pennas sicut columbæ, et volabo et requiescam? (Ps. liv. 7).
[6] Exerce autem teipsum ad pietatem, nam pietas ad omnia utilis est, promissiones habens vitæ quæ nunc est et futuræ (1 Tim. iv. 7, 8).

have only what is strictly necessary, I nevertheless have great riches, if I have piety.[1] I understand when the Apostle St. John calls it his greatest joy. " I have no greater grace than this," he says, " to hear that my children walk in truth " (3 John 4).

In fine, the human virtues of prudence, fortitude, justice, and temperance, utilized by the divine virtues of faith, hope, and charity, are as it were condensed and concentrated in piety. And not only the virtues of the heart, but the knowledge of the mind, the actions of the body, every vital movement, every habit or human act, all these centre and unite in this one and sovereign disposition. Piety is, therefore, the gathering together of all dispositions, forms of knowledge, virtues or human actions, in the sight, love, and seeking of God. The word " piety " sums up all that is made for God, in the same way as the word " impiety " sums up all that runs counter to God.

17. The body and the soul of piety.—And how comes about this gathering together, this living union of my whole activity in piety ?—Piety is a SINGLE . . . WHOLE.—Its totality shows that it has a body, its unity shows that it has a soul. What is its body ? and what is its soul ?

The body of piety is composed of members. These members are all and each of the forms of knowledge of my mind, all and each of the virtues of my heart, all and each of the actions of my powers. There is not one of the manifestations of human life which cannot and ought not to be a member of the body of piety.

The soul of this body is divine charity ; it is this that is its living form, its principle of supernatural animation. And when this soul is joined with this body, the result is the living unity and totality which are called piety. Thus do we get a better revelation of the depth of the saying of St. Paul's already quoted.[2] After having counselled the practice of the different virtues, he ends by saying : But above all these dispositions, to animate them and to bind them into one living and perfect whole, have charity, which is the bond of

---

[1] Est autem quæstus magnus pietas cum sufficientia (1 Tim. vi. 6).
[2] See § 10 above.

perfection. It is not in itself the whole of perfection, for it never goes without the other virtues.[1] But it is the soul which gives them life, the bond which gives them perfection. Thus, in the supernatural order as in the natural order, human life finds its perfection in the union of the soul with the body.

It is thus that piety is profitable to all things, because, in its living unity, it does not allow a single fragment of human activity to be wasted. Everything has an infinite value for God and in God's eyes. Sleep as well as food, work as well as prayer, knowledge as well as virtue, a sigh as well as a smile, little things as well as great things, all things are full of life and glory and merit and eternity. Apart from piety, alas! what waste! what uselessness! what fatality!—O living unity, O living whole, O holy piety, when shall I possess thee? when wilt thou possess me? be thou the concentration and organization of my being, be thou my entire and sole occupation in time and in eternity!

18. **It is a matter of the mind.**—From considering the elements of piety, it appears that it is before all else a matter of the intelligence and of the will. The intelligence sees, the heart loves, and action follows. As long as the intelligence cannot see, or sees amiss, piety is false or null. Piety begins in the intelligence, continues by the will, and ends in action. It is the highest exercise of man's faculties. It has its beginning in truth, its centre and climax in charity, its fulfilment in liberty.

It is, then, no little affair of sentiment. It is a strange abuse of words to attribute the great name of "piety" to the affected tricks (*mièvreries*) which are practised by so many narrow souls in spiritual exercises. The glitter of imagination, the touches of sensibility, however fine and pleasant they may be, are often only the empty amusements of those suffering from illusions, who have some of the appearances of piety, but none of its power.[2]

19. **The function of sentiment.**—Feelings and sensible affections, as well as imagination, are good in themselves; for

[1] Read the whole of 1 Cor. xiii. to see how charity is the bond and soul of all the virtues.
[2] Habentes speciem quidem pietatis, virtutem autem ejus abnegantes (2 Tim. iii. 5).

this inferior part of the soul, which borders on the senses, is still one of God's beautiful gifts to our nature. Imagination and sensibility have great utility in life, and they play a fairly important part in it. Are they not called to embellish the hard outline of duty, to adorn it with refined graces and pure attractions, to impart to it the brightness of the beautiful and the relief of vigour, to clothe it with the glories of art, and so forth ? Their well-ordered function is so brilliant, comforting, and elevating ! They have, therefore, a place to occupy in piety, their help is by no means to be despised ; for grace employs and utilizes all natural resources. To wish to suppress their normal function in piety would be to hurt nature and to hinder grace. Therefore, let them keep their place, let them find their most noble and legitimate expansion in piety,—nothing could be better ; let those sensitive souls, in whom feeling predominates, go to God by this way,— there is no harm in that.

But it must be on condition that sensibility and imagination are not allowed to play a fatal part. If they desire to become the main thing or the whole of piety, that also hurts nature and hinders grace ; for the sensible faculties are only the hired servants of the intelligence and the will. To be led by sentiment is to put the servant in charge of the house, and to get the master to abdicate. It is not sentiment that is bad, but the inordinate part assigned to it. What is a bad thing is the suppression, or at least the lessening, of all the higher part of the soul in its relations with God, and confining oneself to the inferior regions of the sensibility.

20. **The loss of sensible impressions.**—In some souls, emotions are so much the whole of piety that they are convinced that they have lost all devotion when feeling disappears. Oh dear ! I have no piety left ; I no longer *feel* anything !— They only had sentiment : when it is gone, they have, indeed, nothing left. But it is not piety that they have lost ; they never had it. If they only knew that this is just the moment to begin to have it !—The greatest hindrance is gone ; the way which was blocked by sentimentalism, is now clear ! But how little do people know what piety is ! How far are they from suspecting what it is in its fulness !

CHAPTER IV

God's Glory

21. What glorifying God means.—22. The material and formal elements of glory.—23. Intrinsic glory.—24. Extrinsic glory. 25. The fulness of the word "glory."—26. *Crescamus.*

21. What glorifying God means.—I can now define the meaning of the word "glory," and the nature of the obligation which it expresses. What is the meaning of my being made for God's glory?—It means that I must apply the resources of life which I possess to know, love, and serve Him; and refer my whole being to Him by the application of my faculties of knowing, loving, and acting. The servant who has received five talents brings back five others to his master; he who has received two brings them back doubled.[1] Both of them were diligent in using for their master that which he had confided to them; and they bring him back the fruits of their diligence. And it is this diligence and this return that glorify their master. The bad servant was not diligent, and he brought no return; he did not honour his master, and he was punished. Thus, then, to apply the faculties He has given me to know, to love, and to serve Him, and by this diligence to refer my whole being to Him, this is for me to glorify God.

22. The material and formal elements of glory.—In glory, there are two parts: one, which is, as it were, its matter; the other, as it were, its form.

The matter of glory, or the object to be glorified, consists of the qualities of the glorious being. In God's glory, these are all and each of the perfections of the infinite Being. Each one in particular, as well as all together, may be the object of the glorification to be rendered to the Creator.

The form of glory, or the act of glorifying, consists of all and each of the acts whereby the perfections of the glorious Being are acknowledged and exalted. And in the glory which I, for my part, can and must give God, it consists of

[1] Matt. xxv. 15.

all and each of the acts of my life applied to the exaltation of the divine perfections.

Glory, in its proper sense, is constituted of the meeting together and union of these two elements. A being possessed of the greatest of perfections, if these perfections do not receive the honour which is their due, would be glorious but not glorified. In the same way, honour attributed to defects and vices is not glorification but abomination. Glory means the meeting together of glorious qualities and glorifying acts.

23. Intrinsic glory.—God has in Himself, by Himself, and for Himself, an infinite glory, infinitely worthy of Him; a glory which is His own, which is as great as Himself, which is His life, which is Himself. In the unity of His substance, He has all perfections, and all these perfections in infinity, which is the plenitude of the divine Being. In the unity of His Being, God is infinitely glorious.

In the Trinity of the Persons, He is infinitely glorified. In the infinite act whereby the Father communicates to the Son all divine perfections by way of knowledge, and the Father and the Son, conjointly, communicate these same perfections to the Holy Ghost by way of love, there is a glorification in all respects equal to the glorified Being. And this is the intimate, infinite life of God in Himself. And in this life He is infinitely glorious and infinitely glorified. This is what is called the intrinsic glory of God.

24. Extrinsic glory.—The glory rendered to their Creator by creatures is called extrinsic. In this, the object to be glorified still consists of all and each of the divine perfections. The glorifying act is the manifestation and the exaltation of these perfections accomplished by creatures. The object is infinite, the praise is finite. But although it is finite, the praise is nevertheless full, when the being who glorifies spends all the powers of its life in the act.

For me personally, it is possible to exalt my God's perfections, by applying my whole life to know, love, and serve Him. And as knowing, loving, and seeking God constitute piety, my piety is that which finally glorifies God.

And since my piety is an essentially supernatural work,

participating to some extent, by grace, in the nature and the life of God, I am made capable of and responsible for giving my Saviour and my God an entirely supernatural, and in a manner infinite, glory.

The glorious qualities of the infinite Being are all expressed in Holy Scripture by a single phrase—the name of God. The acts whereby I can glorify the divine perfections are all summed up in a single word—piety. Consequently, it is the meeting together of my piety with God's name which constitutes God's glory. And this is what is so magnificently expressed in the first petition of the Lord's Prayer: " Hallowed be Thy name."

25. *The fulness of the word " glory."*—The divine perfections are infinite; and the acts by which I can exalt them are exceedingly manifold. When I speak of God's holiness, power, goodness, etc., I only see one aspect of Him in His totality. In the same way, when I speak of submission, gratitude, or love, etc., I only name one of the particular acts of my being. The word " glory " is altogether general; it indicates at the same time all the perfections which I can glorify in God, and all the acts by which I can glorify Him. The fulness of the word corresponds with the whole of God's being and with the whole of my being.

In explaining the word " creature,"[1] I saw how convenient was the broadness of this expression for enunciating in one principle the universal rule of the use of all things. Nothing possesses the force of a word of illimitable meaning. " God's glory " is also an universal expression, which suffices of itself to formulate in the totality of its comprehension the most absolute rule of my existence.

The " Name " of God says all that is in God. The word " piety " says all that is in me. The word " glory " says at once both all that is in Him and all that is in me in the meeting together in which we unite with one another. It is the most universal term of my life.

26. *Crescamus.*—" Praise the Lord, O my soul," says the Psalmist.—" Yes," replies the soul, " in my life I will praise the Lord: I will sing to my God as long as I shall be "

[1] See Book I, § 27

(Ps. cxlv. 2). It is my life that glorifies God;[1] my life, which means my increase in this world, the fulness of my being in the next. "Increase," said God in the beginning. And the Apostle, taking up and explaining the Creator's first command, says: Let us increase in Jesus Christ by means of all things, by doing the truth in charity. O my God, give me the want, the desire, the will, the strength, to increase for Thee according to the measure of all the resources with which Thou hast endued my being. Thy love expects of me the portion of glory for which Thou hast made me. Oh that I might not in any way frustrate the expectation and desire of Thy heart! Thy glory can grow in me, since I can increase; it ought to grow, since I ought to increase. Oh that my life might be a real, constant, and complete growth; that my being might attain to the full its possibilities for praise. Grant me to live, for it is life that glorifies Thee.[2] The dead shall not praise Thee, O Lord; nor any of them that go down to hell. But we that live bless the Lord, from this time now and for ever (Ps. cxiii. 17, 18). I shall not die, but live: and shall declare the works of the Lord (Ps. cxvii. 17). Thou art my God, and I will praise Thee: Thou art my God, and I will exalt Thee (*ibid.* 28).

CHAPTER V

Zeal

27. *Multiplicamini.*—28. Divine honour.—29. The human bond.—30. The eternal bond.—31. Zeal in one's vocation.

27. Multiplicamini.—To live for God, is the noble ambition of those who are zealous and know how to devote themselves. But if I have this ambition, I shall increase His glory not only within me, but also around me. As all increase of soul glorifies God, I shall dilate as many souls around me as possible. No one in this world is isolated, and no vocation is for self only. When He first laid down the laws of life, its Author

---

[1] Vivet anima mea et laudabit te (Ps. cxviii. 175).
[2] Vivens, vivens ipse confitebitur tibi (Is. xxxviii. 19).

not only proclaimed the law of individual increase, but at the same time He proclaimed the law of social multiplication. " Increase and multiply " (Gen. i. 28). In virtue of this law, the individual has the power and the duty of increase, the society has the power and the duty of multiplying the increase. This privilege of increase and of multiplication, which is realized at the starting-point of every human life, applies to all propagation of life, natural and supernatural. And as a matter of fact, God only intended human intercourse for the purpose of the multiplication of life.

28. **Divine honour.**—God might have reserved to Himself the right of being the sole Author of life ; and He willed to associate man with the power of His goodness. I can give life. By material help and bodily care, I can promote physical life. By counsel, encouragement, and example, I can exert moral influence. By speech, teaching, and writing, I can further the life of truth in the will. By the whole range of my activities, I can attract towards the good, elevate, and sanctify my surroundings. Still more, in virtue of the communion of saints, by my prayers and my sacrifices I can reach all the members of the body of the Church, of which I form a part : I can thus be of use to the just and to sinners, to the living and the dead ; both earth and purgatory are open to my zeal. God has given me this immense power of expanding life on all sides for His glory. Shall I be able to understand my power and to do my duty ? If I love God, if I desire His glory, what a field lies open to my zeal ! If I only consider that God holds as done to Himself what is done to the least of His brethren,[1] and that the least practical service done to the least of those who are His, such as merely giving a cup of cold water, possesses an eternal value in His eyes ![2]

29. **The human bond.**—Such is the honour that is done to me, and such is the happiness that is given me. It is also a divine honour to communicate life, and it is also a human bond. I am bound to all those to whom I give and from

[1] Amen dico vobis, quamdiu fecistis uni ex fratribus meis minimis, mihi fecistis (Matt. xxv. 40).
[2] Et quicumque potum dederit uni ex minimis istis, calicem aquæ frigidæ tantum, in nomine discipuli, amen dico vobis, non perdet mercedem suam (Matt. x 42).

whom I receive, bound by the very bonds of life. We are formed by one another and live in one another. In me there is something of them, and in them there is something of me. What of them is in me is their life; what of me is in them is my life. Our lives interpenetrate one another, and are more or less identified, according to the amount each receives or gives. What I receive from my relations, from my friends, from all those who exercise a vital influence upon me, is, as it were, a part of their life which is formed in mine; what I give those whom I serve is, as it were, a part of my life which is formed in them. How close are these bonds, how strong, and how sweet! It is this exchange, this interpenetration of life, that is the great secret of the charm of our human relationships.

30. **The eternal bond.**—And these bonds go beyond the frontiers of death to reveal all the fulness of their strength and sweetness in heaven. It is only there that they will be rightly revealed. On earth, we are in the region of dimness and enigma; we see such a little way! The mystery of our reciprocal influences remains so darkly veiled from us! But in heaven will be the region of light and of open vision. For there is not anything secret, that shall not be made manifest; nor hidden, that shall not be known and come abroad (Luke viii. 17). In eternity, nothing vital perishes, everything expands and grows. What bonds shall I then have with my parents, who have done so much for my training! What bonds with the masters, who took such care of my youth! What bonds with friends, who gave such encouragement and support to my life! What bonds with my brethren, whose example and counsel so often put me in good heart!

And on the other hand, if I know how to devote myself, what bonds will there be with innumerable souls to whom I had imparted an increase of life by my prayers, my alms, and penances, by my words, my example, my care, and by all my activities! It is just the secrets and the details of this zeal, of this communication of life, which will be proclaimed at the general judgement as the motives and causes of immortal beatitude.[1] O my God, how good art Thou in thus binding

[1] Matt. xxv. 35.

us together for eternity! How I thank Thee for making us live thus in one another, and all together in Thee!

31. Zeal in one's vocation.—To live for God, to cause to live for God, is loving myself, loving my neighbour, and also, loving God. These three loves are but one, since in all three we seek the same one glory of God. Oh that God may give me the grace to live and to cause others to live for Him according to the whole extent of the obligations and possibilities of my vocation! I am right in saying " of my vocation "; for it is in conformity therewith that I ought to glorify God in myself and in my surroundings. Every vocation involves a responsibility; and this responsibility must be fulfilled for God's honour. No one gives himself his own vocation; it is God who outlines his programme of life for each one in creating him.

By Him and for Him it is that I have my vocation. Hence, I ought not only to extend His glory in myself by the full spiritual increase of my being in piety, but also to extend it around me within the sphere of influence which infinite Goodness has been pleased to assign to my destiny. O my God, grant me, for the glory of Thy name, so to increase that I may be capable of fulfilling the whole of my vocation. Make me full of zeal for Thine interests.

CHAPTER VI

Disorder

Adherence to Creatures

32. The journey far from God.—33. Stopping.—34. Adherence.—35. Rest.

32. The journey far from God.—I have just considered the organization of my life according to God's plan. I must now consider its disorganization through human disorder. We are made for life, says St. Paul; and He that maketh us for this very thing, is God, who hath given us His Spirit, the pledge of immortality. This is why we are courageous, knowing that our mortal life is a journey far from God. For we walk by faith and not by sight. But we have courage and good-will and desire to journey away from the body, and to be present with the Lord.[1]

This journey far from God is my passage through creatures in this world. I must pass through them to go to Him. But I must pass through and go beyond them, in order to find Him alone above them, in order to adhere to Him alone amongst all things that are not Himself. If I know how to pass onward in the use of them, my terrestrial pilgrimage is performed according to the divine order.

33. Stopping.—Here, however, is the evil. Instead of passing on, I linger, turn aside, and stop. I linger among creatures, I turn aside from God, I stop at myself. And there is the evil of my life, the whole evil of my life, this is disorder.

Wherein, then, does disorder consist?—In the lingering, turning aside, and stopping of my life, which, in all or in part, does not rise up to God. When a part of my being or of my movement does not attain, at least indirectly, the supernatural union which God intends me to contract with Himself for His glory and for my happiness, when some portion of me does not reach the total and true end in its final term, there is disorder. And this disorder is more or less pronounced, according to the nature and extent of the deviation. The preeminence of the end to which I am called will never allow me to remain outside of or below it. And if I remain outside of and below it, it is an injury done to my life, and a wrong done to Him who is the author, director, and consummation of my life.

34. Adherence.—And whence comes disorder?—Always from one thing, pleasure, pleasure in created things. I am made to be happy, and an intense need of happiness is in all my faculties. And in my earthly journey, far from God whom I cannot see, since I walk by faith and not by sight; in the midst of creatures I can see and by the pleasure of which I

---

[1] Qui autem efficit nos in hoc ipsum, Deus, qui dedit nobis pignus spiritus. Audentes igitur semper, scientes quoniam, dum sumus in corpore, peregrinamur a Domino; per fidem enim ambulamus et non per speciem; audemus autem et bonam voluntatem habemus magis peregrinari a corpore et præsentes esse ad Dominum (2 Cor. v. 5-8).

am affected, I allow myself to be deceived by what I see, and I forget what I do not see. Instead of sustaining my progress by the oil of gladness which is put at my disposal, I desire, in it and by it, to find my satisfaction and repose. Pleasure ceases to be an instrument, and becomes an end. The fascination of this trifle makes me lose sight of the good, and the variableness of concupiscence upsets the good order of my soul.[1]

Pleasure, which ought to ease the passage of my soul through things created, now sticks to it; it becomes a sort of viscosity, which attaches and keeps me to myself and to creatures. I am now delayed, turned aside, stopped, by the very thing which should have most contributed to the rapidity of my ascent. Like some machine the cleaning of which has been neglected, and in which the use of oil ends by so clogging it as first to impede, and finally to stop its going, I contract an adherence to things created; I, who was made to adhere to God alone.

35. Rest.—In heaven, the joy of the blessed is in praising God, their satisfaction comes from this, their rest is in God. On earth, creatures for my use have their manifold pleasures. If I take these pleasures, which are in the creature, to stay in them; if I stay in them to enjoy them; if, in this enjoyment, I take my rest, my joy is no longer that of the just; it is not even that of reason; it is perverted, falsified, debased; it is that of the animal man, of the evil nature, of the world under a curse. This is the joy so often anathematized by God and by His saints.

Every creature, in which I take my rest solely for the sake of the pleasure I find in it, stops my progress towards God, and my union with Him. However noble this creature may be, however high or supernatural I may suppose it to be, even if it were a most pre-eminent gift of God's, since nothing of this kind is God, but only a gift of God's, if I stop therein, if I attach myself thereto, if therein I take my rest, I stop, attach myself, and rest outside God. And He Himself alone is the term of my movement, the place of my rest.

[1] Fascinatio nugacitatis obscurat bona, et inconstantia concupiscentiæ transvertit sensum sine malitia (Sap. iv. 12).

CHAPTER VII

Disorder

Attachment to Self

36. Appropriation.—37. Self-seeking.—38. The evil is not in satisfaction, but in subversion.—39. *Gloria mea nihil est.*

36. Appropriation.—In adhering to the creature and in taking my rest outside God, I stay something of the creature in myself, and I stay something of myself in creatures. I thus take away from God a part of my life and a part of those things which ought to be of use to me for Him. What of creatures I take away from God, and the part of my life that I share, these I appropriate to myself. And from this it is that arise selfishness, self-love, and self-interest. Whatever of my mind and its views stops at myself and goes no higher, constitutes selfishness. Whatever of my will and its affections is attached to myself and does not go to God, constitutes self-love. Whatever of my powers and their actions rests in myself and does not go further, constitutes self-interest.

It is against this undue appropriation, this " propriety " (" *propre* "), that the saints have penned such terrible anathemas : especially do mystical writers show us in regard thereto depths which are alarming, and in which we get a closer view of what is meant by God's all, and by the absolute and essential duty of referring all to Him. He intends the sacrifice of praise to be complete and universal, the holocaust to be entire ; He hates and cannot endure the least robbery in this holocaust.[1] He wills my union with Himself, and this higher, sovereign union excludes all foreign adherence, or any union which makes me stay in things created.

37. Self-seeking.—When in creatures and in their pleasures I rather see means of satisfying myself than of glorifying God ; when I love them rather for my own happiness than for His honour ; when I use them rather for my own pleasure than

---

[1] Ego Dominus diligens judicium et odio habens rapinam in holocausto (Is. lxi. 8).

for His, my life is no longer applied to seeing, loving, and seeking God; it is applied to seeing, loving, and seeking myself.

Self-seeking, seeking self instead of God, this is my great temptation; my satisfaction before all else, this is the continual tendency of my nature, its primary need, its strongest inclination. To satisfy myself in and through creatures, to the point of dividing, neglecting, forgetting, hurting, and trampling under foot God's glory, this is the leaning of my vitiated nature. In satisfaction of the mind by pride and of the body by sensuality, lies the whole of the evil; and, since sensuality and pride are at bottom only the same thing, self-seeking, in naming self-seeking I have named what hinders my piety and God's glory, the source of my defects, the cause of my sins, the deep root of the evil in me and in my life. Every time that I stray from the law of my creation, it is by seeking myself in the pleasure of things created, and because my selfish satisfaction is put in the front rank instead of God's glory.

38. *The evil is not in satisfaction, but in subversion.*—The evil in itself does not lie in seeking my satisfaction. Neither the final satisfaction of my increase in God, nor the instrumental satisfaction of pleasure in created things, is bad in itself; on the contrary, both are good, and very good. God having willed and made them for me, neither the one nor the other can be bad in itself. All that comes from God is good. The evil is not in my satisfaction in itself; it is in the manner in which I seek it, it is in the subversion which I bring about in order to secure it. My satisfaction must remain below the glory of God, must come after it, and help it; and as for me, I try to get it in creatures and set it before and above God. The evil lies in the displacement and subversion.

39. *Gloria mea nihil est.*—" It is true," says St. Francis of Sales,[1] " that what we do for our salvation is done for God's service, *provided that* we refer our salvation to His glory as its final end. It is also true to say that our Saviour has made our salvation in this world only a secondary end, but that He has referred it as a final end to His Father's glory; Himself saying that He came not to seek His own glory, but the glory

[1] *The Spirit of St. Francis of Sales,* Book XVIII, ch. xii.

of Him that sent Him ; and He went so far as to protest that if He sought His own glory, His glory would be nothing, which means it would be vain if God's glory were not its chief end."[1] Our Saviour's glory indisputably holds the most pre-eminent place among created satisfactions and goods. What is my glory compared to our Saviour's glory ? And if our Saviour declares that His glory is vanity and nothingness apart from His Father's, how must it be with all other satisfactions of creatures ? Vanity, nothingness, disorder, such is every satisfaction sought apart from God's glory.

CHAPTER VIII

Disorder

Its Effects

40. Perversion.—41. Evil —42. Lies —43. Vanity.—44. Slavery.—45. Universal groaning.—46. Death.

40. **Perversion.**—What I do contrary to God's glory, and which does not go directly or indirectly to this end, is perversion and evil, lies and vanity, slavery for myself and for creatures, and lastly, death.

Whatever in me goes contrary to God's glory is radical perversion and iniquity : it destroys God's plan, breaks down the order of my life, and annihilates the very thing for which God made me, and for which He made all that in any way concerns me. This is the perversion that puts me at variance with the essence of things—and which, by destroying my *raison d'être*, would destroy my being and all beings, if God's works could be destroyed, and if God, by His power, were not to bring back my being to render to Himself in another manner the glory which I am seeking to destroy. No creature will ever be able to understand what is the meaning of a single sin ! The perversion of sin ! This is an unfathomable mystery ! This is *evil !*

---

[1] Ego non quæro gloriam meam . . . si ego glorifico meipsum, gloria mea nihil est (Joan viii. 50 and 54).

41. **Evil.**—For there is only one evil—as there is only one good.—The one essential good is God's glory. The one essential evil is that which destroys this good, that which attacks God's glory,—sin.—This is the evil!—All created goods have in them only that of good which procures God's glory. All the evils in the world have in them only that of evil which participates in sin.—In all evils that which is evil is the portion of sin which has crept into them.—Nothing is evil except sin and what belongs to sin. God's glory is the one and universal good.—Sin is the one and universal evil.—O God! what a quantity of evils there are in the world! and yet there is only one!—If I only knew how to understand this!

God's glory is God's one good, since He can only act for His own glory; it is also my one good, since it is my entire end. Apart from this, there is no other good than that which leads to this highest good. In the same way, sin may be called God's evil, since it attacks God's one good; and it is my highest evil, since it deprives me of my highest good. Apart from sin, there is no other evil than that which leads thereto or comes therefrom.

Good and evil! God alone has a real knowledge of them. " You shall be as gods, knowing good and evil " (Gen. iii. 5). Such is the perfidious promise of the tempter. Of a truth, if I knew good and evil as they are, I should become like God by participating in His knowledge; knowing in all things how much good and how much evil there is, how much is for His glory and how much is contrary thereto, this is, indeed, the great thing to know. Oh, how much I need to acquire this knowledge!

42. **Lies.**—Disorder may exist in my mind, in my heart, in my actions. In my mind, it produces lies; in my heart, vanity; in my actions, slavery.

When my sight is centred on myself and wanders away from seeing God, my mind belies its destiny; for it is made to see God. In the creature, when I look at that only which can give me satisfaction, when I consider it merely from the point of view of my human utility, my mind is once more in error and lies; for it is made to see in the creature the means of going to God. Is it not the great falsehood, indeed, to look for myself in creatures, to think that they are made mainly for me, and to put myself in God's place ? Thus, I deceive myself, and make creatures belie their destiny.

Moreover, the great murderer from the beginning, the devil, the father of all those who refuse God's glory and seek it for themselves, stood not in the truth, the truth is not in him ; he lies, and has his root therein ; for he is a liar, and the father thereof.[1] He is the liar, the great liar, because he seeks in all things to usurp the glory of God. He is the father of lies, because he urges men to look for nothing but their own satisfaction in all things, and prevents them from considering their Creator's praise.

43. Vanity.—Love, if it stop at idle enjoyment, only cleaves to vanity and emptiness. Oh, how empty are creatures, if I do not try to find in them that which is their fulness and essence ! " Vanity of vanities," said Ecclesiastes ; " vanity of vanities, and all is vanity " (Eccles. i. 2). Vanity means the creature when void of God. Every created thing that I love exclusively for my own satisfaction is vanity to me, because to me it is void of God. How empty are the pleasures of the world, and what a void do they create in the soul ! We must, indeed, have experienced what fulness means in order to feel the meaning of emptiness ! It is only after having felt something of the fulness of God, the fulness that comes from the love of His glory, that a soul begins to feel the vanity of its own selfish satisfaction ; it knows what emptiness is, it feels its depth, it knows what a burden it is.

Yes, indeed, everything in my life which is no help, which does not somehow contribute to the love of God's glory, is useless and null and wasted. Being made, and made only for that, if I do it not, I am no good, I am worthless, I am nothing. Vanity of vanities, and all is vanity ! O God ! am I not entirely vanity, I, who live so little and so rarely in the love of Thy glory ?

44. Slavery.—When I seek my human pleasure in things

---

[1] Ille homocida erat ab initio et in veritate non stetit, quia non est veritas in eo ; quum loquitur mendacium, ex propriis loquitur, quia mendax est et pater ejus (Joan. viii. 44).

created, when I seek in them my life's repose, I become a slave. There arise in me deep, insatiable, constantly growing needs. I no longer have any control over my own appetites, nor over the witchery and tyranny of the influence of things around me. A sad servitude is this, and it makes my existence the plaything of what is meant for my use!

In fact, what has become an ultimate necessity to me is a form of slavery. I cannot withdraw myself from the dominion of the end which has become a necessity to me; I am under it, it is my master, and I am its servant. As soon as I set the end of my life in the enjoyment of things created, they become the dominant necessity of my life, they bind me with an imperious tyranny, and I become their slave.

And I see clearly that this is the case. For what is the source of my uneasiness, of my trouble, of my disturbance, of my sadness, all of which are signs of my slavery?—The one source is seeking my own pleasure. I am uneasy, when I am afraid of having it taken from me; troubled, when I have lost it; disturbed, when it is difficult to get it; discouraged, when I no longer see how to find it; sad, when it is altogether wanting to me.

I am a slave in the measure in which I seek my own pleasure; unhappy, exactly in proportion to the way in which I desire to place human happiness in the forefront of my life. Such is the just punishment of broken order! For, says St. Augustine, he who does not give God His due by doing as he ought renders it to Him by suffering as he ought. Nor is there any interval between these two things; at the very moment when he does not as he ought, he suffers as he ought. For the beauty of the universal order cannot endure to be defiled for a single moment with the ugliness of sin without being made good by the beauty of punishment.[1]

45. Universal groaning.—Creatures, all created things, so far as I am concerned, are essentially only instruments—instruments ordained for God's glory: this is their essential

---

[1] Si non reddit faciendo quod debet, reddit patiendo quod debet. Nullo autem temporis intervallo ista dividuntur, ut quasi alio tempore non faciat quod debet, et alio patiatur quod debet; ne vel puncto temporis universalis pulchritudo turpetur, ut sit in ea peccati dedecus sine decore vindictæ (*De libero arbitrio*, iii. 44).

destination. If I use them for another end, if I employ them mainly for another purpose, the use I thus make of them is, as far as I am concerned, always foolish, usually hurtful, and often wrong. So far as created things are concerned, it is a use which violates order and is contrary to nature; for I turn them aside in a disorderly way from the great purpose for which they were created. St. Paul, in his energetic way, speaks of the way in which they are violated. The whole of creation, he says, waits with great expectation for the revelation of the sons of God, because it is now subject to vanity, not willingly, but by reason of Him that made it subject, in hope that itself also shall be delivered from the servitude of corruption into the liberty of the glory of the children of God. For we know that every creature groaneth and travaileth in pain as of child-birth until now![1]—What a word is this!—St. Paul sorrowfully heard this universal groaning: "we know," says he. And what do I know of it?—I make the whole of creation groan, and, thrice deaf, I hear nothing.

46. **Death.**—Finally, if order is life, disorder is death. And what is death?—It means separation, disintegration, annihilation; separation from the principle of life, disintegration of the true elements of being, and the annihilation of its existence. Death is complete, when this threefold work is finished; death has begun, wherever this threefold work has begun. Its reign extends wherever there is separation, disintegration, and annihilation.

Disorder is a kind of death, because it makes me leave God, establishing a more or less pronounced separation between Him and me. It is my death, because it disintegrates the oneness of my faculties, which it scatters and disperses amidst creatures. It is my death, because it hinders my growth for God, lessens my being, and dries up or annihilates my merits. Thereby I am separated from God, dispersed amidst creatures, lessened in myself. The reign of death is within me, and it works baneful destruction just where life alone

[1] Expectatio creaturæ revelationem filiorum Dei expectat. Vanitati enim creatura subjecta est non volens, sed propter eum qui subjecit eam in spe; quia et ipsa creatura liberabitur a servitute corruptionis in libertatem filiorum Dei. Scimus enim quod omnis creatura ingemiscit et parturit usque adhuc (Rom. viii. 19-22).

should be increasing. Alas! how lamentable do I feel the works of death within me to be! I am far from God, so scattered amidst creatures, so weak in myself!

CHAPTER IX

Disorder

Its Degrees

47. The descent.—48. Division.—49. Domination.—50. Exclusion—51. The three stages of evil.—52. The three stages of life.

47. The descent.—Disorder is very extensive; it stretches from heaven to hell. What a distance there is between a soul which almost touches heaven and only bears the least trace of the dust of earth, and one about to be flung into eternal fire! Hence, disorder has various degrees; can they be measured in any way?—It is clear that I cannot calculate each of the increases which my soul may gain, nor each of the losses which disorder may inflict upon it. What is possible and useful is to characterize in its broad outlines the progress of evil which separates me from God.

And since there is deviation, in order to appreciate it, I must first of all see where it begins, so that I may afterwards be able to ascertain where it ends. Therefore, by proceeding from above to below, *i.e.*, by following the downward descent of the soul in its deviation, I shall be able to form an idea of its disorder. If I would then consider how it is to be corrected, I shall have to proceed from below to above, *i.e.*, to follow the progress of the soul in its return. Let us first look at its descent.

48. Division.—Since disorder is radically an aberration of the soul, which permits itself to be bewitched and taken up with pleasure in creatures, a division occurs in this first deviation from God. The stream of life no longer sets wholly towards God, it is severed, and one part of it is diverted towards creatures. And in this way, my divided interest, my human pleasure, is put very nearly on the same footing as God. I no longer consider God as my one *all*. I think of Him as no longer being sufficient, in *Himself alone*, for my hope, my happiness and my life. I find in myself something apart from Him, something that divides with Him the honour of being, to some extent, the end of my life's progress. I get attached to myself and to creatures, and in me there occurs a sort of rupture through which something of my personality escapes; and this leakage frustrates God of the all which He has a right to expect and to require, in reality, from me. *Diliges ex toto*.

What an astounding wrong is done to God, if He is compared with the creature, if the latter is allowed to share my life with Him, and thus to frustrate Him of a part of my being, and of a part of those beings destined to glorify Him through me, and which I appropriate to myself!

49. Domination.—But appropriation does not stop short at division; it "goes further still," as St. Francis of Sales would say, it comes to domination. Then, it is no longer a juxtaposition of false human interest with the divine interest, there is superposition. The pleasure of created things ends by getting a more or less pronounced preponderance over immortal glory. In the mind, certain ways of looking at and judging matters, assign to things human a higher place than things divine. In the heart, certain affections give the preference to human satisfaction. In the actions, certain endeavours put selfish interests above sacred interests.

This is a still greater disorder, it means subversion, it means that man is higher than God. It is no longer merely a failure to understand God's all, it is also the misunderstanding of God's sovereignty. It is a more or less extended, a more or less conscious subversion, whereby that which ought to be only an instrumental facility, subordinate even to the use of the instrument, comes to predominate over God's glory; that which is very secondary thus tends to become the chief thing, the accidental to become the essential, selfish satisfaction to take the first place; the servant to put himself above his Master, the creature before the Creator.

50. Exclusion.—And with the still further encroachments of pleasure upon God's rights, disorder finally is carried to

such an excess that the Supreme Master is supremely misunderstood, and His rights are excluded. The direction of the soul towards disorderly satisfaction is so great that it becomes totally turned away from God. The supernatural union is broken, the divine life is lost, the divine glory is annihilated. Destruction of life, exclusion of God's glory, such is the last depth of the abyss.

51. **The three stages of evil.**—Here then are the three successive stages in the long descent from God : division, domination, exclusion ; false pleasure first divides, then dominates, and finally excludes God's glory. And these are three real stages.

For division has a long way to run before it gets to domination. And domination itself has far to go before reaching exclusion. And exclusion finally increases with the multiplication of iniquity. Consequently, these are the three stages of evil.

52. **The three stages of life.**—Piety, which is the journey back to God, reascends these three stages, starting from the depths to attain the heights.

It begins by restoring life to the soul, and drags it forth from the deeps of evil, from excluding God's glory. This is the first stage of its ascent : it may be called the reawakening of life, or the recognition of God. It is the recovery of union.

It will next correct the disorder of my satisfaction predominating over God's glory; it will go on to efface and abolish the falseness of human preferences, the usurpation of the divine by the human. This will be the second great stage, which I shall call the growth of life, or God first. This will be the perfecting of union.

Finally, it will desire to purify and wipe out all traces of division ; it will not allow false human interests to come into comparison and to mingle with divine interests. And this will be the third and last stage, which I shall call the summits of life, or God only. And this will be the consummation of union.

These three stages of life are to be found in spiritual writers under various names. Thus, some say : the states of beginning, advancement, and perfection. Others: the purgative, illuminative, and unitive life. Others: the fundamental Christian life, the ascetic, and the mystic life. St. Ignatius says: the first, second, and third degrees of humility. These various names are not, however, synonymous; for they consider life from different points of view, and they do not uniformly attribute to each of their three degrees the same extent and the same character. Nevertheless, they approximate to one another, in that they all divide the entire elevation of the spiritual edifice into three stages.

We must now consider these three stages of life. The last chapter of this second Book will be briefly devoted to the first stage of the reawakening of the soul. Then in the third Book there will be studied at greater length the growth of life, and the fourth will be taken up with the summits.

CHAPTER X

Avoiding Mortal Sin

The First Degree of Piety

53. Sin. — 54. Restoration. — 55. Habit. — 56. The multiplicity of actions and the oneness of disposition. — 57. Eagerness to be avoided.—58. The height of this first step.

53. *Sin.*—If I set my own satisfaction before God's glory in such a way as to break with Him altogether and to separate myself entirely from Him, that is mortal sin. Mortal sin is the domination of human satisfaction to the point of a grave and formal infraction of a divine commandment. It is the complete and radical subversion of the essential order of my creation, it is the destruction within me of God's plan, it is disorder in all its dreadful perversity. I face God, and trample His glory under foot, by sacrificing it to my own pleasure. All those who sin are devoid of God's glory.[1]

This is the evil which must be lamented with the tears

[1] Omnes enim peccaverunt et egent gloria Dei (Rom. iii 23).

which Holy Scripture so rightly callsirremediable.[1] Such were the tears of Jeremias. " Consider diligently ; and see if there hath been done anything like this. If a nation hath changed their gods, and indeed they are not gods : but my people have changed their glory into an idol. Be astonished, O ye heavens, at this : and ye gates thereof, be very desolate, saith the Lord " (Jer. ii. 10-12).

54. Restoration.—To restore order herein, means to place my satisfaction below God's glory and service, and never to allow the former to subvert it mortally and to exclude it ; this is the first degree of piety. The lowest depth in the abyss of disorder consists in seeing, loving, and seeking my pleasure in created things to the point of breaking with God and of destroying His glory. The first degree of piety consists in seeing, loving, and seeking God's glory in preference to my own pleasure in all grave circumstances in which my pleasure would tend to separate me from God ; in maintaining this divine glory in its place as the principal object of my sight, of my love, and of my search.

And as for my own pleasure, if I can harmonize it with God's glory, I shall be satisfied with putting it in its place, and of assigning it its function. But if I could not reconcile it therewith, if it is absolutely bad, I shall sacrifice it. And even if I had to sacrifice my life in doing this, I should sacrifice it : such is the price which I must be ready to pay for maintaining God's glory in the first place in my existence. No pleasure, not even that of life itself, ought to take its place.

55. Habit.—Piety will have attained this degree in me when I have sufficiently acquired readiness and facility in making the sacrifices necessary for avoiding mortal sin. When I have the disposition to rectify and to sacrifice, if need be, every satisfaction rather than to commit a single mortal sin voluntarily ; when, if occasion so require, I act thus with promptness and facility ; when this disposition is perfectly established in my soul, I have reached the first degree of piety.

In order to be perfect, this disposition must be established throughout my being, dominate all my faculties, and affect

[1] Flebat irremediabilibus lacrymis (Tob. x. 4).

my whole life. "Thou shalt love the Lord thy God with thy whole heart, and with thy whole soul, and with thy whole mind, and with thy whole strength" (Mark xii. 30). Mortal sin must have no place in my mind or heart or soul or body: no creature and no circumstance must be able to make it enter therein, unless it be by surprise. I say, surprise; for our poor human frailty is so great that such wretchedness is always possible, even in the best and strongest dispositions. But these passing accidents do not prevent the acquired habit from subsisting, and do not make the soul fall away from the state which it has attained. In speaking of a state of soul or a degree of virtue, we must never take into the reckoning mere somersaults arising from sins of pure frailty.

56. The multiplicity of acts and the oneness of disposition.— It is, indeed, with the state of the soul and with the degree of virtue that we here have to do. For now I do not mean to study acts, or the practice of any particular virtue. I intend to consider only the sole and unique central disposition, the universal resultant of all acts and of all dispositions, which concentrates and sums up in its living unity all the virtues, and which is called piety. It is upon this whole and this unity that I fix my regard; and its developments and degrees of increase are what I now mean to look at. The avoidance of mortal sin is the first degree of it, the first stage of the return to life.

This degree, like all those that come after it, is not characterized by the greater or less multiplicity of the acts produced, but by the oneness and perfection attained by the disposition. The soul, indeed, only succeeds in getting established in a definite state in the measure in which it attains to the oneness of its characteristic disposition. I know well that this disposition is acquired by the repetition of acts; but the repetition of acts, if it contributes to form habits, is, nevertheless, not the habit itself. In fact the habit has its natural root in the tendencies of the soul, and its supernatural root in infused graces. And it is developed not only by my human work, but above all by God's work in me. I shall see this in the second part. Hence, the repetition of acts enters only as the fourth and last factor into the formation of piety. There are, indeed, the following factors in my life ; first of all, natural tendencies, then, supernatural graces, next providential action, and lastly, my personal action. Piety is the final result of these four factors.

57. Eagerness is to be avoided.—These reflections, which will be given their necessary explanation later on, must be recalled here, in order to put me on my guard against the impatience and disquiet of human tendencies. Indeed, with the mania for feverish fuss which carries away souls of goodwill in these days, I shall be immediately borne off to plunge headlong into anxious or impatient agitation, leading me either to dread the impossibility, or else to expect to find a too speedy possibility, of getting established in a state the beauty of which attracts me. And I should find myself left amidst anxious and vain fears, and should wear myself out in thoughtless and fruitless proceedings.

No, no, let there be not too much eagerness ; we do not begin to build before making our design, we do not start before knowing the end. The architect takes his time to draw out his plans in full detail ; he only sets the workmen to build after the plans are all ready. The traveller takes his time to study and prepare for his journey ; he only makes a start after all the preparations are quite finished.

Thus, here, I am going to forearm myself against any attacks of fear or precipitation. I am going to consider in all its height the divine plan of my life, and I am going to take stock of it with calmness, without asking myself at the outset how I shall succeed in carrying it into execution. For it is not a good thing to mingle and confuse the two kinds of work together. I intend, then, to be diligent in studying, first of all, the end ; and I mean to study it thoroughly. Questions of ways and means will afterwards come in their place at the proper time. Whatever impatience or uncertainties there may be, whatever fears and improbabilities and discouragements I may experience, these are hares I shall not start. There is a time, and there is a place, for everything.

This much being laid down by way of precaution, I return to the consideration of the first degree of piety, which is the avoidance of mortal sin.

58. The height of this first step.—The avoidance of mortal sin is already one degree of piety, since it is seeing, loving, and seeking God that make us avoid sin. Wherever these three things are united: sight, love, and seeking for God, there is piety. However weak its beginnings may be, these beginnings always belong to this great disposition, which is the summing up and the living unity of Christian life.

Besides, it is not the work of a day to succeed, not only in driving away mortal sin in practice, not only in possessing the disposition which avoids it at all costs, but in establishing, securing, and fortifying this disposition in such a way as to give me facility and readiness in making all the sacrifices which may be actually *necessary*, even the sacrifice of life itself, in order to avoid a single mortal sin. And this facility and readiness must be established in the senses, in the heart, in the mind, and in my whole being.

Have I reached this point ?—Do I not still halt between two sides, and do I sufficiently understand to what extent the Lord is my God, and to what extent I ought to serve Him ?[1] In my struggle against sin, have I resisted to the blood ?[2] Can I even say, O my God, I have ascended only the first step of piety ?—Am I sure that I have done that much ?—What facility do my mind, my heart, my senses, possess in the rejection of sin—and of the thought of sin ?—I have lived in sin—have I quite got free from it ?—Has it not left behind in me secret and deep affections ?—Am I really restored and quite purified ?—What am I, O my God ? . . . A heap of earth and ashes: be Thou glorified ![3]—What is my piety, if I have not reached the first rung of the ladder ?

[1] Usquequo claudicatis in duas partes ? Si Dominus est Deus, sequimini eum (3 Kings xviii. 21).
[2] Nondum enim usque ad sanguinem restitistis, adversus peccatum repugnantes (Heb. xii. 4).
[3] Quid superbit terra et cinis ? (Ecclus. x 9).

BOOK III

GROWTH

When it has eliminated the evil of mortal sin, my soul has restored within itself the foundations of order and recovered life. And when it has become sufficiently steadfast to remain habitually in a state of grace, it leads a fundamentally Christian life. The deepest part of its disorder, which I have called the "exclusion" of God's glory, has been got rid of; the first stage of life, which I have called "the re-awakening of the soul," has been traversed; God has been found once more.

Now opens the second stage, that of "growth." The evil to be expelled is the "domination" of the human over the divine, the falseness of certain preferences for created things, dominating and therefore hurting and lessening God's glory. When this part of the spiritual journey is designated the ascetic life, which means the life of exercise, we consider primarily the human side, man's efforts, which, more especially in this part of one's career, are exercised in setting one free from what is human and in seeking the divine by various practices of prayer and penance. If we call it the illuminative life, we consider primarily the divine side, the gifts of God which impart eternal enlightenment to the soul. Since I am not now anxious to ascertain accurately the function of human efforts nor to define God's gifts, which are the two factors of life, but to follow life itself in its halts and advances, I characterize this stage as "domination" of the human, with regard to the things that bring it to a standstill; and as "growth," so far as its forward movement is concerned.

In what does domination consist?—It seems to me to have two steps, venial sin, and imperfection. Growth will therefore consist in the elimination of this twofold evil. It is this evil and this elimination that I am about to consider in this third book.

CHAPTER I

Avoiding Venial Sin

The Second Degree of Piety

1. Sin.—2. Its gravity.—3. Restoration.—4. The height of this step.

1. Sin.—What is venial sin?—It is the domination of human satisfaction to the point of a formal infraction of a divine precept.

It is domination. Being fastened to creatures by the mucilage of pleasure, my soul prefers its satisfaction to God's order; it is satisfied with itself and dissatisfied with God. The commandment is there, and it is binding; my soul perceives it, at least to some extent; and it chooses its false satisfaction. This is the dominance of pleasure.

But it is not so far dominant as to exclude God's glory altogether, and the infraction it produces is but slight; whether the levity comes from the matter, which is not grave in itself, or through the weight of the prohibition that forbids it; or whether it comes from a want of sufficiency in my advertency or in my consent. And just because the offence does not amount to being grave, it does not deprive me of life; my soul is not altogether turned aside and separated from God. It is a sort of injury done to the soul, and it is also an injury done to God.

2. Its gravity.—Although not nearly so grave by nature and in its effects as mortal sin, this evil is nevertheless essentially a disorder, in other words, an evil compared with which all others do not deserve to be called evils. Unfortunately, pleasure is so much my rule of life that it is difficult for me to understand it, and still more to feel it. I so easily understand the evils that attack my pleasure, and I feel them so strongly!—I understand so hardly the evil which attacks God's glory, and I feel it so little! Who can understand sins (Ps. xviii. 13)? Who is wise, and can understand these things?

Who is intelligent, and can know them?[1]—O my God! in what aberration do I live, when I call evil that which is hardly so at all, and when I find it so difficult to think that is evil which is so very ill!—The evils that afflict me are often so good for me! Venial sin is never this! The greatest ills always involve some good; in the least of venial sins, so far as it is sin, there is not the least trace of any good!—Who can understand sin?

3. **Restoration.**—The second degree of piety consists in the rectification of this disorder. In the circumstances in which there is venial sin, *i.e.*, where my own satisfaction, coming before God's glory, injures and wounds it, I shall succeed in reserving for the divine glory its proper place and rights. No forbidden pleasure will usurp its position.

What constitutes this degree is a thoroughly acquired facility and readiness in putting my own satisfaction in its own place, and in assigning to it its proper function, without allowing it, of deliberate intention, the least venial exhibition. And this facility must dominate and sway my whole mind, my whole heart, and my whole body. *Diliges ex toto.*—It must extend to all circumstances and to all creatures. And if I must sacrifice my own satisfaction, if I must immolate life itself, rather than commit voluntarily and deliberately the least venial sin, I am ready to make the sacrifice. Nothing, not even the fear of death, should make me commit a venial sin voluntarily. When this disposition is established in the soul, when I make the necessary sacrifices with readiness and facility rather than deliberately allow my satisfaction a venial deviation, then I have reached the second degree of piety, which is the avoidance of venial sin. Such a life is solidly Christian.

4. **The height of this step.**—The perfection of this degree is by no means so easily attained. For finally to purify the mind, the heart and the senses, from all affections and attachments, even those which are venial; to undo one after the other the meshes so closely interwoven by the venial habits, which enclose my poor human nature; to purify so many inward sinuosities which conceal thoughts of pride, affections

[1] Quis sapiens et intelliget ista, intelligens et sciet hæc? (Os. xiv. 10).

for creatures, and sensual leanings; to raise all my powers to such a facility and readiness in restoration as prevents any venial recurrence, in all this, it must be admitted, there is work which is almost infinite. From the first degree of piety to this second step in its perfection, what a course has to be run!—If, indeed, it is already a difficult matter to become established for good in the entire avoidance of mortal sin, what is to be said of the entire avoidance of venial sin ? The occasions of venial sin are far more numerous than those of mortal sin.

And where am I ? Alas! how numerous are my venial sins!—Does not self-seeking lead me at every turn to wrong God?—and this, although I know it well?—although I fully take it into account?—And how many sins there are which I am almost unaware of, arising from habits over which I keep no watch!—How often my evil instincts, but little or scarcely repressed, increase the number of my affronts, and I hardly take any notice of them!—Oh, these venial sins! I do not consider how many they are! they are more in number than the hairs of my head.[1]

CHAPTER II

Imperfection

The Domination of the Human

5. Its definition.—6. The domination of human pleasure.—7. What is the harm of it ?—8. The source of the evil.

5. **Its definition.**—Along with venial sin does all trace of " the domination of the human " disappear ?—The work has already made progress, but it is by no means yet finished. The first part of the stage of growth is over; but a second part remains, and this is also higher and more extended. After having got rid of the hurts resulting from venial sin, I have to break away from the bonds of imperfection.

[1] Comprehenderunt me iniquitates meæ et non potui ut viderem ! multiplicatæ sunt super capillos capitis mei (Ps. xxxix. 13).

Wherein does this evil consist ? What is imperfection ?—It is the domination of human satisfaction up to the point of the simple transgression of a counsel, or the non-culpable transgression of a precept. It is seeking myself and my own pleasure before God's glory in things naturally good or even bad in themselves, but without there being any formal offence against God. When, without any formal offence against the divine Majesty, I use some created thing primarily for myself, staying at self to some extent, directing my act too much towards my own satisfaction, or too much dominated by the influence of my own nature, I commit an imperfection.

Two signs clearly characterize this disorder: 1. the domination of what is human ; 2. the absence of what is called a formal offence against God. And these two signs must be explained. The first, the domination of the human, will be the subject of this chapter. The second, the absence of any formal offence against God, will be treated in the next chapter.

6. The domination of human pleasure.—This domination, known or unknown, intended or not, actual or habitual, may influence an act or the mode of its doing. This fact gives rise to involuntary and to voluntary imperfections: the latter known and intended, the former wanting in advertence or consent. Without causing the act to go beyond the limits of the useful and the honest, this domination nevertheless makes it stop short, to some extent, at myself primarily. There is too much adherence and stopping short at pleasure, which ought, indeed, to be only a means of inspiration ; and it is this adherence and this stopping short which deprive my movement of some of the relationship which it should possess, at least virtually, with God's glory in the first place. And thus I am led to fall short of the fulness of the counsel given by the Apostle : " Whether you eat or drink, or whatsoever else you do ; do all to the glory of God " (1 Cor. x. 31).

Nowhere, and in nothing, must God be given the second place. The intention of my act may go to Him first, either actually or virtually ;[1] the essential thing is that it should go

---

[1] See § 50 further on, for the question of actual and habitual intention.

to Him in some way, and that my own satisfaction should be subjected to His service. Without going so far as to offend Him formally, I must also not act with regard to Him, even in what is good, like some unmannerly person who always pushes into the first place, and who speaks and helps himself first. Impoliteness is quite out of place in dealing with men, it is much more so with God. It is certainly less lamentable to fall short in human decorum than to be wanting in what is due to God.

7. *What is the harm of it?*—This evil arises from a habit of our evil nature which recoils upon itself through selfish anxiety. According to the energetic words of Holy Scripture, the soul is here to some extent " bowed down."[1] It yields to the tendency towards self-seeking which makes me look instinctively first of all for that in the creature which cajoles me. And though I am often unconscious of it, the strength of this habit leads my eyes to see, my heart to love, my senses to act, by and for a sort of personal preference, so that good itself is seen, loved, and sought for, under some human aspect. And the viscosity of things created fastens to myself, in some measure, the employment and the care of my faculties. In all this, I am in reality following natural instincts rather than the leadings of grace.

8. *The source of the evil.*—Hence, the source of imperfection must be sought in the tendencies, instincts, and habits of our evil nature. And I must look for this source. Here, indeed, I desire to study my inner life. And since the question at stake is for me to define the steps of my soul's ascent towards God by way of interior purification, I cannot be satisfied with characterizing my acts by their external and objective disagreement with the divine order, and by their pernicious effects. It is far from being all to ascertain that such and such an act is opposed mortally, venially, or imperfectly, to the intended order of God, and that it produces unhappy results within me; I must also know why and how my soul is led into this opposition and into this unhappy state. I must discover the source.

First of all, I tried to find this source in the case of mortal

[1] Incurvaverunt animam meam (Ps. lvi. 7).

sin, and then in the case of venial sin, and now I must try to find it in the case of imperfection. And I find that it is in what is the sole reservoir of the manifestations of disorder in all its stages. It is the more or less close adherence of my being by means of pleasure to things created. Thus it is that I have come to recognize the domination of human satisfaction up to the point of excluding the divine life and glory, by the grave and formal infraction of a divine precept in mortal sin. In the case of venial sin, I saw human pleasure dominating me up to the point of the slight breach of a precept. Here, in the case of imperfection, I again find this domination of false satisfaction; the adherence to what is created is still strong enough to set up a preference, a predominance of the human, which leads to the neglect of a counsel, or to the non-culpable infraction of a precept.

CHAPTER III

Imperfection

The Absence of Formal Offence

9. The second characteristic of imperfection.—10. The transgression of a counsel.—11. The non-culpable transgression of a precept.—12. "Go behind Me, Satan."—13. The Saviour's reasons.

9. **The second characteristic of imperfection.**—The first characteristic which essentially constitutes imperfection is, then, a certain dominance of the human over the divine. A second characteristic, which is inseparable from the first, is the absence of any formal offence. Since, according to the language of the School, a definition is made by way of genus and species, I should say that, in the definition of imperfection, the domination of the human is the genus, and the absence of formal offence is the species. The predominance of the human causes it to resemble sin, the absence of formal offence is what differentiates it.

Hence, in imperfection, the predominance of the human never rises to the point of inducing my soul to commit a formal offence against the divine Majesty. And the imperfection may come about in two ways: either by the simple transgression of a counsel, or else by the non-culpable transgression of a precept.

10. *The transgression of a counsel.*—I call the simple transgression of a counsel that which is not complicated either by a venial or a mortal sin; for it is clear that sin, too, leads to the neglect of counsels. But no doubt I may happen to leave a counsel undone without any admixture of sin in the omission: whether this transgression occur through omission or commission, by an act of the mind, or of the heart or the senses, through some internal habit or external accident. And thus it is that so many defects and eccentricities are kept up, as well as inclinations and whims, low natural views and worldly estimates, curious and futile fancies, human preferences and hampering connections, precipitate actions and careless behaviour, and so forth! In a word, all our earth-bound existence, wherein the human is too often dominant, and the divine has not wholly the first place which it should hold in a Christian's life, lies here.

11. *The non-culpable transgression of a precept.*—" Here is an instance of it," says St. Francis of Sales.[1] " I come to tell you that such and such a person sends you his kind regards and best wishes, and that he has spoken highly of you. Well, all this is far from being the case. This is a venial sin which is quite voluntary. But suppose I am telling a story, and, as I am speaking, some words slip in which are by no means true, and I only notice it after I have spoken them: that is an imperfection." How often do I thus happen to forget a duty, or not to observe a precept, from the fact that I have been humanly carried away and swayed by some natural instinct! It is this kind of dominance that makes me imperfect. If grace had a stronger influence over me, even these involuntary outbreaks of disorderly tendencies would be less frequent.

12. " *Go behind Me, Satan.*"—The Gospel affords me a truly striking example of this domination of the human over the divine, without there being any formal offence against

[1] *Conversations*, xv., Annecy Edition, p. 284.

God. It is in the episode in which St. Peter is addressed as Satan by his divine Master. Our Lord was announcing to His disciples all the sufferings of His Passion. "Peter taking Him aside, began to rebuke Him saying: Lord, be it far from Thee, this shall not be unto Thee. And Jesus turning said to Peter: Go behind Me, Satan, thou art a scandal unto Me: because thou savourest not the things that are of God, but the things that are of men " (Matt. xvi. 22, 23). Here Peter is addressed as Satan by the gentle Saviour, although he was the very man whom, a few verses higher up, this Saviour had called " blessed," and chosen as the foundation-stone of His Church. What crime, then, can he have committed to draw upon himself such a lively rebuke after having merited such sublime praise ?—He wanted to show his Master his affection, and he did so sincerely indeed. Peter was a man of reckless generosity. Who is going to bring any accusation against the Apostle for testifying his affection to his Master ? And is he addressed as Satan for thus testifying his affection ?— Yes, just for this testimony.—Why ?—Our Saviour explains. Thou puttest man, says He, before God, man's thoughts before God's thoughts, man's likings before God's. And when thou actest in this fashion, thou art a scandal unto Me; and because thou actest thus, I call thee Satan. Give God His place, keep thine own, go behind Me. Cease to put the human above the divine, and learn that in all things God must be above man.

13. **The Saviour's reasons.**—These two scenes, which are placed side by side in the Gospel, wherein Peter is first of all addressed as blessed, and then as Satan, are singularly instructive. On the one hand, Peter acknowledges and confesses the divinity of Christ, and Jesus says to him: " Blessed art thou."—Why blessed ?—Because thou hast heard and listened not to the voice of flesh and blood, but to the voice of the Father who is in heaven. Here is the divine above the human.

On the other hand, Peter, following human likings and not God's wisdom, goes so far as to run counter to the Passion of the Son of man, and his Master calls him Satan. Here we see how our Saviour praises and extols faithfulness in reserving the first place to the divine. And here, too, we see how He rebukes the domination of nature's views, affections, and tendencies, even in those manifestations which are free from sin.

CHAPTER IV

Imperfection

Its Evil

14. Why is not imperfection a sin ?—15. Its connexion therewith.—16 Its frequency.—17. Its evil.

14. *Why is not imperfection a sin ?*—Why is it, and how is it, that there is no formal offence against the divine Majesty in imperfection ?

Is it because God, in His mercy, condescending to my weakness, willed not to lay upon my poor fallen nature difficulties too great for its strength ? He knows the clay of which He hath framed us ;[1] and He, who was so strict towards angels, can be so merciful towards men !

Or else, is it because there is not enough consent in the deviation of my will ? I am so full of impotence ! and I meet with so many appeals from without ! and the coming together of the two produces so many upsets and distractions and yieldings !

Or again, is it that this stage of disorder does not sufficiently affect the reality of the act to prevent it from going to God nevertheless in some manner, although in an incomplete fashion ? In spite of the taint of imperfection, the act retains a substance and accidents, which leave it so far in relation with God's honour that it does not incur the defilement and the penalty of formal sin.

God, man, the act which brings man into relation with God ; in God, His goodness ; in man, his frailty ; in the act, its morality : such are the three points, outside of which it is difficult to push our enquiry, and in which it is doubtless

[1] Quoniam ipse cognovit figmentum nostrum, recordatus est quoniam pulvis sumus (Ps. cii. 14).

possible to find the reason of this absence of formal offence in the disorder of imperfection.

15. *Its connexion therewith.*—However this may be, it is nevertheless a fact, that sin and imperfection are very near neighbours. For on the one hand, things bad in themselves become simple imperfections through want of knowledge or of will. And on the other hand, we see in the lives of the saints, for instance, that God sometimes punishes infidelities as if they were real sins, although they would be mere imperfections in any ordinary soul. Are they real sins in the saints, and that especially on account of the immense enlightenment with which their souls are illumined ?—I cannot tell. But the fact that God punishes them so rigorously is very significant.

16. *Its frequency.*—Hence, although I may succeed in avoiding sin fairly faithfully, I may nevertheless still live in almost continual disorder !—I shall commit no voluntary sins, or but very few of them, and nevertheless I may be almost constantly misunderstanding the order of my creation !—It is, indeed, a very high and rare thing to avoid deliberate venial sin ! — And, nevertheless, my life may still be spent in continual disorder !

I say : continual disorder ; for truly the circumstances in which a sin has to be avoided are much rarer in life than those in which I have to do good actions. The ordinary texture of life is made up of an uninterrupted succession of acts which are honest in themselves and naturally good ; the temptations to be overcome and the sins to be avoided are relatively much less numerous. I am not always confronted with a temptation or a sin, but I am always doing something, in mind or heart or body. What an amount of details there are in a single day ! thoughts, words, and acts follow one another by the thousand.

Well and good ! If, in this incessant work which constitutes life, I habitually make use of things for myself primarily, stopping short in a way at myself and my own pleasure, forgetting God more or less, and giving Him practically the second place, I am living in continual disorder ; my life, without being a sin, is nevertheless the subversion of the order which assigns the precedence to God. O my God! how frightful must sin be, if imperfection is indeed so far the upsetting of the order Thou hast established in Thy creation! —Nothing has ever enabled me to fathom so deeply the malice of sin!

Imperfection is a subversion of God's plan!—What then is sin, which so deeply offends God and makes Him complain with such bitter lamentations?

17. **Its evil.**—Imperfection is once more the great evil, the essential evil, the evil I ought to avoid to the utmost at the cost of my blood and my life!—If I have understood the design of my creation and the purpose of my life, I must be convinced of this, I was about to say, overwhelmed at the thought of it!—for, of a truth, what have I done until now? —If, abominable and unprofitable man that I am, I have drunk iniquity like water,[1] have I not breathed in imperfection like the air?—Does it not enter into my soul as the air enters into the lungs, at every breath?

St. Catherine of Genoa[2] relates that one day "God gave her a clear view of herself, *i.e.*, of such of her bad inclinations as were contrary to pure love. And she understood that she would have rather chosen not to exist than to have offended God's love, not only by the least sin, but even by the least defect."

CHAPTER V

Perfection

The Third Degree of Piety.

18. Its proper object.—19. The scope of the word.—20. *Ex toto.*—
21. Perfection according to St. Francis of Sales.

18. **Its proper object.**—To correct the disorder of imperfection, *i.e.*, to restore order in the good or indifferent details of my life, so as to see, love, and seek God first, and myself

---

[1] Quanto magis abominabilis et inutilis homo, qui bibit quasi aquam iniquitatem? (Job xv. 16).
[2] *Dialogues*, Part I, chap. xvii.

only afterwards, this is the proper object of perfection, and it is the top of the second stage of piety. Up till now, we have been correcting or redressing bad acts; perfection corrects good acts, and drives out from them all disorder which may impair them. When good acts are thus corrected, there no longer remains in my life any trace of the second part of disorder which is characterized by the dominance of my pleasure over God. The whole of this evil has disappeared, and this is why the third step of the whole ascent is called perfection.

19. The scope of this word.—The word perfection does not by any means signify that the good has attained its fulness of intensity, and that it is capable of no further increase. In this sense, perfection is only to be found in God, in whom the good has no limits. Nor does it by any means signify that the good is entirely pure; for there still remain in my soul secret attachments apart from God, the multiplicity of which I shall see later on. Nor does it at all show that the last traces of disorder, what I have called the *division* between human satisfaction and God's glory, have disappeared. But it indicates that the good is free from the evil of human *preferences*, that nothing remains of the sin of the subversion of God's glory, nor of the disorder of the dominance of human satisfaction. Seeking self before God is totally excluded; and thus, in this kind, the good is perfect. It has attained a first and relative perfection, the work of restoration is fulfilled; it is therefore the perfection of restoration, or of the ordinary ways of spiritual advance. This is the meaning of the word " perfection."

20. Ex toto.—What, then, is perfection?—Perfection is nothing else than seeing, loving, and seeking God first *in all things;* it is piety which has reached that state of relative perfection, which excludes *all* subversion. "All whatsoever you do in word or in work," says St. Paul, "all things do ye in the name of the Lord Jesus Christ, giving thanks to God and the Father by Him" (Col. iii. 17). "Therefore whether you eat or drink, or whatsoever else you do; do all to the glory of God" (1 Cor. x. 31). All, absolutely all, says the Apostle; each thing in particular, and all things taken together: *omne*

quodcumque . . . omnia . . . Each thing, first of all, in its own and particular entirety, in such a way that the whole of this one thing may be truly and fully ordered towards God primarily : *omne quodcumque.* This is the particular perfection of the act. Next, all things taken together generally, as an organic whole, in such a way that the entire texture of my life as a whole may be effectively subordinated to the honour of God's name : *omnia :* this is the perfection of one's state.

It is this ALL that characterizes the perfection of the act as well as of the state. *Diliges ex toto.*—Here we have no longer only all the faculties of the soul and body avoiding all sin, but also avoiding all usurpation of God's rights. This disposition of seeing, loving, and seeking God first, here really reaches all things without any exception whatever. God is truly in His place, at the very highest point of my life.

It is putting God fully in the first place that befits His dignity as my Saviour, and putting myself totally in the second place that befits my humility as His servant. One of my life's acts is perfect, when it entirely realizes this subordination ; and the state of my life is perfect when my whole existence is thus ordered.

21. Perfection according to St. Francis of Sales.—" I hear nothing but talk of perfection," sometimes said St. Francis of Sales, " and I see very few who practise it. Everyone has his own idea of it. . . . As for me, I know of no other sort of perfection than that of loving God with all one's heart. And if we really love God, we try to procure Him the good of His glory by ourselves, referring thereto our being and all our actions, not only the good, but also the indifferent ; and not satisfied therewith, we use all diligence and put forth all our efforts to try to get our neighbour to serve and to love Him, so that in all things God may be honoured. It is in this that our end and final consummation consist, it is the end of all consummations and the consummation of all ends.[1] They who fashion for us any other sort of perfection, do but deceive us."[2]

[1] Omnis consummationis vidi finem (Ps. cxviii. 96).
[2] *The Spirit of St. Francis of Sales*, Book I, ch. xxv and xxvii.

CHAPTER VI

The State of Perfection

22. The external state.—23. The internal state.—24. Religious perfection.—25. Episcopal and sacerdotal perfection.

22. The external state.—In speaking of the state of perfection, it is necessary to distinguish between the external state and the internal state, between the state of perfection to be acquired and the acquired state of perfection.

The external state of perfection is something constituted with an organization of external means fitted for the more prompt and full realization of the state of internal perfection. The religious orders, in conditions as diverse as their vocations, have realized this external state of perfection. They are institutes of perfection. The different ordinances and practices of worship and discipline are generally organized in them for the special purpose of facilitating to chosen souls the ascent towards the total restoration of their lives. And those who come to submit by enduring engagements to these ordinances of worship with regard to God and of discipline with regard to themselves, by this fact constitute themselves in an external state of perfection.

They are constituted therein, and it is a state, because they contract engagements which establish them in a permanent position. And it is a state of perfection, because everything in their condition, their vows, and their rule, imposes upon them and facilitates for them progress towards the full restoration of the honour of God.

23. The internal state.—The internal state of perfection is acquired perfection, it is the practical realization of the full scheme of the ascetic life. It is the soul living habitually and universally, in mind, heart, and senses, in the sight, love, and search of God in the first place. It is piety come to the end of its second stage.

But the state of perfection is not finally established in my soul until I have acquired facility and readiness in seeing, loving, and seeking God first in all things, until I can easily and readily make such sacrifices as are necessary for keeping my own satisfaction constantly in its place. And the state is by no means complete and finished until I feel that I am disposed to sacrifice even life itself rather than commit a voluntary imperfection. Rather let me die than seek myself voluntarily before God, even in the smallest thing: such is the language of perfection.

24. Religious perfection.—The state of internal perfection is, then, that towards which a religious binds himself to tend by his vows. To aim at eliminating imperfection little by little, at keeping God's glory definitely before him in the first place, and at loving and seeking it primarily in all things, and at never allowing his own satisfaction to usurp its place, such is the purpose of the religious life.

The still higher ways of holiness do not come under the obligation of the vows in the same way as the vow of perfection. Doubtless, the religious who has set the mysterious ascent and its upward steps towards virtue in his heart, will put no limit to his career, just as God puts none to His appeals and to His grace. He will be glad to enter into the narrower ways, if God invites him to do so. But it is important for him first of all to measure at a glance the way he has to run, and to consider the end towards which he must tend. This end is perfection, the third degree of piety.

25. Episcopal and sacerdotal perfection.—It is in this state, according to St. Thomas, that Bishops should be established; for they have received the *magisterium* of perfection.[1] Perfection in them must be in a state of activity, *i.e.*, they must not only be perfect, but "propagators of perfection," whose office it is to lead others thereto.[2] Perfection in the religious is in the passive state; he tends thereto, he receives it. The Bishop has perfection, and gives it.

This is the state that befits the priest, not on account of the essential obligations laid upon him by his ordination

---

[1] Status autem episcopalis ad perfectionem pertinet tanquam quoddam perfectionis magisterium (2, 2æ, q. 185, a., 8).
[2] Secundum Dionysium (*Eccles. Hier.* 6) perfectio pertinet active ad Episcopum, sicut ad perfectorem; ad monachum autem passive, sicut ad perfectum (*Ibid.* art. i., ad 2um).

or his office, but because of the sacred acts he fulfils; for, if he would fulfil them worthily, he ought to possess internal perfection.[1]

CHAPTER VII

Perfection and Sacrifice

26. Perfection is not sacrifice.—27. Aberration.—28. Failure.—29. Would not sacrifice be more perfect ?—30. Sacrifices necessary.—31. To what extent ?—32. The fear of sacrifice.

26. Perfection is not sacrifice.—Perfection *in itself* does not demand the sacrifice of my pleasure; it only requires me to put it in its proper place, the second place. Thus, for instance, in the use of food and drink, it does not demand any extraordinary sacrifices from me; I may use what God provides for me in a fitting manner, without being in any way wanting so far as perfection is concerned. The essential thing is that my first intention should be to use these things for God's glory. " Whether you eat, or whether you drink," says the Apostle. He does not bid us not eat or not drink. Eat and drink, these things are not contrary to perfection; do this, but when you do it, do it to God's glory. Neither the pleasure nor the need of eating and drinking must be the dominant or ultimate incentive, nor, above all, in any way whatever the exclusive intention of the act; for therein lies imperfection. But the effectively preponderant incentive, the virtually, if not actually, principal intention, must be God's glory; therein lies perfection. The question of actual and virtual intention will be explained later on.[2]

The specific idea of perfection does not consist in the sacrifice of my satisfaction. Since I assume that my satisfaction is permitted and void of offence towards God, it does not contradict His glory, and there is no incompatibility between them; it is enough for me to reduce the one into obedience

---

[1] Ex hoc quod aliquis accipit sacrum ordinem, non ponitur simpliciter in statu perfectionis; quamvis interior perfectio ad hoc requiratur, quod aliquis digne hujusmodi actus exerceat (*Ibid.* q. 184 a. 6, c).

[2] See § 50.

to the other, and to set each of them in the order belonging to it. I repeat that perfection does not consist in sacrifice, but in restoration.

27. Aberration.—Oh, how easily do I make mistakes on this point! As soon as I get the least idea of perfection, I run off to sacrifice, and hence the idea of perfection is almost confused by me with the idea of deprivation and of sacrifice. I scarcely have any other notion of it. When an impulse of fervour fills my heart, at once I am off on the road to penance and self-denial, where I expect to meet with perfection. Poor wanderer! perfection is not on this road.

These sacrifices are often a kind of red herring. For, while I am greeting privations, I am not thinking of repairing my ways, I go on seeking self, and disorder remains within me. Often my sacrifices are chosen through caprice, or through momentary tastes; even in the selection of them, there is self-seeking; and my very act of choosing becomes too easily a matter of disorder. As being satisfactory acts, they may possess a certain value; to lead me to perfection, they have none; at least, very often.

28. Failure.—On the other hand, the sacrifices of my choosing frequently labour under the disadvantage of being above my strength and of not corresponding with my actual spiritual needs. For, so long as I have not effected the rectification of my intentions, I am not up to the level of such sacrifices, my strength is not equal to bear them; and moreover, grace, the influence of which is proportioned to the growth of my soul, has not been given me for this purpose; and then, what happens?—Since these generous impulses do not produce the results which I desire, because my soul is not strong enough for this, I get discouraged and lose ground, and the saddest outcome of my lamentable effort is this, that I come to think perfection is impossible. It seems to me as if I had done everything, not even shrinking from sacrifice, and I have only succeeded in falling lower than before!

Nor could it be otherwise: I have done everything except just what I ought to have done. What is the use of making great strides, if I am off my road? The faster we walk on the wrong road, the more we go astray. Why should we go to find perfection where it is not to be met with, and not look for it where it really is ? Why should we try to find it a long way off, when it is close to us ? Instead of sacrificing my satisfaction, let me correct it : how much more simple this is ! And it is just here that perfection lies.

29. **Would not sacrifice be more perfect ?**—But would it not be more perfect to sacrifice my satisfaction ?—*Perhaps;* but before aiming at the more perfect, it is quite enough in the usual order of things to aim in the first place at what is merely perfect. To make higher sacrifices which perfection does not require, while I am not making the rectification which it does require, is a flagrant contradiction. It is a case of the best being the enemy of the good.

This is one of the most treacherous ruses of the evil one so far as souls of good-will are concerned. How clever it is to put anyone on the wrong scent, to upset the question at issue and to turn aside anyone's attention from the true purpose, under the pretext of some greater good which it is clearly quite impossible for him to realize ! Hence, it must be repeated that I may enjoy legitimate satisfactions on this sole condition, that if I would be perfect, I must order, co-ordinate, and direct them, actually or virtually, but effectually, to God's glory.

30. **Sacrifices necessary.**—I said that perfection *in itself* does not require the sacrifice of my satisfaction ; because the idea of sacrifice and of the renunciation of my satisfaction does not constitute the specific idea of perfection and is not of its essence. But, from the fact of my nature being vitiated, I shall often be obliged to practise certain renunciations for the sake of repairing and preserving order within me. But these sacrifices are not at all desired for their own sake as constituting perfection, they are only used as the indispensable or useful means for attaining it. And it is because they are means that they will be especially dealt with in Part III.[1]

31. **To what extent ?**—Thus, to return to the example already mentioned, if in eating and drinking I desire to cut off only that which is, strictly speaking, sin, without cutting off one of those satisfactions which are allowed, I shall get

[1] See Part III, Book I.

attached to them contrary to God's glory, and I shall become plunged in disorder. If, on the contrary, I do not hesitate to deprive myself voluntarily of such satisfactions as may be usefully sacrificed for the re-establishment or the preservation of order within me, I make rapid progress.

The essential thing is, then, neither for me to deprive myself, nor to avoid depriving myself; the essential thing lies not herein, but higher. It lies in the rectification of my intentions, so that they should all go in the first place towards God and His glory. This is the essential thing: this is the end. For this purpose I must not shrink from any necessary or useful sacrifice; and I give no thought to any sacrifice which does not lead thither. As to optional sacrifices, I employ them freely and simply under God's good pleasure. To know how to use everything is more perfect than depriving oneself of a great deal; and there is often more virtue and more profit in making use of and sanctifying a pleasure than in doing away with it. The reason for this has been already given.[1]

32. **The fear of sacrifice.**—Under the pretext of merely ordering my satisfaction below God's glory, or of putting it at His service, I may easily miss my way; and, under the cloak of God's glory, I may in reality rather hold to myself than to God, and seek myself rather than God. The ruses of self-love are so subtle, and the cheats of the tempter are so treacherous! How often does it not occur to me to use even the very specious pretext of God's glory to justify not only imperfections, but even real sins? What can be done in such dangerous circumstances? for they are dangerous, and very dangerous.—I must merely be on the watch to maintain my intention very upright, and look carefully to see that I am not trying to deceive myself, a thing which conscience will show pretty clearly to anyone who is ready to interrogate himself seriously; and, for the rest, I must leave things to God. For where illusions are involuntary, God undertakes to dissipate them. He undertakes to take away from anyone such satisfactions as deceive him; and when such a satisfaction is forcibly torn away from him, he then perceives how far he had become

[1] See Book I, ch. vii.

attached to it. The hardship felt in being separated from it reveals the degree of cupidity existing in the possession of it.[1] In dealing with the examination of conscience,[2] I shall consider the practical means of dissipating the illusions of self-love. And in Part II,[3] I shall consider what are the two kinds of sacrifices demanded by God's will signified, on the one hand ; and by His will of good pleasure, on the other.

CHAPTER VIII

The State of My Soul

33. Where am I ? — 34. Human utility. — 35. In ordinary life.— 36. God's interest and mine are not incompatible.—37. In the spiritual life.—38. If I would only go down deep !

33. Where am I ?—And now, where is my soul so far as perfection is concerned ? ... Alas ! do I not live in constant disorder ? Is not my life a perpetual subversion of order ? Let us consider : what is my habitual motive for acting ? Is it not primarily and far too much—self ? What is the first object of my thoughts ? What is the favourite tendency of my affections ? What is the preponderant incentive of my actions ? Is it not myself, my own pleasure, my own convenience, my own interests, my own humour or whim or taste ? always self ? self everywhere ?

I am speaking of the good I do or think I am doing, for here there is no question of formal sin. Yes, in this, which is far the most important part of my life since it occupies almost the whole of my time, in this continuous succession of indifferent or good actions which makes up the texture of my days, what I usually look at in the first place is myself ; what I seek is myself. I generally take precedence of God, and my pleasure comes before His glory.—Such is the instinct of our evil nature ! ... Subversion ! ... Disorder ! ... O God ! is it possible for my life to be nothing but perpetual disorder ?

---

[1] Non est in carendo difficultas, nisi cum est in habendo cupiditas (St. Aug., *De Doctr. Christ.* iii. 27).
[2] See Part III, Book II, § 26 *ff.*
[3] See Part II, Books I and II.

Alas! all that I take to be good, my acts and my justice, all that is only a filthy rag![1] And if what I thought was good in me, and what I perhaps was too ready to consider laudable, if this good is but sordid, what a subject of shrinking must I afford to God when the most repulsive infection of numerous sins constantly contributes to increase my perversion? ... If my justices are only impurities, what must I be in myself, O God? ...

34. **Human utility.**—But it is well to look closer. In everything, it should be my rule of life to see, love, and seek divine before human utility, and to subordinate human utility to the divine. When did I ever take account of the divine utility of things, and of their efficacy in helping forward the divine life in the soul? What do I know of it? In what creature am I accustomed to see, love, and seek chiefly God's glory?— My *human*[2] interest is the universal, constant, primary, and instinctive rule of my judgements, affections, and actions; for that is what I see clearly, easily, and everywhere. And as I see it, I love and seek it, and stop short at it.

But God's glory! ... Too commonly I judge events, persons, and things as being good or bad according to the greater or less amount of human benefit that I find in them either for myself or for others. The habitual rule of my thoughts and words is human utility. I generally love or detest events and things according to the greater or less amount of satisfaction they bring me. The ordinary rule of my affections is human utility. I seek or avoid persons, events, and things habitually according to the pleasure or displeasure they give me, according as they help or hurt me or others from a human standpoint. The most universal rule of my actions is human utility.

35. **In ordinary life.**—If I were resolute in confronting my judgements and tastes and habits with the maxims of the Gospel, should I find them in harmony with these maxims? Thus, poverty, gentleness, tears, hunger and thirst for justice, mercy, the love of peace, persecutions, calumnies and evil speaking, all the things included in our Saviour's beatitudes,

---

[1] Quasi pannus menstruatus universæ justitiæ nostræ (Is. lxiv. 6).
[2] See Book IV, § 7, the definition of the *human*.

these are called misfortunes or follies by the world. Are my actual talk and conduct really more in accord with our Lord than with the world ? ... As to the love of enemies, of crosses and privations, of a hidden, simple, and sober life ; as to confidence in divine Providence, the efficacy of prayer, the advantage of fasting, self-denial and alms-giving ; in a word, as to the evangelical counsels, am I thoroughly worthy to be called a follower of Jesus ? ... In the vicissitudes of daily happenings, whether general or particular, how far do I try and how far am I ready, to look at the advancement of God's kingdom within me and in mankind ? For therein consists the great significance of what happens. Thus it is that they are regarded by God, and by the men of God. But how far am I still from the thoughts of God ! and how far am I from the thoughts of the men of God ! The world of man lies before me open enough, the world of God is far too much closed to me.

36. *God's interest and mine are not incompatible.*—Once more, the evil does not lie in my thinking of my own interests and in my considering the human utility of things. My own satisfaction, even my instrumental satisfaction, may quite well be united with God's glory ; often it ought to be so united. I cannot too often say to myself : for His own glory and for my happiness in Him, God wills me to grow, and to develop my mind and heart and senses for Him. And in order to grow, He wills me to make use of instruments, He wills me to use pleasure in things created. Hence, there is no incompatibility between my satisfaction and His glory ; the one does not exclude the other, the one calls for the other ; but satisfaction must not become dominant, and it must not remain purely human. And this is just what in my case it usually does. No, in my ordinary run of life, I really fear that there is not one thought or affection or action wherein God's glory entirely has its proper place, unless, perchance, on those rare occasions when I fully accept some suffering.

37. *In the spiritual life.*—Are my paths any straighter, at least in the region of the spiritual life ?—There, no doubt, I seek God's interests rather more. But how often are they supplanted by views of personal interest ! My devotional

exercises seem good when I am satisfied with them. If a day has given me a great deal of satisfaction, I call it a good day. But if I have experienced no satisfaction, I think something must be wrong. What guides me in such judgements ?—My own satisfaction.

I very readily try to find consolation in Communion, in meditation, and in prayer ; and this is all very well, if in such consolation I am trying to find means to encourage and strengthen me in my duties ; the soul has so much need of joy to be alert in God's service ![1] . : : But my reason for preferring one exercise to another is often only the pleasure it affords me, on which I feed, and in which I repose. It is myself that I see and love and seek in all this. And what is the reason that I have been faithful for so much longer to such and such an exercise, or that I have constantly been irregular in the use of some others ?—My own consolation. When I find the consolation I am looking for and which brings me satisfaction, I flatter myself as to the success of these exercises, I think them just the thing, and myself too ; and as long as this lasts, I do not give them up. But if dryness comes ! then, all is lost, everything is empty, the exercises are no longer of any use, and I am still more good-for-nothing ; I give them up and get discouraged. This is how I judge even my devotional exercises !—They are too full of self, and too wanting in God.

In other supernatural works, in those of zeal or charity for instance, what place do I give to considerations of being thought well of, to the desire for praise, to seeking for gratitude, to wishes for success, and so on ! What a need I feel of finding self-satisfaction in what I do !—Am I not ordinarily depressed and discouraged when I do not reap this harvest ? Do I not too readily measure the value of my work by the amount of enjoyment it brings me ? Is not my liking for it propoitioned to the consolation I meet with in it ? Is not my zeal according to my satisfaction ? Here, too, our judgements, our likings, and our actions are too much ruled by self-seeking.

38. If I would only go down deep !—My natural life, my spiritual life, nearly everything within me, is ruled, directed

[1] See Part II. Book II. § 13.

and dominated by my own satisfaction. How dreadful were my examination of conscience, if only I were ready to enter into the inner details of my thoughts and likings and actions ! ... How I should find the accursed instinct of selfish satisfaction more or less supplant God's glory in everything, everywhere, and always ! ... In everything ! ... Oh, I shall never know how deep is the disorder of my life ! ... Myself everywhere the first ... God constantly in the second place or set aside. In what I do, in what happens to me, in what I seek for or avoid, it is myself whom I consider in the first place ; I love for my own sake, I hate for my own sake.... Of what use is this to me so far as God's glory is concerned ?—This is what I should be accustomed to ask myself in all things, and this I ask myself so rarely ! ... Of what use will it be to me for my own advantage or for my own pleasure ?—This is what I always look at in the first place, and this I should only consider in the second place, and as a consequence or as a means to God's glory.... Have I ever known the meaning of perfection ?

CHAPTER IX

The General State

39. The state of society.—40. Bible ideas.—41. The ages of faith.—42. Ideas of to-day.

39. The state of society.—This evil is also the great evil of society. In social conditions everything is organized for man ; human interest dominates everything, inspires everything, directs and sums up everything. What place is given to God's glory in families, associations, and corporate bodies ? Where is the idea of God in industries, in commerce, in science, in politics, in history, and the rest ?—In human relationships, it is human interest which universally engrosses people's thoughts, feelings, and efforts. All converges towards this. The thought of God and His glory gets weaker and weaker and disappears ; man is driving out God.

I take what is, perhaps, the most striking example, that of

history. History should be nothing else than a picture of God's glory amidst human vicissitudes, of divine action amidst the agitations of human affairs. To-day it is no more than the miscoloured picture of the convulsions of mankind. Thus everything belies its origin and its end. It is the great and revolutionary heresy, man put in God's place.

40. **Bible ideas.**—Contrast all this with the Bible! In the life of the patriarchs, we feel that God, their God, is everything to them. He dominates, inspires, and, in practice, guides their lives. In their history, we feel at every moment a sense of the Spirit of God. It is the same throughout the history of the chosen people. It is God who is the centre of everything. If human passions cause His memory to be forgotten, punishments recall it; and, beneath the rod, the cry that arises and begs for victory over enemies is always in the first place God's honour. "For the glory of Thy name, O Lord, deliver us" (Ps. lxxviii. 9). And when the victory is won, they rejoice above all, because God is glorified.[1] When Moses,[2] Judith,[3] and Esther[4] wish to obtain the salvation of their people, they do it by invoking God's glory, and this is the motive which moves God to save His people.[5] In the Psalms, what a place is given to the glory of God! It is the supreme and constant end of these sublime songs.

41. **The ages of faith.**—In the ages and countries of faith, how much more real and living was the place assigned to God in the customs of His faithful peoples! Nothing expressed it so vividly as popular speech. It is in the turns of everyday conversation that we find the best reflection of this state of mind. But how and when was God spoken of in the times and ages in which the notions of faith prevailed?—The name of God perpetually occurred with an appropriateness and reality which were indeed admirable. They used to say with such simplicity and sincerity: "Thank God", "God be praised", "Please God", "With God's help", and so forth. Private documents began with the sign of the cross, and public deeds were drawn up in the name of the Blessed

---

[1] Cantemus Domino, gloriose enim magnificatus est (Ex. xv. 1).
[2] Num. xiv. 13.   [3] Judith ix.   [4] Esther xiv.
[5] Et salvavit eos propter nomen suum, ut notam faceret potentiam suam (Ps. cv. 8).

Trinity, and laws were promulgated in God's name; the custom of giving first-fruits, inherited from the ancient faith, consecrated to God the first-born of everything; paternal, judicial, and civil authority acted as a delegation of that which is divine; there was respect for persons and solemnities and things sacred; the dread of the punishment of blasphemy and so many other customs, unfortunately so far removed from our days; all these testified in practice how far the thought of God held the foremost place in everything. God lived in people's thoughts and conduct, in their customs and institutions. Human wretchedness no doubt made its appearance, for it always does. But God also was manifested above human wretchedness. It was felt that He was the King of souls and bodies, of individuals and peoples, of time and eternity, and His sovereignty remained above all.

42. Ideas of to-day.—In our utilitarian age, if we still have recourse to God, it is rather because we need Him than because of His glory. We still know what carnal love means, but what of the love of benevolence! . . . To ask above all else that God may be glorified, and to rejoice above all that He is glorified, this is the case of a few, but they are daily becoming fewer. And the great heresy which breaks asunder the union of God with man, the co-ordination of the One with the other, is drunk in by everyone, it enters everywhere, it darkens the mind, it misleads the feelings and perverts action. " The Lord knoweth the thoughts of men, that they are vain " (Ps. xciii. 11). Even in the sanctuary and in the cloister this cloudy and unwholesome atmosphere has found its way; and slowly, in small doses, but constantly and surely, its poison filters in.

Oh, how terrible it is to have to walk in this fog which is as thick as darkness, and to inhale this air which is as heavy as death ! . . . And how hard it is to cast out the virus from the spiritual organism, and to render mind, heart, and act, completely sound ! . . . If, however, we mean to live, it must be done at all costs; otherwise the virus, daily creeping in more and more deeply, will kill us, will kill all Christian vitality in us, and induce the putrefaction of death itself Alas ! how sick we are !

CHAPTER X

The State of this Evil

43. The centre of the evil.—44. We do not see or see amiss.—45. The worth of sentimental books.—46. Dogmas make nations.

43. The centre of the evil.—In the light of these principles I can better analyse the evil of my life. The evil lies not only in the lower part of the soul, where it suffers from the tyranny of the passions which demand irregular satisfactions. There, no doubt, are to be found many disturbances, many wounds, which make me groan bitterly and sigh with St. Paul: " Unhappy man that I am, who shall deliver me from the body of this death ?" (Rom. vii. 24). The evil lies there, but it is to be found still higher.

The will, too, is sick. Being full of fluctuations and feebleness, it does not know how to look to God for support ; and being left to itself, it has not enough energy to resist the perverse appeals of nature ; and its cowardice brings about many falls. The evil lies there, too, but it is still higher.

The intelligence is, perhaps, more affected than the will and the sensibility. It does not see, or it sees wrongly. And when I do not see or see amiss, of what use are my will and sensibility, unless it be to carry me astray through following the false directions given by the mind ? And if the blind lead the blind, both fall into the pit (Matt. xv. 14).

44. We do not see or see amiss.—The deepest evil is, then, in my intellect and ideas. For I judge things from the point of view of my own interest or pleasure. This is the light in which I see them ; and because I thus look at them, I thus appreciate them, and act accordingly. My action is vitiated, and my will is vitiated, and this above all on account of my intelligence being vitiated. My actions depend upon my feelings, and my feelings on my ideas ; and directly my ideas are wrong, my feelings and actions are wrong. " Certainly," says Father Surin, " nearly all our defects arise from the perversity of our judgements, and from the fact that we do not refer things created to their first principle, which we ought to do, as being children of God."[1] "The way of justice is, indeed, our way," says St. Augustine. "How can we help stumbling in the way, if we have no light? And this is why it is our first business in this way to be able to see; in this way, the great thing is, to see."[2] If seeing is the great necessity, if seeing is the great business, then not to see is the great misfortune, and seeing wrongly is the great danger. Hence, my greatest evil is not to see, or to see amiss.

45. **The worth of sentimental books.**—I can now take account of the worth of the books of piety which swarm on all sides, the whole skill of which consists in stirring up our sensibility. To cure the soul by means of the emotions when the great evil is in the intelligence! ... Really, this is like trying to cure consumption by rubbing a little ointment on the foot! This is what all the worth of such books amounts to. Who will give us back the devotion based upon theology of the great ages of faith?

Verily, we may ask ourselves if the unfortunate and too copious production of sentimental books of devotion is not as disastrous a plague as that of the unclean literature which splashes us with its disgusting popularity! For, after all, the unclean books only appeal to those who grovel in the gutter. But devotional books are addressed to higher souls whom God calls to raise and elevate the masses. By lowering and withering their spiritual life, do not such books deal a more damaging and disastrous blow to society, by preventing these higher souls from raising it, since they do not elevate themselves? And this all the more, because higher souls are relatively scarce, and the evil which is done to them is felt by all those whom they ought to attract. Sentimentalism in piety is the explanation of materialism in society, and there is much to be learnt from the parallel advance of these two kinds of literature.

46. **"Dogmas make nations."**—So says M. de Bonald: such is one of the most profound remarks of this profound thinker. And if they make nations, they also make men.

---

[1] *Fondements de la vie spirituelle* (Book II, ch. ii).
[2] Ipsa est enim via nostra juste vivere. Quomodo autem non offendat in via, cui non lucet lumen? Ac per hoc in tali via videre opus est, in tali via videre magnum est (*Tract. in Joan.*, xxxv. 3).

"I shall never cease saying or thinking," says another deep thinker, M. de Maistre, "that a man's worth depends upon his belief."[1] Man's worth does, indeed, depend upon his ideas, and he is what he thinks. It is the weakening of truth that makes sanctity vanish from amongst mankind.[2]

Hence, my most urgent and primary necessity is to rectify my ideas as to myself, as to creatures, and as to the use I ought to make of them. As long as these remain uncorrected, nothing will be restored in me; as long as my efforts are not directly brought to bear upon this point, they will remain fruitless. It is faith that purifies the heart.[3] Faith is the vision of the truth; truth is God's glory seen in everything. And truth is the primary element which directs piety. When I have this clear, habitual, and dominant vision, my heart will soon be purified, my life devout.

CHAPTER XI

Restoration

47. Knowing and seeing.—48. The influence of habit on actions.—49. The morning intention: its value.—50. Actual and habitual intention.—51. Complete subversion.

47. Knowing and seeing.—And nevertheless, did I not already know that everything ought to be done for God?—I knew it, no doubt; but did I see it? ... It is one thing to know, another to see. What is the good of a more or less speculative knowledge, entrusted to the memory where it sleeps? ... What is the good of knowledge which does not direct the will? ... What is some good is seeing; seeing practically, definitely, vitally; seeing, not by means of constantly repeated acts, which would be impossible, but by means of an acquired habit of soul, a trained interior disposition.

---

[1] De Maistre, *Lettres à Mme. de Stourdza.*
[2] Defecit sanctus, quoniam diminutæ sunt veritates a filiis hominum (Ps. xi. 2).
[3] Fide purificans corda eorum (Act. xv. 9).

Have I any practical insight into the perpetual struggle between my own satisfaction and God's glory ? . . . into the habitual dominance of my selfish interests ? . . . into my habit of seeing everything from the point of view of my human pleasure ? . . . The evil lies in not seeing that, in not thinking of it, and in perpetuating in myself, by the actual fact of my daily conduct, *habits* of mind which are more or less errant.

48. The influence of habit on actions.—Now, the worth of my actions depends a great deal on my habits ; for the interior state of our faculties deeply modifies the nature of their actions. Thus it is that the state of mortal sin quite deprives even heroic acts, if done while in such a disposition, of their eternal and meritorious worth. The best of intentions and the finest actions, says St. Paul, do not prevent me from being nothing and having nothing, and from being worthless, if I have not charity.[1] Moreover, how many sins does this habit draw in its train !

In the same way, if my interior habits, if my ordinary tendencies are venial, without depriving my good actions of all their value, they nevertheless singularly diminish the merit of them, and they are a source of numerous sins. And if I live in a state of imperfection, this state inevitably reverberates upon those acts which are not withdrawn from it by a contrary intention. Whatever this intention may be, whether actual or habitual, it must at least have the property of affecting the act and of withdrawing it from the opposite influence.

49. The morning intention : its value.—But once more, do I not rectify my intention every morning by directing my actions to God's glory ?—No doubt ; and that is all very good. But what I thus do in the morning is an act. Now, an act does not destroy a habit ; it may interrupt it momentarily, and produce some effect, until the habit regains the upper hand. This act does not destroy the habit I have formed of judging everything from my own point of view. And this all the more, because it is an act of the will, and an act of the will is not directly contrary to a habit of mind. If I had no contrary habit, the morning intention would normally

[1] 1 Cor. xiii. 1.

cover the whole of my day's doings with its virtue. But the habit of self-seeking is there, and in possession; and it is only momentarily interrupted by right acts, as long as the habit of piety has not succeeded in supplanting it.

The fact remains that, in spite of this good morning intention, I continue habitually to look at my own interest primarily; the thought that practically inspires and directs my conduct is always too much that of my own interest, and so far the good intention has hardly corrected it; and it was all the less capable of correcting it, in that I did not see clearly enough the chief seat of the evil.

What then? is this direction of my intention in the morning no good?—It is of very great use. First of all, it is a very meritorious act, wherein there will be no dominance of self-seeking. Lastly, by constant repetition it may help to create in me the great habit of seeing, loving, and seeking God first in all things.

50. *Actual and habitual intention.*—Then, is it necessary to think ACTUALLY . . . of God's glory in each one of my actions?—By no means; it is no more necessary than actually to see my own interest in everything in order to seek myself habitually nevertheless. Is it not true that, from the very fact of habit, I consider, love and seek my own interest without hardly any thought of it, unconsciously, as it were, and instinctively? It goes on of its own accord. It is the property of any habit which is definitely set up in the soul to produce action without the soul's noticing its influence in any definite manner; the habit is all the less perceived, the more thoroughly it has been acquired. I act for self so habitually, that I no longer notice it; the habit dominates me so thoroughly that I no longer perceive it.

Very well! it is just such a strong habit that must be formed within me on behalf of God's glory. The vision, the love, and the seeking of God must so take possession of my powers and so fully dominate them that I shall no longer need to think of them definitely. Piety must become the first instinct of my soul in the same measure as self-seeking is at present. The impulse of grace must take the place, the function, and the sway, now possessed by the impulse of nature; the divine

THE END : GROWTH

must work within me in the same conditions as the human does now. Like the needle of a compass the soul must be set and magnetized so as to point constantly towards God, and finally to be fixed on Him. Then I shall have reached perfection, and I shall go to God as easily, as readily, I was about to say, as naturally, as I now go towards myself. Oh, when will this be ? . . .

There is the end. In Part III, I shall consider the means of attaining it.[1]

51. **Complete subversion.**—In fine, there is almost an entire subversion to be made. My whole life has to be more or less revolutionized : my thoughts, feelings, and actions have to be turned upside down. It is the deep and radical modification of my hitherto too human manner of seeing, loving, and acting. I must form new notions about everything, new feelings about everything, and a new behaviour with regard to everything. The old man must be stripped off once for all and the new man must be put on.[2] How deep are these simple words : seeing, loving, and seeking God in all things, and all things for God ! . . .

Without knowing or reflecting on it, by the inclination of my nature, I have come to see, love, and seek everything for self. The place unduly assigned to my own satisfaction must now be given to the glory of God. What a work ! It is only when the latter has been put in the first place in my thoughts, in the front rank of all my affections, at the root of all my actions, that I shall be able to say : I have reached perfection. When shall I attain it, O my God ?

[1] See Part III, Book II.
[2] Exspoliantes vos veterem hominem cum actibus suis, et induentes novum, eum qui renovatur in agnitionem, secundum imaginem ejus qui creavit illum (Col. iii. 9-10).

BOOK IV

THE SUMMITS

WE have now reached the higher regions of piety. It is a question of making *division* disappear, of getting rid of the juxtaposition of the part of human interest which still remains by the side of, and outside of, the divine. And this separation must vanish altogether, so that my life may have no purpose apart from God, and that the union of my life with His life, of my being with His being, may be absolute.

I am about to consider, in two successive stages, how the separated and stray interest at first languishes in oblivion, and then perishes in annihilation. The decay and death of the *human* are the two higher degrees of piety, and these upward steps belong to what is called the unitive life.

In these higher regions, certain states of soul are called the mystical life, because the soul then enters into the secrets of the divine intimacy. God hides it far from human disturbance in the secret of His countenance.[1] And in the mystery of this intimacy, God works operations as mysterious as the secrecy itself. And it is from these mysterious or mystical operations of God that these higher states of the soul have received the name of the mystical life.

[1] Abscondes eos in abscondito faciei tuæ, a conturbatione hominum (Ps. xxx. 21).

CHAPTER I

Holiness

The Fourth Degree of Piety

1. Work done and work to do.—2. The acts of holiness.—3. The state of holiness.—4. The greatest glory of God.—5. Indifference.

1. Work done and work to do.—When I have reached the blessed state of the soul in which all is in order, at the third degree of piety which is perfection, shall I be at the top?— I shall be already far up, but nevertheless a long way from the summits. I am on the first peak, which is very difficult to attain and which is reached by too few. But beyond this height rise others; these are the high summits that touch heaven itself.

Above ordinary perfection, there is holiness. Perfection has already shaken off the first evil, it has driven away the disorder of human preferences; and it is called perfection, because it has purified the state of my soul from all subversion. The good is then upright, God is first; but interior purity is far from having attained its full expansion. There are infinite degrees in the higher development of my purification in its integrity.

In the three degrees hitherto considered, the soul was successively purified from the evils of mortal sin, venial sin, and imperfection. From these it is now set free, delivered and cured; it can enter upon the career of the good without alloy, of light unclouded, and of love undivided.

A great work has been done, the disorder of self before God has vanished; but my union with God is still far from being consummated. My satisfaction is put in its proper place, but still it is not all lost in God. There is a fresh work to be taken in hand; or rather, the upward steps of the soul continue to rise; for the principle of life within goes on unfolding its activity in an uninterrupted movement.

It enters into holiness.

2. *The acts of holiness.*—What is holiness ?—An example will enable me to grasp it clearly. If a merchant can gain a hundred pounds by a lawful transaction, is he likely to be satisfied with fifty ?—Certainly not. The fundamental condition of commercial negotiations is that each party shall honestly do his best for his own interests. This is what secures rivalry, progress, and success.

I am bound to procure God's glory; it is the essential object of my life, and creatures are given me for this. But, amongst creatures, it is certain that some help towards this end better than others. If I do not mean my conduct to be more unreasonable than that of the most ordinary merchant, I am bound to choose those creatures which best procure God's glory. If I am not at all anxious to choose those which are most advantageous for this end, I am clearly going against reason, and by my conduct I am contradicting the fundamental principle of my existence. If to this one essential business I am only willing to bring the ordinary amount of faithfulness which men bring to their material affairs, I must distinguish between creatures and choose those which contribute most to God's glory. The choice of the most perfect is the act which is proper to holiness.

3. *The state of holiness.*—But holiness is a state; and a state is constituted by a habit, and a habit is characterized by facility and readiness in doing the acts belonging to that state. Holiness is, then, a readiness and facility in seeing, loving, and choosing in all things that which is most for the glory of God. *Diliges ex toto.* . . . When all our powers, mind, heart, and senses, have acquired this facility; when in all things the greatest glory of God is readily and easily seen, loved, and embraced, holiness is established in the soul.

The proper work for the realization of this state is seeing in created things no longer merely God's glory, which is the object of the three preceding degrees; but it is seeing to what extent each created thing contributes to His glory, and to make choice of those which give the greatest share. The motto of St. Ignatius: " To the greater glory of God," is the prescription for this work. We are bound thereto when we make what is called the vow of the most perfect. It is the vow which has been made by many of the saints, and, amongst others, by St. Teresa, St. Jeanne de Chantal, and St. Alphonsus of Liguori.

4. **The greatest glory of God.**—This state is characterized by two things: first, by a sole anxiety for the greatest glory of God: secondly, by forgetfulness of self. First, anxiety for the greatest glory of God. Throughout the three preceding degrees, the soul's principal anxiety was to set up an equilibrium between its own satisfaction and God's glory, to hinder the usurpation of the former, and to establish God's honour at the highest point in one's life. Now this order has been realized, peace is secured, and satisfaction finally put in its proper place. No longer having to strike a balance between my satisfaction and God's glory, I put the latter in a still higher place. I busy myself only with God's interests, and I weigh each created thing to see which possesses most value for Him.

This is a great ascent of the soul. Its whole life consists in the care and the need of glorifying God by the best possible means. The zeal of God's house has eaten it altogether up;[1] it aspires only to honour Him, and it lives only to please Him. God is its all, it hungers and thirsts only for His glory;[2] His good pleasure is its sole food.[3] In heaven it finds nothing, on earth it desires nothing apart from God and His glory. He is the God of our heart, and all our riches, even unto eternity.[4] The desires of the heart and the manifold needs of the body are all summed up in this one thirst.[5]

5. **Indifference.**—Thus dominated and absorbed, the soul forgets its own satisfaction, *human* and created satisfaction, the false enjoyment which comes from created things, and which tends to stop short apart from and aside of God's glory. Thus is realized the indifference so much recommended

---

[1] Zelus domus tuæ comedit me (Ps. lxviii. 10).
[2] Beati qui esuriunt et sitiunt justitiam (Matt. v. 6).
[3] Meus cibus est, ut faciam voluntatem ejus qui misit me (Joan. iv. 34).
[4] Quid mihi est in cœlo et a te quid volui super terram ? Deus cordis mei et pars mea Deus in æternum (Ps. lxxii. 25, 26).
[5] Sitivit in te anima mea, quam multipliciter tibi caro mea (Ps. lxii. 2).

by St. Ignatius, and this is the second characteristic of holiness. "Man," says he, "ought to make himself indifferent with regard to all created things in all that is left to the choice of his free will and that is not forbidden him; so that, so far as he is concerned, he does not wish for health rather than sickness, riches rather than poverty, honour rather than contempt, a long life rather than a short one, and thus with all the rest, desiring and choosing solely what leads him most surely to the end for which he has been created."[1]

Thus, in this state, my human pleasure is indifferent to me; I no longer think of it, I forget it, and my thoughts are raised still higher. I am as ready for sorrow as for joy, for contempt as for honour, for want as for abundance, for death as for life; all these things are all the same to me: I have only one thing at heart, the greatest glory of God. If there be more of this divine glory in sorrow, the saint accepts sorrow with joy; if there be more in happiness, he receives happiness with simplicity. One thing alone differentiates creatures so far as he is concerned: the greatest glory of God. Whether this is to be found here or there matters little; wherever he sees it, thither he flies without any care for joy or sorrow. He would fling himself into hell, if more of God's glory could be found in doing so.

CHAPTER II

Mystical Death

6. The mystery of life and death.—7. The human —8. It must die.—9. *Seminatur . . . surget.*—10. Passing away.

6. The mystery of life and death.—What! Can the soul succeed in forgetting all satisfactions, and live purely for God without any return to its own interests?—Here is a great mystery, which it is of importance to explain in order to escape the errors of quietism. It is a mystery of life and death. There is in me what ought to die, and there is in me what ought to be set free from this death, in order to return to life. What

Exercit. Spirit., Fundamentum

is it that ought to live ?—All that is right, and all that comes from God.—And what is it that ought to die ?—All that is false, and all that comes from man. What thus comes falsely from man is what is called the *human*.

7. **The human.**—What, then, is the human ?—The *human*, understood in a sense which is exclusive and opposed to the divine, is that in me and in my activity which is separated from God and which runs counter to union with God, who is the true end of my life. When false satisfactions attach me to things created, when the independence of my activities withdraws me from the action of God, I am dwelling in the human. Thus, my satisfaction is human when it rests contented apart from God. Thus, my movement is human when it takes place in me and through me independently of the divine action. In a word, everything in my vital movement which is not reached, animated, and directed by the divine life, everything which is outside of union, all this is human, it is *the human*.

8. **It must die.**—And all this must die : why ?—Because I am made for God, and for Him only ; because my life consists in being united to Him, loved by Him, ruled by Him : and all that separates me from Him must disappear. Hence, on what point must I bring to bear those operations which in the language of mysticism are called unclothing, annihilation, death, etc.?—They should exclusively be brought to bear upon what separates me, and universally upon what separates me, from God.

This does not mean the destruction of my soul or body, or faculties or aptitudes, or aspirations or activities, or instruments or pleasures, or hopes or happiness. It rather means their purification by the destruction of a certain viscosity which fastens me to created things, and of a certain independence which keeps me at a distance from God. It means the setting free of my being by the breaking of the ties which bind it to the things of earth. What has to be broken, destroyed, and annihilated, is not myself, it is these ties ; as for myself, I have to be set free. And if, according to the protestation of the Fore-runner, there is an " I " who must decrease and vanish from before God, in order that He may increase;[1] this is the " I " of self-seeking apart from God, it is the " I " of nature which lives without God.

9. *Seminatur . . . surget.*—Hence, all that tends to *keep* my life in a state which is purely natural, human, and isolated from God, must die; all this must die, *i.e.*, it must undergo that transformation which is most strikingly illustrated by the death of the body.

" The body," says St. Paul, " is sown in corruption, it shall rise in incorruption. It is sown in dishonour, it shall rise in glory. It is sown in weakness, it shall rise in power. It is sown a natural body, it shall rise a spiritual body. . . . Now this I say, brethren, that flesh and blood cannot possess the kingdom of God; neither shall corruption possess incorruption. . . . For this corruption must put on incorruption: and this mortal must put on immortality. And when this mortal hath put on immortality, then shall come to pass the saying that is written: Death is swallowed up in victory " (I Cor. xv. 42-54).

10. **Passing away.**—" Yet," says St. Francis of Sales,[2] " we speak with peculiar propriety of the death of a man in our French language; for we call it ' passing away,' and the dead, ' those who have passed away '; signifying that the death of a man is but a passing away from one life to another, and that dying is nothing else than passing beyond the confines of this mortal life to enter into that which is immortal."

The body does not perish, but it is transformed; it passes through a progressive dissolution, and through that kind of annihilation which is death. All that is *human* and mortal, all that belongs to corruption, abjection, weakness, and to the animal in man, undergoes the same law. All this is condemned to waste away and die in order to be transformed and rise again in incorruption, in glory, in power, and in a being which is all spiritual.

Thus it is that what is merely *human* satisfaction disappears little by little in order to die and rise again in God's glory. We have seen how this satisfaction falls into languor

---

[1] Illum oportet crescere, me autem minui (Joan. iii. 30).
[2] *Treatise of the Love of God*, Book IX, ch. xiii. The two French words are *trépas* and *trépassé*.

before dying : how it falls into forgetfulness, indeed, and into indifference, which is one of the characteristics of holiness; for this is nothing else than the languor and wasting, whereby natural satisfactions journey towards their final passing away. Further on, in Chapter IV, we shall see how this passing away comes about.

CHAPTER III

Transformation

11. *Quotidie morior.*—12. Renewal.—13. Rising by degrees.—14. The vow of the most perfect and trifles.

11. Quotidie morior.—But the death of our satisfactions is not quite like the death of the body. We die daily : this is as true of satisfactions as of bodies ; daily a few fragments fall away until the last remnant of the wall of separation has crumbled away in death. For the body resurrection is deferred, and it will only take place at the end of time and all at once. As for satisfactions, in proportion as they die, they rise again in God's glory ; and thus it is that, in forgetting our own satisfaction and in immolating it to God's glory, the saint finds it transfigured, re-arisen, and purified in this same glory.

Hence, the saint is never without satisfactions ; the original plan of putting God's glory in the first place and man's happiness in the second, is never impaired. Forgetfulness of self, hatred of self, annihilation of self, and death also, are only the transformation of death into life, and the swallowing up of death in victory. " He that will save his life shall lose it ; and he that shall lose his life for My sake, shall find it " (Matt. xvi. 25). We must lose all to find all ; for we can only find what we have lost. We lose the human to find the divine.

12. Renewal.—" It is impossible," says St. Francis of Sales,[1] " to remain long in this state of denudation, stripped of all kinds of affections. And this is why, as the holy

---
[1] *The Treatise of the Love of God*, Book IX, ch. xvi.

Apostle remarks, after putting off the clothes of the old man, we must put on those of the new man, that is to say, of Jesus Christ; for having renounced everything, and even affections for the virtues, so as not to wish for either these or those, except so far as God's good pleasure shall carry us, we must straightway put on several affections, and perhaps the very ones we have renounced and given up; but we must put them on straightway, not because they are pleasing to us, useful, honourable, and proper to satisfy our self-love, but because they are pleasing to God, useful for His honour, and intended for His glory." Thus every day our outward man is corrupted: yet the inward man is renewed.[1]

13. Rising by degrees.—Oh, what a high thing is holiness! . . . and how perfect must one be to attain unto it! Yes, perfect: for we must have gone over the road of perfection, at least in the sense in which it has been explained in Book III, to reach the regions of holiness. The following remark is general: these degrees of piety rise one above another, and are like steps whereby the soul makes its upward ascent towards God; so that it is impossible to rise to a higher degree unless one has passed through those that are below it.

It is clear, indeed, that a soul could not become established in the avoidance of venial sin, unless it were first strengthened to resist mortal sin; nor could it habitually avoid imperfections as long as it does not avoid venial sins; nor become holy until it had become perfect. No doubt the higher degree begins to be formed whilst the one before it is attaining its perfection; no doubt in the lower degrees we practise the acts of those above them: a sinner, for instance, will sometimes emerge from his unfortunate condition by an act which is worthy of the highest degree of holiness; but, in general, we can only contemplate and attain one of these states by following the several degrees that lead up to it.

This is an important fact for the direction of souls. Each degree has its special duties and enlightenment, and to set it to do duties which are above it is to lay oneself open to the risk of making grave mistakes. The vow of the most perfect,

[1] Sed licet is, qui foris est, noster homo corrumpatur, tamen is qui intus est, renovatur de die in diem (2 Cor. iv. 16).

for instance, should not be allowed to a soul unless the state of perfection has been soundly established in it.

14. **The vow of the most perfect and trifles.**—An important observation made by St. Teresa : He who binds himself by the vow of the most perfect ought not to stop at small trifles and at the minutiæ of life to ask himself every moment in which of these petty details the greatest glory of God is to be found. This would be puerile and ridiculous. Life would thus become full of worry, and subject to scruples and illusions. No, it is not a question, as she says, of running after little lizards ; but the matter in question is some great disposition of the soul. The soul must become established in a great forgetfulness of self, in a great contempt for anything created, in an immense desire for God's glory. Then, let there be simple and constant fidelity in little things, and a generous choice of the most perfect in circumstances of some importance.

As for the rest, as I have said, our enlightenment is proportioned to our duties. A soul in the lower degrees, if it has not a light which corresponds to its condition, will easily be subject to illusions in looking for the most perfect, and will fall into exaggerations and scruples. On the contrary, one who has reached this height will not fear these reefs, because he has light enough to keep clear of them. God's sunlight shines on him with greater intensity, so that from afar he can discern between what is great and what is small, and see it in its true light. Oh, how happy is he who knows how to be satisfied with God's light, how to reckon on it for his guidance, and how to open his eyes to its rays and to follow it as it increases !

Moreover, St. Teresa in practice was led to modify her vow in such a way as to regard as the most perfect only what her confessor had confirmed to her as such. It was the surest way to cut short all worries and scruples.

THE END: THE SUMMITS

CHAPTER IV

Consummation

The Fifth Degree of Piety

15. The two crowns.—16. Immolation.—17. The supreme conclusion—18. *Beati mortui.*—19. The rational man.—20. St. Francis of Sales's wish.

15. **The two crowns.**—We have seen how, in the preceding state, *human* satisfaction languishes in forgetfulness; we shall now see how it dies in immolation. This is the crown of holiness, the very top of the ladder which is set up between earth and heaven.[1] An example will again show us what this state is: it is a well-known fact in the life of St. Catherine of Siena. This is the report given of it by her confessor.[2]

"The Saviour of the world appeared to her, holding in His right hand a golden crown enriched with precious stones, and in His left hand a crown of thorns.—Know, My dearest daughter, said He to her, that thou hast to wear both the one and the other at different times and seasons. Choose the one thou preferrest: either in this life to wear a crown of thorns; and then I will keep the other for thee in that life which has no end; or else, now to enjoy the use of the precious crown, and the crown of thorns shall be reserved for thee after death.—It is a long time, O Lord, since I renounced my own will in order to follow Thine alone; hence it is not for me to make any sort of choice. Nevertheless, since it is Thy will that I should answer, I tell Thee that I choose to be in this world unceasingly conformed to Thy blessed Passion, and for Thee ever to seek my joy in suffering.—And in saying this, in an outburst of fervour she takes the crown of thorns from the Saviour's hand, and with both hands forces it upon her head so energetically that the thorns pierce through on all sides."

Thus did she choose suffering, through a supreme need of

---
[1] Viditque (Jacob) in somnis scalam stantem super terram, et cacumen illius tangens cœlum (Gen. xxviii. 12)
[2] *Acta Sanctorum*, II, p. 901.

absolute purification even in this world, and of being conformed to our Lord, in order that all might be stripped off and consummated before death.

16. Immolation.—Here the soul has not to strike a balance between the lesser or greater glory of God; it has done this work in the preceding state. It has now attained to see, love, and seek God's greatest glory in all things with facility and readiness. It easily sees where this greater glory is to be found, it loves it firmly, it chooses it readily; this habit has been thoroughly acquired by it. It does not shrink from any sacrifice, in which there is rather more honour to be procured for its God.

What remains to be done? What degree can it find higher up?—There remains the human satisfaction which it has forgotten, and as to which it was indifferent. It has already sacrificed this, as soon as it saw the divine good pleasure rather more clearly; but still there remains much of it behind. These are the last traces of those adherences which hamper and hinder its upward flight. It now wishes to complete its holocaust, to detach, burn, and consume everything, through a supreme need of immolation, of denudation, of disengagement from things created, and of union with God.

That which characterizes this state is the need of immolation, the hunger for suffering, the passion for the cross. "Suffering or death," is St. Teresa's cry. "Not death, but suffering," is the still more amazing cry of St. Mary Magdalene de Pazzi. The soul neither will nor can allow anything created to remain in it any longer, nor any attachment to things created or to itself: GOD ONLY!... GOD ONLY!

It immolates itself and everything else, all that it is and all that it has; it annihilates itself so that Jesus only may live within it. I live, now not I; but Christ liveth in me (Gal. ii. 20). With Christ I am nailed to the cross (Gal. ii. 19); the world is crucified to me, and I to the world (Gal. vi. 14); I am dead; and my life is hid with Christ in God.[1]

17. The supreme conclusion.—This sublime state, the last word of all earthly holiness, is further a logical conclusion

[1] Mortui estis et vita vestra abscondita est cum Christo in Deo (Col. iii. 3).

to be drawn from the first principle of creation: God is my sole essential end, my sole all. The soul says to itself in fact: If God's glory is my one essential good, if God is the sole all of my life, if in His glory is all my happiness, the more He is solely the one object of my anxiety, the one aim of my love, the one purpose of my efforts, the more shall I attain my end. Consequently, the more I disappear in Him, the more the satisfaction I have in what is apart from Him is swallowed up in His glory, the more all that proceeds from self gets annihilated in Him, the more God only remains. Hence, I shall annihilate everything within me which proceeds from self, I shall annihilate all that proceeds from things created; and I shall not rest, until I feel that everything has been finally annihilated and that God reigns the sole master within me over the ruins of my *attachments* to things created. It is written: Blessed are the dead who die in the Lord (Apoc. xiv. 13).

Then the saint, arming himself with indignation against himself, summons to his aid self-denials and macerations. God above all assists in this destruction of the creature by interior devastations, and the saint's supreme happiness is finally to be able to raise a hymn to the sole glory of God upon the débris of all earthly satisfactions. *Diliges ex toto.* . . . Thou shalt love the Lord, thou shalt sing to His glory with all thy heart, with all thy mind, with all thy soul, and with all thy strength. . . . With ALL ! . . . O victory ! this is where the saint has attained ! . . . Yes, now all, all is for God, since for him there is nothing left except in God ! . . .

18. Beati mortui.—I can understand the joy and the intoxication of the saints in their immense sufferings. The more suffering works in them, the more does their joy break forth ; because they see the last remains of the created fall one by one in themselves under the blows of sorrow. They see God finally invade their whole being, they see death swallowed up in victory. They see the supreme vision of love, wherein God is all in all,[1] realized within them; and, in proportion as some fragment of the wall of separation falls,[2]

---

[1] Ut sit Deus omnia in omnibus (1 Cor. xv. 28).
[2] Medium parietem maceriæ solvens (Eph. ii. 14).

they triumph with fresh joy. Their sorrow is their greatest joy. Blessed are the poor, blessed are those that mourn, blessed are the clean of heart, blessed are they that suffer persecution, blessed are the reviled and persecuted and calumniated. The Saviour has said it, and they enjoy it. All the beatitudes are in them. O supreme happiness of the saints! O ineffable pleasure of suffering! O holy blessedness of death! *Beati mortui!* . . . Whoever has not had some taste of such things knows nothing of joy nor of the true meaning of happiness.

19. The rational man.—The saint who has reached this supreme conclusion of all holiness is the only man who is really and entirely rational. He is, indeed, the only one to draw all the true conclusions, to gather all the consequences, from the great fundamental principle which should guide every human life; he is the only one to reach in an absolute manner that end for which he was created. Alone he has seen the consummation of every end, and the end of every consummation;[1] alone he knows the infinite breadth of the great command to see, love, and seek God in all things.

And if he has had to pass through numberless experiences of denudation and destruction, he feels that nothing of his real being has perished in these agonies; that nothing which ought to live has been lost. On the contrary, his life, his true life, has become emancipated in its purity and freedom; it is a bath wherein his body has left its defilements behind; it is a crucible in which the gold has shed its dross. Here again is one of the seals of true holiness; its penances are able to immolate what ought to be sacrificed without doing any harm to what is really vital. How many of the mortifications of the saints are health-giving, first of all for the soul, and then even for the body! Diabolical exaggeration always ends in destroying what ought to be preserved, and in preserving what ought to be destroyed. The saint, being led by God, strikes where he ought, destroys where it is fit to do so, and builds up with wisdom. He is the absolutely rational man *par excellence*.

[1] Omnis consummationis vidi finem, latum mandatum tuum nimis (Ps. cxviii. 96).

20. St. Francis of Sales's wish.—" O my daughter !" writes St. Francis of Sales to St. Jeanne de Chantal, " how much I desire that we may one day be altogether reduced to nothingness in ourselves so as to live wholly unto God, and that our life may be hidden with Jesus Christ in God ! Oh, when shall we ourselves live, and yet not ourselves, and when will Jesus Christ live wholly in us ? I am about to make this the subject of a little mental prayer, and I shall pray the royal heart of the Saviour for ours."[1]

CHAPTER V

Purgatory

21. Nothing defiled enters into heaven.—22. The duration of purgatory. — 23. Purification and glorification. — 24. Glorification stopped.—25. Purification continued.

21. Nothing defiled enters into heaven.—How earnestly should I make the desires of St. Francis of Sales my own ! For this entire purification of human nature, this complete transference of my whole self to the rule of the love of the Son of God, which renders me worthy and capable of entering into participation with the company of the saints in light, must be wrought and fulfilled in me before I enter into heaven. None shall enter there until this work has been accomplished. What has not been done in this world will be done in purgatory ; at all events, if the work has been already begun, for mortal sin remains eternally the spoil of hell. We must pass by death to reach life.

Yes, all this almost infinite work of the purification of my being, this stripping off of the created, this annihilation of false adherences, this transformation of the human, has to take place as a preliminary condition of entering heaven. Flesh and blood shall not inherit the kingdom of God, neither shall corruption inherit incorruption, says St. Paul. The corruptible must be clothed with incorruption, and the mortal must put on immortality. Until it has been entirely purified,

[1] *Letters*, Book IV, Letter 106, Ed. Léonard.

says St. John of the Cross, the soul cannot possess God on earth in the pure transformation of love, nor in heaven in the beatific vision.[1] If God cannot in this world consummate with the soul that complete union which is called the mystical marriage, until the human has been totally annihilated, how can He consummate the eternal union of glory in heaven without this?

22. The duration of purgatory.—O God! what then will purgatory be? ... What! must the flames burn up everything in me? ... not only my sins? ... not only my imperfections? but also all the human? ... all the created? ... and that in all adherence which is apart from God? ... Have they to bring about the complete transformation of my being? ... If even in the saints in this world, these operations are so long and so painful; if so many crosses and tribulations are required to accomplish them; if the stripping off of everything in their case makes me shudder; then, O my God, what will purgatory be to me! ...

Now I understand how few souls enter directly into heaven, and the doctrine of the Church as to purgatory, and her extraordinary insistence on making us pray for the dead. When I shall take a time, on the threshold of eternity, says the Lord, I will judge justices.[2] Such is the judgement of justices.

23. Purification and glorification.—So far as interior purification is concerned, all souls will be on the same footing in heaven; one will not be more pure than another, since all must be absolutely pure. From this point of view, all have the same vocation, all are called to attain the utmost height. In this sense, the command which binds me to love God with my whole being has the same absolute breadth for me as for saints and angels. The word of God in His great commandment, *ex toto*, has no limit to its strictness. No spot, no imperfection, no speck of dust, may remain in my soul any more than in an angel. I am then called to perfect purity, to the supreme consummation.

But here we must recall a distinction. There are, indeed, in the work of the interior life and in its ascent through the five degrees of piety, two parts: one negative, which is that

---

[1] *The Ascent of Mount Carmel*, Book I, ch. iv.
[2] Cum accepero tempus, ego justitias judicabo (Ps. lxxiv. 3).

of purification; the other positive, which is that of glorification. During this mortal life, these two parts of the divine education are never separated. All purification is accompanied by an expansion of soul and by an increase of merits.

24. **Glorification stopped.**—I have just seen in what measure purification takes place in going through the five degrees of piety, since these five degrees are indeed characterized by the progress made by interior purification. But the measure in which the soul increases its divine capacities and eternal merits is God's secret. I know what are the miseries of which I strip myself, but I do not know what are the riches which I am acquiring. What may be the height of virtue reached in me, what may be the extent of my merits, what may be the level attained by my soul, what its place in heaven will be: all these mysteries will only be revealed to me in the brightness of the life to come.

I know that in this world, grace is given to every one according to the measure of the giving of Christ.[1] I know that in the next life, glory will answer to the measure of the grace which I shall have turned to good account here below; I know that in eternity, I shall possess that amount of growth that I have reached in time; I know that in getting my evil defilements washed away, I increase at the same time; and this is all I know.

I am mistaken, I know something more. I know that here below each one has his own measure, and that in heaven, among the elect, star differeth from star in glory (1 Cor. xv. 41); I know that the work of growth and glorification ends irrevocably with death, and that each one will be left eternally with the amount of merits in his possession at the time of his passing away.[2] I must work the works of Him that sent me, whilst it is day : the night cometh when no man can work (John ix. 4).

25. **Purification continued.**—Consequently, of the two works which go on simultaneously during the time of our earthly existence, one stops instantly and absolutely at death,

---

[1] Unicuique autem nostrum data est gratia secundum mensuram donationis Christi (Eph. iv. 7).

[2] Si ceciderit lignum ad austrum aut ad aquilonem, in quocumque loco ceciderit, ibi erit (Eccles. xi. 3).

and this is the work of glorification; the other, if necessary, continues beyond the grave until its supreme completion, and this is the work of our purification. Its operations are carried out in a place determined by the merciful justice of the supreme Judge, a place which has therefore been given the name of purgatory. What there takes place is a purification which is altogether barren of any increase of merits or of being, without any other benefit than that of the purification itself. Purgatory will lead me to the degree of absolute purity required for my appearance before God, and on leaving it, I shall have the same degree of merit as I had on entering. Ah, how important it is for me to come to an agreement with my adversary betimes, whilst I am in the way with him in this world, and before he delivers me to the judge, and the judge delivers me to the officer, and I am cast into prison! Once there, I shall not go out from thence till I have repaid the last farthing.[1] How mad and faithless must I be if I condemn myself to such rigorous confinement and to such an unprofitable expiation while it is still possible for me to gain so much by becoming more holy!

CHAPTER VI

A General View

Unity

26. Unity.—27. Simplicity.—28. Strength.—29. Division.—30. The three struggles.—31. Nothing to give unity.

26. Unity.—In this first principle of my creation I find the real foundation of my spiritual life; the whole building of holiness rests entirely upon it. The ultimate consequences of the most perfect heroism as well as the first beginnings of the avoidance of sin are conclusions from this first principle. It is the centre of everything in the spiritual life. All truths,

---

[1] Esto consentiens adversario tuo, cito dum es in via cum eo; ne forte tradat te adversarius judici et judex tradat te ministro et in carcerem mittaris. Amen dico tibi, non exies inde, donec reddas novissimum quadrantem (Matt. v. 25, 26).

even those which appear to be most fundamental, can be reduced to this principle and deduced from it. It is, indeed, easy to see that the spirit of faith, the love of God, zeal, purity of intention, conformity to the will of God, etc., humility, self-denial, mortification, etc., are but the conclusions from, or applications of, this principle.

When I have attained to the full light of this truth, which is the mother and mistress of all the rest, I seem to have ascended to the top of the mountain of God; and from this height, I can begin to comprehend, with all the saints, what is the breadth, and length, and height, and depth (Eph. iii. 18). This light illumines more fully the truths of the faith and the Christian virtues. How much better can I fathom with its help the texts of Holy Scripture, the utterances of the Church, and the writings of the saints! No other truth is as general, universal, and central. It gives me the key of all spiritual doctrine. Without it, I can only confine myself to some particular and more or less important truth, which can never be the all of my interior life. The first fruit I gather from it is therefore unity; unity of thought, unity of aspiration, unity of effort, unity of my whole life, which is directed towards this one end.

27. Simplicity.—Unity engenders simplicity; unity of view implies unity of way and unity of means. Thus disappear the manifold complications of devotional practices, the incoherent and tiresome details of exercises, in the maze of which the soul fails to find guidance, light, and life. Oh how complicated is an ill-instructed piety, and how simple is that which is true! This will be seen still more clearly when I have to speak of devotional exercises.

28. Strength.—The fairest fruit of unity is strength. The great source of interior weakness is disturbance and division. Every kingdom divided against itself shall be brought to desolation (Luke iii. 17). The soul which is dispersed and divided amidst the thousand anxieties of the senses consumes its powers in detail and wastes them. But when these are concentrated in unity and in God, what strength do they possess! Seek ye the Lord, and be strengthened: seek His face evermore (Ps. civ. 4). Seek ye God, and your soul shall

live (Ps. lxviii. 33). Thus saith the Lord to the house of Israel : seek ye Me, and ye shall live (Amos v. 4).

No power is comparable to that of a soul unified in the vision, love, and seeking of God. First of all, I get the initial strength that comes from the very gathering together of all the powers of my being. Who can measure the power of one, all of whose faculties are entirely united in the same effort ? When the intelligence, the will, the passions and powers of the body, are concentrated and as it were compressed together upon the same object, no earthly might is comparable to it. And when this strength is reinforced by God's, for in concentrating himself in God man acquires God's strength, how can we be astounded at the prodigious sway exercised by the saints ? How can we be astounded at the potency of their prayer and at the might of their action ? O my God ! when shall I thus be wholly united in Thee, so as to be strong by Thee ? . . . I will keep my strength to Thee (Ps. lviii. 10) ; and Thou, O God, who art wonderful in Thy saints, Thou the God of Israel art He who will give me Thy power and strength (Ps. lxvii. 36).

29. Division.—We need not look further than our inward division for the amazing weakness with regard to the good which is in our midst. If it may be said with truth that the strength of the wicked is the weakness of the good, what is the cause of this weakness ?—Division and want of unity. Not only the division which separates man from man and which hinders any unity of view, any cohesion of will, and any concentration of effort. This division is but the product of another which is still deeper and more lamentable : the division that exists in the depths of each soul. It is often enough to enter into the inner state of a single soul to appreciate the state of society. For the general state of society is but an outward reproduction, and the pattern in a lower sphere, of what takes place in the higher region of piety.

30. The three struggles.—I have considered my soul, and what have I found therein ?—My tastes and whims as the practical rule of my thoughts, my determinations, and my conduct. But what suits me is not the rule followed by God in His governance of the universe. Hence, by this fact

I am divided in thought, will, and action, so far as God is concerned. This is the first struggle.

Then, what suits me is not the rule laid down for my fellows and followed by them. Each one has his whims and his notions, and if each one finds his rule in himself, this means a universal division of thought, resolution, and effort. This is the second struggle.

Lastly, what suits me is not the rule laid down for my own life. My tastes are unstable: momentary whims are not abiding, bodily needs are not those of the soul, manifestations of passion cross one another and are endlessly multiplied; and this means inward division. On the other hand, my whims cast me outside of myself to seek the creature with its infinitely multiplied divergencies. And all this still more divides my mind, and causes my feelings to scatter and struggle with one another, and gives my actions incoherence and precipitancy and disturbance and feverishness. The soul wastes at every pore; it is like a pair of bellows full of holes, a well that leaks and lets out the water at every stone, a machine out of order in every part. I am divided and fighting against myself. This is the third struggle.

31. *Nothing to give unity.*—Where is the thought of God to control and concentrate all these ideas? the love of God to control and concentrate all these affections? the seeking of God to control and concentrate all these actions? The thought of God, the love of God, the seeking of God, these are but a small section, which has its place amidst all other fragments that make up life, which works and struggles with them, and is scarcely any more than they. This means division without end, and the multiplication of weakness to the last degree.

Disunion and impotence become the state of each one, and are the state of all together; and they are the state of all together because they are the state of each one.[1] The barrenness of the efforts of each individual as to himself and as to all as a whole; the impotence of one's work upon one-

---

[1] Here I repeat a remark made at the outset. The words " all " and " each one " must be taken in a sense broad enough to allow for numerous exceptions which are our consolation in the present and our hope for the future.

self and upon society : the cause of all this lies in inward division. I make a number of efforts, and yet I am always going backwards ; such is the complaint of many souls. What a quantity of efforts are made on behalf of society, and yet society daily goes backward. O piety, thou divine unity, give us back the ascending steps of life ! O my God ! grant that in me and in all others the splendid promise of Thy prophet may be fulfilled : that Thy glory may gather up and restore and restrain all our life in unity ![1]

CHAPTER VII

A General View

Peace

32. Liberty.—33. Equanimity.—34. Peace.—35. Glory and peace.

32. **Liberty.**—When God becomes my one thing needful, He also becomes my one sole Lord. I know that when I become anyone's slave to obey him, I am the slave of him whom I obey, whether it be of sin, unto death, or of obedience, unto justice. Now I am made free from sin, and am become the slave of God only.[2] What do creatures matter to me ? What do happiness or sorrow matter, peace or suffering, abundance or want, honour or contempt, health or sickness, life or death ? What do they matter ? None of these things are my necessary end, I am free from them all, above them all.

The all of my life is higher, and all creatures, whether agreeable or disagreeable to me, are equally the means of my reaching my one necessary end. I know that God will always afford me these means as far as they are necessary to the one end of my life. I therefore cast all my care upon Him, for

---

[1] Gloria Domini colliget te (Is. lviii. 8).
[2] Nescitis quoniam cui exhibetis vos servos ad obediendum, servi estis ejus cui obeditis, sive peccati ad mortem, sive obeditionis ad justitiam ? . . . Nunc vero liberati a peccato, servi autem facti Deo (Rom. vi. 16-22).

He makes it His business to care for me.[1] And I have only to take what He gives me; I make use of it as far as I need it; and when it is of no more use, I throw it away. I am master. Thus I am not the slave of any being or event; I am independent of them, indifferent about them. When truth is revealed in me, the truth which is the highest term of piety, it sets me free, truly and totally free.[2] When the truth, by way of charity, issues in liberty, piety is complete. O holy liberty of the children of God! are all the toys of vanity too high a price to pay for thee? These toys are like the meshes of the net in which I was caught. The bird escapes from the net: the snare is broken, and I am delivered.[3]

33. **Equanimity.**—Along with liberty, I win equanimity and peace. My soul's affections being transferred to God, my one necessity, are no longer drawn hither and thither by being divided amidst creatures; disturbances from below can no longer affect my soul, which is disengaged from them and dwells in a higher region. They may be manifested in the lower sphere of the senses and of the sensibility, which border on the inferior part; but they never rise to the higher part of the soul, which lives in God and dwells in the region of tranquillity. Through all things, whether pleasant or the reverse, my soul preserves its equanimity of temper and action. Now that all brings it that increase of life which is its sole ambition, now that by means of piety it has learnt to make use of everything in view of the one end, human vicissitudes cease to communicate to it those interminable tossings hither and thither from which we suffer while we are lost in the crowd.

34. **Peace.**—When piety has established order in everything,[4] I rest in that tranquillity of order which is peace. And this is real peace, deep peace, the peace of God, which rises far above all that belongs to the senses.[5] This is the peace

[1] Omnem sollicitudinem vestram projicientes in eum, quoniam ipsi cura est de vobis (1 Pet. v. 7).
[2] Cognoscetis veritatem, et veritas liberabit vos; si ergo vos Filius liberaverit, vere liberi eritis (Joan. viii. 32, 36).
[3] Anima nostra sicut passer erepta est, de laqueo venantium. Laqueus contritus est et nos liberati sumus (Ps. cxxiii. 7).
[4] Pax est tranquillitas ordinis (S. Aug., *De Civ. Dei.*, I, 19. § 13).
[5] Pax Dei quæ exsuperat omnem sensum (Phil. iv. 7).

which Jesus Christ calls His own, and which infinitely differs from that of the world.[1] When I have done what is just, giving to God what is God's, and to the creature what belongs to the creature, justice brings forth its fruit, which is peace.[2] I cross over the hills of justice to get to the mountains of peace.[3] The Angels proclaimed it at Bethlehem: man's peace ever follows upon God's glory.[4]

Peace: this is the last word of man's happiness. It is the final summing up of the divine promises, the last hymn of the Church's triumph sung at the grave of her children. When one of the faithful leaves death behind to enter into life, the representative of God and of the Church says in the name of God and of the Church three words which are the connecting-link between time and eternity: *Requiescat in pace.* Rest in peace !... What words, what a wish is here !... It is the wish of eternity, for peace will not be ultimately realized except in heaven.

35. **Glory and peace.**—And, in the last analysis, this is how my life comes to be summed up in the two words which were sung by the Angels over our Lord's crib, as the full message of His coming into the world: " Glory to God in the highest: and on earth peace to men of good-will." There, indeed, is the whole purpose of the Incarnation and of Redemption: to procure and to repair the glory of God and the peace of man. Glory is all that man can render to God, and peace all that God gives to man. Glory means man dwelling in God: peace means God dwelling in man. For there is this double indwelling of man in God and of God in man, and the one is inseparable from the other and always follows the other. Abide in Me: and I in you, says the Lord (John xv. 4). He that abideth in charity, says the Apostle of charity, abideth in God, and God in him (1 John iv. 16). I must abide in God by glory that God may abide in me by peace. And this abiding, this interchange of glory and peace, this is my life for time and for eternity.

[1] Pacem relinquo vobis, pacem meam do vobis ; non quomodo mundus dat, ego do vobis (Joan. xiv. 27).
[2] Et erit opus justitiæ pax (Is. xxxii. 17).
[3] Suscipiant montes pacem populo, et colles justitiam (Ps. lxxi. 3).
[4] Gloria in altissimis Deo et in terra pax hominibus bonæ voluntatis (Luc. ii. 14).

CHAPTER VIII

For Priests

36. The duel between the ministry and spiritual exercises.—37. The priest seeks self. — 38. He also seeks the good of others.—39. Destroy the common enemy.—40. Centre and circumference.—41. Exhortation.

36. The duel between the ministry and spiritual exercises.—This principle further throws light upon an important point in the ministry of the priest. Is it not a strange paradox that an ecclesiastic should be hindered in his interior life by the work of the ministry? . . . The ministry of the priest is essentially spiritual, it has to do with nothing but the things of God and with such as lead to God. All day the priest, devoted to his ministry, is given up to the service of God, and occupied with supernatural work. The normal effect of this employment should be to unite the priest deeply, intimately, and constantly, to God. How does it happen that it keeps him at a distance? for it is impossible to disguise the fact that such is the too common result of his work to-day.

Whence comes this antagonism, I was about to say, this duel to the death, between exercises of piety and the ministry, the one killing the other? How can two things which are so much alike contradict one another? Their reconciliation is a difficult problem, and counsels and recommendations recur year by year on this capital question without securing any entirely satisfactory conclusions. In order to stop the strife, priests are advised to assign to each its share in a careful manner, and not to allow the one to infringe on the domain of the other. Nothing is so unstable as this factitious equilibrium, since it rests upon convention and not upon principle.

37. The priest seeks himself.—To go to the root of things, there can be no setting up of a reconciliation or harmony between two things which are absolutely alike. Would it not be wiser to look for a common enemy, who slips in between them and divides them, and kills both? For the ministry is no better off than the exercises of piety; as soon as one suffers, the other suffers with it ; the evil that befalls the one, comes to the other as well. This mortal enemy may be discovered by the help of a principle which I have already meditated upon.

What, in fact, does the priest, whose piety is becoming paralyzed, look for in his ministry ? what has he in view ? what does he love ?—Two things. The first is himself. He sees, loves, and seeks himself far too much. He is far too much in the front rank in many of his intentions. How many are his personal seekings and views ! . . . How many of his ideas are neither those of God nor of His Church ! . . . how many customs and practices there are, which are not exactly in the spirit of the liturgy and of discipline ! . . . And then, there are the joys of success, the satisfactions arising from gratitude, the want of praise, and all kinds of other things. . . . A host of different kinds of self-seeking. All this tends to get the upper hand within, and what is inspired by this spirit does not go towards God.

38. **He seeks the good of others.**—In the priest's views as to himself, his eye does not keep enough to the simplicity and clearness which make the whole body full of light. But, as is plain, he also looks at others. And he has to look at so many souls . . . and so many things ! . . . Since his eye is not simple enough, he does not know well how to reduce all this multiplicity to the great centre of unity, and he allows himself to get divided. God is no longer so clearly seen in souls, nor are souls so clearly seen in God, as is demanded by the ascents of the divine glory. The very idea of salvation to be procured assumes a sort of aspect which is too utilitarian and human ; it becomes mingled with a crowd of other advantages and considerations which are more or less temporal, the direction of which is finally set too much towards the creature. Certainly, the priest cannot remain totally apart from any of the interests of human growth, since it is his function to set them towards God. He must not be unconscious of what he has to direct. But let him take care, in busying himself as to this, not to get himself set in the direction of the creature instead of directing the creature towards God.

From the moment I regard the creature, is it to be wondered at, if I find what I am looking for? Seek and you shall find (Matt. vii. 7). As soon as I make the least little slant away from the one way, I set myself in a wrong direction, and the farther I go, the more I get astray; and this is fatal. And if sometimes it happens, *ut cum spiritu cœperitis, nunc carne consummemini* (Gal. iii. 3), this terrible misfortune does but prove that those who end thus have gone on in the wrong way until the utmost. And to what do those who have been preserved from this owe it?—Solely to getting themselves wound up from time to time by the exercises of a retreat. To get wound up is the term used, and how significant it is ! ... And yet, if we were in the right way, on the one way, we should not need any winding up, but only have to go straight upwards.

39. Destroy the common enemy.—If one sought God, one would find Him. Here again we have perverted our way, the secondary has taken the first place, order has been subverted. What then must be done?—There is clearly no reconciliation to be brought about between the exercises of piety and those of the ministry: they are not enemies. One thing need not be sacrificed to the other, the one does not live at the expense of the other. Get rid of the common enemy, self-seeking and looking at the creature, which kills both the ministry and exercises of piety.

Let there be unity within, look at God, and love God: seek God, God and His glory before all else, both in your ministry and in your exercises: when you have reached the centre, you will see how everything converges there. The ministry will then strengthen your exercises, and your exercises will stimulate your ministry. They will be various acts of the same work. Instead of being drawn hither and thither in opposite directions, your soul will pass from the one to the other without shock, without effort, without distractions,[1]

[1] *Distraction* means being drawn hither and thither in different directions. How many souls complain of distractions in their prayers ! Do they know the reason of this? Distractions are the inevitable condition of a soul which is away from its centre. In proportion as it returns to the central unity of its life, distractions vanish. Consequently, the most thoroughly effective means of escape from being drawn hither and thither is to draw towards the centre of unity.

in the deeper etymological sense of the word. Then prayer will be nourished by the ministry and the ministry will be kindled by prayer, and you will see and find God in the ministry as well as in prayer: this wonderful unity will be the truth, apart from which the soul is perpetually divided and weakened.

40. Centre and circumference.—Therefore, regard God more in souls and souls more in God. In the words of Jeremias, see in the high and glorious throne from the beginning the place of all sanctification.[1] Seek your satisfaction and contentment less; rest in God, not in yourselves, nor in creatures; there is your centre, and then all, all will converge towards the same end. Towards this point converge all the points of the circle. This one point is the sole bond of all the rest. Directly the centre is left, there is no more union or concentration. In piety, too, there is but one centre, one point, which draws all, unites all, binds all together: the pure and single view of God and His glory. If I abide at this one point, if I am established at this one centre, all converges and finishes there. The infinite multiplicity of the points of the circumference, in other words, the manifold anxieties of the creature, all end in God and His glory. Nothing draws me away from it, all brings me back to it. Apart from that, there is no unity, all is division.

Oh, remain, remain at the centre, and thus the ministry will have the same effective result as prayer, every one of the external occupations will be as sanctifying as prayer, and then, what potency of sanctification there will be! All the day's acts concurring in the same end and producing the same result, the soul is borne to God simultaneously on the two wings of work and prayer. What ascents and what progress flow from this! Oh, how soon would the priest be sanctified, if he thus understood his ministry!

Thus was it understood by the saints. They were observed passing without any transition from prayer to action and from action to prayer, hardly making any difference between them, because in both they found God. God was sought and

[1] Solium gloriæ altitudinis a principio locus sanctificationis nostræ (Jer. xvii. 12)

found in the necessary succession of different occupations, but in the unity of a single view.

41. Exhortation.—O priests of God ! see and hearken. . . . There, indeed, is the secret of your strength, the treasure of your power. . . . Oh, if you only knew it ! . . . Be then united and unified in God, and nothing can stand against you. For whatsoever is born of God overcometh the world : and this is the victory which overcometh the world, our faith (1 John v. 4). O priests, if you only willed it ! . . . Faith, the vision of God, the seeking of God ! . . . Then you would be invincible ! . . . Against a single soul unified in God, the whole world can do nothing ; alone it is stronger than the world. Against it all powers are powerless, all strength is weak. Learn where is wisdom, where is strength, where is understanding : so that you may know where is length of days, the true food of the soul, victory and peace.[1] O priests ! if you only knew it !—if you only willed it ! . . . Faith, the vision of God, unity . . . and victory is yours. . . .

[1] Disce ubi sit prudentia, ubi sit virtus, ubi sit intellectus, ut scias simul ubi sit longiturnitas vitæ, et victus, et lumen oculorum et pax (Baruch iii. 14).

CONCLUSION

Here, then, is what St. Paul calls the goal of our supernal vocation in Jesus Christ. It only remains for me to fling myself into this career after the example of the great Apostle. " But the things that were gain to me," he says, " the same I have counted loss for Christ. Furthermore I counted all things to be but loss, for the excellent knowledge of Jesus Christ my Lord : for whom I have suffered the loss of all things, and count them but as dung, that I may gain Christ. . . . Not as though I had already attained, or were already perfect : but I follow after, if I may by any means apprehend, wherein I am also apprehended by Christ Jesus. Brethren, I do not count myself to have apprehended. But one thing I do [for the sake of this unity,] . . . forgetting the things that are behind [the secondary], and stretching forth myself to those that are before [the main things], I press towards the mark, to the prize of the supernal vocation of God in Christ Jesus. Let us therefore, as many as are perfect, be thus minded : and if in any thing you be otherwise minded : this also God will reveal to you. Nevertheless whereunto we are come, that we be of the same mind, let us also continue in the same rule. Be followers of me, brethren, and observe them who walk so as you have our model "[1] (Phil. iii. 7-17).

[1] Unum autem, quæ quidem retro sunt obliviscens, ad ea quæ sunt priora extendens meipsum, ad destinatum persequor, ad bravium supernæ vocationis Dei in Christo Jesu.

The Vulgate is given of that part of the above quotation in which the author has inserted the gloss printed in brackets. The rest is from the Douai version.

PART 11
THE WAY

PRELIMINARY

The Will of God

1. Who must mark out the way ?—2. The kingdom of heaven.—3. The two entrances.—4. The two wills of God.—5. The two dwellings of the Holy Ghost.—6. Their union.—7. The division of this Part

1. **Who must mark out the way ?**—I know the goal of my supernal vocation, the one end of my life; I know where I have to go, and whither my efforts must tend. But to get there, there is a way to follow, a path from which I must not deviate, unless I would miss the end. This way is one, like the end to be attained. What is it ?

In the *Pater noster*, I saw that the way is the will of God.[1] It is this will that marks out for me the path to take. In the manifold variety of spiritual and corporal creatures, some are useful for my end, others are harmful; some are more useful than others. There is, then, a choice to be made. How am I to make it ?

If I wish to make it myself, I can only make it according to my own tastes and ideas, and this will be a fresh disorder: myself before God, the disorder to be avoided at all costs. On the other hand, what do I know as to what there is in creatures ? How am I to know what is useful for the service of God, and what is not so ? God, who made the creature, alone knows what it has in it. It is, then, for Him and His will to determine what creatures I must use for His glory.

2. **The kingdom of heaven.**—*Not every one that saith to Me, Lord, Lord, shall enter into the kingdom of heaven: but he that doeth the will of My Father who is in heaven, he shall enter into the kingdom of heaven* (Matt. vii. 21). The kingdom of heaven is that in which is sung the glory of God, for it is the characteristic of heaven to shew forth the

[1] See Part I, Book I, § 51.

glory of God![1] Wherever the praises of God resound, there is the kingdom of heaven. Heaven begins here below in holy souls, and is continued in its fulness in the splendours of eternity. The kingdom of heaven is, then, the kingdom of the praise of God.

And what is the entrance into this kingdom?—It is the beginning of the praise of God. When I begin to glorify God, I enter into the kingdom of heaven, and each time I begin a new praise, a new manner of glorifying God, it is as it were a new entrance, or rather, an entrance into a new mansion of the kingdom; for in the kingdom of the heavenly Father, there are many mansions.[2] The last entrance will be that which establishes me for eternity in the mansion where I shall praise God unto the end of the ages.[3]

3. The two entrances.—But there are two kinds of entrances into this kingdom: either I enter into it, or it enters into me. Our Lord, in fact, says two things. I enter into it, when I procure the glory of God; and in this way, I begin here below to live in heaven,[4] since here below I begin to sing the glory of God. It enters into me, when I receive the gifts of God. Thus it is that Our Lord says: "Lo, the kingdom of God is within you" (Luke xvii. 21); and thus it is that in the *Pater noster* He makes me say "Thy kingdom come." Already here below, the kingdom of God enters into me and I enter into it. And when the hour of eternity strikes, then I shall finally and totally enter into it to praise God through eternity, and it will enter into me to flood me with endless felicity.

But how and in what way does this entrance come about? —Our Lord says that it is not by prayer. Prayer is not the way: later on, I shall see that it is a means, and a great means, but a means which is only of use if I am on the way. Outside of the way, he who takes this means and says, "Lord, Lord," shall not enter. What then is the way?—It is one only, it is the will of God. He who does the will of My Father, it is he who will enter, he alone, and no others.

[1] Cœli enarrant gloriam Dei (Ps. xviii. 1).
[2] In domo Patris mei mansiones multæ sunt (Joan. xiv 2).
[3] In sæcula sæculorum laudabunt te (Ps. lxxxiii. 5).
[4] Nostra autem conversatio in cœlis est (Phil. iii 20).

4. **The two wills of God.**—This is the road I must take and follow. But to take and follow it, I must know it. The will of God is one; " but," says St. Francis of Sales, " although His divine Majesty has but one very singular and simple will, yet we denote it with different names according to the various means whereby we know it, a variety which obliges us to conform to it in ways as various."[1]

All the varieties of the manifestation of the divine will may be reduced to two, which are like the two hands of God. With one hand, God indicates to me the rules of what I have to do; He sets up the barriers, He keeps the channel which has to confine, protect, and contain my vital movement. This is the fixed part, the statical element of the supernatural life. All laws, rules, directions, and institutions, the use of which is to direct and contain my action, belong to that divine will which is called the will signified. It is thus called, because it puts along my path signs which indicate the line I have to follow.

With His other hand, God acts within me: He stimulates and animates me, He impresses upon me the impulse of a supernatural movement. This is the motive power, the dynamical element of my divine life. All that comprises inspiration, right movement, God's inner action, belongs to this side of His will which is called His will of good pleasure. It is thus called, because, in its vivifying action upon me, God manifests the good pleasure of the mercy and loving-kindness which inspire His will.

5. **The two dwellings of the Holy Ghost.**—And, at bottom, what are these two manifestations of the divine will but the twofold dwelling of the Holy Ghost, promised by the Lord to His Church? The will is the peculiar attribute of the Holy Ghost. And in announcing His mission, Our Lord said to His Apostles: " The Spirit of truth shall abide with you, and shall be in you " (John xiv. 17). He shall abide with you, this means dwelling in the house which is the Church. This is the public, external, official presence, whereby the Spirit of truth maintains the laws, and guides the persons who interpret the laws of God. He will be in you, this

[1] *Treatise of the Love of God*, Book VIII, ch. iii.

means the inward dwelling, the personal indwelling of the Spirit of holiness, acting in the soul and producing in it the mysterious seething of eternal life.

Hence on the one hand, there is a regulative power which gives me the outward form of what I have to do : and on the other hand, there is a stimulative movement, imparting internal activity to me. On the one hand, social authority, intended to contain ; on the other, individual action, intended to vivify. On the one hand the body, and on the other the soul of Christian life.

6. Their union.—Consequently, it is plain that these two sides of the divine will, these two hands of God, these two dwellings of the Holy Ghost, cannot be separated in the formation of my life. My activity must be at once contained on the one hand, and animated on the other, by the Spirit of God. Whilst the rules of the signified will, being stable, fixed, and firm, act as an external mould, the living, mobile, and varied operations of the will of good pleasure animate, knead, and transform the dough, and make it enter into all the shapings of the mould. It is thus that the two hands of God combine to confine and to arouse my movement.

7. The division of this Part.—Here then are three things : the external rules of my action for God, the internal secrets of God's action in me, the living combination of the two elements which form my life. Consequently, I have three questions to put to myself here : 1. What rules are laid down for my action by the will signified ? 2. What part does the action of the sovereign good pleasure play in my life ? 3. How do these two actions come to unite and combine ? The three Books that follow will be entirely devoted to answering these three questions. When I know what my action ought to be, what God's action is, and what the union of my action with God's should be, I shall know my way, I shall know the road whereby the soul rises to glorify its Creator.

Thus it is that Part II is divided into three Books entitled :

      I. The Will Signified.
     II. The Will of Good Pleasure.
    III. The Concurrence of the Two Wills

It is well to remark that if the need for clearness necessitates this division of the three ideas, and their separate explanation, it does not follow that the will signified can appear apart from the will of good pleasure, since, in the living reality of my progress towards God, they are allied and united as is steam to the pipes that contain it, and as is the stream to the channel in which it runs. Nor must it be inferred that piety which is active and piety which is passive, as they will be here understood, are two successive states of the soul. They are two factors of the same movement. In order to understand them better, I shall first study each of them separately, as it were by the method of analysis; and after the partial consideration of each in two distinct Books, in the third Book, I shall come to see their living synthesis.

BOOK 1

THE WILL SIGNIFIED

It is this will that lays down duty, that marks out the way of right in which man has to walk, and which protects him from the by-ways of evil, which he has to avoid. It is this which marks out the road to heaven, and indicates both the direction to be taken and the barriers that must not be crossed. Its indications are indispensable to man, poor lost wanderer in the wilderness of the world, for, without them, he would be incapable of finding his way to the fatherland.

Two points must be considered here. First, where and how is this will of God manifested and expressed? Next, how must I answer and correspond thereto? Hence, in the first place, there is the manifestation of God, in the second, the answer of man: the manifestation of the divine orders and desires, the rule of my activity; the answer of my activity and of my life to the orders and desires of God. In other words: on the one side, the signs of the divine will; on the other, active piety: such are the two things I have to meditate upon in this first Book.

CHAPTER I

Commandments and Counsels

1. Divine manifestations.—2. The commandments of God.—3. The commandments of the Church.—4. The counsels.

1. **Divine manifestations.**—God, who at sundry times and in divers manners spoke in times past to the fathers by the prophets, last of all in these days hath spoken to us by His Son, whom He hath appointed heir of all things, by whom also He made the world (Heb. i. 1). God has spoken, and He speaks; for He never leaves Himself without testimony.[1] He hath spoken by His prophets and by the men He has inspired; He has spoken Himself by coming to live our human life, and He continues to speak by His Church. This word of life, which God in His goodness has multiplied in so many ways and at so many times, is practically condensed in matters of conduct in the Commandments of God, the Commandments of the Church, and in the Evangelical Counsels.

2. **The commandments of God.**—They manifest to me the most general and the most absolute will of God my Father. This will applies absolutely to all. Therein is the source and rule of all obligations. It is what is binding on piety in quite the first place, and the other manifestations of the will of God only help to explain, to determine, and to apply the general prescriptions laid down by the commandments. The commandments of God, then, are the primary and fundamental rule of piety, and their observance is the first duty.

In the commandments there are two parts, written formerly by the finger of God on the two tables of the law: the first, the rule of the interests which are divine; the second, of the interests which are human. God and man, divine relations and human relations, these constitute the whole of religion. And the commandments govern that which concerns God

[1] Et quidem non sine testimonio semetipsum reliquit (Act. xiv. 16).

and that which concerns man; they are finally summed up in the love of God and in the love of our neighbour. Not only what God has written on the two tables of Sina, but all that He has said in the law and the prophets is ultimately condensed into these two precepts.[1]

3. The commandments of the Church.—They are the voice of my mother, explaining to me and determining certain points of the will of God my Father. It is the mission of the Church to adapt to times and persons the divine prescriptions, and, according to necessity, to specify certain of their practical details and certain particular applications. Here is the second rule of piety.

Since complete piety is at once truth in the mind, charity in the heart, and liberty in action, the Church, whose office it is to mark out and to protect her course, has at once the *magisterium* of truth, the sway of charity, and the discipline of liberty. By virtue of this triple power, which is infallible, she promulgates the laws of her dogma, her morals, and her discipline, and these three categories of laws are at once the rule and the protection of piety. By the laws of her dogma, the Church is the guardian of truth for my mind, and lays down its ways. By the laws of her morals, she is the guardian of charity for my heart, and shows it the path. By the laws of her discipline, she is the guardian of my liberty of action, and determines my use of it. By her commandments, the Church is then the fosterer and guardian of my piety. And if I would have truth in my mind, charity in my heart, and liberty in my actions, in a word, if I would have piety in my life, I must conform to the laws of the Church. Piety is only kept in truth, charity, and liberty by the protection of Holy Church, my mother.

4. The counsels.—God is not only manifested by His absolute declarations of will, binding under pain of sin; He also condescends to make known His wishes. And as the commandments express His absolute will, the counsels indicate His wishes. The commandments determine what is the evil to be avoided and what is the good to be done. The

[1] In his duobus mandatis universa lex pendet et prophetæ (Matt. xxii. 40).

counsels, being based in the first place on the commandments, rise above them and mark out the way of the better and of the perfect. They reveal to man the secrets and the higher ascents, and they mark out for him the paths by which he may rise to consummation in God.

The way of the commandments is obligatory, in such a way that every voluntary deviation becomes a formal disobedience to the supreme Master. The paths of the counsels are free in the sense that negligence in going forward in them does not constitute an offence properly so-called against the divine Majesty, and remains a simple coming short of the good and a diminution of perfection.

The counsels are numerous, for they exist interiorly for all states of the soul, and exteriorly for all social positions. They are extensive, for they reach as far as the highest point of the mystical marriage of the soul with God. That is to say, that all are not adapted to all, that they vary according to the external position of different souls, and that they are graduated even for the same soul according to the level of its interior ascents.

CHAPTER II

The Duties of One's State of Life

5. Twofold object.—6. The application of the commandments.—7. The choice of counsels.—8. For priests.—9. For religious.—10. For laymen.

5. The twofold object.—Practice requires an application of the commandments, a choice of the counsels. There is no choice to be made between the commandments, since they must all be kept; but they have to be applied, and this application is as various as are one's external conditions and interior disposition. As for the counsels, since all of them cannot be carried out by all, a choice has to be made.

What is it that determines both the necessary application of the commandments and the fitting choice of the counsels?—The duties of our state of life. These duties are not a category of obligations or of directions distinct from those which are contained in the commandments and the counsels. Their proper object is to specify in a very concrete way the practical mode of execution, and what personally applies to each individual.

Hence their object is twofold. It is in them that I find these two things determined: 1. The proper and personal manner in which I have to practise the commandments; 2. the special part of the evangelical counsels which it is possible and a good thing for me to conform to.

6. **The application of the commandments.**—Though identical for all and absolute in substance, the commandments cannot be practised by all in the same conditions. The principle is general, its application must be special. The precept proclaims the general principle, the duty of our state of life determines the special application.

The fourth commandment, for instance, which has authority for its object, universally applies to all men. For, in our social organization, no one can exist without having some amount of authority to exercise or to submit to. Hence the commandment is indeed universal. But, as to its fulfilment, what a difference there is between master and subject! And for masters: fathers, professors, heads, superiors, chiefs of all kinds, what differences there are in the exercise of their manifold social authorities! And for the subjects: children, pupils, servants, workmen, inferiors of all sorts, there are as many varieties in the conditions of their obedience to authority! All have to observe a general precept, and each one does this differently according to his state of life. The laws and special rules of each state tell each one how he must adapt himself to the common precept.

So much for authority. And it is the same with regard to the adoration, reverence, and worship of God, and charity, chastity, justice, and truth, governed by the other commandments, and practically determined by the duties of each state.

7. **The choice of counsels.**—With regard to perfection and the ties by which one may be engaged thereto, men may be classified into three states: priests, religious, laymen. There are doubtless counsels, such as those of patience, humility, gentleness, etc., which are fitting for all these states. Many

of the general principles of the spiritual life may be studied and meditated on in the same books by priests, religious, and laymen. Nevertheless, the practice of these counsels cannot be separated from the surroundings of professional duties with which they must be in accord.

But there are also, especially in the matters of prayer and detachment, counsels which are quite peculiar to each state. Sacerdotal, religious, and laic perfection does not strip off the human and go towards the divine by the same way in each of these states. Nor do all priests fulfil the same functions, nor do all the religious follow the same constitutions, nor do all laymen practise the same professions. And the practice of the principles of perfection has necessary variations, and they are often fairly characteristic of the different specialities of sacerdotal functions, religious constitutions, and social professions.

8. For priests.—The duties of his state in the case of the priest are contained in ecclesiastical laws. These laws are of two kinds: liturgical laws, and disciplinary laws. The liturgical laws, and the word is here taken in its broadest sense, govern his relations with God; disciplinary laws govern his relations with the creature. One set strips him of himself, the others lead him to God. Here there are two operations which, in reality, are only one, and which refer man to the glory of God.

It is the liturgical rules that determine for him the sense of the three commandments, as well as of the counsels, which have to do with his relations with God, and it is these rules that give them their sacerdotal form. And in the same way, it is canon law that determines the commandments of the second table, and the counsels which govern his relations with creatures, in such wise as to give them their sacerdotal form. It is, then, in this twofold classification of the laws which properly belong to his state that the ecclesiastic must look for the rule that touches clerical piety most nearly, and for its most appropriate form.

9. For the religious.—The duties of their state are expressed in the Rule. It contains the authentic collection and the complete form of the obligations which are specially binding

on them. God has shown a loving care, even in the smallest details, to indicate His will to them. Two essential parts sum up the Rule of the religious, whatever it may be: one, which is ritual, governs their offices with regard to God; the other, which is disciplinary, strips man of himself and of all that is created, in the degree and in the manner which are peculiar to each institution. Here, again, we have the two fundamental operations of all piety.

Precepts and counsels, then, in the case of the religious also, are fused into and become embodied in his Rule, in order to assume that special form which imparts its proper character to the religious life. And the piety of the monk will be manifested in its true religious form, if he is able to find in his Rule the most immediate law of his advance towards God.

10. **For laymen.**—The duties of their state are laid down for them by the professional rules which belong to each person. The magistrate has his rules of duty, the soldier has his regimental orders, the merchant, the doctor, the workman, the father of a family, the mother, the children, all and each in their several positions have obligations specially belonging to them, and which are marked out for them by rules which are more or less explicit, or by unwritten customs having the force of law.

These professional obligations are the nearest rule for the piety of laymen. If the piety of the priest only becomes sacerdotal by its conformity with ecclesiastical laws, if the piety of the monk only becomes religious by the observation of his Rule, the *piety* of the layman is only real in and through the practice of his professional duties. Thus each state has the form which properly belongs to its piety, and this form is willed by God, in such a manner that the piety of the priest is not that of the religious nor of the layman, and that of the layman is not that of the priest nor of the religious.

CHAPTER III

The Knowledge of Duty

The General Obligation

11. Practical piety.—12. Knowing, loving, executing.—13. The necessity of knowing one's duty.—14. Ignorance.—15. Illusion

11. **Practical piety.**—Such is the general will of God. To this will correspond the obligations which constitute what I may call the practical part of piety, since they determine what I ought to *do*, and they point out to me the portion of personal action which God asks of me in the work of His glory and of my own sanctification.

I must, in fact, act and exercise my faculties in the execution of God's orders and desires. I must walk in the way that is marked out for me. And how can I walk?—By means of the three groups of faculties within me. I can know, and love, and execute. But I have seen that when the direction of my sight, my love, and my seeking is set towards God, that is called piety.[1] The part of this direction which is brought about by the concurrence of my personal activity must then be called piety in action, or the practical part of piety. Hence, practical piety is the part in action which I have to develop in seeing, loving, and seeking God.

12. **Knowing, loving, executing.**—If I have to know my end, I must also know my way; if I ought to love my end, I ought also to love the road thither; if I must try to attain the final summit of my life, I must also follow the paths which lead me thereto. Now, I have seen[2] that the glory of God, which is my end, requires: that my intelligence should know it; that my will should be attached to it; that my action should seek it. This triple obligation is equally binding so far as the will of God is concerned. My intelligence must know it; my will, respect and love it; my action, execute it. The seeing, loving, seeking the glory of God, constitute the essence of piety; the seeing, loving, seeking the will of God, constitute its way.

[1] See Part I, Book II ch. ii.   [2] *Ibid*, ch. i.

THE WAY: THE WILL SIGNIFIED

13. The necessity of knowing one's duty.—I must first of all know the will of God. I must know it, if I desire to follow it and not to walk in darkness,[1] and if I desire not to be entirely wanting in prudence and wisdom.[2] Knowledge is here again the first condition of the good. I must ask God to fill me with the knowledge of His will in all wisdom and spiritual understanding, so that I may walk worthy of God, please Him in all things, be fruitful in every good work, and increase in the knowledge of God.[3] As the eyes of servants are on the hands of their masters, and as the eyes of the hand-maid are on the hands of her mistress; so must my eyes be fastened on the Lord my God,[4] so that I may inquire for and come to know His will in all things.

14. Ignorance.—There are two evils to be feared: ignorance which does not see, and illusion which sees amiss. First of all, there is culpable ignorance which is not at all anxious to refashion its feelings anew, but which, conforming to the world, does not try to ascertain what is the will of God, leading from the good to the better and the perfect.[5] Next, there is the ignorance composed of distractions and frivolities, which cannot stay to give thought to anything and lets its life glide with the stream. Finally, there is involuntary ignorance, the fruit of the darkness of our weak intelligence, and against which we have to struggle our whole life long, asking God above all to set His light in the little lamp of our minds, and to enlighten our darkness.[6]

---

[1] Qui sequitur me, non ambulat in tenebris (Joan. viii. 12).

[2] Nolite fieri imprudentes, sed intelligentes quæ sit voluntas Dei (Eph. v. 17).

[3] Orantes et postulantes, ut impleamini agnitione voluntatis ejus, in omni sapientia et intellectu spirituali, ut ambuletis digne Deo per omnia placentes, in omni opere bono fructificantes et crescentes in scientia Dei (Col. i. 9, 10).

[4] Ecce sicut oculi servorum in manibus dominorum suorum, sicut oculi ancillæ in manibus dominæ suæ, ita oculi nostri ad Dominum Deum nostrum, donec misereatur nostri (Ps. cxxii. 2).

[5] Et nolite conformari huic sæculo, sed reformamini in novitate sensus vestri, ut probetis quæ sit voluntas Dei bona et beneplacens et perfecta (Rom. xii. 2).

[6] Quoniam tu illuminas lucernam meam Domine; Deus meus, illumina tenebras meas (Ps. xvii. 29).

15. Illusion.—Illusion is perhaps the commonest evil. We are so fond of feeding ourselves on illusions ! . . . Indeed, we live in them . . . and we also die in them ! . . . To feed oneself up with illusions is the great need and the constant anxiety of self-interest. It is so skilful in manufacturing them ! . . . But nowhere are illusions so frequent or so fatal as concerning the will of God. It is so much to our interest not to see too much of it, or to see just enough of it to quiet our conscience without overloading it ! . . .

I am so accustomed to looking at things through the prism of self-interest and to brinigng my obligations into harmony with what suits me ! Before God's will, I consult my own interests : they are so near and so insistent ! Their voice makes itself heard so readily, and the noise they fill my ears with deadens the sound of God's voice, which no longer quite reaches me. And when my eyes perceive the divine will through the distorting prism of my sensual instincts, my vision is perverted, things no longer appear as they really are, and I fall into illusions. And how often does this happen ! . . . My loins are filled with illusions (Ps. xxxvii. 8). My loins, *i.e.*, my carnal nature ; there is the reservoir, a reservoir which is always full. . . . And what an abundance, O my God ! of illusions ! . . . How I need, O God, to keep my loins girded so that the reservoir may not allow its sad fulness to overflow into my soul, and to have in hand my lamp always burning,[1] so that I may be able to see plainly ! Lord, make me to see ![2]

[1] Sint lumbi vestri præcincti et lucernæ ardentes in manibus vestris (Luc. xii. 35).
[2] Domine ut videam (Luc. xviii. 41).

CHAPTER IV

The Knowledge of Duty

Special obligations

16. Knowing the commandments.—17. The spirit of the commandments. — 18. Knowing the commandments of the Church.— 19. Knowing the counsels.—20. Knowing the duties of one's state.—21. The necessity of direction.

16. **Knowing the commandments.**—I ought to know my duty, and I therefore ought to know the manifestations that define it for me. And since the will of my Master is manifested in the commandments of God and of the Church, and in the counsels, I must be diligent in acquiring a knowledge of the precepts that are binding on me and of the counsels that concern me. And since precepts and counsels for me are defined and determined by the duties of my state of life, I ought above all to give myself to getting a clear, enlightening, and exact knowledge of the duties of my state of life. I shall be more or less enlightened as to my duty, according to the light that is given me on these four points.

Knowing the commandments of God, learning the divine law, knowing the obligations it lays upon me, getting a knowledge at least of its essential points: my piety will depend necessarily on my knowledge of all this. If well instructed in my duties, I have an enlightened piety; whereas if my duties are dim, my piety is left in darkness and error. True piety loves the light, because he that doth truth, cometh to the light (John iii. 21). I now know what doing the truth means.[1]

17. **The spirit of the commandments.**—But we must know their spirit more than their letter. It is both a great mistake and a great weakness to know nothing but the external details of the law, to see the material side of the prescription, without taking account of the motive that inspires it, and the end towards which it tends. When one only knows the

---

[1] See Part I, Book II, § 9.

law in this fashion, one observes it with a mechanical and pharisaical fidelity which imparts no life to the soul. I know that the end of the law does not come under the law;[1] but I know also that the law is not laid down for the just, but for the unjust.[2] If then I am attached to what falls under the law, I fall under the law myself, and I am convinced that I am not in justice. But if I am not led by the spirit, then I come under the law.[3] We know that the law is good, if a man use it lawfully according to its spirit.[4] In fact, if I submit as it were by necessity, and by constraint of will, to external obligations, I am a slave of the detail that fetters, a victim of the letter that killeth.[5] And if I am killed by the letter, what life is left in me? ... The spirit alone giveth life.

18. **Knowing the commandments of the Church.**—Piety which is truly right seeks to know the laws of the Church as much as possible; it takes pleasure in studying them, knowing that the Church, assisted by the Spirit of God, has the office of throwing such light as times and needs demand upon the way Christians have to go. The voice of the Church is the shepherd's voice; the sheep know the voice of the shepherd; and they follow him because they know his voice; but a stranger they follow not, because they know not the voice of strangers.[6] The true sheep who have real piety willingly listen to the voice of the Church; any other voice sounds false in their ears. This predilection for the Church's voice, this need of hearing it and hearkening to it, this repugnance for any particular voice and spirit, is one of the most characteristic signs of true piety. It is a mark that never misleads. It is one of the worst signs, when it is wanting.

19. **Knowing the counsels.**—Had I no other anxiety than to know the formal precepts, I should no doubt know enough to avoid sin; but I should not know enough to rise to the

---

[1] Finis legis non cadit sub præcepto (Axiom).
[2] Scimus quia lex justo non est posita, sed injustis (1 Tim. i 9).
[3] Quod si spiritu ducimini, non estis sub lege (Gal. v. 18).
[4] Scimus autem quia bona est lex, si quis ea legitime utatur 1 Tim. i. 8).
[5] Littera occidit, spiritus autem vivificat (2 Cor. iii. 6).
[6] Oves illum sequuntur, quia sciunt vocem ejus. Alienum autem non sequuntur, sed fugiunt ab eo, quia non noverunt vocem alienorum (Joan. x 4, 5).

heights of virtue. I might manage not to offend God too seriously, but I should be unaware of the great secrets of how to please Him. I should be just about able to succeed in keeping my soul from sickness and death, but I should not know how to take it to the great fountains of life. I should know the grand lines of God's designs as to myself, but the heights of His thoughts, the magnificence of His desires, would remain hidden from me. If, like the saints, I would know them in all their breadth and length, in all their height and depth, above all, if I would know the charity of Christ which passeth all knowledge, and thus attain to all the fulness of the life of God,[1] I need to meditate on the counsels : I must meditate on them to grasp their divine meaning and their infinite scope.

In this manifestation of His desires, God has revealed beauties and grandeurs and riches, which have enchanted the eyes of saints. Oh, how unknown are God's secrets ! The eyes of man are no longer familiar enough with this light. If only I knew how to meditate upon the Gospels, and the Epistles of St. Paul ! If only I knew how to become intimate with the writings of the great masters of sanctity, who have said such splendid and wonderful things about the counsels on which they have lived ! What things are to be learnt in the school of St. Francis of Sales, for instance, and in that of St. John of the Cross, St. Teresa, and the two Saints, Catherine of Siena and Catherine of Genoa !

20. Knowing the duties of one's state.—Here we have the knowledge which is practical *par excellence*, a knowledge wherein what we have already learnt comes to be defined and applied. These unfortunate duties of one's state of life ! how often they are unknown ! . . . or misunderstood, or distorted by the illusions of self-interest ! . . . How often special obligations are fabricated which are quite unjustified, whilst no care is taken as to the real obligations imposed by the duties of one's state ! Ah, if only I knew the duties of my state of life,

[1] Ut possitis comprehendere cum omnibus sanctis, quæ sit latitudo, et longitudo, et sublimitas, et profundum ; scire etiam supereminentem scientiæ charitatem Christi, ut impleamini in omnem plenitudinem Dei (Eph. iii. 18, 19)

I should not busy myself with creating external ones, I should not have to bind myself under any obligation of my own making; for these duties lay down for me all that is necessary to satisfy the aspirations of my soul.

The duties of one's state, as I have said,[1] specify for me the particular way in which I must personally keep the commandments, and the proper portion of the counsels which I must personally practise. Why should I then go looking beyond these? Do they not contain the whole of God's will? If I go beyond them, what am I trying to find, unless it be my own will, leaving God's? A fine advantage, indeed, to put my own will in the place of God's! Here are only the devil's trickeries and the folly of my own pride. Under the pretext of a greater good, I am led to do my own will and to lose sight of the sovereign and single rule, which is the will of God.

21. The necessity of direction.—It is as to these duties of one's state, especially in the case of laymen, that *direction* is often an indispensable source of light. It does not enter into our plan to deal with this question; in this matter we refer the reader to what has been said by St. Francis of Sales and other masters of the spiritual life as to the necessity of a director, and as to how to choose him, and to work with him, etc.

It must be said again and again, that the one and only way is the will of God. It alone marks out my action, and all my actions, for me. Whatever I do, if it is not laid down thereby, is outside of the way.

CHAPTER V

Love and Practice

22. Loving duty.—23. The divine yoke.—24. Human appearances.—25. Fidelity in practice.—26. Breadth in fidelity.

22. Loving duty.—It is not enough for the mind to see, the heart also must love; for the end of the law is love.[2]

We must love obedience more than we fear disobedience: this is one of the favourite maxims of St. Francis of Sales.

---

[1] See ch. ii.   [2] Finis præcepti est charitas (1 Tim i. 5).

As soon as I know the will of God, I must be attached to it, and I must love what helps it to be manifested to me. The book of holiness is entitled, "Doing the will of God"; there I shall find what I must set fast in my will, and it is the law which has to be planted in the fair garden of my soul.[1]

23. The divine yoke.—The will of God is often painful to nature, since it runs counter to its perverse tendencies. It is the yoke we must take upon us, the burden we have to bear. If I get attached to it, if I love it, the yoke is sweet and the burden light.[2] If I submit to the law under constraint; if, as St. Paul says, I am under the law,[3] it crushes me; if I embrace it heartily, it bears me up. It is the precept in the law that is hard; it is the obligation that weighs us down. But it is the will of God that is sweet, and this I know how to discern and to love in spite of its apparent hardness; it is His good pleasure that is light, and this draws me to Him under its painful exterior.

24. Human appearances.—Hence, my love ought not to stop short at the outward appearance, but to become attached to the supremely lovable will of God, which is manifested by the law. In the same way, I shall love the Church and her laws, because to me she is God's instrument. I shall love my superiors, because to me they are the living interpreters of the will of God. I shall not stop short at the human accidents, which may be far from lovable; but I shall look beyond at the divine fact which is manifested to me even by these means. I shall be reminded, according to the fine thought of a Russian writer, " that in the Church, under the *appearances* of a visible and human society, is hidden the divine substance, and that all that may seem abnormal in the history of the Church belongs only to the human appearances, and not to the divine substance."[4] Oh, what a sign it is of a pure and upright heart to know how to discern and love the divine substance under the human appearances, the will of God in men full of defects! Unfortunately, it is easy and

---

[1] In capite libri scriptum est de me, ut facerem voluntatem tuam: Deus meus volui, et legem tuam in medio cordis mei (Ps. xxxix. 8, 9).
[2] Jugum enim meum suave est et onus meum leve (Matt. xi. 30).
[3] Si spiritu ducimini, non estis sub lege (Gal. v. 18).
[4] Soloview, *La Russie et l'Eglise universelle*, Part II, ch. x.

common to make human defects a pretext for setting oneself free from the will of God !

25. **Fidelity in practice.**—Finally, love must result in fidelity in action : a constant and generous fidelity to all that is the will of God : fidelity in the least things, not for their own sake, for this is the mark of small minds, but for the sake of the great thing, which is the will of God, and which I respect greatly in little things. It is in this sense that St. Augustine says : " Little things are indeed little ; but to be faithful in little things is a great thing."[1]

Thus, in the sometimes irksome details of the laws of discipline or of the rubrics, the priest recognizes, loves, and respects the great and holy thing, which is God's will. Thus, in the rather minute prescriptions of his Rule, the religious is able to see and respect this will, which is always great, always infinite, even in the most minute details. Is not our Lord whole and entire, as great, as living, as adorable, in a small host as in a large one, in a little particle as in an entire host ? Do I not receive the smallest particles with the same adoration as the large host ? And thus is it with the will of God. The smallest fragments of my Rule contain it whole and entire, and therein I adore it and embrace it with the same devotion as in great things. I will not let slip the least part of this sacred good.[2]

26. **Breadth in fidelity.**—And just as in Holy Communion, however small the host may be, I am increased by my contact with our Lord, thus in my fidelity to duty, however small the observances may be which I carry out, I feel that I increase and expand through my contact with God. So great a thing it is to come into contact with God ! . . . And this is the only thing I seek in my fidelity in little things : to establish between God and myself a contact that will be more adequate, more continuous, more absolute, in such a manner that at last there may be no sort of deviation left.

Hence, it is not fidelity to the prescription or to the practice for its own sake that attracts me, no : for this would be a

---

[1] Quod minimum est, minimum est ; sed fidelem esse in minimis, magnum est (*De Doctrina Christ*, xiv. 35).

[2] Particula boni doni non te praetereat (Eccles. xiv. 14).

paltry thing; but it is fidelity to the prescription and to the practice for the sake of the divine contact, and that is an infinite thing. Moreover, what breadth, what ease, what freedom, there are in the souls of the saints! I see them faithful in all, and at the same time so free in all things. How one feels that they are attached to God alone, and their soul clings to nothing but Him! They are exact in everything, but with a living, broad, and supple exactitude, which yields to all necessities. They know nothing of pharisaic rigidity, paltry scruples, and petty fidgets.

When I understand, like them, that my purpose is not to adjust myself to the prescription, but to God by the prescription; like them, too, I shall get this breadth with precision, this ease with fidelity, and this greatness in little things. Like them, too, I shall feel that I am not imprisoned but delivered, not stifled but dilated, even in the most insignificant details of the rules I have to keep. The more I run in the way of the commandments, the more I feel my heart enlarged.[1]

CHAPTER VI

The Piety of the Priest

27. Vocations.—28. The forms of vocation.—29. Liturgy and canon law, the form of sacerdotal piety.—30. The good priest knows this.—31. The liturgical and canonical spirit.

27. Vocations.—In the Church, the mystical body of Christ, there are manifold functions to be exercised according to the multiplicity of the necessities of the body. Just as in my natural body there are various organs to meet the various requirements of life, so in the Church there are different vocations assigning to each one the special portion of activity committed to him for the general advantage of the body. Each person has his vocation, *i.e.*, each one is called in life to such and such a position; in that position, he has such and such a function to fulfil. God does not create men at haphazard;

[1] Viam mandatorum tuorum cucurri, cum dilatasti cor meum Ps. cxviii. 32).

in time and space there is a wonderful reciprocity between souls and vocations.

As we have seen in Chapter II, vocations may be subdivided into three general groups. Some, the most numerous section, have the ordinary vocation of a life taken up with the duties of family surroundings. Therein occupations are very various; but, in general, the care of human interests is the universal material of them.

Others have the higher vocation of the priesthood, and become the representatives of divine interests. Others have the more special vocation of the religious life, and are as it were prophets of the union between God and man.

28. The forms of vocation.—A special form must correspond to a special destiny. Not every instrument is fitted for every kind of work. Hence the soul must receive a training in conformity with its mission. And what just gives this training is the laws peculiar to each state. In these laws I find not only the practical determination of the work I have to do in my life for God, but also the adaptation of my soul to this work. If I earnestly wish not to make any mistake in choosing my road, and not to lead a useless existence, if I am anxious to live, I have only to take the laws of my state of life, and they will plainly mark out for me my personal share of duty, and they will form and transform me and adapt me to all the needs of my vocation.

What then is vocation?—It is the special form in which God wishes each one to grow up, so as to glorify Him in the body of the elect. And each one has his own physiognomy, and all are united together.

29. Liturgy and canon law, the form of sacerdotal piety.— The truly pious priest takes great pleasure in knowing, studying, and getting a mastery of the laws of his state. Does he not find everything in his liturgical and disciplinary laws? Seeking God, forgetting self: this is the whole of piety. Does he not find that seeking God is admirably marked out for him by the liturgical laws? and forgetfulness of self, by disciplinary laws? Hence, here he has the entire form of his piety. Whatever he looks for outside this is mistaken and misleading; any other form of piety is not sacerdotal piety.

Call it worldly piety, modern piety, or by any other horrible name, but, however much it may desecrate this fine word, it will never be cutting enough to lash the wretched mania for hunting after piety where it is not to be found. Sacerdotal piety is made up of the observance of liturgical laws and disciplinary laws, all of these, and nothing more.

30. **The good priest knows this.**—He knows what a wonderful treasure he has in these grand laws of the Church his mother. Moreover, he makes them the favourite subject of his meditations, spiritual reading, and silent studies. Therefrom he draws instructive illumination and abundance of strength. The books of the Church are the books of his choice; their official text is the favourite food of his mind. And where could he find anything more beautiful or more wholesome? Above all, where could he find the voice and will of God better expressed?

Oh, what a lovely thing is the piety of the priest! . . . lovely, great, and strong! . . . And how far it surpasses the " consumptive piety"[1] of those who go in search of their incentives amidst all the smart trifles of to-day, which are as empty as they are dazzling! O priests, you have the fountain of life: drink deep thereat! . . . Why should you forsake the fountain of living water to dig wells for yourselves? broken cisterns, that can hold no water?[2] Ah, if only your life were wholly informed by ecclesiastical laws, entirely moulded thereby, if only you were to allow no strange thought or habit to disfigure it, how great would you be! Your greatest weakness and your most dreadful punishment are to neglect the laws of your state. Everything that falls short of this is not up to your level and lowers you.

31. **The liturgical and canonical spirit.**—The priest should make the liturgy so far enter into his relations with God, and canon law into his relations with men, that he comes at last to get into the spirit of them. Only the spirit is living, for the letter is dead. Liturgy and canon law are not forms which are purely external and dead; under this rind flows a mighty

---

[1] *Vie du Père Aubry, Missionnaire en Chine*, p. 210.
[2] Dereliquerunt me fontem aquæ vivæ et foderunt sibi cisternas dissipatas, quæ continere non valent aquas (Jer. ii. 13).

sap. And, if it is important to have the rind, it is much more so to have the sap. Oh, what a consolation for the present, and what a hope for the future it is, when we see priests, and especially sacerdotal associations, diligent in reviving within them this rind in all its integrity and this sap in all its fruitfulness! Liturgy and canon law, taken in the letter and in the spirit, mean sacerdotal life in its fulness of form, the priest raised above the human and brought near to God, the ministry of holy things lifted above the lower conditions of humanity and established in the region of things divine;[1] in a word, it means that the priest has entered into the fulness of the truth and power of his vocation.

CHAPTER VII

The Piety of the Religious

32. The piety of the religious has its form in his Rule.—33. The religious does not overstep his Rule.—34. The rind is hard.—35. The book to be eaten.

32. The piety of the religious has its form in his Rule.—The true and holy religious knows that, for himself, the most faithful and complete expression of his duty is to be found in his Rule. He, too, desires to go truly to God and to strip himself of self. Is not this the sole purpose of his becoming a religious? Charity and humility are the two virtues which sum up all for him, if indeed these two virtues be not one and the same virtue, or rather, two poles of the world which is called piety. For he can only love by stripping himself, and he only strips himself to love.

One must go out of oneself to go to God. It is like the two motions of spiritual breathing, which cannot be separated, and which, although quite distinct, constitute only one act of breathing. He ceases to look at, love, and seek himself, to look at, love, and seek God. There lies his piety, and thus it is that he goes to God.

But does not he, too, find in his Rule this one and twofold

[1] Omnis namque pontifex ex hominibus assumptus pro hominibus constituitur in iis quæ sunt ad Deum (Heb. v. 1)

duty, outlined in its two parts, which he never separates in action ? Charity, seeking God, finds its way, its perfect form, in that part which contains the rules for the divine offices. Humility, the stripping of oneself, has its way, its perfect form, in the part which contains the disciplinary statutes. There is the form of his piety, such as God looks for it from him. Any other form is not his, and is not that which God requires of him. God wills that his humility and his charity, in other words, his piety, shall be clothed in this form, and He has taken care to draw its outlines in his Rule. Consequently, for the religious, any other form of personal piety is mistaken, and contrary to God's will and to his own perfection. Oh, how sad it is to see a religious go so far astray as to try to find in particular practices, or in uses unknown to his rule, a perfection which is merely a hybrid and ill-assorted compound ! . . .

33. The religious does not overstep his Rule.—"There is," says St. Francis of Sales, " a certain simplicity of heart, wherein consists the perfection of all perfections; and it is this simplicity that brings it about that our soul looks at God only, and that it keeps entirely gathered up and recollected in itself to apply itself with all the fidelity of which it is capable to the observance of its rules, without overflowing to desire or wish to undertake anything beyond that."[1]

No, the true religious does not overflow to desire or undertake anything beyond his Rule ; this alone is enough for his piety, and it contains for him all the will of God. Moreover, what love he shows in studying it, in meditating on it, in ruminating over it, finally, in transfiguring it into himself, or rather, in transfiguring himself into it ! He knows that he will only find God in following the liturgical ordinances of his Rule ; he knows that he will only strip himself by the prescriptions of the disciplinary statutes. On any other way, he would not find God, he would not strip himself of self ; and he knows this. He knows that there, in his Rule, is his perfection, and nowhere else ; and it is there that he looks for it with all the energies of his being. Oh, what a power of

[1] *Entret. Spirit.*, 13 (Édit. Annecy, p. 235).

holiness and what a fulness of life there are in the religious " who keeps entirely gathered up and recollected in himself " to get inspired with the spirit of his Rule, to suck in its sweetness, to extract its marrow, without overflowing to desire or to undertake any other thing ! ...

34. **The rind is hard.**—The Rule, in its expression, usually keeps a severity of demeanour, a coldness of appearance, which appeals directly neither to the imagination nor to the feelings. It is none the less the perfect expression of the will of God, nor does it contain any the less the essential form of the piety of the religious. He who knows how to break through this rind and to discover the substantial fruit beneath, knows what rich and invigorating and wholesome food is to be found therein. There are only those who have gone astray in sentimentalism who are unaware of the treasures of piety contained in the Rule.

There is nothing in it for the heart, it is said. Well, what sort of a heart have you ? ... Is it only fed upon " Ohs !" and " Ahs !" ? ... and can it do nothing but send up dove-like sighs ?[1] If we are to reckon thus, piety would find next to nothing in Holy Scripture, nothing in the laws of the Church, and nothing in the writings of several of the great Doctors.

35. **The book to be eaten.**—" Take the book, and eat it up : and it shall make thy belly bitter, but in thy mouth it shall be sweet as honey !" (Apoc. x. 9). The angel of the Rule says this to every religious. The true religious understands this speech, he hearkens to it, and puts it into practice. He finds nothing strange in having to eat up a book ; he eats it up. This process of manducation is, indeed, neither easy nor pleasant, it is dry and hard ; but he has been told to " take and eat," and he takes and eats. And he has no fear of bitterness in the belly, in other words, of the work of stripping himself of self, which is always the first thing done by the Rule. And he experiences the sweetness of honey in his mouth, in other words, he finds God, the true honey and the true sweetness of the soul.

The religious who is a sentimentalist is astonished at having to eat up a book ; in his opinion, such things are not fit to eat.

[1] *Vie du Père Aubry*, p. 215.

And then, he is altogether too much afraid of the bitterness in the belly, which is the first fruit, the first result of such manducation. Further, why does not God put the honey in his mouth all at once? Oh! that honey! ... this is all he is in earnest about. Very well: if you will have the real sweetness of honey in your mouth, that is to say, the charity that relishes God, you must eat the book of your Rule; and when you have eaten it, it will first of all be bitter in your belly; it will give a severe shock to the lower part of you, to bring about the stripping of yourself of self; but, lastly, in the higher part, you will find God, who will be the honey and the sweetness of your soul.

CHAPTER VIII

The Spirit of Piety

36. The divine encounter.—37. Knowing how to pierce the veil.—38. Making no distinction between things ordered.—39. Leaving my own practices for God's.—40. The children of God are born of God.

36. The divine encounter.—In fine, what it is most important of all to see, love, and follow in the law, is not the law itself, but the will of which it is the expression. There is what we have to see, what we have to love, what we have to seek. If I see that, I see everything; if I do not see that, I see nothing at all. If I directly attach myself to God's will, I get to my end directly. And what is my end?—To go to God and to be united with Him to glorify Him and to be happy myself. It is in this encounter of my soul with God that His glory and my happiness are found. But where is God encountered?—Where His will is. The union of my soul with God is a moral union, *i.e.*, a union of wills. Hence I encounter Him when my will meets with His; and I unite with Him, when my will is united with His. Where I do not see His will, I do not unite with Him. In the sphere of my union with Him, God is only, so far as I am concerned, where His will is

The animal man, because he does not understand what the Spirit of God is,[1] sees only the material side of his obligations; and his soul, being entirely absorbed by the material side, is drawn away from God. Whatever may be the occupation which God demands of me, whatever may be the kind of work whereto His will calls me, even were the occupation the commonest, the work the roughest, God is there, because His will is there. He is there, quite near, transparently clear behind the thin veil. The soul with dull eyes does not see Him, it only sees the material obligation, which occupies and arrests its looks. And when it desires to find Him, it turns elsewhere to see if it can find Him in a few devotional exercises. And there it does not find Him, since His will is not therein: His will is only to be found in the obligation that presses at the moment.

37. **Knowing how to pierce the veil.**—When I have any obligation to fulfil, if I knew how to look through the veil, I should not look a long way back to find God, just when He was there before me, quite close. If I were to look more carefully, if I tried to see behind the veil, I should see God there, calling me: "Come," He is saying to me, "I am here, My will is here, My grace is here"; for His grace is wherever His will is. How blessed is the man whose help in his work comes from God![2]

When I thus understand my obligations, when I see God present in His will, when I know that I can meet with Him there, I plunge fully into the fulfilment of my duty in order to immerse myself fully in God. O God, how blind must I be not to see Thee in every obligation Thou layest upon me! A veil is on our hearts: but when we shall be converted to the Lord, the veil shall be taken away.[3]

38. **Making no distinction between things ordered.**—If the will of God is what I am seeking to know, what I am attaching myself to, and what I strive to follow, I find it always great, always perfect, always like itself, always holy and adorable.

---

[1] Animalis homo non percipit ea quæ sunt Spiritus Dei (1 Cor. ii. 14).
[2] Beatus vir cujus est auxilium abs te (Ps. lxxxiii. 6).
[3] Velamen positum est super cor eorum. Cum autem conversus fuerit ad Dominum, auferetur velamen (2 Cor. iii. 15, 16).

It matters little whether it be in important matters or in small details, in dispositions which irk me or are agreeable to me ; as for me, it is always the same will that I am looking for, the same will that I find, and the same will that I carry out. The difference in the importance of the precepts or the counsels shows me the order I must follow in my observance of them ; but I adore the will of God in the one just as much as in the other. Whether God send me to work or to pray, whether He demand something honourable or the reverse, whether His law be manifested to me in this way or in that, all these things may change, but I do not worry about it too much : I know that HE Himself does not change,[1] and it is to Him and to His will that I am attached. " Good heavens ! how often are we mistaken !" says St. Francis of Sales, " I tell you once more, you must not look at the outward aspect of your actions, but at their inner motives ; that is to say, whether God wills them or does not will them."[2]

39. **Leaving my own practices for God's.**—But I never make a more foolish mistake than when I want to make piety consist in certain devotions and practices of a particular nature. What do I look for from practices of my own choosing ?—Unfortunately, my own will, my own likings and whims. It is useless for me to put any amount of good-will into them ; this good-will will never be anything more than a very indifferent sort of will, since it is not in conformity with God's.

" Cry, cease not," says the Lord to His prophet, " lift up thy voice like a trumpet, and shew my people their wicked doings, and the house of Jacob their sins. For they seek Me from day to day, and desire to know My ways, as a nation that hath done justice, and hath not forsaken the judgement of their God : they ask of Me the judgements of justice : they are willing to approach to God. Why have we fasted, and Thou hast not regarded : have we humbled our souls. and Thou hast not taken notice ? Behold in the day of your fast your own will is found " (Is. lviii. 3 *ff*).

40. **The children of God are born of God.**—The children of

---

[1] Tu autem idem ipse es (Ps. ci. 28)
[2] *Letters*, III., 3rd ed., Léonard.

God are born, not of blood, nor of the will of the flesh, nor of the will of man, but of God (John i. 13). "It is as if he said," says St. John of the Cross,[1] "The power to become sons of God and to be transformed into Him is given only to those who are not born of blood, *i.e.*, of natural dispositions; nor of the will of the flesh, *i.e.*, of the caprice of nature; nor even of the will of man. And here, by the will of man, we are meant to understand all human ways of judging and estimating according to man's reason only. To none of these is it given to become those who are children of God. This happiness is reserved to those who are born of God." Thus, the practices, prayers, or mortifications suggested by our natural dispositions, caprice of nature, tastes of the human will, are not in the one and only way of true piety. Piety is born of God alone and of His will; it sees, loves, and follows the will of God, and it is by this road that it procures His glory.

[1] *The Ascent of Mount Carmel*, Book II. ch. v.

BOOK II

THE WILL OF GOOD PLEASURE

I now know the rails of the road that leads me to God, I must next know about the steam. The train cannot move along the rails without the steam which imparts motion to it. Hence, after having considered the will signified, which lays down and maintains the rules of action, I must consider the will of good pleasure, which imparts the divine impulse.

As to the will signified, I saw two things: 1. how it is manifested; 2. how I ought to correspond with it. I have to look at the same two things with regard to the will of good pleasure.—How is this will manifested?—It is no longer by words and precepts, but by operations; it is the part of God's action which God reserves to Himself in the building up of my life.—How ought I to correspond with it?—No longer by action, but by submission. Then, what in me and upon me are the operations of the divine good pleasure? this is the first question. How ought I to submit to these operations by passive piety? this is the second question. And these two questions make up the whole of the subject-matter of this Book.

Is there any need to say once more that passive piety is only one of the sides of complete piety, that it is not a superior and successive state following that of active piety which has gone before, that the one and the other are simultaneously joined together, that they are constantly in combination and alliance in the progress of Christian life? Their alliance cannot be clearly shown until we come to the next Book.

CHAPTER I

Divine Action

1. In God's arms, and my own little steps.—2. God's care for me.—3. The fresco.—4. All works together for the good of the elect.—5. The wonderful appropriateness of God's work.

1. In God's arms, and my own little steps.—" The rest of us, Théotime, like little children of the heavenly Father, can go to Him in two ways. For, in the first place, we can go to Him walking with the steps of our own will, which we conform to His, holding all the time with the hand of our obedience that of His divine intention, and following it wherever it leads us, which is what God requires from us by signifying His will. . . . But we can also go to our Lord by allowing ourselves merely to be carried by His divine good pleasure like a little child in his mother's arms."[1]

" For our Lord in our pilgrimage throughout this miserable life, leads us in these two ways: either He leads us by the hand, making us walk with Him, or He carries us in the arms of His Providence. He holds us by the hand, when He makes us walk in the exercise of the virtues. His divine goodness gladly leads us and holds us by the hand in our way, but it also wishes us to make our own little steps, that is to say, that we for our part should do what we can with the help of His grace. But when our Lord has led us by the hand . . . He afterwards carries us in His arms, and does within us work in which we seem to do nothing."[2]

Thus speaks St. Francis of Sales. In studying God's will signified, I saw how God wishes me " to make my own little steps." Now, in studying His will of good pleasure, I shall see how " He carries me in His arms."

2. God's care for me.—God cares for each one of us.[3] Are not five sparrows sold for two farthings, and not one of them

[1] *Treatise of the Love of God*, Book IX, ch. xiv.
[2] *Sermon on the Presentation.* [3] Ipsi cura est de vobis (1 Pet. v. 7).

is forgotten before God? Fear not therefore: you are of more value than many sparrows (Luke xii. 6, 7). This care of God's is that of the hen for her chicks,[1] of the shepherd for his sheep,[2] of the mother for her child. I will carry you at My breasts, and upon My knees will I caress you; as one whom the mother caresseth, so will I comfort you.[3] Can a mother so forget her infant, as not to have pity on the son of her womb? and if she should forget, yet will I not forget thee![4]

This will of God, always busied with my sanctification,[5] follows me in all the details of my life to lead me to the supreme end of my creation. There is so much to be done in my soul that God works in it without ceasing. Thus, it is not I alone who work for the glory of God with the help of grace; it is much more God who works Himself in me for His own glory, and who works in me without me, and sometimes in spite of me.

These divine operations more than anything else work to realize holiness in my soul. What I do in the way of practical piety is but little with regard to my sanctification. It is not in this way that I make great progress. Therein I am making my own little steps; very small ones in reality, and such as help me forwards but little. My great progress is made when God carries me in His arms. It is the action of His good pleasure which is the principal means of my interior progress. Here, there are no longer my own little steps, but the great strides of God Himself. He carries me much more than I walk.

3. *The fresco.*—A splendid fresco was covered with rough plaster. A fortunate accident one day made the plaster fall off, and the fresco appeared in all its beauty. But what a quantity of spots of the remains of the plaster were left behind! Who was to take them away? Who was to touch

---

[1] Matt. xxvii. 37. [2] John x.
[3] Ad ubera portabimini et super genua blandientur vobis. Quomodo si cui mater blandiatur, ita ego consolabor vos (Is. lxvi. 12, 13).
[4] Numquid oblivisci potest mulier infantem suum, ut non misereatur filio uteri sui? Et si illa oblita fuerit, ego tamen non obliviscar tui (Is. xlix, 15).
[5] Hæc est voluntas Dei, sanctificatio vestra (1 Thess, iv. 3).

up the little details, and to restore the freshness and finish of the original design?—Here an artist was needed, an artist possessing the skill of the original designer. Any other would run the risk of doing irreparable injury to the picture by his touches.

My soul is the likeness of God: a splendid portrait, in which God has portrayed His own image.[1] By original sin at the outset, by mortal sin afterwards, the image of God has been covered up, His likeness destroyed. Once Baptism, and later on Penance, brought out afresh the features of the divine likeness. But, alas! what a quantity of tainted details are left! how many spots remain! Who is to get rid of them?—He alone who made the portrait; he alone is skilful enough to touch the picture. And He reserves the right of doing so to Himself: no one but God can touch the soul. He who first made it alone can restore it.[2]

4. All works together for the good of the elect.—If I would know the general mode of such action, I have only to recall the Apostle's words: " All things work together unto good to such as God's will calleth to be saints."[3] " All things," this expression is quite absolute; all things, and therefore, all the details of the movements of the world, whether physical or moral; the influences put forth by all beings, angels, men, animals or plants, on the very smallest developments of my physical, moral, intellectual, and supernatural life, work together in this operation. God acts by all these instruments; for if creatures are my instruments, much more are they God's.

If I would know to what extent all things work together for the good of the elect, I have only to compare the text of St. Paul already quoted with the words of the Saviour: " But a hair of your head shall not perish "[4] without the permission of your heavenly Father. The falling of a hair is

[1] Faciamus hominem ad imaginem et similitudinem nostram (Gen. i. 26).
[2] Quem ipse creavit ut homo sit, eum ipse operatur ut justus sit (S. Aug., *De Genesi* ad litt., viii. 23).
[3] Omnia cooperantur in bonum iis qui secundum propositum vocati sunt sancti (Rom. viii. 28).
[4] Capillus de capite vestro non peribit (Luc. xxi 18).

certainly not an event which takes up a considerable place in my life. Well, even this event, about which I do not care in the least, is a matter of God's care ; He calculates things to such a nicety, that the very hairs of my head are all numbered.[1] So thorough is His care.

God never ceases acting upon my soul ; His care for it is unceasing ; He makes use of everything for purifying and dilating it. And with what wonderful delicacy does He proceed ! All is so tempered, and so infinitely measured, in what He does ! He always gives just the right touch at the happy moment, and in the happiest manner. If I accept His action, He proceeds rapidly and increases the number of His touches ; if I repel Him, He withdraws gently, waits with patience, and returns at another time and in another way. Sometimes He uses gentleness, sometimes strictness.

5. The wonderful appropriateness of God's work.—He knows how to adapt Himself to all the states of the soul, how to use all possible means, how to choose the happy moment, how to take all the best ways. He that keepeth Israel shall neither slumber nor sleep (Ps. cxx. 4). He is never inattentive nor careless. He pursues the execution of His plans without interruption. He has laid down the scheme of my life, and He guides it towards fulfilment without ever being turned aside by anything, unless it be my want of correspondence, which runs counter to His work and designs. Oh, what wonders will there be to be contemplated, when God, on the great day of eternity, reveals the secret springs of His action on the soul ! ... How beautiful will it be, how infinitely and eternally beautiful, to contemplate in detail how *all things* have worked together for the good of my sanctification ! ... It will be one of the delights of heaven, one of the themes of eternal praise.

Here below, God shows very little, and as it were regretfully, the secrets of His action. My eyes are too dull to see beneath the surface, to discern anything beyond the outward reflected glitter of human movements. But what do we know of the design which God is fulfilling, of the divine springs that set in motion and guide us, of the divine action which orders and directs all things for the sanctification of His elect,

[1] Vestri autem capilli capitis omnes numerati sunt (Matt. x. 30).

of the mysterious depths in which He hides the movements of His wisdom from our observance? I can hardly see anything except outward appearances which mislead me and seem to be incoherent, because I do not know their origin or order, nor their purpose. Oh, what an ecstasy will thrill me, when there shall be revealed in the full light of God in all their detail both the truth and grandeur of the words: "All things, yes, all things work together for the good of those whom the will of God hath called unto holiness! . . ."

If the fulness of light is reserved until the day of the great revelation, it is still none the less true that God has a mind to reveal to me, even now, according to what my progress may require, some of the mysteries of His action. He means me to see them so that I may correspond with them. And I can see them and ought to be on the look out for them, so far as He pleases to reveal them to me, and for the purpose of bringing my action into harmony with His.

CHAPTER II

The Purpose of the Divine Operations

6. God's action.—7. His idea.—8. His desire.—9. *Ipse faciet.*

6. God's action.—One has already entered into some understanding of the gift of God, when one has intuitions which make one feel or anticipate God's action in the outward and inward events of life. Nevertheless, it is possible and it is good for me to enter more fully into the understanding of this divine mystery. If, indeed, God acts within me, it is not for the mere sake of acting. His action is no passing play, bearing no fruit, it is intended to have an effect, and it has a purpose; and it is intended to have an effect, because it has a purpose.

In itself it is transitory; some of God's touches are as flashes of lightning, and those that last longer have an aim. My life is an uninterrupted succession of incessantly changing, incessantly fresh occurrences, wherein the action of the divine good pleasure is unfolded concerning me. And my soul must

THE WAY: THE WILL OF GOOD PLEASURE

yield and adjust itself to this fugitive, changing, and manifold action; I must indeed get to learn, to recognize, to welcome, and to submit to it.

7. *His idea.*—But, must I ultimately adhere to, stop at, and rest in this transitory side of my relations with God ?— No: what passes away, passes away; and it passes away to go on to eternity. Beyond the temporal side, there is the eternal side. In this action of God's which passes like the time wherein it takes place, there is a germ of eternity. When He acts, God always has a desire and an idea; He acts, because He is urged by the desire to realize His idea. If I mean, as far as it is permitted and possible, to understand and follow His action, it is a good thing for me to know what is the desire which makes Him act.

And to know His desire, I must come to what He thinks. It is His idea which is eternal. And here, since I am especially taken up with His action on myself, it is His actual desire so far as I am concerned, and His eternal idea so far as I am concerned, which I need and intend to know.

His eternal idea concerning me is that which governed my creation; and I saw it at the outset, in the preliminary chapter of Part I of this book. His idea is, that I should live: live by Him, for Him, and in Him.

I am to live, that is to say, I am to grow up to the full measure of knowledge, love, and being for which He has created me, and according to which He intends me to glorify Him in the body of the elect and to find happiness in Himself. His idea is to realize this building up of my being in charity,[1] to form the one and living whole which is piety. There is His idea. And never for a single moment, nor in any one of His operations concerning me, is He diverted from this idea, the realization of which He pursues by all means and at every encounter in which He meets with me.

8. *His desire.*—God's idea concerning me is, then, a general idea, since it extends to my whole life, the entire plan of which it comprehends. It is this that inspires, directs, and links together the events of my whole existence. But in detail, in each event, at each moment, there is a particular desire.

[1] ... In ædificationem sui in charitate (Eph. iv. 16).

It is this desire that determines and marks the extent of His special action at any given time. And what is this desire?— It is to lay in the edifice of my life the stone which is there and then needed, which is demanded by the plan, according to the actual state of the building. This stone may be—in the mind, for instance, a view to be corrected, or created or completed; in the heart, a habit to be amended or to be got rid of, a virtue to be aroused or strengthened; in the senses, a purification to be effected, or an energy to be exercised, etc. And God knows well the actual state of my piety, and what is wanting in it; He sees what must be done, and what can be done. He yearns, wants, and is tormented, as the saints say, to bring His work to completion. And, urged by this yearning, He acts in each event, proceeding according to the ductility or resistance I offer Him. Ah, if He were only always free to find His satisfaction in me! . . . If He could only follow up and accomplish all His desires! . . . and realize all His ideas! . . .

9. Ipse faciet.—Throw open the way for God, have faith in Him, and He will do [it].[1] HE WILL DO [IT]: I am struck by this verb; it is absolute, and has no object to confine its sweep and to limit its application. He will do, not this or that, not now or at another time, but everything and always: everything, *i.e.*, all His work, which is His own, in the fulness which befits Him. And His work, His own work, is life: life comes from Him. He will bring life to pass.

He will do it, HIMSELF. He will busy Himself with it, and make it His care; He will carry it through, beginning and completing it: it will be His work. He has the idea of it, and the desire of it, and He acts. The work is so great! and He so much desires to carry it through to the end! And how mighty is His operation, and how great is the progress of those who put no opposition in the way of His designs! The proof of this is the life of the saints.

And what about myself? . . . His idea concerning me is so lofty, His desire so urgent, His action so incessant! . . . If I only knew this! if only I understood it! at least, if I only understood it as much as is possible and necessary!

[1] Revela Domino viam tuam, et spera in eo, et ipse faciet (Ps. xxxvi 5).

CHAPTER III

The Two Modes of God's Operation

10. Putting off and putting on.—11. Consolations and trials.—12. God's intention.—13. The divine effects of joy and sorrow.—14. The divine witness of love.

10. Putting off and putting on.—It is possible in fact, and it is indispensable, to know at least a few of the great main lines of the sovereign Artist's work. Now, as I saw in Part I,[1] there are two things to be done, if I am to bring about this development of life within me: I must leave death and go towards life; I must get rid of the evil by the purification, and build up the good by the glorification, of my being. Hence God, who works to lead me to life, has two simultaneous operations to carry out, until His work in me is completed. He has to put off and to put on: He has to put off the human, and to put on the divine in me. And He cannot put on the one without putting off the other. When the wheels of a machine are encrusted or rusty, cleaning must be done. There must be taking away, detaching, and purification. Then, when the metal is clean and bright, a suitable amount of oil or other lubricant is applied to make the wheels move with ease and rapidity. This is just what has to take place in me. The corruption of pleasure in creatures has more or less deeply rusted the wheels of my faculties, adherence to creatures has made my soul cling to them; there is cleaning to be done. Then comes the oil of sweetness which imparts ease of movement and power to go forward.[2]

And the two operations must take place in all my faculties, and touch my being at every point, until my life is completely finished and finally realized.

[1] See Book IV, § 23.
[2] It is well to note that there is this difference between machines and men, that machines must often be stopped for cleaning, whereas the purifying operations of God do not cause a moment's hindrance, but, on the contrary, always stimulate my own action; since, according to what has been already said, and as will be still more fully explained in the next Book, passive piety is constantly united with active piety to animate the latter.

11. Consolations and trials.—It is in this twofold work that God makes use of the instruments which He has in hand. All the creatures which come in contact with me are manipulated by Him for the carrying out of this work. These contacts are manifold and infinitely varied; for the divine procedure is immeasurably diversified according to souls and according to their state. Nevertheless, since the touches of the eternal Artist and the strokes of His instruments have no other ultimate object than the purpose of liberation and imparting an impulse, the different impressions received by the soul on which God is working may be reduced almost universally to two: suffering and consolation. It is under these two modes that I can classify and consider all the proceedings of God's action. There are creatures He makes use of to try me by detaching me from them, and there are others He gives me for my consolation and encouragement.

And He alternates and combines these two ways of acting, intermingling sorrow more or less with joy, prolonging a pleasure or a suffering, replacing the one with the other, just as in the material sphere, He makes sunshine follow rain, the calm succeed storm. And, in fact, I shall see in the next chapter how the divine operations are almost always an alternation of gifts which console, enlighten, and kindle, and of deprivations which bring desolation, blindness, and impotence. But the most delightful mystery involved in these operations is the sweetness that springs out of bitterness, the honeycomb in the lion's mouth.[1] In Chapter VIII, I shall see how the torrent of joy can break forth from amidst the waters of bitterness.

12. God's intention.—Why, then, do God's instruments, directed by His own hands, bring about in me, some of them sorrow, and others sweetness? What is the reason of the joys and trials of my life? He does not send consolation, indeed, for the puerile purpose of amusing me, nor does He send suffering for the cruel purpose of torturing me. God acts neither as a child nor as an executioner, He acts as a Father; His conduct towards me is always that of one who is serious and fatherly. Essentially at heart He keeps a purpose,

---

[1] De forti egressa est dulcedo (Judic. xiv. 14).

from which as a Father He cannot depart, He intends to be a Father to me in all things, that is to say, He wishes to give me His life. And to lead me unto life, He is bent upon liberating me and encouraging me. He is bent upon liberating me, and this is the chief reason of my sufferings. He is bent upon encouraging me, and this is the chief reason of my consolations. It is His intention that no creature shall inflict sorrow upon me except so far as detachment, expiation, and reparation are necessary for me: and no creature brings me joy, except so far as I need heartening up. Sufferings detach one from creatures, and consolations attach one to God. This is His intention.

13. *The divine effects of joy and sorrow.*—And what effects holy joy produces! ... and also sacred suffering! ... in a soul in which God's operations do not meet with too many voluntary hindrances! ... Joy imparts such energy and vigour, such heartiness and ardour for the good! It results in such a flow of generosity and zeal, such a desire for elevation and growth: it is the sun of life. It enters into the very bones and marrow,[1] and carries with it a sense of well-being and imparts fruitfulness.

And does sorrow go less deep? Of a truth, we may exclaim: How does it divide asunder soul and spirit, joints and marrow, even to the innermost depths of the heart's intentions! It is all-powerful for the sundering of ties, the purifying of defilements, and the purging of dross. It is this that brings to the soul the holy freedom of denudation, the robust energy of self-denial, and the masculine heroism of self-sacrifice. How beautiful and great and precious are the fruits of trial, at least such fruits as it brings me from the hands of God!

14. *The divine witness of love.*—In joy, it is not too hard for nature to recognize one of God's smiles. The soul which is consoled by God thinks that He is pleased with it, and it is pleased with Him. It is indisputable that consolation is, on God's part, a proof of His love. But what of suffering? ... Ah, suffering! ... the supreme mystery of love! Suffering

---

[1] Auditui meo dabis gaudium et lætitiam, et exultabunt ossa humiliata (Ps. l. 10).

in all its forms: interior and outward suffering, suffering of the mind, the heart, and the senses: all this is but one more witness of the love of Him who loves me so deeply!

God never loves me more than when He sends me suffering. It is not at all difficult to be convinced of it. Among friends, is it not the highest proof of affection, the climax of friendship, to render to one's friend, out of loving devotion, a service which will give him pain, but which is necessary for him? To please and to flatter do not in any way demand more than can be asked of the most foolish feelings. But to speak a painful truth, to tell a crushing piece of news, to give a disagreeable warning, to ask for a heart-rending sacrifice —and to do all these as a friend and because friendship gives one not only the right but also the strength to do them, this is the last word of friendship! And thus it is that God acts with regard to me. It is love that induces Him to make me suffer; His love urges Him thereto, and constrains Him thus to act. It is an operation which is necessary for my purification and for the expansion of my life, and His love will never allow Him to let me waste away far from Him, without using every means of making me live in Him. So far does His love for me go. O my God! how little do I understand Thy love!

CHAPTER IV

The Progress of the Divine Work

15. The needle and the thread.—16. The threefold outward denudation.—17. The threefold inward denudation.—18. Its correspondence with the five degrees of piety.—19. God's gifts becoming hindrances.

15. **The needle and the thread.**—And now, if I would take some account of the manner in which God intermingles joy and sorrow, and of the way in which He makes the soul advance, I must study the progress of the divine work. No one, I think, has given a more profound summing up of it than Father Antony of the Blessed Sacrament[1] in his Ten

[1] *The Works of Père Antoine du Saint-Sacrement* (Poussielgue).

Days' Retreat. I am going to follow his teaching in what I now write.

God alone is God; His gifts are not Himself, they are but the instruments of His operations. The gifts themselves, which enter into and penetrate the soul, enter into it as the fore-runners and preparations of the place they have to make ready for God. Hence, they are not intended to remain, but to pass away. They can only be the means by which God enters; and if they remain in the soul, they take God's place. According to the graceful comparison of St. Francis of Sales,[1] as long as the needle remains in the stuff, the thread cannot pass into it. The needle only goes through the stuff to drag the thread after it. Thus, the gifts of God must merely pass through the soul to make God enter into it. Consequently, every gift must be annihilated to make room for a higher gift. "If I go not, the Paraclete will not come to you" (John xvi. 7). It is the function of that which is a fore-runner to vanish to let God increase.[2]

16. The threefold outward denudation.—The first gifts, whereby God begins His operations in the soul, are usually consolations. They are intended to subdue the inferior part of the soul, the sensible part, and to detach it from creatures and to attach it to God. When this result has been obtained, consolations disappear, so that the soul may no longer be attached to them, for they are not God. If the soul is attached to them, it stops all the work of the divine life. This is why consolations must disappear in times of dryness, which comes to annihilate this first gift of God's.

When dryness has accomplished its work, *i.e.*, when it has sufficiently denuded the soul of all attachment to consolations, God sends a higher gift: this is the enlightenment intended to subdue the intelligence, to detach it from creaturely views, and to give it the view of God. The soul then gets profound views as to the mysteries of faith. When its intelligence has been strongly established in the faith and turned away from creatures, the enlightenment vanishes, and darkness supervenes; this is a fresh denudation.

[1] *Treatise of the Love of God*, Book XI, ch. xvi.
[2] Illum oportet crescere, me autem minui (Joan. iii. 30).

The darkness, which has displaced enlightenment, is followed by great yearnings and burning ardours, the mission of which is to subdue the will to God. The soul, under their influence, is devoured by a yearning for the glory of God, it has vast designs for the salvation of souls and for the spread of the Church. When they cease to operate, these ardours give way to distaste and impotence.

When this new denudation is finished, God grants the soul a greater potency of action, a great readiness to do what it had previously desired. But the soul might become still self-satisfied in this readiness for action, it might stay in it, and become attached thereto, and this is a danger. Without taking it away, God takes away the joy of it; the soul retains no joy in its actions, because it has neither calmness nor peace. God, in fact, is making it pass through fresh denudations.

17. *The threefold inward denudation.*—By the gifts already given, God has successively acted upon the sensibility, the intelligence, and the will. He has detached them from creatures and attached them to Himself. He has stripped them of perversities of vision, of love, and of seeking creatures to bring them back to the vision, the love, and the seeking of Himself, that is to say, to piety. Now He is about to shake and jolt these powers, to test the solidity of His work; and He will set about underpinning it in order to complete it.

These powers, indeed, are quite detached from creatures, but they are not yet detached from themselves. They still retain deep traces of the vision, the love, and the seeking of self apart from God. And the falsehood, the vanity, and the servitude of this egoism must altogether disappear in order that piety may attain its supreme fulfilment.

God is going to work for this. He begins by stirring up the lower part by dreadful temptations of impurity, anger, and all sorts of other things. All is upset in the region of the passions.

After that, God goes further still. He devastates the intelligence and the will by darkness, weariness, and inward burdens. There is no peace to be found anywhere.

The work of annihilation goes still further. God now

deprives the soul of active virtue, I mean of the readiness for action which it had kept throughout the former storms. At this time, there is a total impotence of acting. The soul has only one power left ; it is that of suffering and receiving.

This power of suffering and of receiving, or passive virtue, will also be taken away. The poor soul, annihilated, ground to pieces, no longer has, in itself and by itself, the power of enduring and of accepting them ; it has not, in its human capacity, the energy to accept them. It can do nothing, absolutely nothing. It is deprived of everything, everything is destroyed and annihilated. Of itself, it produces no thought or feeling or action. It has no *human* movement, no purely natural life, left ; this is mystical death. All is consummated. At this moment, every hindrance to God's entrance has disappeared ; He enters and takes possession of the soul by mystical marriage, which realizes the state of unity.

In this state, the soul has no movement but God's ; no natural movement takes place in it enabling it to determine any action of itself, at least effectively ; they are all determined by the will of God, who is the one and sovereign motive power of its faculties. It is God who performs all its works in it.[1] Its faculties are absolutely disengaged from the tyranny of creatures and from the tyranny of their own independence, and they are now fully free, supremely full of activity, in the one movement of the will of God.

18. **Its correspondence with the five degrees of piety.**—These different operations of God's cause the soul to ascend by the five degrees of piety. Consolations come at the beginning of the spiritual life, and very usually correspond with the two degrees of avoidance of sins. Enlightenment often accompanies the third degree of perfection. Great yearnings and readiness in action are given at the fourth. The other operations, which sometimes begin in the fourth degree, occur for the most part only in the fifth.

It is a good thing to consider this course of holiness, even to the highest summits. In this way, I get a little insight into the lives of the saints, I see more clearly the distance

[1] Omnia opera nostra operatus es nobis (Isa. xxvi. 12).

between myself and them, and I acquire an appetite for the substantial food of renunciation, which should give me the strength to follow in their train as far as the mountain of God.[1]

19. **God's gifts becoming hindrances.**—But what it is of the utmost importance for me to remember is, that the very gifts of God are a hindrance to His entrance into me, if I get attached to them. So rigid is the fundamental principle of piety: seeing, loving, seeking God alone! . . . To such an extent is my becoming attached to any creature apart from God a disorder! . . . I must see God alone before all else, love Him alone before all else, seek Him alone before all else. His gifts, even the most spiritual gifts, even those most directly destined to make me advance towards Him, become a hindrance to my advance, if I get attached to them. And that I may not become attached to them, they have to be annihilated. Nothing better proves to me how far order is an essential thing, and how far the fundamental principle of my creation is the one foundation of holiness.

Moreover, how luminously clear stands out the distinction between the gifts that pass, and the glorification of the Name that abides! Thus I get a deeper knowledge of the fact that my sole good is to adhere to God alone. I see, too, that God's operations are the only ones which lead my soul to that adherence with Him, which constitutes piety And consequently, it is upon this work of God's that all hope of my advancement must rest. Yes, indeed, my own good consists in adhering to Him, and in putting my hope in the Lord my God.[2]

---

[1] Surge, comede: grandis enim tibi restat via. Qui cum surrexisset, comedit et bibit, et ambulavit in fortitudine cibi illius usque ad montem Dei (3 Reg. xix. 7, 8).

[2] Mihi autem adhærere Deo bonum est, ponere in Domino Deo spem meam (Ps. lxxii. 28).

THE WAY: THE WILL OF GOOD PLEASURE

CHAPTER V

Passive Piety[1]

20. Keeping open —21. Acceptance.—22. Recognizing, welcoming, submitting.—23. Simple acceptance.—24. Peace in acceptance.—25. Rest in God.—26. The definition of passive piety.

20. Keeping open.—To correspond with this will of the divine good pleasure, which operates so mercifully within me, what must I do ?—The direct and immediate correspondence of my soul does not here lie in my action, it lies in acceptance. To the will signified, I have to answer directly and formally by making the little steps of active piety. What the will of good pleasure demands in the way of proper and immediate correspondence is to let myself be carried in God's arms. Leave the way open to God, trust Him; and He Himself will do it. While He Himself is acting, I must correspond with Him. And my correspondence with His action consists in trusting Him, in leaving the way open to Him, in giving Him liberty to enter into and act within my soul.—What is keeping the way open for Him ?—No doubt, on the one hand, it is doing what He requires of me by His will signified, giving Him the share of action which He expects of me, making the little steps along with Him, which constitute active piety. It is, indeed, clear that unless I do what God requires, I cut myself off from His action, since I am in opposition to Him. And it is not less evident, on the other hand, that when I am doing His will signified, I am thereby wide open for the ulterior operations of His good pleasure. The correspondence between my soul and Him is set up. Hence, there is here an opening. Therefore, this is one of the results of active piety, and it is its most sanctifying effect, that it renders the soul accessible to divine influences, that it gives free entrance to the inspiring and

---

[1] In view of Leo XIII's animadversions on the expression "passive" in his Epistle *De Americanismo*, Jan. 22, 1899, it should be noted that the word is used throughout as implying "*voluntary acceptance.*"

vivifying impulses of grace. But this opening has been already preceded by a divine movement.

21. Acceptance.—For finally, and this will be explained at length in the next Book, my action does not precede God's. The first and the principal opening is not, then, made by my action, but by my acceptance. To accept the divine good pleasure, to submit to what God does within me and for me, it is this above all and before all that opens the way to God, it is by this that I give free entrance to His action, and free course to His operations. My part, then, is passive; it is confined to acceptance, to yielding, to letting myself be borne and led, to adoration and thanksgiving. God carries me in His arms, and I go to sleep in them in all confidence. To leave the way free for God, to accept His action, to deny Him nothing, this is what I call passive piety, or the passive part of piety. The one and essential disposition is submission: loving submission, without reserve, without anxiety, without curiosity, without murmuring, to all God's action, to the whole of His will, to His entire good pleasure.

22. Recognizing, welcoming, submitting.—But how does this acceptance come about? In what does this submission consist?—It consists in my mind recognizing, in my heart welcoming, in my senses submitting, to the happenings of the divine good pleasure " as operations of God." When, in events ordained of God, my mind can recognize, my heart welcome, and my senses yield submission to *God's operation*, there is then a perfect acceptance of the sovereign good pleasure.

And what must be recognized, welcomed, submitted to, in such a way as to become attached thereto is not the thing in itself, as, for instance, a consolation, an illumination, a trial, etc. The thing is but an instrument of God's; and I have seen in the preceding chapter, that it is just this kind of attachment to the instrument that becomes a hindrance to God's action. To take consolation for consolation's sake is to waste away in what is merely entertaining; to submit to trial for its own sake is to condemn oneself to being crushed! but to accept consolation or trial as a divine operation, or rather, to accept God's operation in the consolation or the trial is to get an impulse towards growth. Hence, what is to be accepted in the thing, what must be adhered to in everything, is God's action; providential events must be recognized, welcomed, and submitted to as divine operations. Happy is the soul which, while not staying too much in its natural impressions of joy or sorrow, begins to perceive, to relish, and to understand God's need of working within it! In the measure in which one becomes insensible to the human, one becomes more alive to the divine. When the mind is able to leave creatures behind, it succeeds in perceiving and getting a glimpse of the idea of the Creator in what it meets with providentially. The heart, which wishes to become freed from natural affections, succeeds in relishing the desires of God in circumstances. Even the senses, when they are hardened to joy as well as sorrow, feel that they are undergoing an operation which purifies and gives life. Oh, how beautiful are the secrets of life! And how beautified is our very existence, when seen, relished, and felt in this divine radiance!

23. Simple acceptance.—Certainly, it is not always necessary for me to have a clear view of God's designs, and to take account of His reasons and ways of acting. Often He will be pleased to reveal them to me; but He also acts without telling me His reasons. Then it is enough for me to know that He is acting according to His own mind and desire, and to yield to His action purely and simply because it is His, and in order to conform to His desire and to realize His idea. Let me kiss His hand and adore His designs; let Him be free to modify His operation according to the designs of His good pleasure, without being irked by any attachment of mine to a joy or any shrinking of mine from a trouble. Let Him do as seemeth Him good, according to His actual desire and His eternal idea: I accept any action of His, solely because it comes from Him and goes to Him. This is true and perfect acceptance.

24. Peace in acceptance.—But here arises an important question: God is working in me incessantly: must I be incessantly making acts of acceptance?—By no means. In the first place, it would be impossible; for, if I wished to

answer definitely with an act of submission to every detail of the action of the divine good pleasure, every breath I drew would not suffice. Here, under the name of acceptance, we must not bring back that *human* agitation, which is one of the great hindrances to God's action. God loves tranquillity,[1] and His place is in peace (Ps. lxxv. 3). What His action requires of me is repose. Has the child, who is borne in its mother's arms, any need of fidgeting, in order to remain in the arms of her who is carrying it?

One of man's two great infirmities is agitation; and one of the things he can do least is to keep quiet in trustfulness in God's hands. Even when I am required to repose, I go on trying to find out what I must do to secure repose; and I begin to make efforts to succeed in getting it. The only well-known way to secure repose is not to begin to worry. And this is just what is required here. We must go to sleep, say the mystical writers, in the divine good pleasure. I will fall asleep and take my rest in a peace that cannot be disturbed, because Thou, O God, hast established me in unwavering hope.[2]

25. Rest in God.—But this means rest in God, in God's action, in the life of God. It is not careless, idle, selfish, pleasure-loving rest in myself and in creatures, a rest which wants to do nothing, which shrinks from activity, which is disorder,[3] and which is the other form of human infirmity. No, indeed; it is not this sort of rest! this kind of rest is a waste of life; whilst rest in God is the first condition of life, which is made up essentially of repose and motion. In fact, the soul which opens for Him and trusts in Him, is entered into by God: He penetrates it, animates it with His breath, and fills it with His life; He sets all its springs in motion, He guides it, He maintains it, and He makes it produce true acts of holiness.

He who abideth in Jesus Christ ought himself also to walk, even as He walked (1 John ii. 6). If I know how to abide in

---

[1] Non in commotione Dominus (3 Reg. xix. 11).
[2] In pace in idipsum dormiam et requiescam, quoniam tu, Domine singulariter in spe constituisti me (Ps. iv. 9, 10).
[3] See Part I, Book II, § 35.

Him in the rest of true acceptance, He will abide in me by His action, and will make me bear much fruit.[1] When I understand and practise real rest in God, my soul is like an engine the tap of which is wide open. The steam is able to enter into it and circulate throughout it, and to put everything in motion. But when I am agitated or rest outside God, the tap is closed ; God remains at the door of my soul, but His action does not enter into me, and His desire and mind are not realized.

26. **The definition of passive piety.**—The first condition of my life is, then, to keep the way open for God, and this opening is called passive piety. It is the receptive side, the passive part of Christian piety.—Then, what is passive piety ?—It is a disposition of spiritual receptivity, which makes the soul accessible to divine influences, so that it may be animated and led by the operations of the divine good pleasure to do the works which belong to the supernatural life. I shall see more at length, in the next Book, how this passivity leads to true activity, and how both the one and the other only compose one piety.

CHAPTER VI

Waiting for God

27. The state of expectation.—28. Returning to calmness.—29. When God's work is to be known.—30. Avoid curiosity.—31. Attention and submission—32. The spiritual director.

27. **The state of expectation.**—Therefore I have to establish myself in a general, unique disposition or state of soul, or rather, I have to let it be established in me by God Himself ; since, according to the words of the Psalmist, I only sleep and rest in virtue of the hope in which God has established me.[2] Unless you become as little children, you shall not enter into the kingdom of heaven (Matt. xviii. 3). O God, how hard

---

[1] Qui manet in me et ego in eo, hic fert fructum multum (Joan. xv. 5).
[2] In pace in idipsum dormiam et requiescam, quoniam tu, Domine, singulariter in spe constituisti me (Ps. iv. 9, 10).

it is for self-love to become as a little child ! If, in spite of my efforts, I have so far entered but a little way into the kingdom of heaven, is it not because I have constantly gone astray in my activity and agitation, and have not been able to become a little child in God's arms ?

This is how St. Francis of Sales[1] speaks of this supreme degree of indifference and abandonment of oneself to God's good pleasure: " It seems to me," says he, " that the soul which is in this state of indifference, and which has no will of its own, but allows God to will as He pleases, must be said to have its will in a state of simple and general expectation; inasmuch as waiting is not doing or acting, but remaining in dependence on some event. And if you look carefully, the expectation of the soul is really voluntary, and nevertheless it is not an action, but a simple disposition to receive what may happen; and when the events have occurred and have been received, expectation turns into consent or acquiescence; but before they happen, the soul is really in a state of simple expectation, indifferent as to everything which it may please the will of God to ordain."

28. **Returning to calmness.**—Such is the degree of calmness to which one must come in the *acceptance* of God's good pleasure. It is a singularly energetic calm, mighty in expectation, which lifts up its eyes to Him who dwelleth in the heavens. As the eyes of servants are on the hands of their masters, as the eyes of the hand-maid are on the hands of her mistress, so does this calm keep my eyes fixed upon God in expectation of His mercy.[2]

Evidently, I cannot at a single step attain to it in its completeness. It is a work of time, and lasts all the longer, the further I have to return. I have gone astray in the ways of self-will and agitation and distraction; I have been unable to hearken to God's voice, to give Him my attention, to interrogate Him; and He has let me go according to the

---

[1] *Théotime*, Book IX, ch. xv.
[2] Ad te levavi oculos meos, qui habitas in cœlis. Ecce sicut oculi servorum in manibus dominorum suorum, sicut oculi ancillæ in manibus dominæ suæ, ita oculi nostri ad Dominum Deum nostrum, donec misereatur nostri (Ps. cxxii. 1, 2).

THE WAY: THE WILL OF GOOD PLEASURE

desires of my heart, and walk in my own inventions.[1] From there I have to come back. How am I to get this calmness of attention?—By degrees. Piety begins little by little and slowly, with the avoidance of sin, and then rises towards its consummation. Since the will of God is the way that leads to piety, it is quite clear that the way is related to this end. If there are degrees in reaching the end, there must be degrees on the way.

Hence, at the outset I shall only be able to accept God's action very imperfectly: my passions, my habits of self-seeking, my incurable illusion of desiring to act by myself, will often cast me out of God's arms. What must be done? —From time to time I must make an act of acceptance to restore to my soul a little of the watchful calm[2] and trustful self-abandonment which are the distinctive stamp of passive piety. These acts, which at first will be few and imperfect, will become more numerous and perfect by degrees, and the general disposition of accepting everything from God's hands will broaden and get stronger.

29. When God's work is to be known.—Hence, I must make an act of acceptance to restore myself to submission, if I have departed from it; I must also make such an act, if I am tempted to depart from it. God performs many of His operations in me without making any other demand upon me than for my passive consent; but His action sometimes becomes more urgent; there are some blows that fall upon my soul, while it is yet but little established in passive piety, and run the risk of being misunderstood, warded off, and as it were deadened by my resistance, or else turned to the advantage of my own satisfaction and to the detriment of God's glory. It is therefore sometimes necessary to have a more express knowledge of some of the special characteristics of God's action upon me, in order that I may be able at least not to misjudge it. When necessary, God manifests it to me. He knows how to speak; and when He speaks,

---

[1] Et non audivit populus meus vocem meam, et Israel non intendit mihi. Et dimisi eos secundum desideria cordis eorum, ibunt in adinventionibus suis (Ps. lxxx. 12, 13).
[2] Ego dormio et cor meum vigilat (Cant. v. 2).

He can make Himself understood. The soul which is simply desirous of keeping submissive to God's will knows quite well when God speaks, and it knows quite well when He denies it something. Whether He speak by attraction or by remorse, by events or by impressions, by the voice of superiors or by sufferings, His word is always clear enough to be grasped by a soul which is docile to God's teachings.[1] God always is acting, and His action requires the most simple submission ; He speaks less frequently, and when He speaks, to understand Him it is enough to show that amount of attention which is produced in every soul by the desire for progress and of submitting to God.

30. Avoid curiosity. — In order to understand God well, a soul which is animated with good desires must be on its guard against curiosity. I must therefore be forewarned against a certain distrustful or proud curiosity, which makes a kind of pretence of supervising the work of God, and next, against the vain and sensual curiosity which seeks to feed and satisfy itself. God does not reveal Himself to pride or to sensuality ; He does not like being suspected, nor to give up His secrets to be the food of folly. And besides, He has His own reasons and seasons for the revelation of His mysteries : we must be able to respect His silence, and to wait for His illumination.

I must not try to find out what is above me, nor to fathom what is beyond my depth. Let the care of my thoughts be bestowed upon what God recommends to my attention by His general will, which constitutes active piety ; as for the rest of His works in me, I must be on my guard against curiosity. In fact, it is not at all necessary for me to see with my eyes what is hidden from me. I must flee from the multiplicity of desires which lead me to wish to know what is unnecessary, and from the curiosity which fain would fathom the works of God.[2]

---

[1] Et erunt omnes docibiles Dei (Joan. vi. 45).

[2] Altiora te ne quæsieris et fortiora te ne scrutatus fueris ; sed quæ præcepit tibi Deus illa cogita semper, et in pluribus operibus ejus ne fueris curiosus. Non est enim tibi necessarium ea quæ abscondita sunt videre oculis tuis. In supervacuis rebus noli scrutari multipliciter et in pluribus operibus ejus non eris curiosus (Eccles. iii. 22-24).

31. *Attention and submission.*—O my God, I think I am truly desirous of living according to the requirements of Thy good pleasure. Grant then, I implore Thee, that my desire may correspond with Thine ; grant me to know it and to submit to it as far as it is Thy will to declare it. It is Thy will that I should know Thine action in some degree, and that I should submit thereto without measure. Give me sincerity of attention and simplicity in submission. Through sincerity of attention I shall not be unaware of anything Thou desirest to reveal to me ; through simplicity in submission, I shall not seek after anything which Thou wouldst conceal from me. By being attentive, my desire will be in conformity with Thine, and my eyes open to Thy light ; by being submissive, my action will be made to correspond with Thine. By attending, I shall attain to that which I so much need, the divine meaning of the events of my life ; by submission, I shall get a calm assurance of rest in hope. Sincerity of attention will enable me to avoid the deviations that arise from carelessness and distractions, and from cowardly negligence ; simplicity in submission will keep me from indiscreet curiosity and troublesome agitation. O my God, grant that I may understand Thee and follow Thee.

32. *The spiritual director.*—Further, to remove all causes of disquiet and illusions, God has appointed official interpreters of His word. It is the mission of the spiritual director to recognize and explain God's calls. If I would not misjudge any of them, I need only survey myself within with calmness and care, and give an account of the result to my director ; the word will come to me from him. When our Lord cast Saul to the ground on the road to Damascus to transform him into St. Paul, it was an extraordinary sign of His special will with regard to him. The ravening wolf[1] thus flung to earth understood it. "Lord," he asked, "what wilt Thou have me to do ?" "Go into the city, and there it shall be told thee what thou must do."[2] God does not even explain His will to him, He sends him to the man whose mission it was to explain it.

[1] Benjamin lupus rapax (Gen. xlix. 27).
[2] Domine, quid me vis facere ? Et Dominus ad eum : Surge et ingredere civitatem et ibi dicetur tibi quid te oporteat facere (Act. ix. 6)

CHAPTER VII

Joys and Sufferings

33. The difficulty of accepting consolation well.—34. St. John of the Cross advises its rejection.—35. The difficulty of accepting suffering well.—36. Ask for nothing : refuse nothing.

33. The difficulty of accepting consolation well.—In practice, it is a good thing for me to consider the two modes of God's operations separately, and to see how I ought to accept the one and the other. Both are rather hard to accept well. I do not say to accept ; for consolation is easily accepted ; but to accept it rightly is not an easy matter. Really, upon the whole, I know not if the very pure acceptance of consolation is not harder than that of suffering. When God sends some consolation, it is not at all common for God's hand to be seen therein before everything else, for it to be loved above all as God's operation, and to stop only at the spiritual fruit which God wishes to produce by means of the consolation. My first impulse is to stop short at the consolation, to find satisfaction in it, and to confine my liking to the joy it gives me. What I thank God for is the pleasure He sends me, which I feel and enjoy, and in which I rest. But I scarcely think of thanking Him for His own action, nor above all for the spiritual fruit which He wishes to bring forth in me, and which means my advancement towards Him. Thus, consolation becomes to me the end, and ceases to be a means. This, again, means disorder, and the subversion which is so well known and so common.

If I would avoid this disorder, I must accustom myself not to be so eager for consolation, knowing that it is not God, but only one of God's instruments ; I must do nothing to seek it directly ; put up with the loss of it generously, when it is demanded of me ; receive it with simplicity, when God pleases to give it me, so as to enjoy it without agitation and see it vanish without regret ; keeping my eyes fixed solely on the one thing necessary, the glory of God, which ought to be the goal of all consolation ![1]

[1] See Part I, Book III, § 36.

34. **St. John of the Cross advises its rejection.**—St. John of the Cross goes further still. Unceasingly he works to persuade the soul that consolations are not God, but an instrument in the hands of God for the production in me of mysterious ascents towards His glory. The quicker the instrument passes away, the more does the spiritual effect abide alone in its purity and completeness. Further, he advises the rejection of consolation and its renunciation and refusal, even when one is quite sure that it comes from God. In this way, says he, one never runs the risk of becoming attached thereto rather than to God, nor of being deceived by the false consolations of the devil.[1] Thus to refuse consolation presupposes more energy and mortification, and doubtless leads to more rapid progress; to accept it with all simplicity requires more humility, because humility alone is able to keep clear of the illusions of self-seeking in consolation.

35. **The difficulty of accepting suffering well.**—If I am too prone to allow myself to make a wrong use of joy, I am also woefully discouraged and irritated by trouble. Often, quite a little shock is enough to cast me down, a slight bitterness quickly fills me with distaste; and if some trial of crucifying sharpness falls upon me, I am crushed. I am a frail flower which dreads every touch of wind and rain, of sun and frost. The habit of pleasure has given my soul an effeminate temperament, which is incapable of enduring anything. And thus God's purifying operations, instead of bringing forth in me the fruits of progress, through my fault only contribute to increase my evil.

Or else, I become embittered and irritated, and revolt against pain. If I submit to it, it is too often against the grain, murmuring; and I do not notice that by thus showing ill-will, I repulse God and His love. How dreadful is this habit of seeing everything in the light of the senses, and of estimating everything according to my own satisfaction! Thus, I come to misjudge the love of God! . . . to repel it, even to insult it; for is not murmuring an insult to love? Oh, how often have I made barren the efforts of this love

---

[1] *The Ascent of Mount Carmel, passim*, specially ii. 11, iii. 36.

hitherto!... How frequently have I repelled God, just when His love was coming to me in its most austere and yet none the less merciful guise!... O my God, had I only understood Thee!... Shall I understand Thee better henceforward?

36. **Ask for nothing: refuse nothing.**—Under whatever guise it comes, all suffering is from God. Coming from God, it has a mission to fulfil in my soul; it comes to purify it, to set it free, to uplift it. It is sent by God, and I ought to welcome it, and to allow Him to fulfil His work. To accept it is my whole duty. One must never ask for it. Unless there be some special inspiration of the Spirit of God, which is but rarely given before one reaches the fifth degree of piety, it is always a matter of presumption, and consequently a danger, to ask for trials. Ask for nothing, refuse nothing: this is a favourite maxim of St. Francis of Sales, and it may well be a prescription for the Christian life amidst desolations and consolations.

There is, moreover, a very long road to be traversed before one reaches the entire, loving, and grateful acceptance of everything sent by God, without ever refusing anything. Am I not incessantly taken up with avoiding such sufferings as I can get rid of? Is not my principal anxiety this? Constantly I am fleeing from pain; how many means I make use of, how many precautions I take every day! There is nothing in which I show more skill and eagerness. I do not say that it is a bad thing to try to avoid certain sufferings, which it is possible to spare oneself. To use for this purpose the means which God has provided, may even be an act of virtue.[1] In fact, I ought, as far as I can, to protect my being from fatal injuries; the care of my bodily and spiritual health for God is a duty It is also a good thing for me to keep at a distance certain sufferings which, without being an injury or a danger, are nevertheless a real hindrance through the burden they impose on my best faculties. Hence, there are sufferings against which I can and ought to provide.

But after all, if I have any desire for suffering, there are thousands of occasions for it without asking for any from

[1] See Part I, Book II, § 6; Book III, § 27.

God. When I remember that St. Francis of Sales never had a fire in order to feel the cold as God sent it, or else let the flies sting his bald forehead without driving them away ; St. Benedict Labre keeping the vermin, and so on ; I can understand what an infinite field lies open to me for the pure and simple acceptance of daily sufferings. It is, however, a good thing to remember that love of sufferings is proportioned to the degree of the soul's elevation, and that, apart from cases which are exceptional, only souls raised to a high state of holiness are able to face heroic sufferings.

CHAPTER VIII

"I Thank Thee"

37. How to say " I thank Thee."—38. The torrent of joy.—39. Pain extinguished.—40. A wonderful power for progress.

37. *How to say " I thank Thee."*—But how must we accept suffering ?—I reply at once : with thankfulness ; I say, with thankfulness, not with joy : joy often does not depend upon me, but God gives it me as a reward ; still, the reward always depends upon me. In the first place, for a soul which is not accustomed to it, it may seem hard to come to be thankful in the embrace of suffering. Really, I believe it is easier to say a resolute " Thank Thee " than to groan in patience. To say it requires an outburst of generosity. I say an outburst ; because it is only well done, when done as it were by a leap of the heart.

When suffering comes, I resolve to make an act which is very short and generous : " MY GOD, I THANK THEE !" That is all. There is no need to dwell upon the act, to repeat it feverishly, as if to establish by violence some permanent and steadfast state of joyful thankfulness all of a sudden. No, I need only be satisfied with the act itself, with the " Thank Thee," quickly and earnestly uttered. When you give a present, you receive a simple and cordial " Thank you," and this " Thank you " is enough to testify gratitude for your kindness, for it assures you that love appreciates your generosity. And thus it is that I must act towards God, when He vouchsafes to give me His great present, which is suffering. "MY GOD, I THANK THEE!" How eloquent is this "Thank Thee!" ... It tells God that I understand His action and His love. A word between friends says so much!...

38. The torrent of joy.—And what results are effected in my soul! It seems as if this "Thank Thee," in springing up, has made the deeps to open. But this takes place so deep down within me, that never before had I any notion of the vastness of my being. Here the senses have no part whatever. Hence, in these deeps, which had been hitherto unknown to me (it is the "Thank Thee" that reveals them to me), through some mysterious opening (apparently it is the "Thank Thee" that opens it up), I perceive a fountain spring forth which was until now unknown, a fountain which, sometimes at a single spurt, sometimes slowly, fills the inmost depths within me. The soul is flooded with pleasant water, with joy so sweet, so calm, so penetrating, that no other joy coming from without can compare with it.

Whoever drinks the water of external joys will still thirst. On the contrary, whoever drinks of this deep water shall not thirst for ever. "But the water that I will give him, shall become in him a fountain of water springing up into life everlasting!"[1] And it is this "Thank Thee" that has made it spring forth!... As for him that believeth, out of his belly shall flow rivers of living water.[2] No, nothing can compare with this sweetness; and, when one has tasted it, one begins to understand the inebriation of the saints with suffering.[3] In them we find torrents of this living water; they drank of the torrent, and it was this that made them so triumphant.[4] No doubt, the first "Thank Thee" will not make the stream of the river of joy to flow;[5] but what at the

[1] Omnis qui bibit ex aqua hac sitiet iterum; qui autem biberit ex aqua quam ego dabo ei, non sitiet in æternum, sed aqua quam ego dabo ei, fiet in eo fons aquæ salientis in vitam æternam (Joan. iv. 13, 14).
[2] Qui credit in me, sicut dicit Scriptura, flumina de ventre ejus fluent aquæ vivæ (Joan. vii. 38).
[3] Superabundo gaudio in omni tribulatione nostra (2 Cor. vii. 4).
[4] De torrente in via bibet, propterea exaltabit caput (Ps. cix. 7)
[5] Fluminis impetus lætificat civitatem Dei (Ps. xlv. 5).

outset is only an imperceptible rivulet is not long in growing to be a stream, a torrent, and a river. All you that thirst, come to the waters (Is. lv. 1).

39. **Pain extinguished.**—Another result of this "Thank Thee" is to make the soul invulnerable to pain thus accepted. The body will continue to suffer, if the pain is a corporal one ; but the soul does not suffer, it enjoys : the water which floods it drives away all pain. The soul has, as it were, recovered a part of its original impassibility. And if the pain is purely inward, such as an insult, a calumny, a humiliation, etc., the feeling of suffering is as it were done away with. If any bitterness remains, this bitterness is pleasant, because it is this that brings joy.

The "Thank Thee" is like the tree the Lord showed to Moses, and which turned the bitter waters into sweetness.[1] Thus I am in peace in the most bitter of my bitternesses;[2] and every bitterness becomes sweet to me from the moment that it opens to me the sealed fountain, the waters whereof make as it were a paradise of flowers to bloom within me.[3] And thus comes about an indescribable mingling of bitterness and sweetness, of joy and suffering, in which the bitterness gives rise to the sweetness, and the sweetness is kept amidst the bitterness. This is the only true joy, for all joy that is not born and is not kept in bitterness quickly becomes corrupt and corrupting. But this kind of joy is strong and vivifying, and permeates the very marrow of my bones with life ;[4] it is never corrupt or corrupting ; it is the strength and life of my soul. In this way, my sorrow becomes joy, and thus the grateful acceptance of suffering becomes the true means of not suffering. To enjoy suffering is the great secret of the saints ; it is the sealed fountain in the enclosed garden.

40. **A wonderful power for progress.**—Nothing perhaps is so mighty as this "Thank Thee" for the spiritual advance-

---

[1] At ille clamavit ad Dominum, qui ostendit ei lignum quod cum misisset in aquas, versæ sunt in dulcedinem (Ex. xv. 25).
[2] Ecce in pace amaritudo mea amarissima (Is. xxxviii. 17).
[3] Fons signatus, emissiones tuæ paradisus (Cant. iv. 12, 13).
[4] Gaudebit cor vestrum et ossa vestra quasi herba germinabunt (Is. lxvi. 14).

ment of my soul; nothing carries life so abundantly and impetuously into the lowest depths. This is because nothing opens the way for God so widely. This practice alone would suffice to sanctify my soul in a very short time; it would be a guarantee for all my virtues, and the condition of their improvement. Oh, if I only knew it! ... if I only willed it!

But the devil is so clever in arousing my sensibility, and in driving it to rebellion! ... He is so well able to exaggerate the demands of nature! ... Thus he succeeds both in drying up the fountain of my joys which are purest and deepest, and at the same time that of my most rapid progress and of my most precious merits. The ruthless robber! Under the pretext of sparing me the pains of the journey, he strips me, belabours me with blows, and leaves me half dead by the way.[1] This is all that I gain by trying to escape from suffering. Oh, how priceless is a good " Thank Thee!"

CHAPTER IX

The Aloes

41. Look trial in the face.—42. Chew the aloe.—43. Shun imaginary suppositions.—44. One's eyes on God, and one's feet on the ground.—45. Cast all care upon God.

41. **Look trial in the face.**—Another practice which is very useful for the right acceptance of suffering—for since suffering is the most common and the most mighty mode of God's action, it is well to give it closer attention—another very useful practice is to look at it in its most aggravating aspect, and to accept it beforehand. I hold stoutly, says M. de Maistre,[2] to my everlasting maxim of always anticipating evil, and of allowing myself always to be taken by surprise by the good. When I am threatened by some trial, I allow my imagination to be stirred up, my sensibility to be exasperated without fear, and I instinctively permit myself to be

[1] Incidit in latrones, qui etiam despoliaverunt eum, et plagis impositis, abierunt semivivo relicto (Luc. x. 30).
[2] Letter to Mlle. Constance, Sept. 6, 1817.

carried away to hope for the best of results. Thus, I allow myself to go along with the reckonings that gratify me, without thinking of resting in the will of God, which ought to be my sole rule. When my imagination is over-excited and my sensibility stimulated, if the evil I dread comes to pass, I suffer under it a hundred times more, since I have taken the trouble to multiply it a hundredfold by the fears which I have allowed to carry me away.

If only I knew how to rest in the will of God, trial would find me calm and strong. Now, the true means of resting in the will of God, in such a way that nothing may be able to trouble my repose, is this practice of accepting in any actual situation its most aggravating side, if it should please God to lay it upon me. When, in any threatened trial, I have courageously made a survey of the darkest aspect; when, having fathomed my heart, I feel that it is ready for everything by God's grace; when my sacrifice has been made, and made fully, and with all the breadth which God may please to put into His action; when I ascertain that I have in me an energetic resolution to take the chalice from God's hands and to drink it to the bottom, to the very dregs, without hesitation or reservation; and if, above all, I can gaze steadfastly upon the chalice without any wavering, then—God be praised !—nothing further can do me any harm. Then, verily, I feel that love is as strong as death, and zeal as hard as hell.[1] Neither fear, nor disquiet, nor trouble, have any hold upon me. I have an even mind and an assured heart, which cannot be perturbed.

42. **Chew the aloe.**—A young pupil of fifteen years of age, on whom his mischievous companions had played the trick of putting an aloe in his mouth while he was asleep, was so filled with disgust and anger that he vowed vengeance. Finding no other vengeance worthy of him, he bought some aloes, and forced himself to chew them for a week, until he could taste them no longer. " Come now," said he to them, " this taste has no effect on me."

If I only knew how to chew my aloe ! . . . in other words,

[1] Fortis est ut mors dilectio, dura siçut infernus æmulatio, (Cant. viii. 6).

to look upon trouble, until the taste of it no longer affected me!—It is the roughest and the sweetest of remedies. The soul which chews its aloe, which has foreseen a suffering, until it can no longer perceive the taste, such a soul is ready for everything, disengaged from everything, insensible to everything. I believe that no one really knows what peace is, until he has traversed this part of life's road. No one knows as well as he, how far resting in the will of God imparts strength to the soul.

43. Shun imaginary suppositions.—This has been practised by the saints; St. John of the Cross recommends it. No doubt, this practice presupposes a real energy of soul: but it is, nevertheless, only a logical inference from the principle which has been meditated upon throughout this Part II: "The rule of conduct is God's will, and not my own tastes." Further, it is not to be confounded with another practice, which has been rightly condemned by spiritual writers, and which consists in representing to oneself imaginary evils, in exaggerating them, in asking oneself if one could endure them, in order to discover whether one really loves God above all things. Such things are but dangerous reveries of the imagination.

Here, there is nothing of the kind. Here, we must begin by silencing the imagination and the sensibility to make our appeal to cool reason and energetic will. There are no imaginary suppositions; the position is an actual one, which must be looked at in a dry light; the issue is a probable one, and must be accepted with a calm will. It is the will of God, which must be embraced with both the arms of my intelligence and my will, and nothing must be allowed to separate me from it. "Who then," cries St. Paul, "shall separate us from the love of Christ? shall tribulation? or distress? or famine? or nakedness? or danger? or persecution? or the sword? (As it is written: For Thy sake we are put to death all the day long. We are accounted as sheep for the slaughter.) But in all these things we overcome because of Him that hath loved us. For I am sure that neither death, nor life, nor angels, nor principalities, nor powers, nor things present, nor things to come, nor might, nor height, nor depth, nor any

THE WAY: THE WILL OF GOOD PLEASURE

other creature shall be able to separate us from the love of God, which is in Christ Jesus our Lord " (Rom. viii. 35 ff.). " I am sure," says St. Paul. How he had measured all these things with a single eye! ... How calm and sure he is as to his triumph! ... It is true that the Apostle could speak from experience: he had been through all these difficulties O my God! give me the wisdom to imitate him!

44. One's eyes on God : one's feet on the ground.—To sum up : passive piety consists exclusively in submission to all that comes from God's good pleasure. It is especially in this way that piety is formed within me ; thus it is that I mainly come to see, to love, and to seek God in all things, since His will is in all things. If, then, I have my advancement at heart, my attention must be chiefly brought to bear on this habit of practical submission to the will of the divine good pleasure in all things. My eyes are ever towards the Lord, says the Psalmist.[1] Very well, says St. Augustine,[2] if your eyes are thus ever raised to God, what are you doing with your feet, since you are not looking straight before you?—As for my feet, says the prophet, God Himself undertakes to pluck them out of the net. As for me, I have only to fasten my eyes upon God and His will ; God undertakes to look after my progress and advancement.

45. Cast all care upon God.—O my God! when shall I be fully and perfectly conformed to Thy whole will?[3] When shall I be able, like a little child, to let myself be carried in the arms of God's good pleasure, " not entertaining myself with wishes and desires for things, but allowing God to will and do them for me, according to His own pleasure ; casting all my care upon Him, since He careth for me, as the Apostle saith.[4] And note that he says, ' All our care,' whether it be that of accepting what happens, or that of wishing or not wishing. ... No, Lord, I do not wish for any event, for I

[1] Oculi mei semper ad Dominum, quoniam ipse de laqueo evellet pedes meos (Ps. xxiv. 15).
[2] Et quasi diceretur illi : Quid agis de pedibus tuis, cum ante te non attendis ? Quoniam ipse evellet, inquit, de laqueo pedes meos (*Enarrat.*, in Ps. xxxi. 21).
[3] Ut stetis pleni et perfecti in omni voluntate Dei (Col. iv. 12).
[4] Omnem sollicitudinem vestram projicientes in eum, quoniam ipsi cura est de vobis (1 Pet. v. 7).

allow Thee to will them for me entirely as Thou pleasest ; but instead of wishing for events, I will bless Thee for having willed them. O Théotime, what an excellent employment of our will is this, when it gives up all care of wishing for and choosing the consequences of the divine good pleasure to praise and thank the good pleasure itself for such consequences!"[1]

[1] *Théotime*, (Book IX, ch. 14).

BOOK III

THE CONCURRENCE OF THE TWO WILLS

Since I have my own action and God has His, they must be united.—How are they to be united?—This is what we now have to see, and it is a question which is above all vital and practical. The proper subject of this Book, then, is the union of the human movement with the divine, so that the progress of my piety may have a single movement, of which my acts will be the body and God will be the soul. Hence, the question is now, to show the accordance of the will signified with that of God's good pleasure, the correspondence of active piety with passive piety, so as to exhibit in its progress the living unity of piety as a whole. The question is to establish union and to oppose separation. Separation makes *the human*. I saw, in the order of the end, how the separation of my satisfaction from the glory of God brings forth human enjoyment, which has to be striven against and destroyed. In the order of work, the separation of my action from God's results in *human movement* which must also be striven against and destroyed.

Separation makes *the human*, and union makes *the Christian*. In the order of the end, the union of my being with God's, of my life with His, of my happiness with His honour, realizes the goal of the Christian life. In the order of work, the union of my activity with God's constitutes Christian movement; and it is this union that must be preserved and realized in all things. Hence, to exhibit union and to combat separation will be the whole object of this Book.

CHAPTER I

The Necessity of Concurrence

1. Harmony is necessary.—2. It is God who worketh.—3. By His will of good pleasure.—4. In us.—5. Both to will.—6. And to do.

1. **Harmony is necessary.**—God has His action, and He asks me for mine. God's action is the principal thing, mine is secondary. Both concur in the same work; but how, in what proportion, and in what order do they unite? The common result of the two actions is the formation within me of that one disposition, that one view, which is piety. It is of supreme practical importance to know how my action must be united with God's. If I know not that, I run the risk of injuring His action and of substituting mine for it; or else, by not giving mine in the measure He wishes of me, of hindering His action. If my action is not in harmony with His, the work of piety necessarily suffers; for, where two acts concur in one effort, they only issue in a useful result in proportion as they are in harmony. Further, nothing I do outside of the divine movement properly belongs to piety, which is essentially a supernatural life wrought in me by God. Hence, how is active piety united with passive piety? what are their relations to one another? what is their organic connexion?

2. **It is God who worketh.**—If we would enter a little into the mysteries of the spiritual life, we must always return to St. Paul, the great theologian who came back to earth from the third heaven. Though he says he is unable to reveal its secrets, each of his words nevertheless seems to re-echo voices from the depths of eternity. "It is God," he says, "who, by His will of good pleasure worketh in us both to will and to do."[1] It is God who worketh. These words of the Apostle possess a depth of infinite meaning. He does

[1] Deus est enim qui operatur in nobis et velle et perficere pro bona voluntate (Phil. ii. 13).

THE WAY: CONCURRENCE OF THE TWO WILLS 215

not only say: It is God who giveth us the means to will and to do. He says with still more energy: "It is God who worketh." Here, St. Paul is not merely considering grace, which is the means put at my disposal by God and the result of God's operation. I shall consider this means later on; I have not yet come to the means, and am still in the way. With St. Paul, I am here considering the actual working of God in its essential source.

It is God who worketh, God Himself. He it is, says the Apostle: *Deus est*. Hence there is no work which He has not worked, nothing is really living, if He does not enter into it and vivify it. Where He worketh not, nothing is done; and where His work gives animation, life is only to be found in that which He sets in motion. There could not be any life apart from this.

3. By His will of good pleasure.—How does God work?— By the will of His good pleasure, says the Apostle. It is His goodness, His will to do His creatures good, which is the determining cause of all the vital operations which He wills to work in me. In the work of creation, He did as He willed, in heaven and on earth, in the sea and in all the deeps.[1] In the work of providence whereby He governs what He has created, and in the very inward work whereby He vivifies souls, He only consults His own will.[2] He has predestinated us unto the adoption of children through Jesus Christ unto Himself, according to the purpose of His will.[3] And all these various works of holiness, one and the same Spirit worketh, dividing to everyone according as He will.[4]

4. In us.—And where does God work?—He worketh in us. Hence His operation is a personal matter. What God does in me, He does for me, and He only does it in me and with me. He wills to raise up the building of my life according

---

[1] Omnia quæcumque voluit Dominus fecit in cœlo, in terra, in mari et in omnibus abyssis (Ps. cxxxiv. 6).

[2] In quo etiam et nos sorte vocati sumus, prædestinati secundum propositum ejus, qui operatur omnia secundum propositum voluntatis suæ (Eph. i. 11).

[3] Qui prædestinavit nos in adoptionem filiorum per Jesum Christum in ipsum, secundum propositum voluntatis suæ (Eph. i. 5).

[4] Hæc autem omnia operatur unus atque idem Spiritus, dividens singulis prout vult (1 Cor. xii. 11).

to the plan of my vocation which He has laid down. And the plan of my vocation is quite a personal matter, for each one has his own proper gift. Thus God is careful to conduct the operations of building for eternity in each person according to the requirements and the measure of his life.

And this operation is an inward operation. It is the interior life, the divine life, which God works to build up. He wishes to reach even to the most secret powers of the soul, and to make the supernatural vigour circulate throughout the deepest channels of my being. The instruments of this action may be external: I saw[1] how God makes use of all creatures, spiritual and material, as the instruments of His operations. But whatever the instrument may be, His operation always aims at what is inward, and that is where it reaches, if it be not stopped short. What God wishes to build up in me is the interior life of piety.

5. **Both to will.**—And what is it that God worketh in me?—Two things, says St. Paul. First of all, He worketh to will, and then He worketh to do.

He worketh to will, this is the first effect of the action of His good pleasure. It is God's preparatory action, which determines, animates, and sets my action in motion. And what St. Paul calls " willing " is the first movement of my action. And this first movement will only be a movement of the supernatural life, will only be a true act of piety, so far as the action of the divine good pleasure has imparted an impulse to it. The starting-point of the divine life, the first origin of supernatural animation, is, therefore, in this preparatory action of God's. The true fruit-bearing of active piety only begins with the seething of the divine sap. What takes place apart from this influence can only be human willing, and therefore, barren and dead.

6. **And to do.**—The action of God's good pleasure secondly operates in doing, but doing up to the point of its *perfect* accomplishment; such is the inference from St. Paul's words: *perficere*. My soul, which is the life of my body, is wholly in the whole of the body, and wholly in each one of its parts. Thus God, who wills by His action to be the life of my soul,

[1] See Book II. § 5

THE WAY: CONCURRENCE OF THE TWO WILLS

is wholly in all my acts, and wholly in each one of them. And just as the whole body, and just as each of its members only possesses life in so far as it is animated by the soul, thus all my acts and each one of them only partake of the divine life in so far as God's action enters into them. My action throughout is measured by the concurrent action of God; it is sustained, guided, vivified, kept going, and completed by it. My life in general, as well as each act in particular, possesses the amount of perfection and supernatural vitality which it gets from the operation of God's good pleasure. Consequently, I traverse the five degrees of the ascent of piety, according as God's operations are able to seize hold of me and to animate me in such a way as to bear me towards the heights.

CHAPTER II

The Nature of the Concurrence

7. The origin and the measure of my action.—8. The meeting.—
9. Union.—10. Electricity.—11. The divine contact.

7. The origin and the measure of my action.—Part I showed me a twofold relation of origin and subordination between my satisfaction and God's glory. God's honour is anterior and superior to my happiness. The same relations exist between God's action and mine. The divine action is anterior and superior to mine, so that the origin and the measure of mine are to be found in God's.

There is its origin; for no supernatural act can arise, except it be from the inspiration of God. It is the divine impulse that determines, animates, and sets in motion any of my faculties.

There is its measure. My action is kept up, maintained, guided, and measured by God's. I can neither anticipate, nor outstrip, nor leave the divine movement, without falling back altogether or in part into the fatality of a purely human and natural agitation.

But, in this movement of piety, my part of the activity

is what I have called active piety; God's share of the activity, or rather, the correspondence with God's activity, is what I have called passive piety. Hence it follows, that the origin of active piety and its measure are to be found in passive piety. It is this that gives active piety its primary impulse, and animates and determines its primary movement. It is this, too, which afterwards sustains, preserves, measures, and guides the movement which it has created.

It is thus that these two parts of piety unite, and they cannot ever be separated. Separation would mean death, and in death there is no piety. Union is life, and piety is a life. Hence, there are no life and no piety, unless there is union between active piety and passive piety; and this union presupposes that passive piety will animate active piety, just as the soul animates the body.

8. *The meeting.*—And this is how the growth of this union proceeds. God anticipates me, He acts upon me by one of the acts of His good pleasure: the act may be interior or outward, a consolation or a crucifixion; for instance, a suggestion or an accident, a word or a chance meeting, etc.; in a word, any one of the providential acts which are constantly occurring to me. What will this action, which operates on me but without my initiative, which anticipates me and is in a manner imposed upon me, do to me?—It is like a stimulus, an invitation, a solicitation. It suggests an idea,[1] a feeling, or an action. And what does this first movement demand of me?—To accept it, *i.e.*, to recognize it with my mind, to welcome it with my heart, to yield to it the submission of my senses, as if I were being shaped by a divine operation. This is what I saw was the duty of passive piety. It is this first perturbation, which is, properly speaking, actually preventing grace, the grace which works in us to will.

As to this stimulus, my liberty may be used in two ways: I may shut it out, or open the door to it. If I shut it out, if, being too sensitive to my natural impressions, I am refractory under trials or allow myself to be diverted by consolations, if outward dissipation or inward apathy deadens

[1] See Book II, § 22.

me to God's touch, there is no correspondence with God's action. In this case, I remain cold, void, without spiritual animation, easily forgetful, or disinclined, or incapable of doing my duty. I remain in falsehood, vanity, and in the servitude of my own inertia or of my purely human activity; my thoughts and feelings and actions are not taken possession of by the divine influence to which I am closed. There is neither passive piety nor active piety; since submission is a failure, so is duty.

9. Union.—But if I lay myself open to the divine invitation by frank acceptance, I then enter into effective communication with the Author of my life. The operation, whereby He has anticipated me, will be prolonged in me; it will accompany me, sustain me, and fortify me, until I have completely carried out the duty for which this help was given me. And thus, duty is seen in the light of God, loved in the movement of God, and carried out in the strength of God. Then it is that duty gets a finished perfection, if, at least, I do my best to keep in that state of correspondence which enables the divine movement to have free course, and to bring forth its effect. This help, which is thus given me, by the working of Providence, is nothing else than concurrent actual grace.

These divine incentives are constantly renewed throughout the occurrences of life, and they are increased in proportion to my duties, so that no duty is left without some preparation, and without the concurrence of supernatural operations.

When the preparations and concurrence have brought me near enough to God to realize the conditions of justification, the flow of holy animation which circulates within me leaves behind it a kind of divine sap which transforms my being inwardly, and properly communicates thereto supernatural life. This is sanctifying grace. It is thereby that my acts, my feelings, and my ideas are transformed; it is thereby that my activity is really as it were fused into the divine activity; it is thereby that my faculties are qualified, adapted, and raised to the supernatural height of the Christian duty of the interior life. But, as I have said, this is not the time to give an actual estimate of those altogether divine means, which are preventing or concurrent grace, and sanctifying grace; that will be done in Part III. It is enough to have pointed out here the connection of the means with the operations.

Here, then, is how I am led to vital union with God, how my mind becomes united with His views, my will conformed to His will, my action harmonized with His action, my life mingled with His life.

Thus it is that the union of active piety with passive piety takes place, and that my piety is one, sole, most unique and vivifying operation, of which God is the promoter and I am the co-operator. It is God's life in me, and my life in God. He is in me by His action, and I am in Him by my action, and thus I bring forth the fruits of piety in abundance.[1]

10. Electricity.—Although He is everywhere present by His power, His knowledge, and His substance, nevertheless God, for the realization of my vital union with Him, is only accessible to me at one single point, that of His actual operation upon me. That is the point of contact which I must come to and touch, if I would have the current of supernatural life circulate in me. "No man can come to Me," says the Saviour, "except the Father, who hath sent Me, draw him" (John vi. 44). Go to God we must, it is the duty of active piety. But for going to Him, there is a preliminary condition; we must be drawn. To be drawn is the characteristic of passive piety. To be drawn, and to go: this is the whole of piety. But to be drawn, there must be two things: 1. God must act; 2. I must come into contact with this action of God's. How does God act?—By His good pleasure. How am I first to come into contact with this action?—By acceptance. At the very moment of my acceptance, I touch God; and I shall be in contact with Him all the time, while, by my co-operation, I remain stayed upon Him. But, just when I am at the point of contact, communication is established, and there is a thrill of divine electricity. And as long as I am stayed on Him, the supernatural flow continues, and, circulating in me, it causes me to act in a supernatural manner.

[1] Qui manet in me et ego in eo, hic fert fructum multum (Ioan xv. 5).

THE WAY: CONCURRENCE OF THE TWO WILLS

I have no power of myself to put myself in contact with God, it is He who anticipates me and leads me thereto, if I am willing to do my best not to hinder Him.

Electrified by God, I am uplifted, and carried away to fulfil present duty. Whatever the divine operation may be, whether a trial or a consolation, as soon as I accept it and lean upon it, being ready to co-operate with the divine movement, I feel circulating within me the vital energy which is supernaturally necessary and corresponds with the obligations of actual duty. And the divine current will only be broken off, when I cease to correspond with God, and deviate; it will be restored as soon as a fresh acceptance has re-established the contact and renewed my co-operation.

11. *The divine contact.*—And this contact is established in its full perfection by the " Thank Thee " which accepts, by the penetrating " Thank Thee," which, in consolation and suffering, is able to discern the divine operation; and which, dominated by no fascination of pleasure nor apprehension of suffering, is straightway attached to the work wrought by God, and to the result which He intends. The more this " Thank Thee " passes through what is sensible to reach God's operation and thought directly and solely, the more intimate is the contact. And then, what activity results!

Hitherto, I have too foolishly allowed myself to be entertained by consolations, to be too faint-heartedly crushed or irritated by desolations: and why?—Because, being too sensitive to self, not comprehending God's action, I have been unable to set up contact with Him. Thus pleasure has enervated me, and suffering has been my undoing.

When at times I have been able to say a more intelligent " Thank Thee," what an impulse it has given me towards my duty! what light to know it! what heart to love it! what readiness to perform it! In such moments of enthusiasm no duty seems to cost too much: it is so well seen and loved and performed! The divine electricity uplifts the soul.

But above all, when the stroke of some trial is met with a heart-felt " Thank Thee," oh, then! . . . I have already spoken[1] of the joy that leaps up; here we must speak of the

[1] See Book II, § 38.

strength that uplifts, of the ardour that carries away, of the light that floods one. It is this strength that goes to make martyrs triumph in their sufferings, this ardour that carries away apostles in their devotion, this light that at last fills souls who suffer with such deep intuitions. All the heroism of duty, that which is calm and hidden as well as that which is enthusiastic and striking, springs from the great " Thank Thee " which is uttered amidst suffering. It is because nowhere is the contact with God more intimate and powerful. Nothing opens the soul so fully to the circulation of the divine life. All that is most sublime in sacrifice is within the reach of those who are able to set up this contact, and to make this opening. Oh, Lord, if men only knew it! This is what the saints call correspondence with God, which they recommend in so many ways.

Doubtless, this correspondence does not lead at every moment to things so sublime, because such things do not offer themselves at every turn ; but it always leads to the perfection of an action, because perfection becomes every Christian action.

CHAPTER III

The Divine Alliance

12. Solicitation and union.—13. Union grows and becomes complete.—14. *Nisi Dominus.*—15. *Surgite postquam sederitis.*—16. Naturalism, Quietism, Christianity.—17. Acceptance.

12. Solicitation and union.—In fine, a real marriage has to take place between my will and God's, between my soul and God. By a primary action of His good pleasure, God solicits my consent. That consent once given, union takes place. The union which has been contracted is consummated in action, and this mutual action of the two wills united produces offspring, which are acts of piety.

13. Union grows and becomes complete.—But this marriage is not at all complete at the outset. It is renewed, and, by being renewed, it improves at each invitation of God's and at each acceptance of mine: thus it is that the inward man is renewed day by day, until my will, being swallowed up in God's, at last loses its *own*[1] (*propre*) action in God's just as the bride loses her name in that of her husband. It is just when God's will has succeeded by its successive operations in swallowing up and in entirely transforming mine, that what the saints call the mystical marriage is finally consummated and celebrated. This is the state of unity. In human marriage, they are two in one flesh; in the mystical marriage, we are two in one spirit.[2] Here we may recall St. John's words: "But as many as received Him, He gave them power to be made the sons of God, to them that believe in His name; who are born, not of blood, nor of the will of the flesh, nor of the will of man, but of God" (John iii. 12, 13).

14. **Nisi Dominus.**—In Psalm cxxvi,[3] David has wonderfully celebrated the marriage between the human will and the divine, their mutual co-operation, and the offspring of their union. Unless the Lord build the temple, he says, the work of the human builder will be in vain. His work will be only man's work, work without God, and devoid of God, and therefore vain, abiding and ending in vanity; since every creature, which is not filled with God, is void and vain.

If the Lord keep not the city of human satisfaction to preserve it from disorder, vain too will be the human vigilance that watches over it.

Yes, in vain will you rise before light to put your own will before God's, and your own action before His. This is indeed vanity; for man's action, taking precedence of God's, excludes God's. *The human* is but vanity and nothingness, so far as piety is concerned.

O ye who eat the bread of sorrow, ye in whom God's good

---

[1] See Part I, § 36, for the definition of "*propriety.*"
[2] Erunt enim, inquit, duo in carne una. Qui autem adhæret Deo unus spiritus est (1 Cor. vi. 16, 17).
[3] Nisi Dominus ædificaverit domum, in vanum laboraverunt qui ædificant eam. Nisi Dominus custodierit civitatem, frustra vigilat qui custodit eam. Vanum est vobis ante lucem surgere: surgite postquam sederitis, qui manducatis panem doloris. Cum dederit dilectis suis somnum, ecce hæreditas Domini, filii, merces, fructus ventris. Sicut sagittæ in manu potentis, ita filii excussorum. Beatus vir qui implevit desiderium suum ex ipsis, non confundetur cum loquetur inimicis suis in porta (Ps. cxxvi).

pleasure worketh, for it worketh usually more potently by means of sorrow, ye whom God feeds with this substantial bread, take heed. Before rising from your action, rest in the acceptance of God's action. After abiding in the acceptance of passive piety, you can arise with assurance and profit to engage in the work of active piety.

Therefore, be not so agitated and eager. Know that God must give your will, His well-beloved spouse, the sleep of death; your will must fall asleep in His. When He has given it this sleep, oh! then will arise God's heirs and your sons. These will be the acts of life and vigour which belong to true piety, living and fruitful piety. They are both the reward of God who worketh in you, and the fruit of your womb, of yours who work with Him.

These acts of piety, the children of your union, the offspring of your denudation and death, will be mighty and strong, like arrows in the hand of the mighty.

Oh, happy is the man who can fill the one quiver of his one desire with such arrows! (When I come to speak of the rapid glance of the examination of conscience in Part III, I shall see what this one quiver is, and how it is to be filled.) When this quiver is full of arrows, enemies may appear at the gate of the city of man to disturb its satisfaction and to stay the work of the glory of God. Let them come: these arrows will keep them back in respect, and hinder them from entering into the city, and bar the approaches to the temple against them.

15. Surgite postquam sederitis.—Here is the first word, the primary secret of piety: acceptance. Acceptance of the action of God's good pleasure: this is the starting-point and beginning of everything, all depends upon this. *Surgite postquam sederitis;* we must be seated before we can rise up, and we must rise up after being seated. These three words perfectly characterize, at this point, both Christian truth, and the falsehood of the extremes which are opposed to it. Naturalism says: "*Surgite*, rise up"; and it takes away what follows. Quietism says: "*Sederitis*, sit still"; and it omits what goes before. Christianity says: "*Surgite postquam esderitis*, rise up after you have sat still"; and it neither

omits nor takes away anything. Naturalism denies God's action, Quietism gets rid of man's action, Christianity demands the union and submission of man's action to God's. And a wonderful thing is this sitting down and this action, this repose of leaning upon God and this acting with God : they are ever allied and combined to form the divine life in me, which is essentially made up of repose and action. Is not all life action in repose ?

16. **Naturalism, Quietism, Christianity.**—Further, Naturalism and Quietism are not merely errors of the way, they are also mistaken as to the end, and as to the means. Here, a short parenthesis may perhaps not be wasted in describing in a general way these two errors which gather up the divergent tendencies of human fallacies.

As to the end, Naturalism gets rid of, or tends to get rid of, God's glory, leaving nothing but human pleasure behind. As to the way, it does away with, or tends to do away with, God's action, reckoning almost entirely upon human action. As to the means, it destroys or tends to destroy grace, and puts all its hope in human expedients. God more or less banished from man's life and work and instruments, such is Naturalism and such are all of its tendencies.

Quietism, on the other hand, annuls, or tends to annul, man's part in the hope of his salvation, leaving behind nothing but God's glory as the end. It annihilates, or tends to annihilate, human activity, to leave behind nothing but God's action, as the way. It suppresses, or tends to suppress, spiritual exercises and means, to allow nothing but grace to work as a means. Man lowered, and mutilated as to his end and activity and means, such is Quietism and such are all the tendencies that belong to it.

The specific idea of Christianity is to be the union, unimpaired yet subordinate, of the human with the divine. Man's salvation united with and subordinate to God's glory, as the end ; man's action united with and subordinate to God's action, as the way ; man's devotional exercises united with and subordinate to God's grace, as the means—such is Christianity. And it is just these three parts of the co-ordination and of the subordination of the human to the divine which make the subject-matter of the three Parts of this work.

17. Acceptance.—My action must, then, be united with that of God. Just as the soul is united with the body without consuming or impairing it, but gives it, on the contrary, its own perfection by animating and governing it, so God desires to become the soul of my soul, the life of my life. He wills, by His action, to animate and govern mine and, by animating and governing it, to unite it with His own as closely as my bodily action, in my natural life, is united with that of my soul.

But, in my body, it is its receptivity of the soul's action that gives to it its own action; the body acts in proportion as it receives the soul's influence. Thus is it with God and myself. My active piety is living and acting, in proportion as, by the acceptance of passive piety, the action of God's good pleasure succeeds in animating and governing it. And the great word of acceptance is that "Thank Thee."

I have already described how the "Thank Thee" opened up the great fountain of joy, and I showed next how it became a great spring of great activity; in reality, then, it is the great key which opens up the entire way of piety. If, in fact, I accept it fully, God's action has its full effect in me, and my action can also have its full effect. If I only accept it in part, God's action is hindered in part, and mine is lessened at least as much, and generally still more. For if my acceptance does not correspond with the whole of God's action, my action will hardly correspond with all my acceptance. Lastly, if I do not accept it at all, God's action is paralyzed and mine killed; I fall back into the void of my own vanity.

CHAPTER IV

God's Action and Man's Action

18. God's action is just and eternal.—19. Man's action is false and mortal.—20. *Nonne homines estis ?*—21. Christian action.

18. God's action is just and eternal.—God's action is always true, fully and adequately true, because it is totally in harmony with God's mind and thoughts, which are true. Being always in harmony with these thoughts, it is always just and adequate ; it is in every way in accord with all the needs of my soul, as well as with its external conditions. In God's action there is nothing violent, or hesitating, or incomplete ; there are no approximations, or inconsistencies, or contradictions. All is interwoven and reciprocal, all is consecutive and mutually sustaining. Further, God's thoughts are eternal, and all that is in conformity with them participates in their eternity. God's action, therefore, is eternal : what He does has not to be done over again or to be touched up ; it abides for eternity.[1]

19. Man's action is false and mortal.—But man's thoughts are false. Man, so far as he is human only, only sees the creature, the human, the lower, the passing advantage, the lying interest of what is created. Every man is a liar (Ps. cxv. 2), God alone is true.[2]

Man's action, so far as it is in conformity with man's thoughts, is as false, lying, and vain as they are. It is never entirely just and adequate, it is always wanting in some respect, and in many respects. When it seems to be all right in one way, it is often all wrong in every other way.

Man's false ideas are necessarily prone to wane, and inevitably comes a day in which they all perish.[3] And with them perish the actions which are in conformity with them ; for the actions share in the perishable character of the ideas. Consequently, as long as I remain human, I am forced by

---
[1] Veritas Domini manet in æternum (Ps. cxvi. 2).
[2] Ut cognoscant te solum Deum verum (Joan. xvii. 3).
[3] In illa die peribunt omnes cogitationes eorum (Ps. cxlv 4).

falsehood into decadence; all that is human is condemned to die. Thought and action, all that is of human origin, must perish: all passes away, and nothing abides.

20. Nonne homines estis?—What! ought I not to be human?—No. St. Paul reproaches the Corinthians with being men. "Whereas there is among you," he says, "envying and contention, are you not carnal, and walk according to man? For while one saith, I indeed am of Paul; and another, I am of Apollo; are you not men"? (1 Cor. iii. 3) "And what would he have them to be?" asks St. Augustine. "If you would learn, listen to the Psalmist: 'I have said: You are gods, and all of you the sons of the Most High' (Ps. lxxxi. 6). It is to this that God calls us, to be men no more. But we cannot raise ourselves to this higher state, in which we shall be no longer men, unless we begin by recognizing that we are men. It is by humility that we shall ascend to such a height; for if we come to think ourselves to be something when we are nothing,[1] not only shall we not get that which we are not, but we shall lose that which we are."[2]

I must cease to be mere man, to be isolated and to waste away in the human; my thoughts, feelings, and actions must no longer be man's thoughts, feelings, and actions. And what is needed for this? They must be united with the ideas, desires, and action of God.—And how are they to be united therewith?—By accepting God's action. Passive piety is the gate of life to me.

21. Christian action.—As soon as life enters by this gate, my action is taken possession of and governed by God's. It is no longer I who am determining and directing within myself a purely human activity. I cease to be merely human, and

[1] Nam si quis existimat se aliquid esse, cum nihil est, ipse se seducit (Gal. vi. 3).

[2] Quid volebat eos facere, quibus exprobrabat quia homines erant? Vultis nosse quid eos facere volebat? Audite in Psalmis: Ego dixi: dii estis et filii Excelsi omnes. Ad hoc ergo vocat nos Deus ne simus homines. Sed tunc in melius non erimus homines, si prius nos homines esse agnoscamus; i.e., ut ad illam celsitudinem ab humilitate assurgamus; ne cum putamus nos aliquid esse cum nihil sumus, non solum non accipiamus quod non sumus, sed et amittamus quod sumus (S. Aug. Tract. in Joan. i. 4).

I become Christian. The Christian is the man who is united with God. Christianity is the union of the human with the divine; a vital union without deterioration or division; a union wherein man preserves and perfects his activity. And when the whole of the human activity is united with the divine movement that controls it, then a man is perfectly Christian. Then he may say, like St. Paul: " I live, now not I ; but Christ liveth in me " (Gal. ii. 20).

Hence, the ideal for me is to let myself be invaded by the operation of God, until that point of perfection is reached, where all my powers will be possessed and governed by God and guided by Him to work in the fulness of their activity.

Then my knowledge will not consist of purely human, low, and false views ; but, enlightened by divine illumination, it will comprise truer and truer and more lofty intuitions of life. Then my virtues will not be shabby natural and self-interested qualities ; but, permeated with eternal warmth, they will be the rich fruits of holiness. Then my actions will not follow one another at haphazard, like empty and disconnected and commonplace things ; but, taken possession of by supernatural activity, all of them, even the most ordinary ones, will have an infinity of meaning and worth.

CHAPTER V

Divine Guidance

22. God requires duty.—23. The whole of duty.—24. Nothing but duty.—25. Extraordinary ways.—26. God performs all our works.—27. Not a fatalist nor a quietist.

22. **God requires duty.**—If I am able to abandon myself frankly and generously to the divine guidance, I am sure of always being borne on by the operation of the supreme good pleasure to do, and to do well, in the measure and at the time required, what God asks of me. What He asks of me is the fulfilment of the duties of active piety, *i.e.*, the observance of the commandments and counsels in the duties of my state

of life. For the priest, this means fidelity to ecclesiastical laws ; for the religious, conformity to his Rule ; for the layman, zeal in the duties of his profession. God requires this ; duty, the whole of duty, and nothing but duty.

He demands duty, and He demands it absolutely. For, if He works within me, it is not to relieve me of working, but to make me act with Him and by Him. The honour He does me is that of associating my action with His.

23. *The whole of duty.*—He asks for the whole of duty, not all at once. It is just the characteristic of the action of the divine good pleasure, in each circumstance, to make allowance for, and to give the amount of, what the general will of God requires. By His will signified, God does not determine and specify the exact moment, when some particular obligation has to be fulfilled, nor how far it is possible in practice. It tells me in a general way the knowledge I must obtain, the virtues I must practise, the acts I must perform, according to the demands of my calling. Thus it is that their respective rules prescribe to the priest, the religious, the head of a family, etc., the knowledge, virtues, and actions, which are obligatory or desirable for each.

But when and how must this knowledge be acquired, these virtues practised, and these acts performed ?—This is what the will signified does not show in detail, and this is just what the will of God's good pleasure comes to determine. It is this that, by ordering events and calling forth occasions, obliges me to look at, to know, or to learn any particular part of my duty, forces me, or puts me in readiness, to practise any particular virtue, and leads me to perform any particular action. It is this which, at the proper moment, lays upon me or suggests to me such renunciations or services as I am capable of offering, and such as correspond with God's designs concerning me. And if I am ready to follow it, it will guide me one after the other to the most refined details and to the greatest heights of duty, without forgetting anything, or confusing anything, or causing any disorder or deterioration. It is equal to everything : God is such a good guide !

And thus, from the first leaving of mortal sin to the end of every consummation, the degrees of piety ascend through an activity which is incessantly aroused and measured by God's good pleasure.

24. Nothing but duty.—God's action demands nothing but that. The observance of the duties of one's state of life, of ecclesiastical laws by the priest, of his Rule by the religious, of the duties of his profession by the layman, this is all that is demanded of us by God's guidance of us.—What! does God only demand that I should keep the commandments and counsels which correspond with the duties of my state of life?—Nothing else. His action, at least in all ordinary ways, will not lead me outside of that. That is just the stamp of God's action, the characteristic by which it may be infallibly recognized. Any action which takes me outside of the ways of the will signified is open to suspicion.

God, indeed, does not give divergent directions by means of the twofold manifestation of His will; the one is made to explain the other. With its more external, fixed, and certain signs, maintained by the infallible authority of the Church, the will signified always gives me the means of " trying the spirits,"[1] in St. John's words, to see if they be of God and whether the interior impulses I experience are really of His good pleasure. Thus the will signified acts as a check, a guarantee, and as an interpreter of the will of good pleasure. Moreover, this is the general economy of God's plan in the organization of the Church, to give me in regard to what is external: laws, institutions, sacraments, etc., the sensible means which contains, checks, and guarantees the inward, living, and invisible elements.

Those who have the misfortune to separate the two sides of the divine will condemn themselves either to perish in Phariseeism, by keeping to the will signified only, or else to get lost in the illusions of illuminism or in the aberrations of private judgement, by pretending to listen to nothing but God's will of good pleasure. But since I wish them to be always combined, I am sure of having at all times both the inward impulse and the outward guarantee.

25. Extraordinary ways.—If, however, God is pleased to

[1] Probate spiritus, si ex Deo sint (1 Joan. iv. 1).

call me into extraordinary ways, I need only let myself be led by Him, as soon as I am certain that it is really He who is leading me. But it is to be noted that these extraordinary ways, if they are God's indeed, are never contrary to His ordinary ways; they are only superior to, and include the latter. God reveals them to show especially that the letter killeth where the really life-giving spirit is present. He is pleased to disengage this spirit from the cloudiness and impediments of the letter; he makes it shine forth in its purity and breadth and vigour; and He shows it thus to souls who dwell languidly waiting in the darkness and shadows of the letter.

26. God performs all our works.—Such then is the union of the two wills. The will signified marks out the way to follow in a settled and general way for me; the will of good pleasure bears me along this way, sets me in motion, does a great deal without me, and heartens me by its activity to do the little which I have to do, and which it lays down for me and measures out to me in each case. How I now understand the prophet's words: " It is Thou, O Lord, who hast wrought all our works in us!"[1] God takes me, bears me, guides me, marks out the road for me, measures the distance for me, upholds me, and gives me strength and life. All the time I abide in His good pleasure, I am sure to advance.

This is how passivity leads on to activity, how my receptivity of God's action is the vital condition of my own action, and how, in fine, that unity of activity comes about which is the highest point of my union with God. I ought, indeed, to come to this final goal of unity, where God's movement and mine are no longer two but one. Unity at last! . . .

27. Not a fatalist nor a quietist.—What a distance there is between the Christian acceptance of God's good pleasure and the inert resignation of the fatalist! The fact of acceptance, in their case, means death; in my case, it means life. They sink under their resignation, I rise through my acceptance. The stroke which has fallen leaves them in indifference and inertia; the divine touch brings forth in me the vital energy of duty. They yield to the brutal force of facts; I

[1] Omnia enim opera nostra operatus es nobis (Is. xxvi. 12).

THE WAY: CONCURRENCE OF THE TWO WILLS 233

unite with the vitality of the act of providence, whereby God guides me.

And what a distance there is between Christian acceptance, as we understand it, and the barren quietism of certain heretics! They reckon on God so as to have nothing to do themselves, and I reckon upon Him to have the strength to do everything by Him. They look for an absorption by Him, not for an impulse from Him; I wait for the union of my activity with His action, so as to attain to the union of my life with His life. Their way of conceiving everything connected with God lowers and annihilates that which they are, and that which they have from Him; as for me, I conceive of the divine secret as the source of my uplifting, the perfection of my being, and as the cause of my happiness.

CHAPTER VI

Human Resolutions: Their Sterility

28. Broken resolutions.—29. Human activity.—30. Practices of my own choosing.—31. Ruins.

28. Broken resolutions.—Now, a glance at my past life and at my present state. In the past, what a number of barren resolutions! . . . how many endeavours ended badly because they began badly! How often, after being first urged by some truly divine impulse, I have fallen back into the barren fuss of human agitation! During a retreat, for instance, or a feast, or in certain particular circumstances, some divine touch may have stirred my heart. If I had only been able to correspond simply, faithfully, with the energetic calmness of a sincerity which would have kept me in conformity with God, leaning on Him, and guided by Him!

But I was so quickly carried away with the *human* impulse! . . . I gave up leaning upon God, and straightway I found myself plunged in resolutions and regulations, in practices of prayer and of mortification, in which eagerness was at strife with profusion and confusion, and in which I was heaping up indiscretion upon imprudence. This torrent of resolutions had two very grave defects. For, in reality, their agitation was a proof that their impulse came from self and had no longer any source in God. I was reckoning on myself, and I was leaning on my own resolutions to *determine* the flow of good: and all this, just as if the least movement of the divine life had not to be created in me by the anticipations of life-giving mercy.

Their agitation next signifies that, being born of myself, this impulse continued to wish to live in myself. I was reckoning on myself, and I was leaning upon my own resolutions to measure and to sustain God's action: just as if it were not God's action which had to sustain, to contain, and to measure me.

Thus, through the deceptive impulse of my nature, I was led to have faith in myself twice over; my starting-point and my place of arrival were both set within me, instead of remaining in God. This is the twofold weakness of this kind of resolution.

29. Human activity.—These resolutions have thus cast me into my own selfish action, into my own separate initiative, into the sterile commotion of human agitation, neither animated nor directed by God. It was my own action which took the upper hand, and claimed to mark out the way, and to set the limit to God's action. It meant leaning on myself and trusting in myself. Good God! how everything was then turned upside down! How could I wonder at the fragility and the uselessness of all the scaffolding? It was not of Thy building, and all my human work was but vanity, *in vanum laboraverunt*.

30. Practices of my own choosing.—And this misfortune happens to me too often. I try to find penances of my own choosing, devotional exercises of my own choosing, employments and virtues of my own choosing; and, at the same time, I forget, I neglect, and I refuse to look at and to accept the penances which God lays upon me day by day, and perhaps I murmur; I complain of the sacrifices which He lays upon me, in changes of weather, in the perverseness of men, and in corporal infirmities or spiritual trials. Why am I so taken up with myself, and so little with Him? so anxious

to make a commotion, and so little careful to correspond with Him ? What a number of touches, impulses, and good inspirations I misunderstand, put on one side, and make of no effect ! What God sends me is so exactly fitting for my soul's needs, and answers so precisely to my wants ! What I choose by natural instinct possesses the double defect of being in opposition to God's action and of not being in harmony with the needs of my divine growth. Thus, what I do under the pretence of piety is precisely what is in contradiction with piety within me.

31. Ruins.—Then, am I not to make any more resolutions ? They must be made, of a truth, but not resolutions of this kind. For it is a fact, that these resolutions have hitherto had the effect of casting me into diversity and division, into being encumbered and agitated, and of giving me over to my personal action, and of hindering God's action. The fact is that too few of these resolutions have been kept, and that their effect has been quite null. But one result has remained, and that a very unwholesome one ; it is the habit of breaking one's promises to God. How many promises have been made, renewed, and reiterated, with protestations of fidelity, and pledging one's honour in the most solemn circumstances ! . . . And of all this nothing remains but . . . ruins ! ruined promises, ruined pledges, and ruined honour ! When the *will* is not from God, the *act* of man is worthy of man.

Nothing can be more deplorable. It is better, much better, indeed, not to make any vow than to make one and not to keep it. There is nothing that perverts a soul, nothing that deprives it of reverence for God and sacred things and for itself, nothing which dulls every lofty feeling and every sustained energy, nothing which destroys the keen sense of faith and of all virtues, nothing that warps uprightness of judgement and feeling and action, so much as the unfortunate habit of making promises to God and not keeping them. Further, it is not uncommon to find in those who are far from being religious a foundation of uprightness, an energy of resolution, a keen sense of honour, in which truth works wonders when it is revealed. It will never work such results in those who are accustomed to promise much and to perform little.

CHAPTER VII

Human Resolutions: Their Folly

32. The example of St. Peter.—33. God so well knows my needs.—34. I know so little.—35. Negligence.

32. The example of St. Peter.—Then, how foolish am I! As soon as God claims the right of guiding my progress and of carrying me, it is folly on my part to want to act of myself, before Him, and apart from Him; this is casting myself out of His arms. It is pretending to remonstrate with Him, to anticipate Him, and to direct Him. This was St. Peter's mistake in the episode already recalled,[1] wherein, urged on by his human affection, he allowed himself to be so far carried away as to remonstrate with his Master. His human impulse was fatal to him, though he was a man of unselfish sincerity and unhesitating generosity. It was this impulse which afterwards led him to his denial, and which in the actual circumstances brought down upon him the sharp reproach! "Go behind Me, Satan, thou art a scandal unto Me!" (Matt. xvi. 23). A severe reprimand, and hard words indeed, which show how the Man-God detests human impulse; words such as God addresses to every soul which desires to walk by itself, to anticipate His action, and which is thereby a hindrance to Him. How often have I deserved such a reproach?

33. God so well knows my needs.—There is no greater folly. What! I know that God is my light, my activity, my strength, and my life; I know that He is my Father, anxious for my progress, careful of my sanctification, and desirous of bearing me in His arms; I know that He tempers His action according to the actual state of my soul, that He will never permit me to be tempted beyond my powers, and that He will only suffer temptation so far as it will be really profitable to my soul;[2] I know that He is infinitely wise, that

---

[1] See Part I, Book III, § 12.
[2] Fidelis autem Deus est, qui non patietur vos tentari supra id quod potestis. sed faciet etiam cum tentatione proventum, ut possitis sustinere (1 Cor. x. 13).

He sees into my inward state, my needs, the way to lead me, the happiest means, the dangers to be shunned, the end to be attained, infinitely better than I ; I know that He desires my perfection a thousand times more than I, and that this is the bitter trial of His love ; I know all this . . . and yet I am so imprudent, so mad, as to tear myself from His arms in order to walk by myself ! . . . And it is to go to God that I fling myself out of His arms ! . . . Can any madness be more lamentable ? . . .

34. I know so little.—What do I, indeed, know of the real needs of my soul ? What do I know of the remedies it requires, and of the food that will do it good ? My soul, my infirmities, my weaknesses, my capacities, what mysteries are all these to me ! . . . When I claim to cure myself, to take care of my soul, to strengthen it, and to raise it, I pile up imprudence and error and failure one above the other. But God knows my soul so well, and loves it so much ! . . . And His care and His action are always proportioned to its state. " Being incapable," says St. John of the Cross,[1] " of rising by its own strength to the level of the supernatural, the soul is borne thither and established there by God alone, when it gives Him full consent. Once more, to act of oneself is to put a hindrance, as far as one can, in the way of the communication of God—*i.e.*, of His Spirit ; it is to stop short at one's own work, which is quite opposed, and quite inferior, to the work of the Almighty ; it is what is very rightly called ' extinguishing the Spirit ' " (1 Thess. v. 19).

35. Negligence.—Another folly, which is unfortunately quite as human, and which must be avoided with as much care as the agitation of forming resolutions apart from God, is neglecting to form any resolutions, or scarcely any. These are man's two excesses : wishing to act apart from God, and wishing not to act at all with God. If I am not allowed to misjudge the operation of God's good pleasure for the fulfilment of His will signified, it is just as little in order for me to set on one side His will signified, under the pretext of submitting to His will of good pleasure. The one must not be separated from the other. I shall not save myself without

[1] *The Ascent of Mount Carmel*, Book III, ch. xii.

God, but neither shall I be saved without myself. As soon as He signifies His orders to me, it is because He expects work from me. I must then determine to give it Him. If it is not a good thing to wish to anticipate God, neither is it a good thing to hang back. He requires me to follow Him. Following does not mean going before, nor does it mean stopping where I am. It means that I must act, but in consequence of, and in conformity with an action which precedes and governs mine. Ah, if I only knew how to follow ! . . . to follow God ! . . . If only, in fine, the two contrary waverings of my nature in the direction of the agitation of pride which desires to go without God, and in the direction of the slumber of slothfulness which would let God go forward without myself, if these two waverings could settle down into the one vital activity which is called " following God !" . . . To live on God, by God, in God, for God ! . . .

CHAPTER VIII

Christian Resolutions

36. The ease of the Christian's walk.—37. God's yoke.—38. Hope in God.—39. Sobriety in resolutions.—40. Unity.—41. Fitness.

36. The ease of the Christian's walk.—O my God ! how much greater is the simplicity and ease of true piety ! " My yoke is sweet and My burden is light," says the Master of piety to everyone. I must always begin by receiving God's action, so that my action may be animated thereby ; and keep hold of His hand, so that my hand may be supported and guided by His. I shall be diligent to refuse Him submission as little as possible, so that my submission may enable me to correspond as much as possible with Him in my actions ; I shall be on the watch to be animated and guided by Him, so that I may act by Him, with Him, and for Him. How simple is such a disposition ! and not only simple, but strong ! What progress one makes, when, like a little child, one allows oneself to be carried in God's arms ! What ease, what security, and what vigour there will be in my little steps of

THE WAY: CONCURRENCE OF THE TWO WILLS

active piety, when I keep hold of God's hand by the acceptance of passive piety! How fully is the duty of the will signified fulfilled, when I am led thereto by the working of the will of good pleasure! How full of life is my action when it is animated by God's!

37. *God's yoke.*—And it is to this union and to this working that the Saviour invites me. "O thou," He says to me, "who hast so many burdens and labours, come unto Me. Why dost thou remain agitated and isolated in the endeavours of a work beyond thy powers, and crushed under a burden that is too heavy for thee? Come unto Me, and do not remain within thyself; unite with Me, and stay not alone in thy trouble and beneath thy load. Leave the yoke, or rather the collar of thy work, which thou makest for thyself and puttest upon thyself in thine agitation. That is what is hard, what injures thee and crushes thee, because thou art carrying it alone, and because it is not proportioned to thy strength and thy vocation. Take My yoke upon thee; Mine, I say, which I Myself have prepared for thee, which I have made to fit thee, and proportioned to thy strength and thy vocation.

"It is a yoke and not a collar, for I desire to bear it with thee, I desire it to rest upon Me all the time it is upon thee, and on Me much more than upon thee. I desire to be with thee always in thy toil, and I will not unload My burden upon thee, but thou mayest unload much of thy burden upon Me. Take My yoke; we will work together, and thou shalt see how this work, shared between us, becomes easy and sweet. What rest shalt thou find for thy soul! With My yoke, how easy is it to move the burdens which I Myself take care in preparing for thee! For if thou bearest My yoke, thou shalt also share My burdens. Thou wilt cease to load thyself with burdens too heavy for thee. I know what thou canst do, and what thou oughtest to do, and I always proportion thy task according to thy strength and to the requirements of thy vocation. Only give it a trial, and thou wilt feel that My yoke is sweet and My burden light."[1]

[1] Venite ad me omnes qui laboratis et onerati estis, et ego reficiam vos. Tollite jugum meum super vos .... et invenietis requiem animabus vestris. Jugum enim meum suave est et onus meum leve (Matt. xi. 28-30).

O my God! I am Thine, save Thou me! (Ps. cxviii. 94). ...
O my soul, be thou, indeed, subject to God! For He is my God and my Saviour! He is my helper, I will not go away from Him. In God is my salvation and my glory: He is the God of my help, and my hope is in God.[1]

38. Hope in God.—Yes! O my God! I desire to keep near Thee, and to lean upon Thee, in order to receive life from Thee. I desire to reckon on Thee and to have faith in Thee, and my hope shall be living and practical. It shall not be a vague sentiment, which is general and indefinite, and without any fixed support. It shall be a concrete reality. At every moment, I will have faith in the present and living action of my God; I will have faith in the operation of the Holy Ghost within me; I will have faith in the charity which God hath in me.[2]

And my faith will be a real and effectual staying of my whole life on God's life, of all my action on God's action, and of each act upon the activity of God.

And with such a definite support, what sureness will my resolutions have at the outset, and what firmness in their execution! Illuminated with this light, how precisely will they correspond with the needs of my soul, how exactly will they fit in with my plan of life! Animated with this activity, what decision there will be at the start, and what vigour in the following up! Sustained by this strength, what energy will there be in resistance, what steadfastness in perseverance! Connected with this fountain of life, what fruits of sanctification will they bring forth in time, and what glorification in eternity!

39. Sobriety in resolutions.—Finally, however, what resolutions are to be taken in practice? for some must be taken. If there be no fixed resolution, duty runs a great risk of remaining nebulous or forgotten. There must be resolutions, but what resolutions?—In general, few are necessary; and these few must be to the point.

---

[1] Verumtamen Deo subjecta esto anima mea . . . quia ipse Deus meus et salvator meus, adjutor meus, non emigrabo. In Deo salutare meum et gloria mea: Deus auxilii mei et spes mea in Deo est (Ps. lxi. 6 *ff*).

[2] Et nos cognovimus et credidimus charitati quam habet Deus in nobis (1 Joan. iv. 16).

There must be few. There are souls which will always go to God by little successive and circumstantial details, which best correspond with the reach of their mind. They must not leave the road which is good for them. Let them walk thus in simplicity, they will reach their end easily. But such souls ought not to overload or to complicate their duties, so as not to get exhausted. Sobriety is the mother of good health.

40. Unity. — Other souls are specially in need of unity. In the perpetual variety of providential occurrences and of professional duties, they require a governing view, a synthetic idea, by the help of which they may direct their lives. Details kill them, unity gives them life. They cannot find their way through the forests; they love the mountain-tops from which there is a wide view. They, too, need to see, and to see practical duty clearly in its details and applications; they want to see it, to love it, and to carry it out in its finest and most delicate circumstances. But they get their view of things by way of unity. In this light, they see; apart from it, they feel that their eyes are dim and defective. Of a truth, it is to such that this work is constantly addressed. It is clear that the resolutions of such souls have to be more and more simplified and to become more and more unified. Since they are only able to grasp the value of details by contemplating them in their organic position and in the connexion of their functions, it is important for them to acquire that unity of glance which is necessary to them. The next chapter will show, more especially for such souls, how this movement in the direction of unity is carried out.

41. Fitness.—Whatever may be the case, whether one has to walk by way of details or by way of unity, it is important that the resolution or resolutions should be really practical and correspond well with the actually necessary part of one's duty. If my resolution does not fall too far short of duty owing to cowardice, and if it does not overstep it by exaggeration, it will be good and effectual. Let it be, then, on the one hand proportioned to my strength, and on the other to my obligations; let it be measured both by what I can, and by what I must, do; what I can and must do now in the present state of my vital resources and of my responsibilities towards God,

CHAPTER IX

The Fundamental Resolution

42. The one primary and governing resolution.—43. No uneasiness as to the present.—44. Nor as to the future.—45. Prayer for confidence.

42. The one primary and governing resolution.—Since I am persistently searching for unity and I want to advance in this way, I must above all else take and keep THE ONE PRIMARY AND GOVERNING RESOLUTION . . . FROM WHICH MUST SPRING . . . IN SUCCESSION . . . AT THE PROPER TIME . . . AND ON WHICH MUST BE CONSTANTLY SUPPORTED . . . THOSE PARTICULAR RESOLUTIONS . . . WHICH BECOME NECESSARY ACCORDING TO THE PROGRESS OF THE INTERIOR LIFE.

The one resolution which gives and maintains life, belongs to passive piety; it is the practical expression of it. The variable resolutions which arise and are maintained through the influence of the fundamental resolution, belong to active piety; they are its actual and concrete application. Their mutual union realizes the living progress of piety as a whole.

The one and unifying, living and life-giving resolution is that which I am beginning to understand a little better, and the fruits of which I desire to taste; it is that of keeping, by practical trustfulness, in correspondence with God, of taking care, by means of acceptance, to lay myself open to His action, and, in my co-operation, of being diligent to preserve an effectual reliance upon Him.

This resolution will afford an entrance to the divine activity; and through the impulse of its working, I shall be led at the proper time to take the resolution or resolutions in detail, which are necessitated by duty. Thus, being born of God and not of myself, supported on God and not on myself, these particular resolutions will have all the sobriety and truth which befits them. Thus I shall avoid overloading, encumbrance, and illusion. I shall have a better chance of holding good by God's help to what I have undertaken by God's urgency. In my resolutions, there must be nothing of mine for myself only, nothing of my wandering imagination, and nothing of self-will. "In our life, there is nothing that comes of man, and that is why all is of God," says the Venerable Mother Chappuis.[1] What comes of man does not hold good ; what is of God is alone strong and lasting.

43. *No uneasiness as to the present.*—And now, so far as the actual state of my soul is concerned, I see how much correction must be made in two defects, which are two kinds of uneasiness : uneasiness as to the present, and uneasiness as to the future.

As to the present, my good will is easily swayed by a sort of trembling anxiety, which deceitfully tries to persuade me that I shall be unequal to doing my duty. I fear that I shall be too distracted, or too cowardly, or too weak. Yes, of a truth, I shall always be distracted, cowardly, and weak, if left to myself. Never can I distrust myself too much, never can I be too strongly persuaded that duty is above me. But, after all, is that any reason for being uneasy ? Distrust of oneself is not uneasiness, it is just the opposite. Distrust of oneself makes its appeal to confidence in God, and confidence in God leaves no room for uneasiness.

What does uneasiness mean ?—It means that I persist in having faith in myself ; for if I am uneasy, it is only just to the extent that I feel what a ruinous thing it is to be relying on myself. Then, whence comes this uneasiness ?—It comes of my incorrigible mania for relying on myself more than on God. I try to find in myself the enlightenment, the impulse, and the strength which are indispensable to duty, and I fail to discover them and become uneasy and full of doubt. When shall I be able to be straightforward ? When shall I learn to have recourse first of all to God and to rely upon Him ? . . . WE ARE ALWAYS DOING ENOUGH WHEN WE KEEP IN GOD'S HANDS . . . because from His hands we always receive in abundance what is necessary for our duty.

44. *Nor as to the future.*—The disturbing anxiety of looking ahead on the road, of making up suppositions and arrangements for the future, is also a want of trust. The future is not yours, Sir, it is God's. Therefore " be not solicitous for

[1] In a circular of the *Visitandines of Troyes,* p. 42.

to-morrow: for the morrow will be solicitous for itself. Sufficient for the day is the evil thereof " (Matt. vi. 34). It is not my business to regulate my progress. I have to follow God, so as not to walk in darkness, and to have the light of life.[1] I need only have one solicitude, if I may have so much as one; since St. Paul tells us to be solicitous as to *nothing*,[2] and St. Peter exhorts me to cast *all* my care upon Him, who hath care of me.[3] The two disciples, like their Master, condemn uneasy solicitude. But, if indeed there be one calm, grave, and reasonable solicitude, it is that of the present moment. Let me be careful to keep in God's hand; and, in His hand, to do my present duty; that is quite sufficient for my life.

45. A prayer for confidence.—Dear Master, give me the grace to be able to wait, to understand, and to follow Thine impulse, to be able to abide in Thee, so that I may act by Thee and with Thee. Give me the sincerity and the pliancy to correspond with Thine action. Give me the ability to rest in confidence, so that I may be sure of my work. Grant that I may live by Thee, for Thee, and in Thee. Grant that I may avoid the two great sunken reefs, being agitated apart from Thee, and resting far from Thee. O God, let there be no agitation of presumptuous pride in me, nor the repose of careless idleness, but let there be a sincere and living correspondence between my action and Thine. Keep me far from the fits and starts of Naturalism, from the negligent indolence of Quietism, and give me the living union of the Christian.

[1] Qui sequitur me non ambulat in tenebris, sed habebit lumen vitæ (Joan. viii. 12).
[2] *Nihil* solliciti estis (Phil. iv. 6).
[3] *Omnem* sollicitudinem vestram projicientes in eum, quoniam ipsi cura est de vobis (1 Pet. v. 7).

CHAPTER X

Concurrence Restored

46. Deviation.—47. The consequences.—48. To be accepted.—49. Human contrition.—50. Divine detestation.—51. Divine reparation.—52. Thank Thee, O God!

46. Deviation.—Desiring to advance towards the end of my life, I feel how I have to maintain and to improve within me the state of living correspondence with God's action. O God! if I could only keep myself in permanent contact and in perfect accord with Thee!... But, O dear Lord, how many are my deviations! How often the impulses or the inertia of my nature take me away from Thee! And being far from Thee, I cease to be animated by Thee, and I fall.

When I fall thus, what am I to do? Must I be uneasy?—Not at all, this would only be a fresh folly, a new deviation, and sometimes, a fall within a fall. Uneasiness is such a wrong to Thee, O my God! What then am I to do?—The thing to be done is to accept as frankly and as promptly as I can the casting away of my sin with all its penal consequences. Certainly, my deviation was never intended by God, but He has permitted it; and it is immediately followed by certain punitive consequences, which are willed by Him. Often God allows a sin to occur to deduce from it a means of healing: there are evils which can only be cured by a fall. " It must needs be that scandals come " (Matt. xviii. 7).

47. The consequences.—The penal consequences of a sin are, for instance, outward humiliation before other people, inward humiliation before oneself and God, often very grave reaction upon one's soul, which is shaken, weakened, dazed, and the very extensive reactions that a sin sometimes has upon the outward events of one's life, etc. . . . For I never know how far or how seriously the echoes of a sin may resound. These consequences are willed by God; and thus it is that He shows His detestation of sin. He did not will the sin, but He willed its punishment. His will, therefore, is in the latter. The sin is my act; the penal consequences of the sin are God's action, the action of His good pleasure, which immediately avenges the disorder of my act.

48. To be accepted.—In order to destroy the deviation of my own action, I have only to unite with God's action; and I unite with it by accepting it. To say to God " I thank Thee " for the humiliation of my sins, is the true way to learn the ways of justification.[1] In the consequences that avenge my sin, is the whole of God's will. If I accept them, without worrying as to what they may be, submitting to what, in the case in point, is God's good pleasure, I am as practically, as truly, and as intimately as possible united with God.

In this practice of saying " Thank Thee " for the humiliation of a sin, there is a potency of repentance and of calmness which are really divine. All that I could say, ask for, or promise God, all that I could do under the impulses of repentance and regret, will never attain to the height of such a simple acceptance. All these wonderful fireworks are too often only my *human* impulse, my own special way of detesting sin. And this is not at all the right way; because what I am led to detest and regret is just what I ought to accept, that is to say, humiliation.

49. Human Contrition.—And when I detest the consequences of a sin, and the annoyances and discomforts of which it is the cause, I too often keep up secret attachments with my inward disorder. This means that, in reality, I am detesting the avenging action of God, and that I continue to love my own bad action. Of a truth, it is a singular sort of contrition, which would come pretty nearly to irony, were it not for the existence of human folly, which somewhat excuses such a grave misunderstanding. This is what may be called *my* contrition. It is, indeed, too much mine, for it unfortunately hardly comes from God.

Is it to be wondered at, if this human contrition results in such poor fruits of divine conversion? In how many cases is this so-called contrition a sort of pillow for the conscience, helping it to slumber in its own evil! I feel that I have a certain detestation, and without being willing to examine too closely upon what it is brought to bear, I soothe myself as to

[1] Bonum mihi quia humiliasti me, ut discam justificationes tuas (Ps. cxviii. 71).

THE WAY: CONCURRENCE OF THE TWO WILLS

my inward dispositions. Thus I remain in a state of soul, which is rather like that of the thief who has just been caught, and who is very grieved, not at having stolen, but at being caught. This is a dangerous disposition, and, after a sin, it tends to make barren what God does at once to cure the sin.

50. Divine detestation.—But when I accept the penal consequences of my wickedness, I become permeated with God's own detestation of sin; and if I accept them fully and without reservation, I appropriate and make my own all of God's detestation for my sin. Thus I detest it, no longer in the way in which I can detest it myself, but as God detests it; and not merely as God detests sin in general, but as He now detests this particular sin into which I have fallen, and to the same extent as He detests it Himself. Therefore, when I have been unable to accept God's action (hence arise all my sins), I have only to say: "I thank Thee, O God, I thank Thee for this humiliation," and at once I find myself once more in the arms of God, united with Him for penalizing the disorder which has momentarily separated me from Him. This act fills the soul with so much peace, that one is almost tempted to sing with the Church: *O felix culpa!* . . .[1]

51. Divine reparation.—By this act of acceptance I am united with God, not only for the detestation of my sin, but also for its reparation. Repentance is divine, and so is firm purpose. Do I say, firm purpose? Here, it is not only a case of firm purpose to reconstruct in myself the building of divine glory, which has been broken into or broken down by my sin; it is, in fact, the work of building, immediately resumed and restored by the hand of God. He Himself repairs the breaches of the sin; and then, what a reparation is His! He, indeed, knows what harm has been done to the divine edifice of my life; He sees it, takes the full measure of it, and nothing escapes His eye. As for me, I never know how far the cracks and injuries, the breaches and destruction, may extend. I see all this so much the less, because the first result of sin is to blind me. Therefore, I am incapable of making fitting repairs.

But since God is there, not only punishing but repairing,

[1] See *L'Art d'utiliser ses fautes,* by Père Tissot. Librairie Oudin.

I have no more embarassment nor uneasiness. I have only to accept His action, to unite with Him, and to follow up His work with my co-operation. And immediately I see the divine edifice being restored according to the true plan of my creation; and very quickly the evil is repaired, not only the actual evil of the particular sin which I have just committed, but also the evil source from which it arose. For God knows how to take advantage of acts to create habits. He is not satisfied with plastering up the cracks, He starts afresh on the foundations. For His glory, He is not satisfied with a tottering building, covered with a deceptive coat of whitewash. He likes a thing to be solid; what He builds, He builds upon the rock; and what has to be repaired, He repairs thoroughly ... if we leave Him alone. O my God! when shall I know how to leave Thee to build? ... When shall I be able, with a good " Thank Thee " to join in Thy work of building and repair? Oh, what reparatory results follow from a good " I thank Thee !"

52. Thank Thee, O God.—Does this mean that the practice of saying, " I thank Thee," for the penal consequences of my sin constitutes the whole of the essence of contrition, and sums up all that need be done in the way of reparation due to God?—By no means. In speaking of means in Part III, I shall see the necessity of the sacrament of Penance, and the necessity, the nature, and the motives of contrition. Here I am only anxious as to one thing: to restore correspondence with divine action as quickly as possible. The sin has interrupted it, and the " *Thank Thee* " in my case, is the most swift and simple and just proceeding to bring me back into contact with God.

O that " Thank Thee," that divine " Thank Thee ! " how great it is, how fruitful, how powerful, how holy. . . . It contains all the treasures of life and strength, of calmness and peace. It is the inexhaustible mine, in which I find God. I will say it, and say it always, in joy, in sorrow, in ascending, in falling, always and everywhere : " I Thank Thee ! " . . .

Bonum mihi Domine! . . . Thus, O my God, shall I ab de in Thee and Thou in me, and at last I shall bear fruit, yea, much fruit.[1]

---

[1] Qui manet in me et ego in co, hic fert fructum multum (Joan. xv. 5).

PART III
THE MEANS

PRELIMINARY

1. The necessity of means.—2. God's instruments.—3. My instruments.—4. In Him we live and move and be.—5. What is essential and what changes.—6. Division.

1. **The necessity of means.**—I know the end, I know the way, and I have a real desire to walk in this way towards this end ; what do I need ?—Means. For means are required for journeying by this way to this end. I must eat God's bread to follow the way of His will until the coming of His kingdom and the hallowing of His name. Knowing the end and the way, and having the means, I shall possess everything. And what are these means?

At the very beginning of this work,[1] the fundamental principle showed me that, between God and myself, every being, and every movement of any being coming into contact with my life, is destined to serve as an instrument of my growth for the glory of God. This principle had to be declared at the outset, so as to disengage it from the notions of the end and of the way. The knowledge of this principle, as I have been convinced, is indispensable for the understanding of the plan of my life, of order and disorder, and of the laws of my ascent and work.

But this general notion, which is essential to the direction of my life, although it may suffice to show me the plan, does not suffice to realize its execution. The knowledge of the architect who draws up the plan, and that of the contractor who controls the work, must be completed by the skill of the workman who handles the tools. After having studied the plan of my life in Part I, and the rules of working in Part II, in Part III I have to study the procedure of execution, the handling of creatures which are the instruments.

2. **God's instruments.**—And whose instruments are creatures ?—They are the instruments of the workers who are

[1] See Part I, Book I, ch. vi.

building the temple of God's glory. Consequently, they are above all instruments of God, who is the principal workman; and next, they are my instruments, since I am called to be the underworkman.

God knows the use of the instruments which He employs, and He knows how to employ them. It is not at all my business to control His use of them; but what is altogether my business, what to a certain extent is necessary for me, is to look at the contact and the result upon myself of the work of these instruments. Now, whatever in fact the instrument used by God may be, the constant effect of it is grace. With regard to myself, then, grace is the immediate divine means, the sole and constant means, and it is this which it is above all my interest to know, so that at this point of contact I may succeed in bringing my means into harmony with God's.

3. My instruments.—As to those creatures which are my instruments and which I have to handle, it is necessary for me to know their use, their management, and above all, that my faculties should acquire an aptitude and facility for using them well. But, no one is a good workman unless he has acquired a trained eye and hand, which, combined with a love for his trade, bring forth excellent work. And to train the taste, the eye, and the hand, there are in each trade certain procedures, and certain trade secrets. Such also there are to form the sovereign aptitude and skill of soul, which is called piety. What, then, I have to consider, at least in their general economy, are the expedients and practices calculated to put my faculties in a position to make a right use of creatures. I say: " at least in their general economy"; for hitherto, having confined my attention to the main outlines of the end and the way, I shall continue to do the same with regard to the means.

What, then, are the practices which will put me in a position to make a right use of creatures?—I know that the work of my divine growth necessitates a twofold operation; on the one hand, disengagement from creatures, and on the other, adaptation to the divine. Hence, there are two orders of pious practices, the one destined to detach me from things here below, the others to attach me to things above. Those which accustom me to detachment are the practices of penance; those which accustom me to meet with God are the practices of prayer. Hence, I shall have to consider the general principles concerning the practices of penance and the practices of piety.

4. **In Him we live, and move, and be.**—I have seen that the fulness of my essential end lies in the glory of God; that the sovereign rule of my activity lies in His will; and I see that my great and vital means lies in His grace. End, principle, and means, God is all these to me. In Him we live, for He is the means, the food of our life; in Him we move, for He is the rule and first principle of our activity; and in Him we are, for He is the end in which we rest.[1] His glory is the end of my being, His will is the rule of my activity, and His grace is the means of my life. He is the end, He is the beginning, He is the middle, He is all. My God and my all.

5. **What is essential and what changes.**—My satisfaction is united with and subordinate to God's glory; and my personal action must be united with and subordinate to that whereby He animates and governs me. In the same way, my devotional practices must be united with and subordinate to grace. Thus, at the end, on the way, and in the means, God is everywhere essential, first, and master; and I am everywhere dependent, secondary, the servant.

Further, I have seen how my satisfaction, at first going astray from God, returns, gets swallowed up, and is transformed into unity, leaving behind the fallacies of *the human* in annihilation. I have also seen how my action, at first agitated apart from the divine action, returns, gets swallowed up, and is transformed into that of God, destroying the independence of human activity. I have now to see how, in the same way, the multiplicity of my spiritual practices is concentrated and vivified in the unity of the influences of grace. In the three relations of the end, the way, and the means, there is the same movement of subordination, transformation, and union, and there is the same ascent towards unity.

[1] In ipso enim vivimus et movemur et sumus (Acts xvii. 28).

God's glory, God's will, God's grace, by making me more and more supernatural, destroy progressively and annihilate, in my satisfaction and action and means, all that is born of myself and that deviates from God; they swallow up, change, and unite that which comes from God and that which is made for eternal union. Thus, I see the three clouds of my mortality dissolve in the brightness of the broad sunshine which is shed upon my soul; multiplicity vanishes before unity, and the creature adheres to its Creator; and thus God, who was at the beginning Himself first of all, ends by changing all into Himself.[1] He is all in all.[2]

6. Division.—This Part will be divided into three Books:

Book I, on the Practices of Penance.

Book II, on the Exercises of Piety.

Book III, on Grace.

[1] Ipse est ante omnes et omnia in ipso constant (Col. i. 17).
[2] Ut sit Deus omnia in omnibus (1 Cor. xv. 28).

BOOK I

THE PRACTICES OF PENANCE

In the first place I am going to study the means that are those of man, beginning with the means of correcting my former conduct, the stripping off the old man, which is the man of corruption, bad desires, and of error. Next, the means of spiritual renovation, the putting on of the new man, who according to God, is created in justice and holiness of truth.[1] The means of stripping off are the practices of penance, the means of putting on are the practices of prayer. It is necessary to use these two sorts of means, and it is a good thing to unite them,[2] since I must get away from creatures to rise to God ; and the great operations of the evil spirit in me are only victoriously striven against by the union of these two means.

The practices of prayer, or spiritual exercises, will be the subject of the next Book ; in this one, I am about to consider the practices of penance ; their value, their function, and their use.

I consist of mind, heart and senses ; by mind, heart, and senses, I commit sins which must be expiated, I contract adherences which must be destroyed, and I undergo degradations which must be repaired. Hence, I need practices of penance ; I need them for the senses, and for the heart and mind. The work of expiation to God and of reparation within me is done : in the senses, by mortification ; in the heart, by self-denial ; in the mind, by humility. Therefore penance is a general necessity : practices of mortification for the senses, of self-denial for the heart, and of humility for the mind ; and this will be the subject-matter of the following chapters.

[1] Deponere vos secundum pristinam conversationem veterem hominem qui corrumpitur secundum desideria erroris. Renovamini autem spiritu mentis vestræ et induite novum hominem qui secundum Deum creatus est in justitia et sanctitate veritatis (Eph. iv. 22-24).
[2] Bona est oratio cum jejunio (Tob. xii. 8).

CHAPTER I

Penance

1. Justice.—2. Penalties.—3. Mercy.—4. Their union.—5. Redemption.—6. *A limpleo quæ desunt.* ...

1. **Justice.**—According to the remark of St. Augustine which was previously quoted; the loveliness of order is so great that the ugliness of sin cannot endure for a single moment without being repaired by the beauty of punishment.[1] Sovereign justice has its rights, which are imprescriptible. It incessantly adjusts, and cannot exist without adjusting, the activity of free creatures to eternal order. If I do well, it immediately answers my action with rewards of merit. In proportion as I glorify God, I enter into participation of the beatitudes of time and of eternity. If I do evil, and if I rob God of the glory which is His due, justice immediately punishes me for the violation of order; I become subject to penalties to the extent in which I have fallen into iniquity. Justice, then, imposes penance upon me as an expiation of the disorder of my life.

2. **Penalties.**—But why does justice have recourse to suffering as an expiation for sin?—The movement that turns me away from God is a false impulse towards pleasure in creatures; and it is because I desire to enjoy unduly that I deserve to be brought back to order by chastisement. Evil is corrected by its opposite. So far as I turn away towards irregular delights, so far shall I have to undergo torments.[2] This is the law of time, and it is the law of eternity. Such are the demands of justice, which exactly counterbalances the pleasures of sin with the pains of its punishment; so that the injury inflicted upon the divine glory by enjoyment is repaired by suffering. " Man always in the end pays God what he

---

[1] See Part I, Book II, § 44.
[2] Quantum glorificavit se et in deliciis fuit, tantum date illi tormentum et luctum (Apoc. xviii. 7).

THE MEANS: THE PRACTICES OF PENANCE

owes Him," says St. Augustine again.[1] "If he does not pay it by doing what he ought, he pays it by suffering as he ought; hence, in one way or another, his debt is paid." And justice will never let anyone off paying the uttermost farthing.[2] It can no more do away with a penalty than it can do away with a merit. Its inexorable function is to adjust, and it always exactly adjusts merits and demerits.

3. Mercy.—But God is not only one-handed. All the ways of the Lord are mercy and truth (Ps. xxiv. 10). If He has a hand of strict justice, which is inflexible in its adjustments, He has also a gentle hand of mercy, which is supremely supple in its kindly dispositions: if it be the mission of justice to ensure the reparation of the essential order of the divine glory, it is the lot of mercy to repair the soul itself. Its part is to raise up what is fallen, to make good what has been destroyed, and to restore what is lost. God willed to show man mercy, whilst He only did justice to the angels. He did not repair the angels, but He has repaired man. And for this restoration mercy has its kindly dispositions, its delicate invitations, and its infinitely adorable discoveries of goodness. If nothing deceives justice, nothing tires mercy. The latter is as unrelaxing in its benevolence as the former is in its strictness.

4. Their union.—And according to God's designs with regard to mankind, His two hands are destined to cross each other constantly over the head of the sinner. The blessings of mercy are intended to harmonize with the severities of justice. God desires that mercy and truth should always be meeting within me, and that justice and peace should always be embracing.[3] And it is just on the ground of penance that the meeting and embracing occur. Justice will relax none of its penalties; but mercy takes up these very penalties, and renders them reparatory of my life, and meritorious of a better

---

[1] Non sinitur anima non reddere debitum. Aut enim reddit bene utendo quod accepit, aut re ldit amittendo quo bene uti noluit. Itaque si non reddit faciendo justitiam, reddit patiendo miseriam; quia in utroque verbum illud debiti sonat (*De Lib. Arbit.*, Book III. § 44).

[2] Non exies inde, donec reddas novissimum quadrantem (Matt. v. 26).

[3] Misericordia et veritas obviaverunt sibi, justitia et pax osculatæ sunt (Ps. lxxxiv. 11).

life. At the same time as I discharge the debts of justice, my being rises once more to the heights from which it had fallen.

Thus every sin demands a penalty, and every penalty is first of all vindicatory, for such are the requirements of justice; and then, it is remedial, for such at least are the intentions of mercy.

I cannot withdraw from the requirements of justice, but I am able not to correspond with the intentions of mercy. And if, as one of the damned, I undergo, in spite of myself, the penalty of justice, my penance is sterile so far as I am concerned, since it does not make good the degradations of my life. When, on the contrary, by my free concurrence, I adapt myself to redemptive designs, my penance becomes both expiatory and reparatory, it satisfies God and purifies my being, it takes away the evil and builds up the good, it discharges debts and creates merits.

Is it not henceforward a matter of supreme interest for me to know how to adapt myself to the work of reparation, so that the vindicatory requirements may never be separated from the reparatory benefits? O my God! how I long, not to expiate as a reprobate, but to make reparation as one of the predestined!

5. Redemption.—But an intervention of incomprehensible love was further necessary to facilitate the encounter and embrace of justice and mercy. It is in the Person of the Redeemer that this wonder came about, and it was fulfilled on the Cross. God became man, and He came to undergo in His human flesh the trials of life and the torments of death, sanctifying both the one and the other, and by the merit of His divinity imparting to the one and to the other an infinite value for expiation and reparation. "He hath borne our infirmities and carried our sorrows. He was wounded for our iniquities, He was bruised for our sins: the chastisement of our peace was upon Him, and by His bruises we are healed" (Is. liii. 4, 5). Hence, it is His Cross that imparts to penalties their true expiatory value and reparatory power.

He has amassed an infinite treasure, and this treasure, from the point of view of its application, has been still further expanded by the merits of the Virgin of Sorrows, and of

THE MEANS: THE PRACTICES OF PENANCE

the martyrs and saints. There is enough to discharge all the debts of justice and to secure the triumph of mercy for all the souls of all the centuries.

6. Adimpleo quæ desunt.—How then shall I succeed in making reparation as one of the predestined?—By uniting with the reparation of the Redeemer.—How am I to unite with such reparation?—By filling up in my flesh those things that are wanting of the sufferings of Christ. His merits are like a beverage which I must drink up by personal practices of penance. When I know how to take and accept purificatory trials in union and in conformity with the Saviour's intentions and with the mind of God, I complete the work of redemption within me, begun for me but not fulfilled without me.

And I may fulfil it, not only in myself and for myself, but also for others. For in saying that he is filling up in his flesh the sufferings of Christ, St. Paul adds that he is doing it for the whole body of the Church.[1] Thus I may have the consolation of doing a penance that will be efficacious both for myself and for the Church.

CHAPTER II

Mortification and Its Function

7. Lost ease and vigour.—8. Expiation and reparation.—9. Mortification.—10. True and false mortification.—11. The hand of Satan and the hand of God.—12. The mind of the Church.—13. The mind of the saints.

7. Lost ease and vigour.—All the powers of my activity should be kept for God, so as to be placed at the service of His glory. And, in order to serve Him, my senses require inward vigour and outward facility : such is the twofold condition of their liberty and of all liberty. But, so far as they are dominated by the fallacies of pleasure, they increasingly lose this twofold condition of their freedom. First of all, they become the slaves of creatures which govern them.

---

[1]. Adimpleo ea quæ desunt passionum Christi in carne mea, pro corpore ejus quod est Ecclesia (Col. i. 24).

If they maintain their inward vigour, they are nevertheless like the prisoner whose hands are chained, and like the bird with birdlime on its wings. The shackles of pleasure deprive them of the outward condition of liberty ; they are no longer at ease in the service of God.

And soon their inward vigour begins to decay. They become heavy, coarse, slow, and idle ; and then, slack, effeminate, and enervated ; and lastly, degeneracy, infirmity, and all sorts of sickness are the extreme consequences of the abuse of pleasure. Degradation destroys the inward part of their liberty. They no longer have the strength which is necessary for the service of the supreme Majesty. Thus my being is lowered and God's glory is frustrated.

8. Expiation and reparation.—The man who allows himself to be cheated by pleasure, feeling that he is lowered in himself and that he owes a debt to God, perceives the necessity of discharging his debt to God and of lifting himself up again. And a deep instinct tells him that pain is the instrument of expiation and reparation. Every soul that wishes to repair the human within and to get back to the divine, is mysteriously impelled to have recourse to sacrifice. And it has recourse thereto with all the more energy according to the depth of its experience of the need of coming out of evil and of rising up in good. The severity of privations and the austerity of sufferings cast a potent spell over it. The love of the saints for that which crucifies the flesh with its vices and concupiscences[1] is a universal characteristic ; they are all crucified with Christ.[2] They are nailed to the Cross, to pay their debts to God and to become free. " We always," says St. Paul, " bear about in our body the mortification of Jesus, that the life also of Jesus may be made manifest in our bodies. For we who live are always delivered unto death for Jesus' sake: that the life also of Jesus may be made manifest in our mortal flesh " (2 Cor. iv. 10, 11). Mortification must be the pathway of life.

9. Mortification.—Mortification means, " Putting to death." To mortify means " to put to death." And what must be mortified ?—" Mortify therefore your members which are

[1] Qui autem sunt Christi, carnem suam crucifixerunt cum vitiis et concupiscentiis (Gal. v. 24).
[2] Christo confixus sum cruci (Gal. ii. 19).

THE MEANS: THE PRACTICES OF PENANCE

upon the earth," replies St. Paul (Col. iii. 5). What! must we put our own bodies to death?—Such is the chastisement which is certainly well deserved by sin; and, as a matter of fact, it is a chastisement which the body has to undergo without any sort of possibility of escape. Nevertheless, it is a chastisement the dispensation of which God reserves to Himself. He alone, by way of duty, of illness, of accidents, or otherwise, understands how to exercise this power of "putting to death."

I have no right of death over that which God has placed within me; I have only the right of life. But there is in me something which comes from me and not from God; I am a man and a sinner. "A man and a sinner, two words," says St. Augustine,[1] "and in these two words there are two things, one from nature, the other from sin; one made by God, the other made by me. And I must destroy what I have made, in order that God may save what He has made." Mortify your members, says St. Paul; and he immediately defines what has to be put to death. Mortify in your members fornication, impurity, and evil concupiscence.[2] What God wills is not the death of the wicked, but the conversion of the wicked.[3] It is not the dead who praise God, but it is the living who bless Him.

10. **True and false mortification.**—What penetrating discernment is needed if my mortification is to distinguish between the man and the sinner in me, between nature and evil, to destroy death and to save life! The climax of mortification is to know how to break the net and to let the bird go free, to kill the microbe and to cure the sick man, to disengage life from death. All mortification is of the true kind, if it breaks down what ought to be broken down, and strengthens what ought to be made stronger.

[1] Homo es iniquus. Duo dixi nomina, duo nomina: homo et iniquus. In istis duobus nominibus, unum est naturæ, alterum culpæ; unum tibi Deus fecit, alterum tu fecisti. Ama quod Deus fecit, oderis quod tu fecisti (Ps. xliv. § 18).

[2] Mortificate ergo membra vestra quæ sunt super terram, fornicationem, immunditiam, libidinem, concupiscentiam malam et avaritiam (Col. iii. 5).

[3] Nolo mortem impii, sed ut convertatur impius a via sua et vivat (Ezech. xxxiii. 11).

False sorts of mortification, for there are false kinds, strike without discernment; and under the impetus of the evil spirit, they easily succeed in breaking down what ought to be preserved, and in preserving what ought to be broken down. Instead of crucifying the vices and concupiscences in the flesh, they kill the man, whilst leaving him his passions, and often increasing the number of his vices.

11. **The hand of Satan and the hand of God.**—No sacrifice is desired for its own sake.[1] The idea of sacrifice for its own sake is Satanic, because it is homicidal. It logically ends in suicide for the individual, and in the abomination of human sacrifices for social communities. What a host of aberrations and of monstrosities history reveals in the course of the ages among all peoples! Everywhere he, whom St. Augustine[2] calls "death's provost," sows death. One of the triumphs that please him most is to take possession of this notion of sacrifice, which is one of the most fundamental of religious notions, and to turn it into an instrument of death. The seal of Satan is infallibly recognized by the fact that it is derogatory to the dignity and integrity of the members and faculties of man; it is destructive of life, and homicidal.

Nothing divine ever degrades. No doubt God sometimes demands the sacrifice of a member, of a faculty, of health, and even of life itself, but He demands it for the sake of one's general improvement. If He inflicts wounds, they are wounds that heal; if He sends death, it is to make life arise out of it. " I will strike, and I will heal " (Deut. xxxii. 39), saith the Lord. In the case of each man, He knows when suffering and death are advantageous to his life, for life and death are subservient to God in the interest of the life of the elect. He therefore sends them according to the designs of His justice and mercy; and, in reality, sickness and death work for life.

12. **The mind of the Church.**—How instructive it is to consult the mind of the Church on this point! In the building of temples and monasteries, in her ceremonies and feasts, in art and science, the Church encourages, exalts, approves,

[1] See Part I, Book III, § 26.
[2] Diabolus præpositus mortis (*De Lib. Arbit.*, Book III, § 29).

THE MEANS: THE PRACTICES OF PENANCE 263

and blesses all that uplifts and ennobles, all that purifies and liberates, all that refines and spiritualizes the senses. She certainly has her own magnificence, but what a distance there is between her chants and the music of the passions, between the rich decoration of a church and that of a boudoir! The world designs everything to give pleasures that enervate, the Church devotes everything to bring about a freedom that uplifts. The object of the world is pleasure, the object of the Church is elevation. Her encouragement is the same for the severity as for the sumptuousness that ennobles; and she has the same anathemas for the cruelty as for the sensualism that degrades. Such is her mind. And this is the explanation of all that she authorizes or forbids by her discipline with regard to the things of the senses. In dwellings and in dress, in food and in rest, in rejoicings and in relaxations, everywhere her language is that of St. Paul: "Brethren, whatsoever things are true, whatsoever modest, whatsoever just, whatsoever holy, whatsoever lovely, whatsoever of good fame, if there be any virtue, if any praise of discipline, think on these things" (Phil. iv. 8).

13. **The mind of the saints.**—What, again, can be more instructive than the mind of the saints?—They were hard on their bodies, and the history of the Church testifies how they were able, in case of necessity, to hand them over to executioners or to penitential sufferings. Whenever God's justice did not demand the sacrifice of health or life, they took care to look after and preserve the vigour of their members. I have already observed[1] how generally hygienic were their mortifications! Soberness in fasting, simplicity of food, the use of bitter edibles, if they run counter to our taste, are yet favourable to purifying the blood; hard beds, short sleep, rough hair shirts, coarse clothing, and the stimulus of the discipline foster its circulation. Thus is the body set free from the heaviness of the animal life and it is kept from bad humours, and becomes both a more obedient and stronger instrument in the service of the soul. Such was the aim of the saints. And this is why their penances bear the two-fold stamp of severity and prudence: severity, to repress ill-

[1] See Part I, Book IV, § 19.

regulated appetites, sensual instincts, and enervating pleasures; prudence, to avoid injuries and disfigurements, weakness and degeneracy.

CHAPTER III

General Rules for Mortification

14. Love that destroys and hatred that preserves.—15. No cowardly sentimentalism.—16. The liberating agent.—17. No degrading cruelty.—18. Necessary cruelty.—19. The remedy.—20. The will to be healed.

14. Love that destroys and hatred that preserves.—I have no right to consent to any degradation of my life. But I may degrade myself, either by an excess of severity, or by an excess of sensuality. Excess in both directions is forbidden. Therefore, in the use of mortifications, I must keep equally far from cowardly sentimentalism and from degrading cruelty. He that loveth his life shall lose it: and he that hateth his life in this world, keepeth it unto life eternal (John xii. 25). There is, then, according to our Saviour's testimony, a love that destroys and a hatred that preserves life. Love that destroys is cowardly sensualism; hatred that preserves, is wise and prudent severity. Therefore, let there be no cowardly love and no cruel hatred. If I have a sense of justice, I shall be able to master the fear of pain with energy; if I have any sense of mercy, I shall be able to avoid striking any destructive blows.

15. No cowardly sentimentalism.—The rebellion of the senses against the spirit demands that they shall be reduced to obedience by being treated as slaves. "Bread, and correction, and work for the slave," says the Holy Ghost. "If he is idle, punish him and put him in irons: if he is faithful, let him be to thee as thy own soul, and treat him as a brother."[1] Therefore, let there be soberness in eating, austerity in correction, perseverance in work, punishment

[1] Panis, et disciplina, et opus servo . . . servo malevolo tortura et compedes; mitte illum in operationem, ne vacet. . . . Si est tibi servus fidelis, sit tibi quasi anima tua; quasi fratrem sic eum tracta (Eccli. xxxiii. 25, 28, 31).

for unfaithfulness, healthy and devoted affection in faithfulness; for thus it is that the senses are kept and made strong and sturdy, sound and vigorous, supple and alert. Does not our daily experience teach us that life is wasted in disorderly passions or loses its balance in infirmities and sickness, when overfeeding produces bad humours, and when a slack *régime* produces enervation, and when work no longer absorbs our vital energies? Man is always punished by that wherein he sins; slackness and cowardice are the origin of the greatest of bodily banes, whilst wise strictness is the guarantee of solid vigour and of real well-being.

16. The liberating agent.—Being a remedy for the restoration or the conservation of vigour, mortification is also a liberating agent. It is this which, in restoring or maintaining soberness of taste, diminishes our needs, and, along with our needs, our dependence. If I know how to use it to the purpose, I succeed in not yielding to any factitious need, in not creating any fresh ones, and in diminishing as much as possible those to which I am subject. Like St. Paul, " I have learned, in whatsoever state I am, to be content therewith. I know both how to be brought low, and I know how to abound (everywhere, and in all things I am instructed): both to be full, and to be hungry; both to abound, and to suffer need " (Phil. iv. 11, 12). Therefore, if I am to be better guided in the serious and prudent use of mortifications, I must aim at not being a slave of what I take, or of what I leave, at not being dejected either through pleasure or pain, at knowing how to make use of enjoyment and at how to do without it, at being free in fine, as free as possible, in the use of all things.

17. No degrading cruelty.—Whenever the wheels of my spiritual mechanism require some of the oil of gladness to improve their going, it must be given them. What a deep meaning is contained in the essentially Christian words, recreation, refection, repose! . . . to re-create, re-make, re-place (*i.e.*, put back in its place)! . . . and this, indeed, is just the purpose of what ought to be done in the way of relaxation, food, sleep, etc. . . . Life needs to be made good, because its organs get worn out in the exercise of their

activities. Entertainment as well as sleep, food as well as medicine, henceforward assume the gravity, the dignity, and the value of being constructive elements in my life. How beautiful everything becomes when one is able to conform with the mind of God! What seems to be in itself, and what is in fact, for the most part, mere waste of time, becomes to those who are in earnest one of life's gains. Just where fools come to grief, the wise grow strong. What a good thing it is to know the ways of life![1]

18. Necessary cruelty.—Hatred of self must save one's life, this is our Saviour's mind. Therefore I shall never commit any unhappy act of imprudence or hurtful indiscretion. If, however, my eye, my hand, or my foot, scandalize me, *i.e.*, if they become a hindrance to my life, I shall know how to cut them out, according to the precept of our divine Lord, and cast them from me (Matt. v. 29, 30). One member is sacrificed to save the rest, the life of the body is sacrificed to save the life of the soul, just as the cargo is thrown overboard to save the ship. It is an act of cruelty, but it is a wise act: it is an act of cruelty, but to fear and to neglect such necessary sacrifices would be much more terrible cruelty. Every kind of cruelty is lawful, and it is praised by the Saviour, when it is preservative of life.

19. The remedy.—In fine, mortification is a remedy, and in this respect, like all remedies, it must be given in doses, and measured according to the state of the evil to be cured, and according to the capacity of the soul and body to which it is to be applied. Not every mortification suits everybody any more than every remedy is suited to every disease. There must be discretion in the use of it. For instance, it is a mistake, when I am reading the lives of the saints, to think that I can or ought to imitate all their penances. Certainly, if God granted me to follow them in the royal way of the Cross, it would be a remarkable grace. But unfortunately, I am hardly able to endure the energetic remedies which did so much good to these great souls.

And since my capacity is insufficient, what do I want?—I must accustom myself by degrees to endure bitterness, and

[1] Notas mihi fecisti vias vitæ (Ps. xv. 11).

set to work to overcome my shrinking from suffering, and try to keep a little joy amidst the little troubles that are laid upon me, so that I may at last acquire generosity to make the sacrifices demanded of me, especially such as are demanded by the requirements of duty and providential occurrences. Thus it is, in most cases, that the spirit of penance grows and that vigour is regained. And by degrees, the senses, especially when they feel that they have recovered their liberty, shudder less in fear and pain ; they get hardened and strengthened, and inured to the fray. The Spirit of God is then able to govern the carnal instincts. And, in my own very limited way, I may succeed in following the example of the saints from afar.

20. The will to be healed.—Further, there is nothing like having the will to be healed in order to enable one to take the remedies required. He who is more anxious to avoid suffering than to obtain health will never care for any remedies except such as are insignificant and soothing. If the one thing which I will with energy is deliverance, I shall not be too much repelled by the draught which is indispensable. Here again, the point of capital importance is sincerity. I must get to know whether I mean to be entertained, or whether I mean to live, whether I mean to enjoy myself, or whether I mean to work for God, whether my rule is that of pleasure or that of duty. Ah, if one possesses the true meaning of life, how much stronger one is to withdraw from petty pleasures and to face beneficent pain and privation ! Also, how much better one understands how to avoid imprudent excesses ! O my God, grant me the grace to walk in the royal way of the Cross, and to go in the pathway of trial. How do I desire not to love my soul so as to lose it, but to hate it so as to save it !

CHAPTER IV

Special Rules for Mortification

21. Three kinds of mortification.—22. The mortifications of duty.—23. Penances occasioned by duty.—24. Providential penances.—25. The acceptance of death.—26. Voluntary penances.—27. Penance for others.

21. Three kinds of mortification.—But it is a good thing to try to find a few more practical rules. What are the mortifications which are especially to be practised?—There are three kinds, and all three are divine; and they are the only ones which are free from danger. There are, first of all, those which are imposed by duty; next, there are those demanded by providential events, and lastly, there are those which are inspired by the Spirit of God.

22. The mortifications of duty.—In duty, there are two kinds of penances, those which it imposes directly, and those which it gives rise to as an occasion.

As to those which it imposes directly: how many pleasures am I obliged to abstain from, because they are forbidden! First of all, God's law prohibits all that is corrupting or enervating, all that is harmful to myself or to others. Whatever may be my fancies about it, I shall never have any right to take a pleasure in any shape, the nature of which is calculated to be prejudicial to my life or to my neighbour's interests. I must abstain and put myself to inconvenience.

Next, the law of the Church imposes upon me certain days on which I am obliged to abstain and fast; here is another obligatory mortification. No doubt, this law admits of dispensations; but it does not definitely admit of any dispensation except according to the necessities of my life; for I am only exempt from the fast or abstinence to the extent in which their observance would become prejudicial to my health or professional duty.

·Lastly, the Rule imposes on the religious his vow of chastity with all its consequences: the cloister, sobriety, the austerities of vigils, fasts, the discipline, food, clothing, sleep, etc.

All these pains and privations bind as gravely as duty itself, and it is never allowable to take or leave them at will.

23. **Penances occasioned by duty.**—The serious performance of the duties of one's state rarely takes place without some amount of compulsion and weariness. One has often to tax one's convenience or one's sleep, often to go counter to one's tastes and to abandon one's quiet, and sometimes to risk one's health or one's life. Such are the severities of duty, and they have to be taken just as they come, not giving the conscience any right to violate duty by trying unduly to mitigate or to exaggerate them.

This spring of the mortifications of duty, whether they be great or small, flows abundantly and continuously enough to provide a first and plentiful satisfaction for the thirst for sacrifice felt by generous souls. Therefore, love duty with its train of obligatory troubles, such is the first section of the practices of mortification.

24. **Providential penances.**—This first section is often enough seasoned with the trials which come from events. Inclement extremes of weather, accidents, sickness, contrarieties, etc., often scatter their bitterness throughout life! . . . It is the hand of God that directs these events and distributes these trials, according to the designs of His justice and mercy combined. I have already seen[1] how I should be able to say " I thank Thee " in these occurrences.

Not that the spirit of penance consists in undergoing adversity, like an animal sinking under the blow that kills it in the slaughter-house, certainly not. The spirit of penance consists especially in the courageous joy of suffering something for God, in virility in keeping faithful to duty during such a time, in the energy with which it is often necessary to strive against a sickness, or to circumvent a difficulty, or to surmount an obstacle, and in the effort made to pass through a trial and to improve under it. That is true penance, which neither murmurs nor is impatient, which knows both how to submit to disagreeables and how to support them, which is able to discard what is hurtful and to keep what is advan-

[1] See Part II, Book II, § 37.

tageous, and finally, which can find a daily renewal of the inward man, even in those dispositions of inexorable justice whereby our outward man is gradually led to dissolution : for that which is at present momentary and light in our tribulation worketh for us above measure an exceeding weight of glory.[1]

25. The acceptance of death.—Of all the trials of Providence, the most dreadful is the final one, that of death. This passing of my being through dissolution is so repugnant to my natural desire to live ! Although the Faith teaches me that it is only a passing, and that by the merits of the death and resurrection of the Saviour I shall come with Him to the final triumph of an immortal life in my glorified body and soul, nevertheless death keeps its awfulness ; it remains a penalty, and the great penalty of sin. And since this penalty must be undergone, is it not a good and necessary thing to accept it ? If I can rise to the level of a calm, confident, and blind acceptance, fully embracing all God's decrees with regard to myself, I practise one of the most wholesome and meritorious of penances. What a good thing it is to familiarize oneself with the idea of death ! If I could only succeed in attaining the joy which made the saints desire to pay this last due to justice, so that they might be thereupon united with God !

26. Voluntary penances.—Lastly, for generous souls there is the third kind of entirely voluntary mortifications. Happy in having to bear the burden of duty, still happier in saying their " Thank Thee " under providential sufferings, such souls become daily more ready for little acts of self-denial. Their attitude in praying grows more humble, their use of food more temperate and austere, their dress more severely simple, and they make use of secret means of corporal mortification, etc. Hunger and thirst for immolation make them try to find what may best help them to offer their bodies to God as a living sacrifice, holy and pleasing unto God, while keeping within the reasonable limits of a service which is

[1] Sed licet is qui foris est noster homo corrumpatur, tamen is qui intus est renovatur de die in diem. Id enim quod in præsenti est momentaneum et leve tribulationis nostræ, supra modum in sublimitate æternum gloriæ pondus operatur in nobis (2 Cor. iv. 16, 17).

essentially spiritual.[1] And in truth, how ingenious, how varied, and calculated to restrain the disorderly appetites of the senses, are the secret expedients of the saintly!

It is the Spirit of God who suggests these expedients, who gives the desire for them, and who governs their employment. It is He alone who ust be followed in this way, if deviations are to be avoided. And in order to be sure of always following the Spirit of God, the soul should always have its most secret penances approved by its spiritual director. The rules of the religious, which embody a subtle knowledge of mortifications, and are aware of how necessary it is to discern the spirits to know if they are of God, do not allow any extraordinary practice of penance unless it is approved by the superiors.

27. **Penance for others.**—In proportion as it advances in the way of suffering, and advances in it by being exercised therein, the generous soul, itself delivered from the manifold tyranny of the creatures of the senses, feels the need of delivering from them other souls which it pities. It knows that the virtue of sacrifice may go out of it, and extend to others. It knows that it benefits itself from the sufferings of the Saviour and of the saints. And in its gratitude, it is fain to pay back a little of what it has received, feeling that it is a more blessed thing to give than to receive (Acts xx. 35). It is then that it expiates, repairs, and suffers first of all for those who are near and dear to it. Then, as its zeal extends, it wishes to suffer for the conversion of sinners, for missions, and for the whole Church. It is glad to mingle its sacrifice with the sacrifice of the Saviour, and, with St. Paul, it feels the need of filling up in its flesh what is wanting of the sufferings of Christ for the Church and for His body. How wonderful is this enthusiasm for sacrifice! O holy folly of the Cross! O inestimable fountain of reparation! How many souls, in their secret penances, are redeeming our outrages, the lightning-conductors of justice, and the guardians of our lives!

[1] Exhibeatis corpora vestra hostiam viventem, sanctam, Deo placentem, rationabile obsequium vestrum (Rom. xii. 1).

CHAPTER V

The Function of Self-denial

28. Its necessity.—29. The evil to be avoided.—30. Limits to be observed.—31. The good to be gained.

28. Its necessity.—My heart possesses both the potency of affection, whereby it tends to become established and to rest in its end, and the potency of determination, whereby it moves towards the place of its repose.

Its life is a combination of movement and repose. I know that its end, which is the place of its repose, is God, to whom it must adhere above all and solely by charity. I know that its life consists in harmonizing and uniting its activity with the action which God exercises with regard to it, and that this correspondence must become so close that there must be unity of action between them. Such is the absolute ideal of the way and of the end.

Its evil, as I also know, is self-love, which causes the potency of its affection to stop short at, and adhere to the creature, and its potency of determination not to harmonize with God's action, by going astray in independence of agitation or inertia. Neither the activity of its life, nor the resting-place of its end, is fully in God. This is its evil.

And since the fulness of its activity and of its repose must be in God, it requires practices to withdraw it from its evil and to restore it to its good. And what are these practices?—They are the practices of self-denial.

29. The evil to be avoided.—What, then, is the precise function of the practices of self-denial?—They have to get rid of my heart's evil and to promote its good. To get rid of its evil is their first and immediate function. Therefore, to combat, diminish and destroy adherences to creatures; to pursue, efface and annihilate the independent deviations of agitated fancy and lax carelessness; and in a word, to stifle self-love, it is upon this that they must be brought to bear; upon this, and upon nothing else. They must not be allowed to weaken, or to injure or hinder the mainsprings of my affective faculties; on the contrary, they have to set them free from the mistakes which wear them out or waste their strength. How much energy is used up in agitation, or is benumbed by inactivity! How many mistaken affections bring degeneracy to the best instincts of the heart! and what a happy deliverance is that which sets me free from all these causes of weakness and impotence!

30. **The limits to be observed.**—And here again, discretion is needed in our way of understanding the matter. It is quicker work to repress an activity unfittingly than to direct it, and we may well happen to dry up our capacity for affection under the pretext of detaching it. Certain procedures of suspicious supervision, or of harsh restraint, through their unfortunate results make it all too plain how easy it is to go wrong on this question. It is by no means everything to repress, and every kind of repression is far from being the vital matter. There are repressions which are sustaining, and these are good; and there are repressions that stifle, and these are no use at all.

In the same way, it is by no means everything to practise detachment. To break chains that bind one is well; but to break ties that are vital is an unfortunate mistake. The surgeon who plunges his knife into the living flesh must have an intimate knowledge of the various tissues; the least slip would quickly make him cut out some essential organ. In such operations, life and death are so near one another! If he cuts away rightly, he saves a life; if he makes a mistake, it means death.

And every case in which one has to cut into the quick, is somewhat like this. Not all positions are equally delicate and perilous, but precision of treatment is always required. In the moral surgery which is called self-denial, precision of method is of the highest importance to the progress of one's life. If I am suitably controlled by practices hindering any fanciful deviations, if I am stimulated by means that stir the slackness of my idleness, if I am fittingly detached and uplifted by a procedure that bears my affections towards God, my heart will gradually acquire a full development of its energies and vitality.

31. The good to be gained.—To develop moral energy is the second purpose of self-denial. There is a certain vigour and virility which is good for the heart. Strength should infuse one's gentleness of affection and calmness of resolution. The man who can renounce himself and his fancies, renounce his sensuousness and attachments, necessarily becomes a man of firm character and vigorous in service. It is especially by self-denial that strength is imparted. Great hearts are steeped in self-denial; and their temper is all the finer, the deeper they are able to plunge into this bath. What a noble instrument is a heart trained to charity by being tempered with self-denial! That is the kind of heart that can love God and its neighbour and itself! . . . And am I not to desire to raise myself to such a valorous kind of charity, the living centre of all piety? Therefore, I must use the practices of self-denial, which will train my heart for such ascents.

CHAPTER VI

The Practice of Self-denial

32. Duty.—33. The Rule.—34. Personal regulations.—35. Detachment.

32. Duty.—In practice, true and prudent self-denial is formed by faithfulness to duty. It is this that imposes or suggests, in proper measure, the renunciations and detachments which are necessary or advantageous. And, in reality, it is within the limits of duty that I must learn how to sacrifice my independence and my affections. It is to it that I must yield and submit; I must subject my person, my time, and all that is mine to it. It demands laying aside one's comfort, conquering one's caprices, likes and dislikes, and the sacrifice of one's preferences and repugnances. What a school of renunciation is the holy and noble servitude of duty! I shall be a man of duty, loved for its own sake, welcomed as God's will, with its restrictions and restraints, its annoyances and troubles, its obligations and discomforts: such is the resolution which is singularly helpful in repressing the wanderings of the heart.

THE MEANS: THE PRACTICES OF PENANCE

33. **The Rule.**—And in order to govern the protestations of nature, and the demands of cowardice, and the outbreaks of humour more practically, there is nothing like having a Rule. The religious have one, the detailed prescriptions of which bind, restrain, and subject the will to the generous impulses of duty. Being guaranteed by the vow of obedience, the Rule masters the deviations of the will which yields to it. How sure and how full is the self-denial of the religious who allows himself to be guided by his Rule!

The priest, too, has his rules, less strict, no doubt, than that of the religious; but still, how *pregnant!* as St. Francis of Sales calls them, if at least, he is in earnest in conforming to them. And what self-denial is needed to be diligent in studying them and in following them!

The rules and regulations of professional duty, especially in certain professions, subject laymen to extraordinary restraints.

The man who bends his will in a Christian manner to such requirements, with the breadth and frankness that are fitting, will acquire self-denial which may amount to heroism. What fine characters are formed by such a conscientious fidelity! The student, for instance, the professor, the soldier, and many others, are bound to a strictness which is often harassing. Happy are those who are able to submit to such requirements with the spontaneous energy of a generous will, instead of being suffocated with discontent under restrictions. Spontaneity is so ennobling, acting under constraint is so depressing!

34. **Personal regulations.**—Many souls experience a need of completing the rules of their state of life by some altogether personal regulations, which are therefore more immediately adapted to their special needs. And this is an expedient which is much to be recommended and truly praiseworthy, when the garment is well fitted to the figure for which it is made. A little child cannot wear his father's clothes, and a workman setting out to work cannot muffle himself up like a shivering sick man. This shows how all personal regulations must be sober, right, and practical, and adapted to one's outward and inward conditions. If they are thus laid down

and approved by one's spiritual director, they are a powerful instrument for self-denial, and therefore, for spiritual detachment.

35. **Detachment.**—This is the way to struggle against the sham independence of self-love. How are mistaken affections destroyed ?—There are three kinds of ties that weigh down the heart : man is attached to things, to persons, or to himself.

Disorderly affection for things is broken for the religious by his vow of poverty ; and for others, by giving alms.

Affection for persons, so far as it is an encumbrance and a burden, is corrected for the religious and the priest, by breaking off, more or less completely, family ties, the loftiness of their vocation calling for a more complete liberation on their part. And for those who are intended by God to live in a family circle, exercises of self-denial are not wanting. There is the practice of mutual toleration ; the habit of self-sacrifice for the sake of thinking of others, choosing for oneself what is most troublesome or disagreeable, and leaving to others what is easy and pleasant ; being careful not to complain or to give others cause for complaint ; patience, gladness, kindness, and meeting everything with equanimity ; pity for the wretchedness, indulgence for the sins, and forgiveness for the offences, etc., of others : what a school of self-denial is all this ! what a purge of one's affections !

Lastly, for one's attachment to one's self, annoyances and adversities often enough try the heart, and he who endeavours to control his temper as well as his despondency, gets frequent and constantly renewed occasions for doing so.

CHAPTER VII

The Practice of Humility

36. Nothing through self.—37. All through God.—38. Nothing for self.—39. All for God.

36. **Nothing through self.**—The practices of humility ought to liberate the mind, just as the practices of self-denial ought to liberate the heart, and as the practices of mortification

THE MEANS: THE PRACTICES OF PENANCE

ought to liberate the senses. My mind is made to see God, and I am always looking at myself. Humility comes to correct my vision. And the first thing that humility tells me is that I have nothing of myself. It does not say that I have nothing at all, but that I have nothing through myself. I do not exist of myself, and nothing that I have comes of myself. Neither my existence, nor any of the gifts of existence in me, is through myself. What I have of myself is nothing.

Through myself I get sin, the tendency to evil, weakness, imperfection, and all the miseries the witness of which I bear in myself.

And humility, which is truth, makes me see and recognize the nothingness which I am of myself. It does not frown at the lessons of its own nothingness, which are given to man in so many of his experiences and in so many shapes. To acknowledge one's sins and mistakes, not to persist in one's own views, to admit one's imperfections and shortcomings, to accept inward and outward humiliations, to draw conclusions preferably against oneself and in favour of others, etc., this is what is suggested by humility.

Pride, indeed, does not like to acknowledge its defects; it is vexed at its sins, it looks for reasons which are quite unreasonable, to persuade itself that it is in the right. It induces me to lie to myself, and to like others to lie to me or to pay me compliments.

Humility is sincere with that inflexible sincerity which dislikes to listen to lies, and which dislikes lying either to oneself, or to others, or to God. It holds in horror all excuses and subterfuges, pretexts and trumped-up reasons, and hypocrisy and falsehood. To humility, whatever is, is; and whatever is not, is not. It means to see things as they are, and looks at them with a cold, clear, and impartial regard. It has no other interest than that of truth, and its one need is to know it and to recognize it, even when it is disagreeable.

37. **All through God.**—True humility neither misjudges, nor denies, nor lessens any of God's gifts. It too well understands the responsibility for talents received. It recognizes natural gifts and supernatural gifts, and knows whence they come. And when these gifts, which are recognized by it

and used owing to it, yield their fruits, it knows that these fruits are to be attributed to the Giver of the gifts that yield them. It sees so clearly that it has nothing which it has not received, and it takes good care not to glory in them as if it had not received them.[1]

The humility which leads people to ignore or to deny God's gifts is a craven idleness which tends to bury the given talent. It is a suffocating and soporific humility, which is good for nothing except to dry up one's faculties, to weigh down one's soul, to weaken one's activity, and to lower one's vitality.

Very naturally, the gift which is ignored, is not made use of: as I do not see it, I cannot feel the responsibility that belongs to it. I have no idea of the advantages that it brings me, nor of the obligations which it imposes on me. And thus the holy seed is not cultivated and does not bear fruit. I must therefore acknowledge the gift of God. If I only knew this![2]

To acknowledge God's gift does not mean displaying it in public. No doubt, there are works which ought to make our light shine before men, that our Father who is in heaven may be glorified,[3] and such as these cannot be hidden. But there are some, like prayer, fasting, and alms-giving, for instance, which our Master, who is sweet and humble of heart, bids us do as much as possible in secret, and beneath God's eyes.[4] And humility knows how to make public with all simplicity what ought to appear, and how to do in secret what ought to be concealed, aiming in both cases solely at pleasing God. As its sincerity enables it to acknowledge man's nothingness, so does its simplicity make it acknowledge God's gifts.

38. **Nothing for self.**—Humility, which turns talents received to good use, never allows them to stop short at selfish and interested enjoyment. Must I stop short the

---

[1] Quid autem habes quod non accepisti ? Si autem accepisti, quid gloriaris quasi non acceperis ? (1 Cor. iv. 7).
[2] Si scires donum Dei ! (Joan. iv. 10).
[3] Sic luceat lux vestra coram hominibus, ut videant opera vestra bona et glorificent Patrem vestrum qui in cœlis est (Matt. v. 16).
[4] Matt. vi.

attention and esteem and praise of others at myself ?—No, says humility. Ought I to stop my own attention and knowledge at self, and to enjoy myself in self ?—No, says humility once more ; no, nothing ought to stop at myself, at my selfish interests, at my pleasurable satisfaction. Pride can only see its own interests everywhere ; humility sees God's interests above all else, its neighbour's interests before its own, and its own interests in God's. It only desires reputation so far as it honours God, and as for the rest, it prefers disgrace and losses. Any view that stops at man seems to it shortsighted and mean, shabby and contemptible : it does not like an attitude of soul which is given to brooding over itself ; it needs uplifting.

39. **All for God.**—Humility is the great science of knowing how to forget self, it is also the great preparation for the vision of God. The less I regard myself, the better am I fitted to see God. The less my eye is dimmed with the fog of self-interest, the clearer is its view of the light of heaven. With my sight thus enlightened, I refer myself, and, with myself, all things else to God. I see the end, I see the way, I see the means : and I go forward and get to the goal. The practices of humility are thus the true means for freeing the eye from errors and for preparing it for the vision of truth, the highest of the conditions of piety.

CHAPTER VIII

The Greatness of Humility

40. All and nothing.—41. True greatness.— 42. The humility of the saints.—43. Humility, holiness, unity.

40. **All and nothing.** — It is thus that the great virtue upon which all is based and by which all begins, is completed. Nothing for me, nothing according to me, nothing through me ; all for God, all according to God, all through God. In proportion as I go out of myself, so does God enter into and transform me into Himself ; in proportion as I strip myself

of self, I am clothed with Him. In proportion as He becomes all in all to me, I become nothing in all things. Thus my humility increases in proportion as God's gifts increase; I disappear to make room for God; He must increase, and I must decrease (John' iii. 30); until, humility and renunciation being complete, nothing of self being left in me, and all being of God and for God, I am consummated with Him in that blessed unity[1] which Jesus besought of His Father in His prayer, and which is the supreme crown of humility and the supreme end of every human life.

41. **True greatness.**—How true is it, then, that humility is my sole greatness, and pride my sole littleness! Humility transports the whole man into God; should I not say, all God into man? It expands my poor human heart, and makes it capable of receiving all God's gifts, nay, even God Himself. It makes me a partaker of the divine nature,[2] as it makes God a partaker of human nature: *exinanivit semetipsum* (Phil. ii. 7).

Pride reduces man to himself, isolates him in himself, closes his heart against what is not himself, and disperses the gifts which might make him greater. So true is the Saviour's word: " Humility exalts, and pride abases."[3]

42. **The humility of the saints.**—He who understands nought of holiness asks himself how it is that the saint, fully enriched with God's gifts, and radiant with all the precious jewels of God's adorning, can be humble. The truth is that he alone can be perfectly humble, and that Mary, the greatest, the most incomparable of all creatures, was the humblest. What, indeed, is pride, if it be not living by self and for self? And what is humility, if it be not living by God and for God? Pride claims to hold everything from self and to refer everything to self; humility receives everything from God and refers everything to God. Therefore, the more it receives, the greater it is, since it can refer more to God. As for me, I have but few of God's gifts, because pride prevents my receiving them. I think that I have too much of myself,

[1] Ut sint consummati in unum (Joan. xvii. 23).
[2] Divinæ consortes naturæ (2 Pet. i. 4).
[3] Quia omnis qui se exaltat humiliabitur, et qui se humiliat exaltabitur (Luc. xiv. 11).

and I know not how to ask or to receive. Next, I am unable to refer the little that I have to God ; I keep a large share of it for myself, and I refer it to my own satisfaction ; and it is in this that I most show my pride.

The characteristic of holiness is to receive everything from God, and nothing from self ; and to refer everything to Him, without keeping anything for self. It is he who receives the most who refers the most ; and this is why the greatest of saints is necessarily the most humble of men. He has nothing for himself, nothing which is his own. All he has is from God and for God. He has received everything : how can he glory as if he had not received it ? (1 Cor. iv. 7) He does not deny any one of God's gifts, nor does he misjudge any of them ; he knows what he has received, and he knows the greatness of the treasures within him ; but he also knows that they are not for his selfish enjoyment, and he dreads to turn away a single one from its end.

43. Humility, holiness, unity.—Hence, humility is consummated in holiness. Holiness ! this is the end of its progress. At the outset, my satisfaction, my will, my means of acting, predominate. Under the divine action which causes me to ascend the ladder of holiness, God's glory takes the place of my satisfaction and transforms it ; His will replaces mine and absorbs it ; His grace displaces my means of acting and simplifies them in the unity of His action. And this path of justice, as a shining light, goeth forwards, and increaseth even to the perfect day,[1] the day of Jesus Christ,[2] in which I have no satisfaction but His glory, no will but His, no activity apart from His grace. He is my God and my all. And I live, now not I ; but Christ liveth in me (Gal. ii. 20). O humility ! O holiness ! . . . O unity ! . . . How beautiful a thing it is thus to immolate oneself to God's glory, to abandon oneself to God's will, to lay oneself open to God's grace ! . . . How beautiful is it thus to be thrice annihilated and sacrificed to God's glory in God's will by God's grace ! . . .

[1] Justorum semita quasi lux splendens procedit et crescit usque ad perfectam diem (Prov. iv. 18).
[2] Perficiet usque in diem Christi Jesu (Phil. i. 6).

BOOK II

THE EXERCISES OF PIETY

UNDERSTOOD in all its greatness, piety is the entire unity of my life. The word includes in it the twofold notion of *unity* and *life*. It is this unity and this life that I have hitherto been meditating upon. According to what was said in the Preface,[1] I have not tried in Part I to consider one after the other the various dispositions or habits that enter into the constitution of my spiritual being; I have not regarded any virtue in particular, either in substance or in practice. Nor have I, in the second Part, studied any of the rules of action in detail, nor any of God's operations. No, I have not here analyzed any of the parts, but have looked at everything as a whole, both in its unity and in its life. And this is why, in contemplating the end, I concentrated my attention solely and exclusively on that one disposition which is the unity and the life of all the other dispositions. In considering the way, I only looked at the general ordering of the laws and operations of God. Does this mean that, in confining my attention to the whole, I denied the existence of the parts that I did not try to consider? Man cannot attend to everything at once; he can only get a clear view by fixing his attention, and he only fixes it by definitely singling out one thing at a time.

In the same way now, I am about to consider the exercises of piety, not in detail, but only according to the plan which I have followed hitherto. I shall look at them as a whole, and in their relations to one another; and I shall only speak of this or that exercise according as the necessities of unity and life may require. Unity and life in the whole body of exercises, this is the definite subject of this second Book.

Does this mean that the consideration of the whole will amount to a denial of methods and counsels as to details, which

[1] See § 18.

are to be found so profitably and admirably set forth in so many excellent books of devotion ? When did an affirmation of the whole ever involve a denial of the parts ? In truth, we may say and also repeat, that the methods and practices authorized by Holy Church are to be venerated, and none of them in itself can be incompatible with the unity and life here affirmed. And the general declarations, which I now desire to consider, are exactly what will help me to make a fitting use of good practices, good methods, and good counsels, and to ensure their efficacy.

Therefore nothing will be said which is not in the order of the two general ideas of unity and life. And in this Book II, after devoting a chapter to recalling the purpose of these exercises, I shall look at three defects which run quite counter to unity and life : pharisaism, which is more especially opposed to life ; isolation, which particularly destroys unity ; and inconstancy, which hinders both. And after looking at the defects which divide and dry up, I shall consider the means which unites and vivifies.

CHAPTER I

The Purpose of Exercises of Piety

1. Their twofold purpose.—2. Means of formation.—3. If badly used, they are means of deformation.—4. The appetite for God.—5. Exercises of the mind, the heart, and the senses.

1. The twofold purpose.—I have just seen, in the last Book, the means of putting off the human; I must now look at the means of putting on the divine. These are the exercises of piety.

By exercises of piety, I understand all practices of worship, which, by putting me into direct relation with God, become to me channels of His grace and the sustenance of my soul. Practices, whether public or private, obligatory or optional, prayers and sacraments, etc., all these are included in the generic term of practices of piety.

With regard to myself, their function is twofold. In the first place, there are some the purpose of which is to prepare my soul, to turn it towards God, and to set up in it the dispositions which are necessary for the entrance of grace. There are others the characteristic function of which is to convey grace to me, since they are its channels. It is in this twofold sense that holy practices are the sustenance of the soul; not that they are in themselves the light and strength which impart life to me; like John, they are not the light, but they are there to bear witness to the light.[1] And they bear it a twofold testimony, because they adapt me to the divine, and they bring it into me. The practices which especially convey grace will be considered in the next Book, at the same time as the means of grace. Here I shall look at the practices that prepare the soul and form its dispositions, and which properly retain the name of exercises of piety.

2. Means of formation.—The one fundamental disposition which ought to govern my life is piety, *i.e.*, seeing, loving,

[1] Non erat ille lux, sed ut testimonium perhiberet de lumine (Joan. i. 8)

and seeking God. The purpose of exercises is to form, develop, and improve this disposition in me. This is why they are called exercises of piety, *i.e.*, exercises calculated to form piety. They are the means adapted thereto. If they are means, they are not the end; if they are not the end, they are not piety; for piety, as I have seen,[1] consists essentially in the end seen, loved, and sought for. They are the instruments of piety, instruments intended for its formation.

If they are means, their only value is that of being means. Therefore, if I use them for any other end, or if I make an improper use of them, they lose their value. If I do not employ them for the end for which they were made, far from being good for me, they are bad for me. They are only good for me to the extent in which they help me towards attaining my supreme end. I must not either love them or use them for any private fancy of my own, nor systematically for their own sake, but in view of God's glory, of which they are to be my instruments.

3. **If badly used, they are means of deformation.**—When all my piety consists of religious exercises, and I fancy that these are piety, I take the means for the end, and stop short on the road. Thus I feed up my own petty vanity, my need for satisfaction, my sentimentalism, and alas! all my little or great passions of pride and sensualism. It is myself and my own pleasure that I am seeking in the last resort; and if I am seeking for God in them, it is often in view of my own satisfaction. God becomes to me a means of satisfaction. Order is, indeed, fully subverted, and what I practise under the name of piety is its counterpoise. This is called false piety, or false devotion; and very false indeed it is, since it is exactly the opposite.

Thus, I sustain my defects with what ought to suppress them; and I make that contribute to self-seeking which ought only to help me in seeking God. Whence comes this disorder? —From forgetfulness of the end. I forget that the exercises of piety are only means, and I no longer use them as instruments which are useful towards my end; and thenceforward, they become food for my pride, a most deplorable matter; for

[1] See Part I, Book II, ch. ii.

there is no worse pride than that which is fed on spiritual food. Hence, it is of the utmost importance to me not to look for more in my exercises of piety than is in them in reality, and not to employ them for anything else than for what they are adapted, that is to say, the expansion of my life for the glory of God. They ought to form within me the one and fundamental disposition which has been so much dwelt upon hitherto, they ought to sustain, to develop, and to improve it. That is their sole purpose.

4. **The appetite for God.**—Therefore my attention and care should be brought to bear in the first place on this interior disposition ; it is like the appetite which the sustenance of the exercises ought both to sate and to excite. It is this appetite, this want of God, this desire for divine sustenance, which must be kept watch over above all ; for the true mark of spiritual health is to feel within one a supernatural appetite for God, in the same way as a hearty appetite is the surest sign of bodily health.

If I feel this divine appetite within me, if it is this that I sate in taking the nourishment of the exercises, if I feel that it is increased and strengthened by this food, God be praised ! my soul's health is capital, I have only to go on ; and my appetite, constantly sated and stimulated by the exercises, will continue to increase until the day when it will only be satisfied to the full by the manifestation of the glory of God.[1] But if it gets weaker, it is a bad sign ; it must be aroused and stimulated, and whetted at all costs. If it is absent altogether, I am dead or at the point of death, and the nourishment of the exercises will do me no more good than it would to a dying man or a corpse : unless, indeed, I am animated with a desire to recover the supernatural life, and use them with sincerity for the work of my spiritual resurrection ; for thus used, they even have power to raise the dead. " I am the resurrection and the life," saith the Lord, " he that believeth in Me although he be dead, shall live : and every one that liveth and believeth in Me, shall not die for ever " (John xi. 25, 26). Exercises of piety participate in this power of resurrection and life which is communicated to them by

[1] Satiabor cum apparuerit gloria tua (Ps. xvi. 15).

our Saviour. When they are made good use of, they can restore life to the dead, and preserve the living unto life eternal.

5. **Exercises of the mind, the heart, and the senses.**—Since piety is the work of the mind, the heart, and the senses, there must be exercises adapted to these three kinds of faculties, and calculated to train them and to lead them to God. The mind has its own, which train it to see God; such, for instance, as sermons, reading, meditation, examination of conscience, etc. The heart has its own, to train it in the love of God; such as exhortations, prayer, and works of zeal of all kinds. The senses, too, have theirs, to train them in the service of God; such as the ceremonies of worship, devotions, chants, etc.

In the Christian arsenal there is an infinite variety of weapons and ammunition for the spiritual warfare. I need not fear any lack of them. The essential thing is to know how to use them.

CHAPTER II

Pharisaic Regularity

6. Outward regularity.—7. The flowers of the Church's garden.—8. My bouquet.—9. Obligatory practices.—10. Practices which are of counsel.—11. Optional practices.

6. **Outward regularity.**—When I have a clear idea of what practices of piety are, I set myself free from three too common and fatal defects: pharisaic regularity, isolation, and inconstancy.

When I regard these exercises of piety as constituting the whole of piety, I put the climax of perfection in a mechanical regularity of external practices. I imprison myself in a narrow formalism. Regularity in one's exercises is a great and beautiful and holy thing, but when it becomes the real end of piety, it is nothing but a narrow prison, in which the soul merely vegetates without air, without expansion, and without life. It becomes Pharisaism, which strains out the gnat, and swallows the camel.[1] People make scruples about little omissions of little observances, and a very secondary sort of attention is given to their inner being : they become unaware of and lose life itself.

All the outward and mechanical part of devotional exercises is a useful accessory, like the ordering of a good meal. The order of a meal may vary without doing any injury to one's health, if one's appetite is good ; and in the same way, methods, hours, forms of prayer, and outward practices may vary without doing any harm to the inner life, if one is really hungry for God.

7. *The flowers of the Church's garden.*—If I employ exercises for their real purpose, I set myself free from useless practices first of all. Instead of overloading myself with tiresome details, I only take up those which are really useful for my advancement. In the Church, the enclosed garden of the heavenly Bridegroom, there is an almost infinite variety of flowers, in other words, of pious practices, which correspond with the thousands of various wants of souls. All these flowers, when they really belong to the Bridegroom's garden, in other words, when the practices are approved by the Church, are very beautiful and very good. The outcome of the Spirit of God, or fruits of the soul of the Church, or perfumed blossoms of the saints, they diffuse a sweet savour of Jesus Christ and impart to souls an odour of holiness. Oh, how good it is to gather them !

8. *My bouquet.*—But all are not suited to all. Why is the variety so rich, if it be not to satisfy the infinitely varied needs of souls ? Amidst this multitude of flowers, each individual may choose according to his necessities and tastes ; he is always sure to find the full satisfaction of his desires. He must make a selection : for to wish to take everything means to be overwhelmed, and it would be impossible ; to wish to reject everything would be robbing piety of its flowers. A bouquet must be made, and everyone must make his own. The choice of flowers and the blending of them together depend on the state of the soul. For this or that exercise may be good for one and not for another; and one particular assort-

[1] Excolantes culicem, camelum autem glutientes (Matt. xxiii. 24).

ment, though well-adapted to one person's state, might be ridiculous for another in a different state.

But how is this bouquet to be made ? What flowers am I to choose ?—In order to succeed, I should fasten my eyes upon the supreme end and not allow it to drop out of my sight, since each flower has no other use except for this end ; secondly, let me try to find out my soul's needs, its weaknesses, its aptitudes, and its actual condition, so that I may make the selection and arrangement required ; thirdly, let me consult my director : for, without him, I shall pretty often make rather a poor bouquet. If I observe these three conditions, I am quite sure to make a good selection of exercises, and a good arrangement of my life ; my bouquet of spiritual flowers will be good for me, it will draw me, and I shall run after the odour of its perfumes.[1]

9. **Obligatory practices.**—But all the flowers in my bouquet will not be of the same importance : some are brighter and sweeter than others. In the exercises, some are more important than others. Further, such as are obligatory, the sacraments, Mass, and prayer at fixed times for the faithful, Mass and Office for the priest, the essential points of his Rule for the religious, come before everything else. These must go with absolute regularity and invariable love. I must cling to these with all the powers of my soul. They are binding on me ; they are therefore the necessary nourishment of my piety ; without it, I should collapse through inanition and could make no progress on the road I have to traverse. I allow nothing to pass in my estimation before these exercises, they hold an essential place in the ordering of my day. If I am a priest, Mass and Office will have my best and first care, and it is in these that I shall try to find the substance of my nourishment. For mental prayer, too, from them I shall draw the rich material which the Church has prepared in them for her priests ; for the prayer of the priest will hardly possess its sacerdotal essence and value, unless it extracts them above all from Mass and Office.

[1] Trahe me : post te curremus in odorem unguentorum tuorum (Cant. i. 3).

10. **Practices which are of counsel.**—As to those which are of counsel, such as the ordinary points of his Rule for the religious, meditation, spiritual reading, fundamental devotions, etc., I endeavour to be as regular in them as the weaknesses of my nature permit. After exercises of obligation, I am more anxious as to practices which are of counsel than anything else; and I take care not to entertain myself with practices of my own choosing at the expense of the former. I know that practices of counsel, too, are very fruitful for the nourishment of my soul.

11. **Optional practices.**—In our spiritual meals, exercises of obligation are the chief dishes, practices of counsel are the accompanying side-dishes. Then, lastly come the *hors-d'œuvre;* that is to say, the entirely optional practices. A few may be useful, but they must be few and in good taste. A solid meal must not be submerged in such trifles. He who feeds on little side-dishes shows that his health is impaired. Therefore, I shall only make use of optional practices so far as they may be good for maintaining and encouraging my regularity in the more important practices.

Further, in what is optional, I shall keep enough liberty not to bind myself irrevocably to anything. For since the needs of the soul vary according to its ascent towards virtue, practices which are good at one time may be harmful later on; and practices which are not suitable at the outset become necessary afterwards.

CHAPTER III

Isolation

General Effects

12. Definition.—13. The drawers.—14. Distaste.—15. Sterility.

12. **Its Definition.**—The second defect, which is specially damaging to unity, is isolation. Thus I call the habit of dividing one's day into disconnected and separate parts, each one cut off and assigned to one distinct operation,

so that there is no correspondence between them, no influence of one upon the others, and no vital bond linking them together. Here there is no question of the very holy, profitable, and necessary habit of making a harmonious and living scheme, in which the place and time of each occupation is fixed according to the demands of duty and occurrences. Regularity is a great and indispensable quality : he who would live for God must live according to rule. I have given enough attention to the necessity which binds everyone to conform to the rules of his state of life.[1] It is a necessity which was once more recalled in the last chapter.

No vocabulary, I think, will be found to give as synonymous the two words : regularity and isolation. One might as well say that health and sickness are synonymous terms. Isolation, in fact, is the sickness and death of regularity. To isolate, to canton, to partition off, means to stop life's circulation, to set up a fatal separation which acts like a ligature or the amputation of a limb. Regularity must be liberated from isolation, if it is to be free and fruitful.

13. *The drawers.*—A sad sickness, indeed, is this isolation, a real anatomical dissection ! This materialistic perversion of regularity, this mechanical regulation, makes life a sort of chest of drawers. At a set time I open one drawer ; this is meditation : half an hour goes by ; I shut the drawer, and it is done with for the day. I open another drawer ; this is the Office : three quarters of an hour pass away, and I shut it up. Thus it is with the other exercises and occupations : each one has its drawer. In this way the exercises of piety are cantonned off, each into a corner of the day ; they are separated from the flow of life, and they have only a momentary influence on the soul, if they have any at all ! ... My life as a whole is disconnected, and without unity.

The thought of God is shut away in a few drawers of exercises, and it only comes out at fixed intervals. And even if it does appear, it is by no means as a habit of soul, it is as a transitory act. It is a fleeting memory or a flash of the imagination, and not a principle of life. It does not permeate my being, it does not inspire my thoughts, it does

[1] See Part II, Book I, ch. v.

not form my love, it does not govern my actions. It ought to be the life of my life, and it is only an accident. It ought to unify my soul and actions, my affections and ideas, and my whole life, making it a compact and coherent whole. But I live too much apart from it; and in this way, my life and my exercises become a rather disordered succession of details, which are often in conflict with one another.

14. Distaste.—Owing to this, the exercises get badly performed. Since they do not guide my life, and are not the soul of it, they become a burden to me. They are too much out of keeping with my occupations and anxieties as a whole; and my soul, being obliged to do itself violence to stay the current of its habitual dispositions and to raise itself to the feelings demanded by these exercises, is eager to put all this restraint on one side and to have done with them. They are a burden which I shoulder with difficulty, and which I abandon with pleasure, and from which I break away as much as possible. It is thus that I succumb to precipitation and distaste, which is quite the natural result of this lamentable fashion of isolating exercises of piety. If, however, I do not always go as far as this, my exercises nevertheless have no expansiveness, I only give them just as much time as is necessary, I do them approximately, and make no progress.

15. Sterility.—By isolating my exercises, I sterilize and annihilate them. "True and living religion," says Soloviev, "is no special matter, no separate sphere, no corner by itself in a man's existence. Being a direct revelation of the absolute, religion cannot be merely a thing by itself; it is all, or nothing."[1] What Soloviev says of religion, I say of exercises of piety, which are the application of it in practice. If they are not all in my life, if they do not permeate it through and through, they are nothing.

And I am sadly sensible of the truth of all this. Why do my exercises drag out a kind of dying existence?—Because, not being everything in my life, being only a corner apart, they are no longer anything, they are only at the last gasp, ever ready to yield it up, and it is a most difficult thing to keep any breath of life in them. Everything kills them,

[1] Soloviev. *La Russie et l'Eglise Universelle*, Part III, ch. xi.

and they kill one another; because, being disconnected and detached, they come into conflict with everything and with one another. All these conflicts are fatal. Later on, I shall see how they are to be avoided, and how exercises may become living by becoming everything in my life.

CHAPTER IV

Isolation

Particular Effects

16. Meditation partitioned off.—17. The mental prayer of the ancients. —18. Living meditation.—19. Distractions.—20. Unity of work and prayer.—21. The Psalms.

16. Meditation partitioned off.—The encroachment of isolating formalism is nowhere more fatal than in mental prayer. The saints so splendidly extol this kind of prayer! and they counsel it so urgently! And, in order to train oneself in it, the masters of the spiritual life recommend the soul to be diligent in giving at least half an hour daily to meditation. It is a salutary counsel, the fruits of which are incomparable in those who know how to practise it in a living manner. But then comes in this paralyzing defect: isolation partitions off meditation into a formal half hour; the exercise is fulfilled to enable oneself to assure oneself that one has done it; it gets the regular time assigned to it more or less in full, and that is all. The meditation is considered to be done and done with, as soon as it has lasted about the stated time; but it has little or no practical connexion with the day as a whole. People fancy that this little exercise, which is too external and very inferior in character, is about all there is in mental prayer, and they scarcely know what is meant by a *life of prayer*.

It is by partitioning off meditation in this way that contemplation has been killed. There are to-day scarcely any true contemplatives, except a few sincere and upright souls, who, without ever having learnt to meditate formally, have sought God in the simplicity of their hearts. They have kept themselves with humble fidelity under the guidance of the Holy Ghost; and the inner and living action of the Spirit of life has led them to converse with God without effort, and by a kind of natural flow of their being.

17. *The mental prayer of the ancients.*—Formerly, as the Rules of the old Orders testify,[1] people were less formal and exclusive; they were more anxious about the unity of exercises and the circulation of life. First of all, they recited the canonical Office at the different hours of the day; this was the acme of devotion, even for devout laymen. As a private devotion, they recited the Psalms, and no doubt with more relish and intelligence than it is done to-day. They took part in the liturgical functions, and they did so effectually; the ceremonies were far from being a dead letter, as they are to-day in the case of a very large number of souls. And in this frequently repeated recitation during the course of the day, and in this participation in the holy functions, the soul entered into communion with God, and lived in communion with Him, and it drew thence the wherewithal to nourish mental prayer during hours of leisure as well as during the hours of professional duty.

The most living and substantial regularity of this liturgical sustenance set up a great unifying tendency. Ideas, feelings, and actions were fed on the same substance, and were transformed and uplifted. And thus it was that the soul went to God. What, indeed, are the outward prescriptions of worship, but the regular channel of prayer? When the soul is firmly set in this liturgical current, and when, on the one hand, it draws from its original spring divine instruction and feeling, and when, on the other hand, it remains subject to the influence of the Spirit which teaches it to pray, how can it help going to God? As a matter of fact, souls which were faithful to such guidance went to Him. Their inward dispositions, arising from this divine intercourse, became habitual, practically dominant, and effectively governed their lives; the soul lived on them, life was gradually transformed into a per-

[1] See Thomassin, *De l'Office Divin*, ch. iv, § 2.

manent meditative state, and finally attained to contemplation.

18. Living meditation.—If to-day the half-hour of mental prayer, which is customary for any soul which is at all anxious for progress, were less isolated in formalism; if instead of being a separate item like the rest, and set in juxtaposition with them in the course of the day, it aimed more at being the summing up and the core of the day ; if the vitality of the other exercises and actions of the day were to gather life from it ; if, instead of making it spring too exclusively from what is too often merely a conventional method, and from books which are too shallow and too much composed of odds and ends, it were to arise from the soul and from daily life ; if it made use of Office and Mass and prayers, and of the incidents and occupations of life, and referred all that it took from them to God ; if it were less confined to its half-hour and tended more to spread over all the rest of the day, creating in my heart the need of refreshing myself from time to time in converse with God, then it would be both more powerful and more easy. It would cost far less and produce much more. Isolation kills everything, but nothing so much as mental prayer.

19. Distractions.—Lastly, it is isolation that keeps up distractions. My habit of thinking of hardly anything but myself in my occupations, of acting by myself without giving God a place in my life, or rather, without putting Him before everything else, for that is His place, this habit leads to the altogether false notion that in prayer I must think of God only. Thus I divide myself into two distinct parts : one, in which I would live in heaven altogether for God ; the other, in which I claim to live on earth altogether for myself. And I flatter myself, or try to do so, that I can make my soul pass from the one to the other in such a way that, when I am on one side, I can lose sight of the other. I admit that, when I am occupied about my own affairs, I too easily lose all thought of God ; and this is because my own occupations take up so much room in my life.

But when I am praying ! . . . Am I ever really praying, O God ? . . . Distractions swarm . . . and attack and overwhelm me.... My mind falls into them incessantly,[1] and my best endeavours fail to make me lose myself in God. This is because to do so is indeed something contrary to nature. The soul does not change its habits like the body changes its dress. If we only had to take off our working clothes to put on our Sunday suits, prayer would be an easy matter. But most happily, it is not thus with the soul. Habits are permanent, and the soul wears them everywhere. If I am accustomed to think of myself and not to think of God, to think of my work and of all the affairs of my life apart from God, I shall keep this habit in my prayers; and the one way of not retaining it, is to change it.

20. **Unity of work and prayer.**—But how is it to be changed? —By unifying my life, and getting rid of the stupid division into sections which breaks down and spoils everything. Certainly, I require a scheme of life, just as a tree needs its bark, just as a soul needs a body. But, if the tree must have its bark and the soul its body, the bark too must have its sap, and the body its soul. So the scheme must have its spirit. What is this spirit, all-pervading and animating every part of the body?—I have only to recall the great fundamental principle: everything in my life must be directed to the glory of God. I must accustom myself to see and consult God in my work as well as in my devotional exercises; to treat of my business with Him by transacting it as if I was praying; to live with Him in my work as well as in my prayer.

True religion means my union with God; I must live with Him, through Him, in Him. My work must be no more human than my prayer, nor my prayer more divine than my work. I must work with God as well as converse with Him; expect Him to direct my work as well as to inspire my prayer; look at Him while I am working, and pray to Him about my work.

21. **The Psalms.**—When I think over the Psalms, which the Church puts daily in the mouth of her priests as the most perfect form of converse with God, this is what strikes me. Turn by turn, with scarcely any transition and with a

[1] It is not only when praying that I begin to be distracted: I am so, whenever I act by myself and for myself and apart from God. When I am praying and try to get back to God, I observe that I have long been subject to distractions.

wonderful blending, David busies himself with the glory of God and his own personal interests. He sings the praises of God, and utters the cries of his own wretchedness; and all this is blended and broken up together, and is bound up into and makes one single prayer. The soul springs from earth to heaven, and returns from heaven to earth, and all the time it is in converse with God. In the midst of the most beautiful outbursts of love and praise, the prophet intersperses the tale of his miseries and anguish and dangers; and he does not consider that the one, any more than the other, is unworthy of God's hearing. Such is the prayer of the prophet; and one feels that his conduct must have been in harmony therewith. Thus God and he are only one, and man's interests were mingled with God's; and his life possessed oneness.

Why does the Church bid me recite the Psalms daily, unless it be to say to me: There is your model; thus unite your life and your prayer. Oh, if I only knew how to do it! . . . If I only knew how to be with God in my work as well as my prayer! . . . If I only knew how to treat of everything with Him, to entrust everything to Him, to give Him the direction of everything; I should then see all things in the light of God, and things thus seen would not give rise to distractions, since they would not turn me away from God. Thus my actions and my prayers would make up one and the same tendency, one and the same supernatural life; this were piety, yes, true piety. *Fiat! Fiat!* . . .

CHAPTER V

Inconstancy

22. The inconstancy of my fancies.—23. And of my too external procedure.—24. And of my weakness.—25. The remedy: sincerity and confidence.

22. The inconstancy of my fancies.—The third defect is inconstancy. If I seek my own satisfaction in my exercises, it is very usual for them to vary with the variations of my fancy. One day I am regular, because it will please me; to-morrow I am careless, because it is irksome to me. If I experience consolation, I am full of enthusiasm: if I experience dryness, I let everything go. This is being like a weather-cock in the wind. The division of my mind between pleasure and duty makes me inconstant in all my ways.[1]

Or else I flutter from one exercise to another, just brushing them one after the other, and without settling on any of them. To follow St. Francis of Sales's comparison, I shall be like the wasps which, perpetually worrying and uselessly hurrying, fly in all directions rummaging, sipping, and pilfering, at last finding that they have neither any retreat, nor provisions, nor way to live.[2] If, on the contrary, I try to get from the flowers of my exercises the true honey of real devotion, " I am like the bees, which only leave their hives to gather honey, and only combine to make it, and which are eager for nothing else, their eagerness being regulated, and which in their houses and monasteries perform only their sweet-smelling house-keeping of storing up honey and wax. The only object of their sight and smell and taste is the beauty and sweetness and fragrance of the flowers ordered on purpose for them, and, in addition to the nobility of their occupation, they have a very lovely retreat, most agreeable provisions, and an exceedingly happy life amidst the stores of their past labours."[3]

Oh, if I only knew how to settle on the flowers ordered on purpose for me, and tried to find in them nought but the wherewithal to store up sweetly-perfumed supplies of the honey of the divine glory and of the wax of my own sanctification, I also should have a very lovely retreat in my own soul, and most agreeable provisions, and a very happy life! . . .

23. And of my too external procedure.—When I act in my spiritual exercises after the manner of wasps, without looking for the honey of the divine glory, a very little is often enough to stop my work. In fact, as I only hold to such exercises externally, any interruption or irregularity will break the

[1] Vir duplex animo inconstans est in omnibus viis suis (Jac. i. 8).
[2] St. Francis of Sales, *Lettres*, Book VI, Letter 26 (Leonard).
[3] St. Francis of Sales, *ibid.*

chain, and then I have nothing left. Thus I am quickly discouraged, I am easily upset, and my spiritual life is often thrown into disorder. If, on the contrary, I aim above all at the inner life, this, since it is a habit, does not disappear along with a single act or several acts; in spite of certain outward yieldings or infidelities, I feel that I am still holding on to the chain, nothing essential is broken off, and I am not discouraged. I have greater steadiness. My infidelities may retard my progress, but they do not cast me out of the way.

24. And of my weakness.—Here then are two causes of inconstancy: the fancies of my own satisfaction and the deceptions of my too external procedure. There is a third, my own weakness: the weakness of my habits, and the weakness of my nature. I have unfortunately allowed my faculties to be deformed by perverse habits; and I have lost my strength in such deviations; bad tendencies weigh me down with a crushing tyranny, which never seems so heavy as when I desire to break away from it.

On the other hand, my nature is weak in itself; and the devastation of original sin has so lessened my powers and weakened their energies, and has left in me such a host of the germs of disorganization and of death! Is there any need to add that the fascinations that tempt me are numerous and urgent?

For all these reasons, I am weak; and because I am weak I am inconstant. " For I know that there dwelleth not in me, that is to say, in my flesh, that which is good. For to will is present with me, but to accomplish that which is good, I find not. For the good which I will, I do not; but the evil which I will not, that I do. Now if I do that which I will not, it is no more I that do it, but sin that dwelleth in me. I find then a law, that when I have a will to do good, evil is present with me. For I am delighted with the law of God, according to the inward man: but I see another law in my members, fighting against the law of my mind, and captivating me in the law of sin, that is in my members. Unhappy man that I am, who shall deliver me from the body of this death?— The grace of God by Jesus Christ our Lord " (Rom. vii. 18-25).

25. **The remedy: sincerity and confidence.**—This weakness arising from my wretchedness makes itself felt and brings forth inconstancy in all the ordering of my life, and especially in the use of remedies, such as exercises of piety. How is it to be got over? By faithfulness in my exercises? But this presupposes as done what remains for me to do. If I can be faithful to my exercises, I can also be faithful to my other duties. If there is no longer any inconstancy in my exercises, that shows that it is cured.

St. Paul points to a single remedy : the grace of God by Jesus Christ.—What is meant by the grace of God?—It means that I must look for strength to God alone ; and look for it with sincerity and patience. First of all, with sincerity ; with that full sincerity of faith which reckons upon God without wavering.[1] And next, with patience; for the weakness of the child does not give way in a day to manly maturity, nor do the infirmities of the soul vanish in a single flash of sincerity. All really vital work is carried out slowly and gradually. I may be deeply sincere with regard to God, and yet drag myself along heavily and wearily, and be tossed to and fro amidst humiliating vicissitudes. Weakness does not in any way deprive one of sincerity ; I much need to remember this, so as not to get discouraged. Therefore, however great my weakness and inconstancy may be, I only need sincerity to lay myself open to the ways of grace ; and grace will enter in, and strengthen my weakness and correct my inconstancy. No weakness and no inconstancy should be able to damp sincerity. Ah, if only I were humble enough to keep myself in the sincerity of true contrition, then I should not need to be groaning long over my inconstancy. And the power of a wise, sober, firm, and living regularity would assert itself and appear not only in my exercises, but in my whole life.

[1] Postulet autem in fide nihil hæsitans (Jac. i. 6).

CHAPTER VI

Examination of Conscience

26. Exercises must possess unity.—27. Examination of conscience is the guiding bond of unity.—28. The means of unity.—29. The witness of the saints.—30. Acts are transitory.—31. Habits are the strings to strike.

26. Exercises must possess unity.—I have looked at the defects, I have now to look at the means of unity. My soul is substantially one, one and all in the body, and one and all in each part of the body. It is everywhere throughout the body, without possessing width and breadth; it acts throughout it, without any division of its substance. One in its substance, it must become one in the action of its powers: such is the purpose of its life and the goal of its activity. Spiritual exercises, which are the sustenance of this life and the means of this activity, ought to lead it to this unity; they ought to establish in it the great and one disposition, which is the one thing to seek for and the one thing necessary. They ought to unite all its powers by directing them to the glory of God; and to destroy the multiplicity and division which always exist, when the end, which alone unites everything, is lost sight of.

But how are they to produce unity, if they are not themselves united? How are they to destroy multiplicity and division, if they are themselves divided by multiplicity and incoherence? Multiplicity cannot create unity, nor does division promote union. Therefore, it is strictly necessary for them to be united with one another; they require a centre and a common tie. It is absolutely necessary that they should be directed towards their true end; otherwise, instead of being means they become hindrances. This is why there must be one exercise which guides and governs the rest.

27. Examination of conscience is the guiding bond of unity.—What is the central and guiding exercise to be? Which, among the manifold variety of devotional practices, is the one on which the rest depend, and from which they get their guidance and their unity ?—One distinctive characteristic will enable me to recognize it. The guiding exercise must be the one in which there is the least possibility of the general evil, which is self-seeking, creeping in. It can only be an adequate and sure guide, if this evil is absolutely excluded by the very nature of the exercise. If, in fact, it were possible for self-seeking to creep into it, I should be cast out of the way and kept at a distance from my end by the exercise intended to lead me back to them. But is there any exercise in which it is impossible to nourish one's vain satisfaction ? In prayer, in meditation, at Mass and Communion, etc., I may too easily, through human interest, seek for sweetness and consolations; therefore none of them can be the guiding exercise. But what satisfaction can I get from my examination of conscience ?

On the other hand, the purpose of devotional exercises being to lead me to God, the first condition is for me to find out where I am, whither I am going, what way I am following, what hindrances and dangers I am meeting with, and what means I must choose. It is impossible to go forward with sureness without this. But all this is just what an examination of conscience will show me. This therefore is the central and governing exercise.

28. The means of unity.—Therefore I am now about to consider how examination of conscience is the means which realizes unity in the exercises, and by unity in the exercises, the unity of piety. And here especially I must not allow myself to be dominated by any notion of some new and particular method. The purpose of these reflections is neither a method, nor a speciality, nor any novelty. Their purpose is to secure unity.

As to the examination of conscience, whether I follow the order of the commandments, or the order of my duties towards God, my neighbour, and myself; whether I produce this or that act, feeling, or reflection; whether I begin or end with this or that prayer, invocation, or thanksgiving, etc., these are all particular applications, which are to be found in great variety and excellently set forth in a number of capital books. As to these methods and counsels, I am free to follow what really corresponds with the requirements and bent of my soul.

Here I shall consider the examination of conscience under a more general aspect: its influence upon the unity of exercises. The particular mode of making use of it may vary; but what must not vary is its unifying influence. And now I am about to try to consider how this influence is to be maintained paramount and along with all these special ways of proceeding.

29. **The witness of the saints.**—The saints have recognized that the examination of conscience is supremely important for guidance and vital concentration. It is thus that St. Ignatius thinks. During a considerable time, he made use of no other means for the spiritual guidance of his companions than the practice of the examination of conscience and a frequent recurrence to the sacraments. In the constitutions of his Order, the examination is regarded as being of such importance that nothing was ever to exempt anyone from it. Sickness or other grave necessities might excuse from mental prayer and other exercises, but from the examination of conscience, never. Reason had already shown its importance to Pythagoras, who recommended it to his disciples as the true means of acquiring wisdom. St. John Chrysostom had a high opinion of it, and this led him to say that if one did it well for a month, one would become established in a perfect habit of virtue.[1] St. Basil, in his constitutions, says that before all else, in order to keep oneself from evil and to make some progress in the good, this exercise is to be set up as a sentinel over our thoughts, so that they may be checked and guided by the eye of this sentinel.[2] The holy Doctors are of one accord in attributing this capital importance to self-examination.

30. **Acts are transitory.**—But still we must know how to do it. Often, by losing oneself in details, one gives oneself a deal of trouble to make very little progress. Thus one

---

[1] Ex ea re tantum erit emolumentum, ut si id uno mense solo fecerimus, in perfecto virtutis habitu nos constituemus (*Homil. in Ps.* iv. 8).

[2] Primum quidem omnibus modis cogitationem continere debemus, ei pervigilis mentis inspectionem præficientes (*De const. monas.*, c. 2).

easily gets discouraged, and one comes to omit, or even to forsake this most important of exercises. If I desire to give it a really governing and unifying usefulness, it is a good thing to remind myself of a few theological principles.

Theology, in harmony with philosophy, teaches that an act in itself is transitory, and that a habit is permanent: the act passes away, the habit remains. If it is a question of venial acts, I know that, in a state of grace, they are effaced if they are followed by an act of supernatural virtue. Hence, these acts leave no traces behind in a soul which necessarily produces a pretty large number of supernatural acts in the course of a day, since I assume that it is in a state of grace. Hence, what is the good of dwelling in my self-examination on acts of which no trace remains? What knowledge of my soul can such a revision of details give me? The Church teaches that I am not obliged to confess them; why then should I spend a long time in making such things the substance of my self-examination?

All this applies to acts that are quite transitory, and which have no connexion of a close and essential kind with any inward habit. For, as to those which depend on a habit, they can only be wiped out by an act that interrupts the habit and intercepts the influence exerted by the habit upon the act. I shall soon see how they are to be examined.

If there be any question of mortal sins, the act is not then wiped out by any virtue; perfect charity alone can do that, still the sin is wiped out by it. No doubt, such an act, even if wiped out by charity, remains subject to the power of the keys, and therefore it must be a subject for self-examination; but acts of mortal sin do not abound, God be thanked, in a soul which thinks of its perfection; and the trace of them stands out clearly enough to afford no difficulty in one's self-examination.

31. **Habits are the strings to strike.**—The mere knowledge of acts will never lead me to a deep knowledge of my soul; they will never help me to make, in the deepest sense, a real examination of *conscience*. To know them may do some good, it is sometimes necessary, but one must go deeper. Con-

science is what is innermost within me and what is most secret : it is the sanctuary of the temple. If I really desire to make an examination of conscience, it is this innermost secret that I must enter into, it is this sanctuary that I must visit. But, in this sanctuary, it is the habits and dispositions of the soul that are the thing which abides. When I have got to know them, I have got to know the state of my soul ; otherwise not. He who would make progress must bring the investigation of his self-examination to bear upon this point.

"Our examination of conscience," says St. Francis of Sales, " must be reduced to a search for our passions. For, so far as examination for sins is concerned, that is for the confessions of those who are not trying to advance. What affections are a hindrance to our heart, what passions are in possession of it, in what does it chiefly go astray ? For it is by the passions of the soul that one gets to know one's state, by probing them one after the other. For, just as a lutanist strikes all the strings, and tunes those which are not in accord by tightening or relaxing them, so after probing hatred, love, desire, fear, hope, sadness and gladness of soul, if we find them out of tune with the melody which we wish to play, which is the glory of God, we may tune them by means of His grace and with the help of our spiritual father."[1]

The important thing, indeed, is that the heart-strings should be in tune for the melody I desire to play, which is God's glory ; and the essential object of self-examination is to show me whether the strings play that tune well. But my heart-strings are my interior dispositions ; they are the ones to be struck to know what tone they give. Do they re-echo God's glory, or my own satisfaction ? When I know the tone they give forth, I shall have made a real examination of conscience.

[1] *Philothea*, Part V, ch vii.

CHAPTER VII

The Glance

32. Its easiness.—33. Its object.—34. It is the substance of self-examination.—35. The tap.

32. Its easiness.—But how am I to get at the true state of my soul ? How am I to seize what I may call my heart's expression ?—At any moment, if I desire to know where I am, what is the state of my soul, what tone echoes within me I merely ask : *Where is my heart ?* By this question I seek solely to know what is the dominant disposition of my heart, which inspires and directs it, and keeps it as it were in its possession. A number of impressions and yearnings and feelings throng about the heart : it is an unfathomable reservoir ; but whatever be the number and the nature of the dispositions, there is always one that is in an ascendancy. It is not always the same, the heart of man undergoes so many fluctuations ! one feeling takes the place of another, one impression drives out another ; but there is always one that holds the first place, and gives a direction to the heart and governs its activity. That is the one, indeed, which gives the true tone of the soul. That is the one I have to seize before all else, if I am to catch my soul's expression.

In order to seize it, I ask myself this simple question : " Where is my heart ?"—but, at the very moment of putting this question, the answer comes within me. This question causes me to cast a rapid glance into the innermost centre of my being, and I at once see the salient point ; I give ear to the tone echoed by my soul, and immediately catch the dominant note. It is an intuitive proceeding, and is quite instantaneous. There is no need for intellectual inquiries, efforts of will, and ransacking the memory ; I hear and see. It is a glance, *in ictu oculi.* It is simple and rapid. A soul must be quite ignorant of its inner self, and quite unaccustomed to enter into itself, if it does not experience this.

33. Its object.—Sometimes I shall see that my dominant disposition is the want of approbation or praise, or the fear of reproach ; sometimes, the bitterness that springs from some annoyance from some harmful project or proceeding, or else the resentment caused by some remonstrance ; sometimes, the painfulness of being under suspicion, or the trouble felt through some aversion ; or, it may be the slackness induced by sensualism, or the discouragement resulting from difficulties or failure ; at other times, routine, the product of carelessness, or frivolity, the product of idle curiosity and empty gaiety, etc. Or else, on the contrary, it may be the love of God, the desire for sacrifice, the fervour kindled by some touch of grace, full submission to God, the joy of humility, etc. Whether it be good or bad, it is the main and dominant disposition that must be ascertained ; for we must look at the good as well as the evil, since it is the state of the heart that it is important to know. I must go directly to the mainspring which sets all the wheels of the clock in motion.

Sometimes it happens that this mainspring is a persistent and continuous disposition, such as some bitterness or aversion. But, at other times, it is some merely momentary impression, which, however, was strong enough to impress the heart for a considerable time with some characteristic impulse ; such, for instance, as the generous acceptance of a suffering; it was the affair of a moment, yet it imparted something to the heart, which will set it in motion during one or several days.

34. It is the substance of self-examination.—When I have ascertained this dominant disposition, good or bad, my examination of conscience is substantially finished ; I have got what is the essential thing, the core of it. In fact, the dominant disposition, by determining finally the impulses of my heart, is like a resultant of the powers of the other feelings, which are practically concentrated and summed up therein. Hence, strictly speaking, I might be satisfied with this essential glance ; and by it I might strengthen the weak, heal the sick, bind up that which was broken, bring again that which was driven away, and seek for that which was lost.[1]

---

[1] Quod infirmum fuit non consolidastis, et quod ægrotum non sanastis, quod confractum est non alligastis, et quod abjectum est non reduxistis, et quod perierat non quæsistis (Ezech. xxxiv. 4).

And in fact, if, in the course of the day, I wish to ascertain the state of my soul, *i.e.*, make my self-examination, I am satisfied with this single glance, diving right into the centre of my heart : " Where do I stand ? " And it is done : I see. I correct and set straight, if necessary : I humble myself and give thanks, if all is well. And this I can do at any moment, and thousands of times ; it is such a simple act ! a look at the heart, a glance ! . . .

35. The tap.—And this simple glance has deep results ; since it retains or restores the resultant of the powers of the heart in the one way, and directs it to the one end. As a matter of fact, nothing escapes from it, since it grasps the centre of everything. Why need I worry about other details ? I need not cut the branches off the tree, when it is down ; nor need I follow the course of the streams, when I am at the source.

When the water spouts forth in profusion from the host of little holes in the rose of a watering-pot, would it not be a tedious and troublesome matter to shut up each little hole one after the other in order to cut off the flow ? And if there were a tap lower down, enabling one to stop the flow by a single turn, would it not be stupid to tire oneself with trying to stop all the little holes ? and that all the more, because there is always a risk of their coming open again. He whose examination of conscience stops at details and outward things, is passing his time in stopping up the little holes. . . . The inward glance turns the tap. . . . To stop at details and at what is outward, is to remain at the circumference and to manœuvre on the surface of the soul. I go straight to the centre and take possession of my whole soul, when I cast this penetrating glance at my dominant disposition.

CHAPTER VIII

The Examination into Details

36. The examination into secondary dispositions.—37. The process of fructification.—38. Self-examination follows and aids the soul's progress.—39. It is not a matter of statistics.—40. Hunting up details.

36. The examination into secondary dispositions. — But will not thinking of nothing but this principal disposition make me lose sight of the other dispositions of the heart which will thus grow up in the background, so that I shall not notice them? There is no danger of that. How are these dispositions to make their way to the light, since the tap is turned? I mean to say, that the principal disposition of the heart, and thereby all the heart, is turned towards God as a result of the examination. All the secondary dispositions are kept in check by this fact. Further, as I have already remarked, the dominant disposition is far from being always the same; defects make their appearance, according to circumstances; and as soon as they succeed in assuming a dominating prominence, the examination of conscience takes hold of them and checks them.

On the other hand, in proportion as defects diminish and disappear under the influence of self-examination, like ice under the sun's rays, those which first of all remained unperceived in the depths, covered as they were by the upper layers of more striking defects, appear on the surface as soon as those which were above them have disappeared. There are, in fact, in the soul something like superposed layers of dispositions, each of them becoming more fine and subtle the deeper one goes. As in everything else, so in the case of these layers, my eye only beholds what is on the surface. I must learn to be satisfied with this look.

37. The process of fructification.—Nature never proceeds by detail, but always goes from the simple to the compound. It takes a seed, and concentrates its action on the vital principle which is hidden in the unity and simplicity of this primary element. The beginnings of this action are rather indefinite; often they are what appear to be the coarsest of rough-draughts. But as the vital principle expands, the outlines come out, the shape becomes more complete, the different parts are finished, and, at last, the natural progress of the work attains to the finest perfection of each detail in the harmonious proportions of the parts and in the living unity of the whole. Such is nature's work. Who ever saw a tree begin with the tips of its leaves?

Nor does grace follow any other procedure. It is implanted in me like a seed. " The kingdom of heaven is like to a grain of mustard-seed " (Matt. xiii. 31). This seed starts its growth with a few elementary endeavours; these are the beginnings of the spiritual life, the struggle against sins and greater defects. In proportion as the process continues, the work gets to be more perfect, virtues increase, life pervades and reaches to details, until the time when all ends and is fulfilled in holiness.

38. *Self-examination follows and aids the soul's progress.*— My self-examination must necessarily follow this development, since its purpose is both to follow and to aid the work. But I follow this development, if my self-examination does its best to lay hold of the soul's dominant disposition. What, indeed, does this disposition show me, unless it be the actual state of grace within me? In ascertaining it, I therefore see just how the work of the fructification of grace within me stands. I see the real and actual state of my piety. And since the beginning of this work is rudimentary and is only accentuated in its main lines, I shall only be able in my self-examination to note the broad outlines of my dispositions, the boldest features which are displayed at any moment. When the seed is about to send up its first blade, am I to look for the fully-developed leaves or flowers?

But in proportion as the work advances, I have merely to look on: and my attention follows the work and perceives its details so far as they appear. I dive deeper into my inward dispositions following the progress of the work of grace. In this way the saint succeeds in discerning, even in their most delicate distinctions, the most subtle movements of his heart. The saint can do this, because grace has reached this point in him. The purpose of self-examination is, then, to ascertain the state of the work of grace, and to follow it.

But its purpose is also to aid it. I want to see, indeed, in order to facilitate the course of grace, to take away hindrances, and to prevent deviations. Such enquiry would be sterile curiosity, if its purpose were not to develop the vital principle, the movements of which I am watching. The twofold work of ascertaining and facilitating is wonderfully achieved by the glance of the examination of conscience.

39. It is not a matter of statistics.—Would it be done in the same way by the mere examination of details?—By no means. Let me assume, for example, that in my self-examination I had succeeded in counting up exactly the number of my distractions. Will this perfectly exact number, if I am satisfied with simply recording it, reveal to me the cause of the evil? On the contrary, if first of all, by a glance into the depths, I seized the true origin of the evil, what would it matter, so far as the external manifestations go, whether there were ten or twenty? It is of capital importance for mortal sins, the number of which I must know in order to accuse myself of them. But, in what is venial, the number is always an accessory question. Although accessory, it is, however, a useful question. I must not totally neglect it, so as to pay no attention at all to outward manifestations; for often the external acts reveal the internal situation. Their number may, therefore, have a revelatory value, and it has such a value. But, while not overlooking the matter of numbers, I must not make it the thing of main importance in self-examination to the exclusion of other things.

I assume again, that in the sphere of the good, I am diligent in reckoning up the number of little prayers and practices, and ejaculatory invocations, etc., which are so sanctifying and much to be recommended. Am I quite sure that their increase will give the measure of my progress?—The manias that afflict too many devout persons testify clearly enough how illusory is an overwhelming anxiety as to a mechanical matter of figures. No, one must not stay in externals; one must not suppose that the swelling of numbers shows of itself an increase of vigour. And it is the condition and the direction of this vigour which it is so important to further. It is the disposition of the heart that must be known, far more than the number of things; it is a question of testing a situation, not of drawing up a list of statistics.

40. Hunting up details.—I shall never be persuaded enough of the necessity, the simplicity, and the efficacy of this inward glance, which constitutes the essence of self-examination. O my God! what is it that has so often discouraged me in this exercise, and led me to give it up? What was it, if it were not the tiresomeness and uselessness of hunting up details, and of manœuvring on the circumference? Oh! that hunting after details! . . . it takes so long, and is so troublesome and unfruitful: it does not require much of it to fill one with distaste.

And how much more encouraging is the simplicity of the single glance! No doubt, it presupposes an efficacious goodwill, and a sincere desire for self-knowledge and improvement. It presupposes a fundamentally straightforward tendency of soul, and unbiassed freedom with God and even with oneself, an imperturbable resolution to see a thing as it is, and not as my interest would wish to see it. Hence, falsehood must be abdicated and a truce made with petty calculations.

If I am afraid of looking within me, if, by instinctive attachment to a sin which I will not give up, I turn away my eyes for fear of seeing too much, I shall never make my examination of conscience. But is not this fear of seeing too much itself already a glance, and does not its terrible necessity violently urge an examination of conscience upon me, which is the source of all my disquietude and remorse? If I could only resolutely decide upon casting a true and sincere glance within, to check and to purify, I should feel how much less painful it is to make such a self-examination than to endure the sense of the above-mentioned urgency.

CHAPTER IX

Contrition and Firm Purpose

41. Their necessity.—42. Perfect contrition.—43. Imperfect contrition.—44. Rising from one to the other.—45. Firm purpose —46. Union of the three elements of the examination of conscience.

41. Their necessity.—But can I be satisfied with the glance? Is seeing everything?—No, it is not everything, but it is the beginning of everything. Why do I wish to see? —I have already said it :[1] in order to second the movement of grace, the ascending movement towards God, I must correct the deviations, if any arise; establish and develop any good movement that may exist. Hence, seeing should bring with it contrition and good resolution or firm purpose; contrition, which corrects what is wrong; firm purpose, which establishes what is good; contrition, which looks at the road already finished; firm purpose, which looks at the road that is yet to be travelled.

42. Perfect contrition.—Contrition should come to be inspired with perfect love as its essential motive, the love of God for Himself and for His own glory. The one all of my life lies in succeeding in seeking for God's glory in everything: incessantly I ought to get nearer to this end. And contrition is just the impulse which brings my heart nearer to it, by keeping it away from evil. This impulse would be incomplete, if it did not tend to this higher end.

Further, God's glory being the centre and climax of everything, everything brings us thereto, if only we desire to get there. Therefore, all the motives of contrition and love, all the means suited to develop them, lead to this end, if I desire to direct them thereto. The essential thing is to not stop on the way, but to aim at that, and to ascend those heights. According to their helpfulness, I may make use of the expedients suggested by the saints, and the practices recommended for the purpose by spiritual writers; but it must always

---

[1] See last chapter, § 38.

be in order to raise my soul to that vision, love, and search for God, which is the climax of my life.

43. **Imperfect contrition.**—The motives of imperfect contrition, the fear of hell, the desire of heaven, the ugliness of vice, the beauty of virtue, etc., are good and useful motives; the Church approves of them, saints recommend them, God Himself has recourse to them in His holy Word to make men determine to glorify Him. It is a good thing for me to have recourse to them. But how?—Like a tailor who uses his needle to make his thread pass. The needle is necessary, because without it the thread cannot be made to pass. But also the needle must not remain behind; because, if it stays, the thread will not pass. Thus the motives of fear may, and often must, be used to make the pure thread of pure love pass after them; but, if they are to help the thread to pass, they must pass away themselves and leave it behind; for perfect charity casteth out fear (1 John iv. 18). I may, then, ask God to pierce my flesh with the needle of His fear, the fear of His judgements;[1] and this will be a beneficial wound, if it lets out the humours of evil and lets in true piety. Yes, let fear enter in, and introduce love.

44. **Rising from one to the other.**—Therefore, it is a good thing for me to have recourse to the fear of the judgements of God; for they contain a mighty remedy against evil, they are a piercing thorn which helps me to give it up, and an energetic preservative against falls. But further, how much should I be on my guard against the selfish and narrow notion, which would make me only sensible of the loss of the pleasures of which sin deprives me! If I were thus to bend back upon myself, I should condemn myself not to make any progress. I should remain crushed by fear, solely anxious about myself; in God I should see nothing but severity, and I should yield to constraint only, and my life would be an agony threatened by God on the one hand, and by sin on the other. Thus it is that people come to think religion is something burdensome and tiresome.

But when the soul expands with love, when it rises to real

[1] Confige timore tuo carnes meas, a judiciis enim tuis timui (Ps cxviii. 120).

and great piety, when contrition brings it back to the vision, love, and search for God, then, if repentance continues to have its thorn which is felt, the thorn brings with it so much sweetness that the pain is as it were swallowed up in an infinity of happiness. How far must one be one's own enemy to condemn oneself to suffer from imperfect contrition, when one could find so much comfort and expansion in perfect contrition ? Is there any need to add that the one wipes out by itself all sin, while the other only wipes it out with the help of sacramental absolution ?

45. Firm purpose.—Contrition must be concentrated in *one* good resolution or firm purpose. I say : *one* good resolution ; for here again, we must get back to unity. This resolution, on whatever particular point it may be brought to bear, must always be brought back to the one essential thing, that is to say, to the vision of God, to submission to His will, and to conformity with the movement of His grace. This good resolution can and must be particularized by being brought to bear on the special point that stands out in my heart ; it must correct the tendency which deviates most from God, or strengthen the one that draws most towards Him, and thus set my heart most fully face to face with God's glory, under His will, and in His grace. This is the point to which one must always get back.

46. **The union of the three elements of the examination of conscience.**—Such are the three constituent elements of the examination of conscience : the glance, contrition, and firm purpose. But what are these three elements but the constituent elements of piety : sight, love, and search ? The union of these three latter elements in one sole impulse of the heart constitutes piety ; and, in the same way, the union of the three elements of the glance, contrition, and firm purpose in one sole impulse of the heart constitutes examination of conscience in its integrity.

As a matter of fact, in the rapid acts of self-examination which I repeat during the course of the day, these three impulses are not distinct : each act is a single instantaneous impulse, a glance *in ictu oculi ;* and this glance is at once sight, love, and search ; look, contrition, and firm purpose. These three things are only distinguished in the longer self-examination, the evening examination, for instance, in which the infirmity of nature obliges me to separate the impulse into its parts, to analyse them one by one, to go through them one after the other, so that each may be as perfect as possible and the whole as finished as possible.

In reality, what difference is there between the examination of conscience and piety, except that the latter is a state, and self-examination an act? It is the life-giving and governing act which impresses and governs the impulse. And thus a closer knowledge of piety and of self-examination shows me that self-examination is really the eye of piety.

CHAPTER X

The Different Kinds of Self-Examination

47. The habitual self-examination.—48. The general self-examination, its centre and two circumferences.—49. The two fundamental questions.—50. The particular examen.—51. The preliminary examination.—52. The facilitation of confession.

47. **The habitual self-examination.**—The time has come for speaking of the different kinds of self-examination, if, indeed, there are several kinds. Usually distinctions are made between the general self-examination, the particular examen, and the preliminary examination. Before these, we ought to put what I shall term the habitual self-examination. This habitual self-examination is nothing else than the simple rapid glance, which, with the simplicity of a single movement, sums up the three consecutive movements of the examination of conscience. I think I have sufficiently grasped its nature and exercise not to have to insist on it any further. If I desire to make any progress in piety, I must get accustomed to repeat it frequently. It is the repetition of this act which will establish the habit of piety in me. The more ready I become in it, the more my piety will advance towards its full expansion. In the saint who has attained to the summit,

this act often becomes the one activity of his life, and the act gets lost in the habit; he no longer is aware if it is a customary act or an actual habit. He thus draws nearer to God, who is a pure act. O my God! when shall I resemble Thee?

48. **The general self-examination, its centre and two circumferences.**—So far as the general self-examination is concerned, I have said already, that it is necessary to take the different parts of the movement to pieces; or, as St. Francis of Sales says, to try the strings one after the other. Hence, I pass in turn from sight to love and search; in other words, from the glance to contrition and firm purpose, and I stop at each part separately.

As for the glance, I make it take in the whole of the day, and I immediately try to discover what was its dominant disposition. As a matter of fact, each day has one disposition, one feeling, one heart's impulse, which characterizes the state of the soul as a whole, and gives its tone to the day. I am soon aware whether my day was a good or a bad day, and why it was good or bad. That stares me in the face with the rapidity of a glance. When I have once grasped that, I have got at the centre of my heart.

From this centre one sees easily, and almost simultaneously, all the points of the circumference. Thus, continuing to look from the centre towards the circumference, I try to discover, according to the strength of my spiritual life, on the first circumference, the secondary feelings of the soul, those which may have taken momentarily possession of it without altogether dominating it; they come up under the dominant feeling. There it is that I see any particular touches of grace, the temptations of the devil, and the different disturbances of the heart. Then, on the next circumference, the principal things, words or actions, which arose from these dispositions. The examination, which is quite complete considered as a glance, is thus decomposed into three parts; at the centre, the dominant feeling, which I discover first of all; then, on the first circumference, the secondary feelings; lastly, on the second circumference, the principal acts arising from these dispositions.

49. The two fundamental questions.—To take the measure of all this with ease and precision, I have to put two questions to myself. The first looks at my piety on its passive side; the second, on its active side. So far as passive piety is concerned: How have I accepted? So far as active piety is concerned: How have I acted? In other words, and to go back to our comparison of electricity, which throws much light upon the situation, my first question shows me whether contact with the electrical fountain has been set up; and the second, how the apparatus has worked. Therefore, first of all: What attitude did I hold with regard to God? Was I open or closed to His action? And why was I open or closed? This shows the dominant disposition, the central point. Next: How did I see, love, and fulfil the duties of my state? This is the working of the apparatus, the dispositions and acts subsequent to the dominant disposition.

These two questions are vital, they show me how I have walked in the way that leads to God; I thus discover the principal incidents of the way, whether they be good or bad. I say: the principal incidents; for it is important not to get submerged in details, which is the ordinary temptation of people of good-will at the outset. One must only stop at what is characteristic, at what reveals the state of the soul. It is much better not to pick all the flowers than to lose one's way in the wood.

Thus understood, the answer to these two questions is quickly made, and in a few minutes I have a deep insight into my day as a whole, and in detail. I know its living features, and grasp its vital interdependence. Oh, when one is able to see! . . . The difficulty is not to see, but to open one's eyes and to look in the right direction. Oh, if I only desired to see! . . . O my God! give me the will to see! . . .

50. The particular examen.—Its object is to overthrow Goliath, the heart's dominant defect. I do this every time I make an examination in the way already shown. As soon as I have cast my glance within, asking myself how I stand, my particular examen is done. I do not lay down a particular point beforehand as to which to examine myself, I do not isolate myself in one corner of my soul. I have no statistics to compile, but my attention is brought to bear directly on my heart, and on the disposition actually dominant therein. What I am confronted with is a living enemy who is there and acting, and whom I discover and lay hold of, and overthrow.

This chief enemy, this dominant disposition, as I have said, may vary from day to day, even more, he may vary in the same day. But these very changes, these waverings of the heart will teach me to get to know it better, will make me dive into its depths which I should not otherwise fathom, and will enable me to discover in the lowest deeps secret causes, the activity of which can only be perceived by means of the fluctuations it gives rise to. What I thus analyse and hold in hand is my heart as it is, my living throbbing heart, with its alternations of life and sickness. Nothing can be more effective for getting a real knowledge of the real Goliath, and for slaying him. In fine, the particular examen is nothing else than the glance which is the centre and sum-total of every examination of conscience.

51. **The preliminary examination.**—It is to be used at the beginning of the day to ensure its right guidance, and to enable me to avoid the deviations to which I am most liable. If at that hour I use the penetrating look of true self-examination in such a way as to set my heart really face to face with God and to establish it firmly in seeking for the supreme end, the success of my day will be strongly guaranteed. The electric circuit will be open. Before foreseeing details, which is a most useful thing to do, it is important to establish my heart in the search for God and in forgetfulness of self, two things which comprise all else. The forecasting of the circumstances in which I have to maintain this disposition will come afterwards, but it is not the essential thing. Here, as elsewhere, the essential thing is to regulate my heart.

52. **The facilitation of confession.**—If I understand what constitutes the very essence of the examination of conscience, I see that, in reality, it is one and not manifold. On all occasions, I must go to the bottom of my heart; and I always get there in the same way, by the rapid and deep glance which at once shows me how I stand. Thus it is a very simple thing.

Further, it is a very easy thing. No long round-about

ways, no weariness of details, but a quick glance as to the state of the soul as a whole. The greatest hindrance at the outset is that one always wants to go further than is necessary ; to look for midday at two a.m., as the saying goes, and to lose oneself in details. With a little good-will, and as light comes with the exercise, one succeeds fairly quickly in correcting this fault.

And it is very efficacious. For thus I really get to see into my soul and conscience ; I go to the source, and lay bare the roots.

And how good it is for confession. When I have thus taken account of my inward state for a week, I go to my confessor and say to him : During the past week, my inward dispositions were these, and such are their principal results. In a few words, I put the picture of my soul before his eyes. He can read what I say like an open book ; he sees my state and follows the movement of my heart ; he seems to catch, as it were, the beatings of life in me, and in a few words, he too can give me just the advice that is suited to my needs. When I get lost in details, my confession is very long and not at all clear, and always superficial, and is like most commonplace confessions. My confessor is unable to read plainly enough in my avowals what my inner state is, and is obliged to give me the sort of counsels that are roughly applicable to everybody.

CHAPTER XI

The Unity of the Exercises

53. Singleness of eye.—54. Self-examination is the eye of the exercises.—55. It is the obligatory prelude to meditation.—56. And of all the other exercises.—57. The presence of God.—58. The great means of piety.—59. Consult spiritual writers for details of methods.

53. **Singleness of eye.**—Now I must see how the examination of conscience thus made is really the central and governing exercise, and how the other exercises find therein their guidance and their way, their light and their rule, their bond

and their unity. I may apply to self-examination thus practised by a rapid glance what our Lord says of singleness of eye. " The light of thy body is thy eye. If thy eye be single, thy whole body will be lightsome : but if it be evil, thy body also will be darksome. Take heed therefore that the light which is in thee, be not darkness. If then thy whole body be lightsome, having no part of darkness ; the whole shall be lightsome, and as a bright lamp shall enlighten thee " (Luke xi. 34-36). If the eye of self-examination be single and full of light, all the body of the exercises will be full of light and excellent ; but if the self-examination is bad, all the exercises will be full of darkness.

54. **Self-examination is the eye of the exercises.**—The eye of the exercises is self-examination. It is not the whole of the body of the exercises, and it cannot suffice of itself. Nor is it the heart which distributes life. The heart consists of the exercises that produce grace, of the sacraments and prayer, for thence comes vigour. The sacraments and prayer are the reservoirs and channels which pour the torrents of the supernatural life into the soul ; they are the heart and the arteries of the mystical body of piety.

Self-examination is the eye. It is by it that I see and become enlightened, that I avoid dangers and correct faults, and that I set my ways right. It is by it that I flood my soul with light and bring light to bear upon everything ; and thus I cannot abide in evil, but I am bound to do the truth, that is to say, to advance in piety ; for he that doth evil hateth the light, and cometh not to the light, lest his works should be discovered ; but he that doth the truth cometh to the light, that it may be made manifest that his works are wrought in God.[1]

It is of supreme importance that this examination of conscience be not darkness ; for if the light that is in me be darkness, how great shall the darkness be ?[2] If the examination is badly made, what will be the state of the other exercises ?

[1] Omnis enim qui male agit, odit lucem, et non venit ad lucem, ut non arguantur opera ejus. Qui autem facit veritatem, venit ad lucem, ut manifestentur opera ejus, quia in Deo facta sunt (Joan. iii. 20, 21).

[2] Si ergo lumen, quod in te est, tenebræ sunt, ipsæ tenebræ quantæ erunt ? (Matt. vi. 23).

55. It is the obligatory prelude to meditation.—Self-examination is the obligatory prelude, the indispensable preparation, of every important exercise. In meditation, for instance, I shall only escape from such defects as would destroy its value, if I begin by asking myself: "Where is my heart?" Unless I do that, I may listen to the pleadings of cowardice and neglect it, or else try to find pasture for my desire of consolation, and thus foster my own fancies and self-love. I shall not go to God in either of these ways, and my meditation will be a failure. If I have put my heart right by the rapid glance of self-examination, these two enemies, my own cowardice and self-satisfaction, will be turned out; and then, what will hinder God from entering in? Clearly, all difficulties will not be got rid of by the mere fact of doing this; distractions, dryness, and a host of other miseries will still remain; but since none of them is voluntary, they will not hinder me from meeting with God. These very miseries are often most profitable to the soul. Hence, the real success of meditation is assured.

56. And of all the other exercises.—What is true of meditation is true of the other exercises, of Mass, Communion, the Office, etc. Thus each of them is directed towards its true end; dangers are shown, hindrances done away with, the way made plain, the soul given assurance, and one's purpose attained. And not only is each exercise perfected, but all are united, all converge towards the same end, under the common influence of a guiding principle. The action of one is united with the action of another, and sustains and strengthens it: they support one another, like the stones of a single arch; they strengthen one another, like the poles of a single magnet; and, in fine, their manifold action is one. How can the soul help being stronger when fastened up in a single bundle like this? How can it help going forward, when it is uplifted by such power?

57. The presence of God.— And this leads me to make another remark. Every devotional exercise begins with a reminder of the presence of God; this is a general recommendation that applies to all of them. Since I wish to converse with God, plainly I must begin with putting myself in His presence. But, the most practical and the most telling way of putting myself in the presence of God is to examine my conscience in the way in which it is here understood. If I am satisfied to remind myself of the presence of God without entering into my heart to correct it, no doubt such a reminder will be a good thing ; but it will not amend my ways, and I may remain self-seeking ; and, although I shall be close to God, I shall not go to Him. This is just what happens to some people. They acquire the habit of the presence of God and of ejaculatory prayers ; they are full of affectionate expressions and feelings towards God ; and they are at least as full of themselves, and as infatuated with self-love. This is not a problematical case. O that self-seeking !

But if I scrutinize my heart to find out where it is ; if I correct my feelings by directing them towards God and His glory, then I am effectively in the presence of God, I seek Him in reality, and I go towards Him and meet Him. This act lays hold of the roots of my soul, it seizes upon the mainspring of my faculties and directs them towards God ; and if I acquire the habit of it, I shall succeed in loving, seeing, and seeking God in everything. I shall be pious !

58. **The great means of piety.**—To sum up, the glance of self-examination will be the chief means for the formation within me of the one and living disposition, which is piety. To follow the great way that leads to the great end is quite impossible apart from the great means of self-examination ; and I shall only follow it with readiness and facility with the help of this means. The words of St. Francis of Sales are there to affirm, that he who would advance must examine into his inward dispositions. Self-seeking is so subtle : it has entered so thoroughly into our ideas and affections and habits, and has encroached so far upon our inner life ! . . . It is behind these entrenchments that we must follow it ; we must cast it out ; and to cast it out, we must enter in. That is the point to which all we have been saying leads up.

It is easy to see that the constant purpose of our remarks is to turn away the soul from external interests, to draw its attention in the main to what is within. To act upon what is inward, so as to react on what is outward ; to make clean

THE MEANS: THE EXERCISES OF PIETY

the inside of the cup and of the dish, that the outside also may become clean;[1] to lift the soul above details, in which it stays and gets wearied and deceived, to recall it to the first principle which it forgets; to restore to its spiritual activity the true processes of life, the unity and simplicity of the inward work, and the unity of the end, the way, and the means; to lop off too conventional ways of proceeding, the multiplicity of which comes to impede the work of life; such is the object we have been earnestly striving to attain.

59. **Consult spiritual writers for details of methods.**—And now what am I to say of other exercises?—Nothing; for I think that if their general function in piety is understood, and if the examination of conscience keeps them in the right way, they will be excellent, or will not be long in becoming so. Questions of method are, as I have said, accessory, and necessarily changeable, according to the different needs and dispositions of souls. Since here I only wish to touch upon questions which are essentially connected with the one main object of this whole work, I only study the essential relations without going into matters of detail, as to which, moreover, most excellent advice is to be found in the writings of the masters of the spiritual life.

[1] Pharisæe cæce, munda prius quod intus est calicis et paropsidis, ut fiat quod deforis est mundum (Matt. xxiii. 26).

BOOK III
GRACE

I know that all creatures, in the hands of Providence and the Holy Ghost, are instruments for the sanctification of the elect. But all these means, in the last resort, are only vehicles of the great means, which is called grace. It is this that is the vital bond between God and me, this is the real agent of unity and life, this it is that forms my piety in a truly supernatural manner, this it is that stimulates and sustains my soul, accelerating its progress and expanding its vitality ; lastly, it is this that, when transformed in the light of glory, will be my life for ever and ever.

I am going briefly to consider its nature, its origin, and its necessity, my weakness without it, the principal means of its communication to me, and, in conclusion, casting by way of assurance a glance of love at the Mother, and at the Author, of divine grace.

CHAPTER I

The Nature of Grace

1. The necessity of a bond.—2. Its nature.—3. Actual grace.—4. Habitual grace.—5. The effects of sanctifying grace.—6. The two kinds of grace combined.

1. The necessity of a bond.—In Part I, I saw how I ought to adhere to God only, how my life should be identified with His, and how my being should be united with His being. I cannot contract any union except with Him: every other union must be broken off. In the same way, in Part II, I saw how my action ought to be united with that of God, my work with His work and my progress with His.— By what means is so close a union to be realized ?—For He, indeed, is infinite, and I am finite ; and there is no proportion between the finite and the infinite. Hence, there must be a middle term which is related both to the finite and to the infinite, which touches both man and God. There must be a mysterious and incomprehensible bond, coming from God, and reaching to man, and uplifting man to God. God has created such a means, and it is called grace.

2. Its nature.—What is grace ?—Grace, say the theologians, is a supernatural and gratuitous gift of God, given by Him to His reasonable creatures to lead them to eternal life. Grace is like a supernatural flow of God's virtue, which comes to raise man above himself, and to accustom his powers and his nature to direct union with God in this world and in eternity. It is essentially and absolutely supernatural, in such a manner that no creature, whether actual or possible, has or can have any natural right to grace. It remains above everything; above angels and the Blessed Virgin, and even the sacred humanity of our Saviour ; it is a gratuitous and entirely supernatural gift. It is the means of supernatural union with God for Jesus Christ, for the Blessed Virgin, and for angels and men. It is by it, and by it alone, that my life is united with God's, my activity with His.

3. Actual grace.—There are two kinds of grace : the grace that is transitory and the grace that abides, the grace of action and the grace of union, the grace of work and the grace of life, actual grace and habitual grace.

Actual grace is that which unites my action with that of God, it is the passing grace of the way. In what does it consist ?—It consists in a supernatural impulse, in a vital stimulus imparted to my powers in order to make them act with God. Grace, in my mind, is a light which helps me to see God, and beings according to God. In my heart, it is a warmth which leads me to love God, and creatures for God. In my executive faculties, it is a force which helps me to serve God, and to make use of things for God. Supernatural light, warmth, and force, such is actual grace.[1]

It is thus called, because it is active and urges to action, and because it is the actual aid of the present moment, and lastly, because it is given and repeated from act to act. It is like a push from the divine hand, which is given to assist me in each act that duty demands.

Thus God's hand prevents me, to suggest a thought to me, to inspire me with a desire, and to stimulate me at the beginning of any act I have to do. This is preventing grace. Next, it upholds my eye in the vision, my heart in the love, and my strength in the fulfilment of duty, until it is completely performed ; this is concurrent grace : thereby the concurrence of my action with God's is established and maintained. Resulting from God's action, stimulating my own, it is the medium, the connecting-link, the means of union of my work with God's.

4. Habitual grace.—If the stimulus of actual grace stirs to life, it nevertheless does not give life itself in the strictly supernatural sense. Its transitory action does not effect a divine state in the soul. This state is established by another grace, superior to the former ; and it is called sanctifying grace, because it is this that makes sanctity ; and it is called habitual, because it is stable and dwells in the soul, and sets it firmly in a state of grace.

[1] Est quidam effectus divinæ voluntatis, in quantum anima hominis movetur a Deo ad aliquid cognoscendum, vel volendum, vel agendum (S. Thomas, i , 2, q. 110, a. 2, c).

What is this grace ?—It is that which St. Thomas defines as " an inflow of the divine Goodness into the soul, whereby it is assimilated to God, and becomes pleasing to Him, and worthy of eternal life."[1] It is, properly speaking, the gift of divine life. It is this that makes the soul live, and by it I live in God, and God lives in me. It enters into me and transforms me. It is the divine virtue entering into my soul, and animating it in the same way as my soul animates its body.

5. **The effects of sanctifying grace.**—It makes me pure. It wipes out the defilements and defects of my poor human nature. It destroys mortal sin, with which it cannot dwell; it successively does away with venial sins, imperfections, and all adherences to creatures; it is the great means of purification.

It makes me just. It forms within me holy views, divine virtues, and supernatural habits; it perfects the gifts and fruits of the Holy Ghost, and it realizes the beatitudes.

It makes me agreeable to God and like God. Adherence to creatures gives rise to deformities which impair the divine likeness which was imprinted on me by the Creator. Grace restores the features of the likeness, and by it I once more become the object of God's good pleasure.

It gives my actions a meritorious value. Without it, no act has any eternal value; by it, there is no act of my life, however insignificant, which does not become meritorious from the point of view of the infinite bliss of heaven.

Hence, it is this that builds up the edifice of my life in God and for God; it is this that establishes piety in me; and it is this that makes me capable of glory and happiness. It is by this that I expand and increase in such a way as to give God all the glory, and to gain for myself all the happiness, which are my end. It is the vigour of the supernatural life, and it goes on growing and making me grow with every act I do in conformity with God's will under the stimulus of actual grace.

6. **The two kinds of grace combined.**—Before the state of grace is realized in me, actual grace stirs me up and urges

[1] Gratia est influentia divinæ bonitatis in animam, per quam assimilata Deo fit ei grata et vitæ æternæ digna (Opusc. 51 de Sacram. alt. c. 26).

me to do acts which will bring me towards justification. It is then a preparation of the way of life. When I already have the happiness of living by the divine life, actual grace brings into play the powers of supernatural animation which are implanted within me; it exercises them, and makes them grow by exercise. Its continual provocations help me to progress continually, by causing me to make use of the supernatural resources within me. It is by the combined influence of these two kinds of grace that my piety is formed. Both concur in this work.

The one is more active, and imparts movement; the other is more stable, and gives dispositions and facility. The one is more variable, and goes with the mobile side of life; the other is more fixed, and is bound to the permanent side of it. The one passes, and is specialized on a present act; the other is more general, and extends as a fundamental habit to all our acts. The one rather resembles Martha, and goes to and fro according to our necessities; the other is more like Mary, and keeps the soul closer to God. The one extends and prolongs the energy of my faculties, by making it possible for them to perform acts above their strength; the other modifies and transforms the very depths of my nature, by giving it a new being, a divine life. One collects the materials, the other organizes them, and both of them build up.

Thus, aroused and sustained by actual grace, and nourished, increased, and perfected by habitual grace, my will keeps within the law of God and is exercised therein day and night. Thus, I am like the tree which is planted near the running waters, which shall bring forth its fruit in due season, the leaves of which do not fall off; and all that I do furthers God's glory and my own eternal happiness.[1]

[1] In lege Domini voluntas ejus et in lege ejus meditabitur die ac nocte. Et erit tanquam lignum quod plantatum est secus decursus aquarum, quod fructum suum dabit in tempore suo. Et folium ejus non defluet, et omnia quæcumque faciet prosperabuntur (Ps. i. 2, 3).

CHAPTER II

The Source of Grace

7. The Saviour's merits.—8. God's action.—9. The reservoirs.—10. My action.

7. The Saviour's merits.—Being a supernatural gift, grace is essentially gratuitous. "If by grace," says St. Paul, "it is not now by works; otherwise grace is no more grace" (Rom. xi. 6). Given by the Creator, lost by sin, it was redeemed by the Saviour, who came from heaven to seek and to save that which was lost (Luke xix. 10). This divine means to the divine life comes to men by Him who is the Man-God, and who, being God, became man, so that, by participating in both natures, He might raise human nature to participate in the divine nature. In the hypostatic union of the two natures, He is the link, the mediator between God and man;[1] for by Him God comes down to me, and by Him I ascend to God. In Him dwelleth all the fulness of the Godhead corporally, and in Him I am filled with the fruits of grace.[2] All the graces I receive are the fruit of His blood. It hath pleased God that in Him should all fulness dwell; and through Him to reconcile all things unto Himself, making peace through the blood of His Cross, both as to the things on earth, and the things that are in heaven (Col. i. 19).

8. God's action.—Jesus Christ is the source; but by what channels do the streams of grace run into the fields of my soul?—I have already seen[3] that by the operations of the divine good pleasure there is a great and constant influx of graces. Creatures which serve as God's instruments are then instruments of grace. In the manifold encounters of all sorts and kinds I daily experience, I receive a host of supernatural helps, incessantly changed and renewed according to the needs of my life.

---

[1] Unus et mediator Dei et hominum homo Christus Jesus (1 Tim. ii. 5).
[2] Quia in ipso inhabitat omnis plenitudo divinitatis corporaliter, et estis in illo repleti (Col. ii. 9, 10).
[3] See Part II, Book III, §§ 8 and 9.

And not only the operation of God's good pleasure, but also the rules of His will signified, are graces to me. In the Church's teaching *magisterium* which maintains the faith, in the sacerdotal organization which fosters charity, in the disciplinary rule that guarantees liberty, how many graces there are ! Hence, supernatural helps reach me from both aspects of the divine will.

9. **The reservoirs.**—These channels are incessantly open, and the necessary graces flow through them uninterruptedly. They do not close, but unfortunately, I may close myself, and the graces that flow, do not flow into me. If I keep myself open, I receive, according to my measure, the fulness of what they contain for me.

But further, our Lord has instituted special reservoirs for special graces, of which it will be enough to mention the two greatest : prayer and the sacraments. The one is within everyone's reach, and from it everyone can draw at will, at all times and without stint. The other is in the special keeping of the Church, who has to administer it, and who only desires to turn on the overflow and let it run. At the end of this Book, we shall have something to say of these two reservoirs.

10. **My action.**—I cannot, in strict right, merit the first grace, that is to say, the grace that justifies me in coming out of the state of sin. This grace is always absolutely gratuitous. As long as it has not come to transform my nature fundamentally, none of my acts is so adapted to grace as to merit it. No doubt efforts made with nothing but the help of actual grace have a certain merit of congruity, but not a merit of strict right, to receive more abundant graces.

But when once, on the other hand, the divine life has been communicated to my soul, each act animated by that life becomes meritorious for fresh graces. Actual grace and habitual grace may thus be augmented at every moment, in proportion as I make the resources of life which are within me bear fruit.

CHAPTER III

The Necessity of Grace

11. In general.—12. To see.—13. To will.—14. To act.—15. We are not sufficient.—16. The new life.

11. In general.—My all consists in rising to God. Who can raise me to Him except Himself? Without Him, I cannot go to Him. No creature is on God's level, and no creature can raise me to Him. And what can *I* do?—Of myself, I cannot go out of myself. When I rely on myself, I do not go out of myself, I remain within myself in self-seeking. And if I am raised by God, and cease to rely on God, and rely on myself, I fall back upon myself; this is reverting to self-seeking and disorder.

God alone is my strength, my support, my refuge, and my deliverance: He is my helper, my protector, my strength and my salvation.[1] "I am the vine," says the Lord, "you are the branches: he that abideth in Me, and I in him, the same beareth much fruit: for without Me you can do nothing" (John xv. 5). He does not say: "without Me, you can do very little"; but: "without Me, you can do nothing."

Without Him, I can neither do little nor much, I can do nothing.

12. To see.—If I desire to be convinced of my impotence in detail, I have only to remind myself of what I have to do: to know, to love, to seek: God as my end, His will as my way. Now, neither seeing, nor loving, nor carrying out, which constitute piety, is within my own power.

The vision of God, which is my true end, to which I have been called in the merciful design of my Creator, this is absolutely beyond the natural scope of the eye of my intelligence. I am speaking not only of the eternal vision, face to face, which will be the great bliss of heaven, and which will only take place in the splendours of the light of glory; but I am speaking

---

[1] Diligam te, Domine, fortitudo mea. Dominus firmamentum meum et refugium meum et liberator meus. Deus meus adjutor meus et sperabo in eum. Protector meus, et cornu salutis meæ, et susceptor meus (Ps. xvii. 2-4).

THE MEANS: GRACE

of that half-dim vision of faith, of the vision of God as reflected in beings, and of His action as seen in the enigma of their movements. This vision I am incapable of catching the faintest glimmer of, if left to myself.

"We are not sufficient," says St. Paul, to "think anything of ourselves, as of ourselves; but our sufficiency is from God" (2 Cor. iii. 5). Thus, not only the fulness of knowledge, but a mere thought, a beginning of a supernatural notion, does not exist in me, or of myself. To see God supernaturally and God's action in the mirror of things and in the enigma of their movements, I must look at them in God's light. This light alone can give my eye supernatural insight, alone it gives the range of vision which is called faith, with the help of which divine mysteries are revealed to it.

13. To will.—Can my will of itself rise to that love of God which is called charity, which is the most divine of divine virtues, which is the soul of all virtues, and which is the real link between man and God ?—" The charity of God," says St. Paul, " is poured forth in our hearts by the Holy Ghost who is given to us" (Rom. v. 5). It is the work, it is the gift, the great gift of the Holy Ghost. I know that it is God that worketh in me both to will and to accomplish.[1] I know that man's will and endeavours do not reach that mark, and that God's mercy only can attain it.[2] Charity is so much the work of grace that theologians ask if it is distinct from sanctifying grace. Therefore, to will God's good, and to love God's glory, I need God's impulse, without which I get deplorably lost in self-love and in the selfish love of creatures. Grace, which is the light of my eye to afford it the vision of faith, is also the warmth of my heart to impart to it an impulse of love.

14. To act.—Without grace, I am incapable of doing the least saving work, and the utterance of a single word even is beyond my strength. " No man," says St. Paul, " can say, the Lord Jesus, but by the Holy Ghost " (1 Cor. xii. 3). If the mere invocation of the Saviour's name, such meritorious

---
[1] Deus est enim qui operatur in vobis et velle et perficere pro bona voluntate (Phil. ii. 13).
[2] Igitur non volentis, neque currentis, sed miserentis est Dei (Rom. ix. 16)

and sanctifying invocation as constitutes an act of piety, if this simple invocation is so high a thing as to be above the sole powers of my nature, of what work, of what act, am I capable ? I can do all things in the strength of God ;[1] the things that are impossible with men, are possible with God (Luke xviii. 27). Thus in the strength of God, I can carry out the most supernatural works of my vocation. But in the strength of my natural powers, I cannot rise to any act of supernatural piety. My strength needs to be increased and heightened by the supernatural virtue of grace to adapt it to the operations of the divine life.

15. **We are not sufficient.**—By my natural faculties, I can see, will, and act ; but these things do not constitute that vision, love, and search which make up Christian piety. Piety is essentially a supernatural work, and presupposes supernatural life in the soul. The acts of this supernatural life are exercised by my natural faculties, but only in virtue of the supernatural principle which animates them. My faculties lend grace the help of their action ; it is through them that grace acts, but grace is the principal agent, the essential motive, and the vital cause. My body only acts naturally in virtue of my soul, and thus my soul only acts supernaturally in virtue of grace. The soul brings forth natural acts by making use of the organs of the body ; and grace brings forth supernatural works by making use of the powers of the soul. My soul no more suffices for the operations of the supernatural life than my body for the operations of the natural life: both the one and the other possess the primary elements, and as it were the matter of the life ; they lack its form ;[2] they are not of themselves sufficient,[3] in the deeply significant words of St. Paul. In the body, the least of vital operations is impossible without the soul, and in the soul, the same is true without grace ; because the life of the body is the soul, and the life of the soul is God.[4]

[1] Omnia possum in eo, qui me confortat (Phil. iv. 13)
[2] With this difference, that the soul is a substance which animates the body, and grace a quality infused in the soul.
[3] Non quod sufficientes sumus (2 Cor. iii. 5).
[4] Vita carnis tuæ anima tua, vita animæ tuæ Deus tuus (S. Aug., in Joan. tract. xlvii. 7).

16. **The new life.**—Hence, it is a new and higher life that I need, a supernatural life ; and I am created for this life by God, as I am created for the life of the body ; it is a second creation. For it is grace that gives me salvation by faith ; and that not of myself, for it is the gift of God ; not of works, lest anyone should glory. I am His workmanship, created in Christ Jesus in good works which God has prepared for me to walk in.[1] For every good work I am created, and made and drawn out of nothingness. Every good work in me is a creation, that is to say, something that God draws out of my nothingness ; for in myself I am nothingness. I have nothing in my natural being that can give rise to this life. No doubt, it is my natural being that is raised to this divine participation ; but the life in itself is not drawn from me, it is created by God in me.

Therefore, of myself I am as incapable of any good supernatural work as I am of my own creation. When once created to natural life, I can perform its acts ; when once created to supernatural acts, I can also perform its acts ; but the creation itself is God's. This is why St. Paul calls it " a new creature " (2 Cor. v. 17), a new life,[2] " a new man, who, according to God, is created in justice, and holiness of truth " (Eph. iv. 24). What he here calls " justice and holiness of truth " is what he elsewhere calls " doing the truth in charity " ; and here we again have the three terms of piety. For me to have this new life, the life according to God and like God's, the life which is justice and holiness of truth, in other words, if I am to have piety, I must have been created for it ; everything comes from grace ; truth, holiness, justice; seeing, loving, and seeking God ; it is grace that makes Christian piety within me.

[1] Gratia enim estis salvati per fidem, et hoc non ex vobis, Dei enim donum est, non ex operibus, ut ne quis glorietur. Ipsius enim sumus factura, creati in Christo Jesu in operibus bonis, quæ præparavit Deus, ut in illis ambulemus (Eph. ii. 8-10).
[2] Ita et nos in novitate vitæ ambulemus (Rom. vi. 4).

CHAPTER IV

My Weakness

17. Relying on myself.—18. In my knowledge.—19. In my will.—20. In my activity.

17. Relying on myself.—This new life is given me by the vine of which I am a branch; my life comes from the sap, and the sap comes from the vine. Without it I have nothing. I am nothing, nothing but a corpse. On what am I to presume ? on what shall I plume myself ? If I am to presume on myself, I cut myself off from the vine, I stop the sap, and I lose life. The limb which the soul does not animate fully loses its strength, languishes, and dies.

Is not this just what happens to my piety ? Every time I desire to rely on myself, to reckon upon and to act by myself, I feel a languor and weakness, and fall; I cut myself off from life. If I knew how to analyse my heart and to enter into the events of my life, I should find that all my weaknesses and falls were due to self-confidence; I was weak or fell just when I wanted to walk by myself and to let go God's hand; and I fell just as far as I let go His hand. The extent and the secret of every weakness is to be found there. The soul which reckons on itself will always fall; the soul which never reckons on itself will never fall.

And there, too, are to be found the measure and the secret of all strength. " As for me," says St. Paul, " I will glory in nothing but my infirmities; for power is made perfect in infirmity. Gladly therefore will I glory in my infirmities, that the power of Christ may dwell in me. For which cause I please myself in my infirmities, in reproaches, in necessities, in persecutions, in distresses, for Christ. For when I am weak, then am I powerful " (2 Cor. xii. 5-10).

18. In my knowledge.—To get to know my infirmity, I must see how far I rely on myself for knowledge, feeling, and action.

As to knowledge, is it not true that I count especially, and often exclusively, on the powers of my own intelligence ? How far do I have recourse to God in my intellectual labours, in my reflections, calculations, and forecasts ? If I am drawing up a plan, if I am studying some branch of knowledge, even if it be sacred knowledge, if I fathom some consideration, do I trust in grace more than in myself ? Do I recur to it more than to myself ? Is it really a light to illumine and guide my judgements and knowledge ? Is it the mistress of my intellect ? Is it the life of my mind ? In fine, grace has rather a narrow place in the life of my mind. My mind acts too much of its own accord, it relies more on itself than on God, more on its own light than on that of grace. How then can I wonder at my own darkness and ignorance, and at my mistakes and illusions ? " He that followeth Me, walketh not in darkness, but shall have the light of life," says the Author of grace (John viii. 12). We cannot see clearly without God's light.

19. **In my will.**—It is not much better with my heart so far as the practical action of grace is concerned. The touches of grace are not the habitual spring of its impulses. Its affections, its emotions, and its resolutions are too often only natural. I count upon myself for willing and deciding ; I get attached to a number of things through purely human impulses, so that the influence of grace is rarely in the ascendant. How, then, can I wonder at my inconstancy and cowardice, at my failure and discouragement ? Oh, if only grace were to enter deeply into my heart once for all, and to rule and direct it, how strong, and firm and immovable I should be ! But how difficult it is to drive out from the inmost recesses of the heart that self-confidence that arises from self-love, and incessantly reverts to it ! We cannot will properly without a divine impulse.

20. **In my activity.**—Are my actions more permeated with the influence of grace ? I go to and fro, I fuss a great deal, and worry incessantly, and yet make no progress. This is the general complaint : the world seems to be all in a fever. It is the most evident sign of universal materialism. Matter never acts without noise and disturbance ; the action of the mind is gentle, calm, and silent. Matter means noise ; mind means silence. What a noise, what a bustle, what a disturbance there is all about me ! . . . And is there any more

calmness within me ? . . . Grace is so gentle, so peaceful, so full of calm and silence, and therefore it is so powerful and efficacious ! . . .

Human agitation is merely impotence and sterility : God's action is gentleness and power. It has an invincible potency for reaching the end, and an indestructible gentleness in making use of the means that are useful for the end.[1] Power and gentleness, nothing can stay them, and nothing can ruffle them : nothing can stay their advance towards the end, and nothing can disturb them in their use of means. Such is the character of wisdom, that is to say, of grace. When it enters into me, I am less disturbed, and I do something ; when I act apart from it, I give myself a deal of trouble, and I succeed in nothing. What calmness and power there are in the saints ! . . . What disturbance and impotence are in myself ! . . . When shall I be able to let grace bring me peace and strength ? How long am I to be like a sick man ravaged with fever ? He tosses, and in tossing, he gets weaker and kills himself. And his penalty is just ! He who only relies on himself gets very weary and constantly loses ground ; he who relies on God has but little trouble and goes forward quickly. At last let me sleep in peace and take my rest in the singular hope in which Thou hast settled me, O my God[2] ! We cannot act well without God's strength.

CHAPTER V

Remedies for Weakness

21. St. Peter's example.—22. Do not wonder.—23. Hope.—24. Relapses.

21. St. Peter's example.—My great strength lies in knowing my weakness, and my great weakness lies in thinking myself strong. I am nothing, and I can do nothing of myself : the better I understand this, the better I feel it, the stronger I shall

---

[1] Attingit a fine usque ad finem fortiter, et disponit omnia suaviter (Sap. viii. 1).
[2] In pace in idipsum dormiam et requiescam, quoniam tu, Domine, singulariter in spe constituisti me (Ps. iv. 9, 10).

be. The greatest of saints is he who best understands his own nothingness. "Everywhere and in all things, I am instructed," says St. Paul, "for I can do all things in Him who strengtheneth me" (Phil. iv. 9). Man's most obstinate illusion is that of wanting to reckon on himself. This presumptuous confidence is only cured by falls, if it be curable at all.

What an example is that of St. Peter! He had to descend to the depths of apostasy to get to the bottom of his own nothingness and to be cured of presumption: and no doubt he would not otherwise have been cured. The repeated remonstrances of our Saviour were powerless to enlighten him; so obstinate and blind is presumption! O my God! how often have I fallen before now! . . . And how often do I still fall! . . . I constantly find myself down in the depths of disorder, which means looking for my own satisfaction at God's expense! . . . Into this it is that I am always falling back! . . . And why?—Because I am always wanting to trust in myself, and to rely on myself! . . . Presumption and pride! . . . Have all these falls opened my eyes? . . . will they one day be opened? Am I to fall still lower, in order to see my own nothingness? O my God! heal me, and keep me from presumption.

22. Do not wonder.—Henceforward, I will take care never to rely on myself in anything. But how am I to succeed in seeing nothing, willing nothing, and doing nothing, except under the influence of grace?—Indeed, it is not the work of a day: to get to this point is to reach the goal of holiness; for where grace alone sows, God's glory alone reaps.

By the fact of the seat of concupiscence which still remains in me, by the fact of my habits, especially by the fact of self-love, I shall again be led to rely on myself, and to act apart from grace, and I shall fall; the seeking of my own satisfaction will drag me more or less deeply into disorder, according as I have more or less forgotten grace. At any rate, I shall no more wonder, I shall no more be upset, and I shall no more be discouraged. Wonder, trouble, and discouragement after sinning, all this comes from pride. Pride thinks itself good and discovers that it is bad, and it is very vexed and upset about it. It obstinately refuses to go to the fountain-head, which alone gives goodness, beauty, and power. If I listen to pride, it is a still greater evil than the fall itself, since it is a lower depth in the fall; and pride hinders humility from deriving from the fall the saving fruits which it can get from everything, even from sin itself.

23. Hope.—I have fallen; and I know it is because I have been leaning upon the bruised reed of self: I have leant upon it, and it has run into my hand and pierced it.[1] Instead of being filled with wonder and irritation and discouragement, I shall say to myself: "This is a good thing, it will kill my pride." And very soon I cast myself into God's arms, and He at once heals my wound and by His grace gives me back goodness, beauty, and strength. I shall next speak to my fallen soul and say: "Why art thou sad, O my soul? and why dost thou disquiet me? Hope in God, for I will still give praise to Him: the salvation of my countenance and my God "(Ps. xlii. 5, 6). In this way, my shortcomings will crush my pride, and will help to bring me nearer to God.

24. Relapses.—It is another ruse and illusion of pride's to persuade one at the end of a retreat, for instance, that henceforth, owing to the resolutions one has taken, there will be no more relapses. I made such good promises. I took such firm resolutions! I feel myself so full of decision and strength! . . . Now, "I will pursue after my enemies and overtake them: and I will not turn again till they are consumed. I will break them, and they shall not be able to stand: they shall fall under my feet" (Ps. xvii. 38). These are splendid words, if they spring from hope in God. The grand fire of hope would be magnificent, if it had in it no breath of pride. What an amount of confidence there is in self, and in one's own resolutions! . . .

Relapses will still occur, since confidence in self still remains. I shall still be wounded in the fray, and perhaps cast down; I ought to expect, and even to foresee this. The roads of the slave-caravans through the great African deserts are tracked

---

[1] Ecce confidis super baculum arundineum confractum istum . . . cui si innixus fuerit homo, intrabit in manum ejus et perforabit eam (Is. xxxvi. 6).

by the remains of human bones, the wreckage of the corpses of the poor slaves who have fallen by the way. On the road of perfection, my path is strewn with the remains of my pride, fallen wherever I have stumbled myself. It is these falls of mine that are instructive. Often I perceive my own confidence in self only at the moment of my fall. At any rate, in falling, I am able to see my self-confidence and weakness. And I must profit by this: it is a great means of progress to me. And I shall go forward in proportion as I succeed in transferring my confidence to God and His grace from myself and my own means. And I shall be fully sure of my road onward, when divine grace is all my support and all my strength.

CHAPTER VI

Prayer

25. All exercises are productive of grace.—26. The soul's aspiration and respiration.—27. We must pray always.—28. Ask in the name of Jesus.—29. Why God makes us pray to Him.—30. The function of prayer in piety.

25. All exercises are productive of grace.—I now must briefly consider exercises which are productive of grace. I know how much I need divine grace, without which I can neither enter into the way, nor advance in the interior life: I therefore greatly need exercises to produce grace. First of all, it is well to remark that the exercises that dispose my soul towards piety, and accustom it to turn to God, to approach Him and to submit to His action, open up by this very fact sources of grace. What, indeed, is actual grace but an impress of light, movement, and energy imparted to my powers by the operation of divine action upon me? All that subjects me to such action or brings me within range of it therefore contributes to increase the divine impulses of actual grace with regard to me and within me. On the other hand, if my soul is justified from the taint of mortal sin, every act that brings me nearer to

God merits a new sanctifying grace, and in this way, every pious exercise turns out to be a channel of grace in some sort.

26. The soul's aspiration and respiration.—But there is an exercise which is in a manner more divine and substantial, and which has a still greater power of drawing one nearer to God, and is yet more productive of grace,—and this is prayer. Prayer, the great means of drawing near, the great channel of grace! Prayer, the universal means, within everybody's reach in all circumstances! This is the first means of the soul which desires to rise, the supreme means of him who would touch the heights of heaven. It is a means of sovereign efficacy for approaching God and obtaining His grace.

For approaching God.—What is prayer?—It is the lifting up of the soul to God.—What is needed, if one is to rise towards God?—Two things: to leave self, and to go to Him. To leave self, I must feel my own wretchedness; to go to Him, I must feel His goodness. To feel the wretchedness, the emptiness, the want, the nothingness of my being, my lack of resources and of life in myself, to be sensible of my dearth of vital air; and then to fling open upon God's infinity the window which will let in an influx of divine air to my lungs—this is prayer; such are the two movements of aspiration and respiration, exactly corresponding with the two fundamental movements of piety, the putting off of self, and the seeking of God.

27. We must pray always.—Further, prayer is the vital sustenance of piety. The devout soul feeds upon prayer, as the lung is fed with air, or the stomach with food. " We ought always to pray, and not to faint," says the Saviour (Luke xviii. 1). It is as if He were to say: " We must always breathe, and never stop." To stop prayer is the same thing to piety as to stop breathing would be to the lungs, it means to stop life itself.

If I would live the incomparable life of piety, if I would expand in it, I must constantly inhale the divine air, and exhale my soul in God. In whatever way I may do this, by inward or outward acts, by my own words or by using set prayers, it matters little; the essential thing is for me to breathe. This breathing need not be done in any particular fixed way, it may be done by any of the movements of my vital activity. Every act of the mind, or heart, or senses, may be a prayer ; ought I not to say, must be a prayer ?— Yes, it should be so, since our Lord says: *Oportet*—" we ought." And what is required that it may be so ?—The act must be a getting away from self and an approach to God. It is thus that life becomes a prayer, and that prayer becomes *vital*. Forms are only necessary so far as they are ordered in certain circumstances, or so far as they help to keep up my divine breathing.

28. **Ask in the name of Jesus.**—Such is prayer in its function of the preparation and adaptation of my soul to God. It also has its part in the production of grace. It obtains it in virtue of the formal promise of the Author of grace. " Amen, amen, I say to you, if you shall ask the Father anything in My name, He will give it you " (John xvi. 23). Jesus makes a solemn engagement in His own name, and in His Father's name : all that is asked for shall be given. But, says He, only what I ask for in His name. What is the meaning of " in His name ?"—It means that one must be recognized, and recommended by Him, and belong to His fold. And then, it means that the prayer must be made for the same purpose as that for which He has purchased grace. If I ask for God's glory and for my own salvation, I am sure to be answered. Nothing thus asked can be refused, since, in praying thus, one prays in Jesus' name. " Ask, and it shall be given you ; seek, and you shall find ; knock, and it shall be opened to you. For every one that asketh, receiveth : and he that seeketh, findeth : and to him that knocketh, it shall be opened " (Matt. vii. 7, 8). Ask for strength to act, and it shall be given you ; seek for warmth for your heart, and you shall find it ; knock at the door of light for your mind, and it shall be opened unto you. Yes, O my God, I will ask, I will seek, and I will knock, for I desire to live. I will ask for myself and for others, and for all God's Holy Church. There are so many and such great interests to pray for. I will extend my petitions, I will increase the number of my entreaties and endeavours, until those designs, to fulfil which Love means to make use of my life, are realized in me and through me, according to the entire scope of my vocation.

29. **Why God makes us pray to Him.**—But why does God make us pray to Him for His grace ?—Why ? . . . Must I not be near Him, if He is to grant me His gifts ? And is it not the purpose of my life to go to Him ? Had He not bound me to pray, I should have remained all the time in myself, and I should be abusing His gifts far away from Him. Thus I should be spending my life like the prodigal son ; and as long as I had any means to waste afar off, I should never return to Him. It is necessity that brings me back to Him. When I feel my need and the riches of my father's house, I rise and return, that is to say, I pray.

And God waits for me to come quite close to Him to embrace me, that is to say, to give me His grace. This is why He makes me wait before He answers me. The dilatory means which He sometimes uses with regard to me are only intended to make me approach closer still. Oh, how good God is to make me pray, and to make me go on praying long ; thus it is that He stirs me to rise towards Him, to press nearer to Him, and to enter into Him. O my God, when shall I understand Thy mercy and all the loveliness of prayer ?

30. **The function of prayer in piety.**—What a wonderful instrument of life is prayer, with its twofold power of uplifting and intercession ! Especially is this the case, when this instrument is combined with that other of the glance of self-examination. While the glance sets right, overlooks, and directs views and intentions and efforts, prayer elevates, brings near, and establishes that divine contact which is my whole life.[1] This contact it is that makes it firm and perfect, and continuously more intimate, more connected, and more complete.

And the more the soul is uplifted towards and united with God, the more it obtains. Its prayer induces an almost illimitable increase of grace, and the divine current is all the more intense the more fully it circulates. How many and great are the currents thus set up in the Church by the potency of true prayer ! What an instrument is this in the hands of those who know how to use it !

[1] See Part II, Book III, § 11.

CHAPTER VII

The Sacraments

31. Sensible signs.—32. The seven sacraments.—33. The seeds implanted.—34. The rights conferred.—35. The treasures accumulated.

31. Sensible signs.—Here are the great reservoirs and channels of grace, instituted by Jesus Christ for the supernatural sustenance of souls : hence is divine life to be drawn, and hence comes its greatest abundance. The Saviour has been pleased to make use of these sensible means to inundate the elect of God with floods of supernatural life. As in Jesus Christ, so in the sacraments the two extremes are united. In Him God and man are joined together ; in the sacrament divine grace is joined to the sensible sign that effects it. Why ?—In order to declare and realize, from one end of creation to the other, the great divine idea which presided over the great work and determined it—union. God united with man in the person of Jesus Christ, this was the climax of the divine work. He unites and incorporates His grace with material signs, the opposite extreme of creation ; and thus every creature becomes united with the divine current. This divine supernatural life I draw from creatures which are below me. Thus was His loving care able, so to speak, to go the whole round of my being, and to bring back to me, by the lower and material side of it, the grace which is to spiritualize me. Starting from the topmost heights, it springs at last from below me to bear me towards the summits from which it first arose.

32. The seven sacraments.—There are seven sacraments, *i.e.*, seven springs of life, answering to the wants of my terrestrial existence. First of all, the initial sacrament that sows the seeds of eternity, Baptism, which changes a child of Adam into a Christian, a child of God, of the Church, and of eternity. Confirmation fructifies the baptismal seeds by bringing to the soul the seven gifts of the life-giving Spirit. The Eucharist feeds the holy growth with a substance which is none other than the very substance of the Son of God and the Son of man, the sovereign food of the divine life and of the human life in the Christian, since Jesus Christ has the fulness of the divine life and the human life.

Penance repairs what is damaged, and cures what is diseased ; it even brings back from death, since it wipes out mortal sin, which is the death of the soul. It is a wonderful remedy, always healing, never losing its efficacy or disappointing ; always at hand, and in readiness, adapted to every kind of disease or death ; only demanding of the sick or dead man a desire for restoration or revival. Then, there is Extreme Unction, the last of our earth-life's consecrations and purifications, and the preparation for the life eternal, when the soul is standing on its threshold.

Lastly, there are the two sacraments which continue and preserve the sacred seed. Holy Order, which consecrates those who are to propagate the divine life ; and Holy Marriage, which consecrates those who are to propagate human life : these are the two *social* sacraments, *par excellence ;* the sacraments, not of individual growth, but of social increase. God has ordained that all life is to increase and multiply.

33. The seeds implanted.—I have received and participated in the sacraments : have I got any fruit from doing so ? There are three things in the sacraments ; and in these three things I have not faith enough ; and this is why I do not obtain from them a satisfactory return, and why I am unable to have as much recourse to them as I ought. I have not enough faith in the seeds implanted, nor in the rights accorded, nor in the treasures accumulated. For the sacraments produce sanctifying grace with the seeds of the habits that accompany it, sacramental grace with the rights that are inherent in it, and actual grace with the treasures that flow from it.

The seeds implanted :—all the sacraments produce sanctifying grace ; Baptism and Penance create it where it does not exist ; the other sacraments increase it. To what extent ?— According to the capacity of the soul into which they enter ; for, in themselves, the sacraments are illimitable in their efficacy. It is an ocean from which one may draw without ever diminishing it. It is a holy fountain, always flowing for everyone, from which everyone may draw according to the size of the vessel which he brings with him.

With sanctifying grace are connected the infused habits of the Christian virtues: divine seeds implanted at first in Baptism, and afterwards swollen with the sap of all the sacraments received. If I only had a practical faith in these seeds and in this sap, the soil of my soul would not remain barren, and I should bring forth to the glory of God other fruits than those which I bear.

34. The rights conferred.—The sacraments produce sacramental grace. What is this grace?—It is a right, founded on sanctifying grace, and in virtue of which I can demand and receive at the proper time the help of actual grace which is fitted to increase the fruits of the sacrament. Each sacrament has its own purpose and effects, and this purpose has to be realized, and these effects are to be ensured. And for all this, by the very privilege conferred by the sacrament, I receive a right to get the necessary help. In the three sacraments of Baptism, Confirmation and Holy Order, this right rests upon an indelible character. Hence, the person who is baptized has a right to the help needed to maintain him in his dignity of being a Christian; the confirmed person has a right to such help as will sustain his strength as a soldier of Christ; the penitent has a right to what ensures his cure; the communicant has a right to such assistance as enables him to get the benefits of the divine food; the sick man has a right to what carries on his purification up to the moment of death; the priest has a right to the assistance needed for his ministry; and the married person has a right to those helps required for the discharge of his immense responsibilities as a parent.

If only I knew how to preserve these rights and to fall back upon them! Assuredly, if God gives them me, it is not for me to neglect them. He lays duties upon me that I may fulfil them; and he confers these rights upon me that I may make use of them. The rights are correlative to duties: if I make no use of the former, I shall not fulfil the latter. No, I have not enough faith in these sacred rights, I am not aware enough of their value; I do not think of claiming them nor of turning them to the best account. And by neglecting my rights, I allow the fruits of the sacraments to run to waste.

35. The treasures accumulated.— Every time I receive the sacrament, it effects a wholesome stir in my soul: it brings light to my mind, warmth to my heart, and strength to my energies. It is an impulse imparted to my life by God. If I only had faith in God, faith in His grace, and faith in the instruments of His grace, should I then be so cold and cowardly and backward in receiving the two sacraments which should be more especially my daily food and the restoration of my inward life? All the treasures of sustenance and cure are there. All calls upon me to make use of them: the wretchedness that I feel, and the facilities put in my way, and the exhortations I receive, and the examples that are given me, and my own experience and the experience of others, and the desires of the Church, and those of God Himself.

And in spite of all this, I am so cold! Can it be that I am so careless as to living for God and according to God! O holy treasures of piety, should I neglect you so, if I wished to advance in you? He who means to get rich does not shrink thus when he can take from the store of treasures in front of him with both hands. Henceforward, let me have a more living and effectual and practical faith in the seeds, the rights, and the treasures of the sacraments.

CHAPTER VIII

The Blessed Virgin

36. The Mother of piety.—37. *Hail, Mary!*—38. *Full of grace.*—39. *The Lord is with thee.*—40. *Blessed art thou among women*

36. The Mother of piety.—I know how much I need grace, and how weak I am of myself; I know to what heights of humility God calls me, and how far I am from attaining to them. When such heights rise before one and such weakness is within one, it is a good thing to feel the hand of God ever near, and ever acting. It is a good thing to trust in this divine Providence, who by the works of His good pleasure comes to raise our death to life, to give strength to our weakness, to encourage us in our cowardice, and to uplift us in our humility. And how good is it to see on the highest peaks of holiness a Mother who bends towards me to support me with her hand, to cheer me with her heart, and to guide me with her look! Mary is on high close to God, the Queen of humbleness, the Mother of divine grace, God's Mother and mine. She bends towards me to say : " I am the pure Mother of fair love and fear and knowledge, that is to say, the Mother of piety, since these three things constitute piety. And I, too, am the Mother of holy hope ; for piety which, as thy Mother, I form and feed in thee on earth, shall only expand in all its fulness in heaven ; trained on earth, enjoyed in heaven. I am thy Mother in time and in eternity. For thee I keep all graces, graces of the way, and graces of the end ; and all hopes, hopes of life above, and hopes of strength on earth to carry thee to heaven. O come to me, all ye that desire me ; come, and I will fill you with the fruit of my womb. My spirit, which will give you life, is sweeter than honey, and the inheritance to which I will lead you is sweeter than the honeycomb."[1]

37. **Hail, Mary!**—O sweet and holy Mother, I desire to come to thee : yes, I desire to place my hand in thine, my heart in thine, and to fix my looks upon thine. I yearn and want so much to live the life of piety, the treasures of which are in thee ! Hail, Mary ! Hail ! O Queen and Mother of mercy, thou art my life, my sweetness, and my hope, hail to thee ! A poor child of death, exiled from the life of God, to thee do I cry. To thee do I send up my sighs, mourning and weeping in this vale of tears. O my dear Mother and Protectress, turn thine eyes of mercy towards me. Be a Mother to me : create in me that life which I cannot make for myself. Thou canst form in me this life of God, since thou art the Mother of God ; thou canst create it, since thou dost possess it in its im-

---

[1] Ego mater pulchræ dilectionis, et timoris, et agnitionis, et sanctæ spei. In me gratia omnis viæ et veritatis, in me omnis spes vitæ et virtutis. Transite ad me omnes qui concupiscitis me et a generationibus meis implemini. Spiritus enim meus super mel dulcis, et hæreditas mea super mel et favum (Eccli xxiv. 24-27).

measurable fulness; thou canst create it, since God has bidden thee be my Mother, and entrusted to thee all life's riches for me. O Mother of God, Mother of divine grace, and my own Mother, make me live by God, with God, and in God.

38. **Full of grace.**—From the first moment of her immaculate conception, Mary, preserved from every taint, was adorned with graces proportioned to her vocation : she was full of grace. And during the whole of her mortal life she was faithful to her vocation, and perpetually referred to the glory of the Most High all that she received from Him. No atom of the sacred gift was lost or turned aside or unused. The immensity of the talents entrusted to her bore fruit in its entirety, and no sin or imperfection, no turning aside, no attachment to creatures, came to check their increase. Mary from the beginning was in a perfect state of unity, and at the highest height of sanctity. Preserved from original sin, she never had any need of purification : none of the divine gifts granted to her were swallowed up by the needs of self-stripping ; hence, all went to increase the treasure of her merits, and helped to glorify and increase her in God. What a life, what merits, and what holiness ! . . . She was full of grace. In myself, what soul-sickness swallows up the resources of life ! in her, nothing is swallowed up. I allow so much of my time to pass away in unfruitfulness ! she, on the other hand, made use in all its fulness of every moment God gave her.

Having thus made use of God's gifts, she can teach me how to use them. Set at the head of the way, she can show me how to get there. A perfect model of all virtues, she can raise her children. A mirror of justice, she can correct their faults. Yes, I may indeed have confidence in such a Mother ! God made me her child, and I am sure that my Mother will not allow a child who wishes to love her, to be near her, and to be like her, to become too far off or too unworthy of her. The higher she is, and the more perfect she is, the better I can hope Mothers do not like being separated from their children.

39. **The Lord is with thee.**—No one can be a mother, unless she gives life : maternity presupposes a communication of life. Mary is a Mother, and she is the Mother of God ; for

of her was born Jesus, who was called Christ.[1] She gave life to Him who is the life of the world. She is thus pre-eminently the Mother of my life; for, for me to live is Christ.[2] Christ came to be the head of the body, of which all the redeemed become members. He is the Vine, I am the branch. Mary, the Mother of the Vine, is also Mother of the branches.

By the privilege of her divine motherhood, Mary's place in the divine intimacy is above that of all creatures. Angels and men, all are inferior to her; for no dignity, whether angelic or human, is comparable with the dignity of the Mother of God. The Lord is with her, and she is with the Lord in a supereminent way. And, in order to be raised to this dignity, Mary had a fulness of grace and a fulness of humility, before which the united greatness of angels and men fades away. The greatness of the Mother of God! . . . all the ages have echoed forth its praise, and yet have not told what it is. All the ages shall proclaim her blessedness, as she has herself foretold :[3] and yet they will never declare it as it is. And no creature will ever tell what it is to be the Mother of God, and what were the grace and humility that made her this.

40. **Blessed art thou amongst women.**—Full of grace in the incomparable privilege of her perpetual virginity, entering into the Saviour's intimacy by the still more incomparable privilege of her divine motherhood, Mary is blessed amongst women in the privilege of her human motherhood. The great benediction of womanhood is motherhood. And Mary amongst all women is the Mother, for she is Mother of all the sanctified. It is she who is used by God for the purpose of giving supernatural life to all the elect; for He has made her the universal distributor of grace. He has made her the channel of graces distributed to angels and men. Our Father, who is in heaven, willed that all His favours should pass through the heart and hands of a mother, so that His children may have all the sweetness of family relationships.

I am of the family of God.[4] God, who is my Father, gives me

---

[1] De qua natus est Jesus, qui vocatur Christus (Matt. i. 16).
[2] Mihi enim vivere Christus est (Phil. i. 21).
[3] Ecce enim ex hoc beatam me dicent omnes generationes (Luc. i. 48).
[4] Sed estis cives sanctorum et domestici Dei (Eph. ii. 19).

all things through Mary my Mother; and all together, both angels and men, participate in the graces of our Father and Mother. Who would dare to be discouraged, if he only understood a little the heart of his God and the heart of his Mother? O my God, I hope in Thee, I am sure that Thou wilt sanctify me; O my Mother, O Mother blessed amongst women, I fling myself into thy arms, and by thee I hope to obtain all things, grace and strength, virtue and life, purity and glory. By thy help I shall become worthy of thee and of God, worthy to sing with thee the praises of our common Father, and in Him to enjoy with thee the bliss eternal.

CHAPTER IX

Jesus Christ

41. Invocation.—42. God and man: their union in Jesus Christ.—43. In myself.—44. In this book.—45. Which is only a Preface.

41. *Invocation.*—O my Jesus, hitherto I have spoken but little of Thee. To begin with, it is so hard to speak well of Thee! and I am so poor a speaker! I would contemplate Thee and get to know Thee in order to be able to say a little about Thee. But, like Simon Peter, I am wholly astonished, and I can only cast myself at Thy feet and say: " Depart from me, for I am a sinful man, O Lord!"[1]

I have said little of Thee, and yet I have spoken only for Thee. I have only attempted one sole thing: to find the secret of becoming like Thee. And I have tried to fathom the depths of this secret, for it is a secret that seems to me exceeding deep. I did not strive to discover with the saints what is the breadth, and length, and height, and depth.[2] I am too small to reach to such greatness.

At any rate, I desired to discover something of the depth

---

[1] Simon Petrus procidit ad genua Jesu, dicens: Exi a me, quia homo peccator sum, Domine. Stupor enim circumdederat eum (Luc. v. 8).
[2] In caritate radicati et fundati, ut possitis comprehendere cum omnibus sanctis, quæ sit latitudo et sublimitas et profundum (Eph. iii. 17, 18).

and to find out the primary roots and foundations of charity, which will finally succeed in attaining to all this greatness.

42. **God and man: their union in Jesus Christ.**—In the Preface,[1] I said that this book was itself only a Preface; and, in conclusion, I have to say the same thing. "The real central dogma of Christianity," says Soloviev,[2] "is the intimate and entire union of the divine with the human, without confusion, and without division."

For His own glory and for His creature's happiness, God willed the union of His creature with Himself. The absolutely perfect consummation of this union lies in the adorable Person of our Lord Jesus Christ. He is both God and man. He is perfect God and perfect man; God and man united together in a personal, indissoluble union; united without confusion, and without division. This is the climax of the divine idea.

During seven centuries, the Church strove against heresies which were perpetually renewed, and which attacked one after the other every side of this primordial and fundamental dogma of Christianity. From the first of the Gnostics to the last of the Iconoclasts, heretics raged sometimes against the integrity of the divine nature in Christ, sometimes against the integrity of His human nature, and sometimes against both. And truth emerged from the darkness, and the union of the divine and the human in Jesus Christ remained the foundation of the Christian faith.

Why were there these struggles? Why was the whole force of the Church so intensely concentrated on this point through so many centuries?—Because Jesus Christ is the foundation of the human and divine edifice, and because the divine and human union, if it were broken in Jesus Christ, would be broken up throughout humanity.

43. **In myself.**—It is through Jesus Christ, and in His body and in His likeness, that every man must participate in the divine union. What is a Christian?—He is a man who bears the likeness of Jesus Christ, and is a member of His body. And how am I to become a member of His body and to bear His image?—By realizing within me, as far as I can, that

---
[1] See § 3.
[2] *La Russie et l'Eglise universelle.*

union which is the specific idea and the essential characteristic of Christianity: union with God, without mixture or confusion, without deterioration or lesion, without separation or division : the union of my being with the divine being, of my life with the divine life : union through the perfection of my being and of my life by my uplifting to participate in the divine nature : union by the subordination of my being and of my life to the being and the life of God. For the divine is superior and anterior to the human ; and, in the union of the two, it is the superior that must govern the inferior. As the soul governs the body, so must God govern man.

And that is the basis and the substance of the Christian idea, it is the foundation of the structure, the skeleton of the body, the root of the plant. If the Christian structure is wanting in this substance, it will only be a lovely outward polish. Polish is easily found : substance is more rarely met with.

44. In this book.—Here I have tried to employ but little polish, and a great deal of substance. In fact, it seems to me that I have only desired, pursued, and considered one thing : divine union, the union of my whole being with God only. How ?—By disclosing the divine glory as the supreme end, hovering above, shining down, and attracting ; by liberating my satisfaction and my whole being, separating it from the fascination of creatures, perfecting it by purification, and by this process of improvement applying it to the glory of God ; by reducing creatures and their pleasures to the sole instrumental function assigned to them in God's plan :—such is the purpose of Part I.

And what is the endeavour of Part II ?—To subject the human activity to the divine, in order that the divine may succeed in ruling the human absolutely, since the union between the two cannot exist unless the one is controlled by the other.

And in Part III, the simplification and the unification of the exercises of piety, and their relations to grace and divine activity, also show how far the one tendency of all the means is towards divine union.

Hence, here there is, indeed, the primary substance of the

Christian life from its first growth to its full expansion, and the fundamental secret of the formation of the divine-human life.

45. It is only a Preface.—But here is only the skeleton of the body, the framework of the building, the root of the tree. O Jesus, Thou art the vine and I am the branch.[1] Thou art the head, and I am the member.[2] Thou art the cornerstone and the foundation,[3] and I am only a very little stone in the building.[4] In Thee must I grow, in Thee must I be built up, for the eternal glory of Thy Father and my Father, of Thy God and my God. Thus art Thou my end, since in Thee I am to be consummated in unity. Therefore I ought to study Thy eternal life in God and Thy mystical life in the Church, so as to contemplate my end therein.

But Thou art also my way. For Thou camest into our midst to live our life, doing the will of Thy Father who sent Thee, so as to lead us in the eternal way[5] by the example of Thy conduct and by the words of Thy teaching. And no one goeth unto the Father, but by Thee.[6] Therefore, I ought to study Thy mortal life and Thy teaching, in order to find my way therein.

And Thou didst will, in Thy humanity, to become the mediator between God and men,[7] that is to say, to become our vital means by winning for us the graces of life by Thy sufferings and death. Therefore, I ought to study Thy sufferings and death, in order to find the means of life therein. . . .

Thou art the vine, and I am the branch; Thou art the body, and I am the member. The branch lives with the tree on the life of the tree; the member lives with the body by the life of the body. Thus, O Jesus, my life, I live in Thee, and by Thee. From Thee I receive the divine blood, and the divine sap; from Thee I await my growth.

Hence, Thou art my end, my way, and my means. Thou

---

[1] Ego sum vitis, vos palmites (Joan. xv. 5).
[2] Et ipsum dedit caput supra omnem Ecclesiam (Eph i. 22).
[3] Ipso summo angulari lapide Christo Jesu (Eph. ii. 20).
[4] Et ipsi tanquam lapides vivi superædificamini (1 Pet. ii. 5).
[5] Deduc me in via æterna (Ps. cxxxviii. 24).
[6] Nemo venit ad Patrem nisi per me (Joan. xiv. 6).
[7] Unus et mediator Dei et hominum, homo Christus Jesus (1 Tim. ii. 5).

Thyself hast said: "I am the way, and the truth, and the life" (John xiv. 6).

O Jesus, be unto me indeed Jesus, and lead me with Thee in the ways of piety, wherein I shall serve, love, and see God in the enigma of this life and in the brightness of the life eternal. *Amen. Fiat!*

CHAPTER X

General Résumé

46. Unity.—47. Life.—48. A commandment which lies very close to me.—49. An easy way.—50. Prayer.

46. Unity.—To sum up : three points stand out very prominently from this exposition as a whole ; they are the marks for piety to aim at : the glory of God, the dominant purpose of my life ; the "Thank Thee" in acceptance of the will of God, ruling the way of piety ; the glance of self-examination, ruling the means. These three things are interdependent, and unite piety in one. Thus is all piety reduced to unity ; unity of end, unity of way, unity of means, unity of the whole. There is only one Lord, one faith, one baptism, says the great Apostle. There is only one God and Father of all, who is above all, and towards whom we must rise, who is in us all to raise us to Himself, and who gives us all things as means to go to Him.[1]

How easy is it for a soul who has understood this to go forward by this means on this way and towards this end ! Is not piety, of a truth, thus understood, thus delivered from the manifold complications in the maze of which people so often get lost, brought within the reach of all who are eager for perfection ? It seems to be great, really great and infinite, like God ; and I see more clearly the breadth of our Lord's words : "Be ye perfect as your heavenly Father is perfect" (Matt. v. 48). But this greatness is so simple in its unity !

---

[1] Unus Dominus, una fides, unum baptisma. Unus Deus et Pater omnium, qui est super omnes, et per omnia et in omnibus nobis (Eph. iv. 4, 5).

THE MEANS: GRACE

47. Life.—Hence, unity is everywhere, and everywhere, too, is life. The opening chapter of Part I is headed: " Life " And what, indeed, did I do all through the four Books of Part I, except meditate on the elements, the organization, the growth, and the crowning of my life ? Part II showed me the ways of life, and the means of life are the subject of Part III. The whole work is entitled " *The Interior Life.*" It is, indeed, this that I have been trying to discover without stopping or swerving ; life in its first springs, life with God, the interior life ; not a life of external agitation, and which, in its separation, is only a waste of existence.

O God, in these meditations I feel that I have found a real desire to live ; to live, which means constant growth, and growing by every means ; growth in Thee, by Thee, for Thee ; growth unending, unresting, until I rest in the peace of eternity.

48. A commandment which lies very close to me.—No, indeed, " this commandment, that I command thee this day, is not above thee, nor far off from thee : nor is it in heaven, that thou shouldst say : Which of us can go up to heaven to bring it unto us, that we may hear and fulfil it in work ? Nor is it beyond the sea ; that thou mayest excuse thyself, and say : Which of us can cross the sea, and bring it unto us, that we may hear, and do that which is commanded ? But the word is very nigh unto thee, in thy mouth and in thy heart, that thou mayest do it. Consider that I have set before thee this day life and good, and on the other hand death and evil : . . . Choose therefore life, that both thou and thy seed may live : and that thou mayest love the Lord thy God, and obey His voice, and adhere to Him—for He is thy life and the length of thy days " (Deut. xxx. 11-20). He is thine everlasting life.

49. An easy way.—" And a path and a way shall be there. and it shall be called the holy way : the unclean shall not pass over it : and this shall be unto you a straight way, so that fools shall not err therein " (Is. xxxv. 8).

There it lies before me, the path of perfection : there goes the great way of holiness. It is the only way, the way the saints have trod. Few there are who find it (Matt. vii. 14) ;

for he who is tainted with seeking self and creatures knows it not. He, indeed, goes by the manifold and hard ways of creatures, but he is unaware of the way of God.[1] The latter is not hard, it is but one, direct, straight, short, easy, and sure. One can go forward in it without fear and without danger. It does not need wisdom of judgement, nor skill in execution. The most simple, the most ignorant, the most stupid, run no risk of going astray therein. It is within everybody's reach In conclusion, let us listen to the advice of wise Tobias: " Bless God at all times: and desire of Him to direct thy ways, and that all thy counsels may abide in Him " (Tob. iv. 20).

50. **Prayer.**—O God, the Father of my life, grant that, in all the perfection whereof I am capable, to-day and all the days of my life, docile to the grace of Thy Holy Spirit, and faithful to the means of sanctification, I may ever conform to the dispositions of Thy Providence and be true to the duties of my state of life, in order that for Thee above all, and for Thee alone, I may grow in Jesus Christ by the working of truth in charity, and that I may rejoice in the sole and supreme glory of Thy holy name. Amen.

[1] Ambulavimus vias difficiles viam autem Domini ignoravimus (Sap. v. 7)

SUMMARY
OF THE INTERIOR LIFE SIMPLIFIED

PREFACE

To-day there are, unfortunately, too many who, though they are called to live a serious life and have serious desires, are stifling in sentimentalism and becoming dispersed in incoherent and disconnected practices, sinking beneath the pettiness of poor ideals. And yet they were made for the heights, and their ascent would uplift those around them towards the things of God.

It is for such that I would outline the framework of the Christian life, showing it from foundation to roof, setting forth its structure, the work to be done, and the tools to be used. Such is the aim of this work, which is divided into three parts.

Part I is entitled THE END, and deals with the life to be lived. It gives the *building* to be erected, and shows the *plan*.

Part II is entitled THE WAY, and deals with the work to be done. It gives the *mode* of erection, and shows the *rules*.

Part III is entitled THE MEANS, and deals with the instruments to be used. It gives the *materials*, and shows their *use*.

This Summary is intended (1) to give a single rapid general view of the whole of the larger work, (2) to serve as a handy reminder for retreats, the numbers and titles always enabling reference to be made for amplification to a corresponding chapter of the complete work.

PART I

THE END
(p. 1)

Life (p. 3).—An examination of all kinds of life shows that life is nothing else than the development of a vital principle. The principle is one, its developments are many : the many developments spring from a single principle.

What is the principle ? what are the developments ? how do these developments spring from the principle ? These three questions are at the root of all life.

Like all life, the spiritual life is the development of a principle. What is this principle ?—It is well known ; its developments are less so, and especially the way in which the developments spring from the principle is too little known. To consider the principle, its developments, and their mutual connexion is what I here propose to do : thus I shall go down to the very roots of the interior life.

In this Part I, I am going to look at life, which is my end : and I shall consider it : 1. in its elements ; 2. in its organization ; 3. in its growth ; 4. in its summits. Hence four Books.

BOOK I

THE ELEMENTS
(p. 7)

1. The purpose of creation (p. 8).—The fundamental principle which is developed throughout the spiritual life is that which is set at the beginning of religion, at the head of the Creed: " I believe in God the Father Almighty, Creator of heaven and earth." All flows from this.

God has created everything: all things are the work of His hands. But if He created them, it was for a purpose; for He is wise, and He created them in His wisdom.

God had a purpose, and could have had one only. This purpose is Himself and His glory. God's creation was for His own glory.

He could have had no other than this essential end. For had He referred His action to any other than Himself, He would have referred Himself to this other, who would have been greater than He: and then God would not have been God.

God's glory, which is the one essential end of all beings, is also their one and only good; for a being cannot have any true good apart from its end.

Every being is made to glorify God, and every being finds its happiness in glorifying God.

2. My end (p. 10).—Further I am created by God, and I am created for God. His glory is my essential end, the reason of my existence, my only good, my whole self.

My essential end: nothing else in my life is essential.

The reason of my existence: it is the reason of my life, the reason of my death, and the reason of my eternity.

My only good: I have no other good than this, and than what leads me to this.

My whole self: if I do not work for the glory of God, I do nothing, I am good for nothing, I am nothing.

With His own glory God has united my happiness, so that in giving glory to God I am made happy in Him. This blessedness begins here, and is completed hereafter.

3. Union (p. 14).—Amidst the infinite number of ways in which He might have been glorified in His creature, God chose the mode of supernatural union, of participation in His divine life. This was quite a free gift of His goodness! It is by my union with Him, by the union of my life with His, that I am called to give glory to my Creator.

This supereminent mode of union is freely proposed to me:

SUMMARY

I may rise to such a height, just as I may fail to do so. If I do not attain to it, I shall lose my happiness; but God will not lose His glory, which will make good its rights over me by the justice of punishment.

4. **The order of my relations with God** (p. 17).—In this union to which I am called, there is God's part, and my part; there is His glory, and there is my happiness. Are these two things on the same footing?—No: His glory is essential, before all, and above all. It is the first and dominant end.

5. **The dependence of my satisfaction** (p. 20).—My temporal and eternal happiness is annexed thereto, as a secondary end. It is so united therewith that it springs from it alone. It is subordinate thereto, so that I may not seek it before God's glory. God comes first, self second.

6. **The use of creatures** (p. 22).—To secure my end, God has put means into my hands, instruments adapted for the purpose: these are creatures.

By creatures, I mean all that has been made, and all that continues to take place daily, whether in the spiritual order or in the material order.

All these creatures, *i.e.*, all things outside God, are for me means and instruments, to attain my end. They are this, and for this only.

Means and instruments for God's glory, essentially and before all else: means of satisfaction, secondarily.

7. **Satisfactions in creatures** (p. 27).—There are in creatures pleasures which are very varied and agreeable; spiritual, intellectual, moral, and material pleasures.

Whose work are they?—God's.—Why has He scattered them amongst creatures?—For me to use them, and not to rest in them.

What is their function?—It is the function of the drop of oil in machinery. Wherever there is a duty, there is a creature which is its instrument, and a pleasure which makes it easier. This pleasure is not final, it is only instrumental.

8. **The order of my relations with creatures** (p. 30).—This is the order to be kept in the use of the instruments of my life. Pleasure, subject to utility; human utility, organized according to the worthiness of the vital interests, and referred to divine utility. I must so take things and the enjoyment of things as to increase my life and to rise towards God.

9. **The essential order of creation** (p. 33).—God's glory, the essential end, first: my satisfaction in God, the secondary end, annexed thereto: creatures, the means and instruments: their proper pleasure, an instrumental facilitation. Such is the order of creation, such is God's plan.

And this plan shows me my greatness: all is mine, and I am God's.

10. **Explanation of the Pater Noster** (p. 36).—This plan is summed up in the *Pater Noster*. It sums up everything.

First petition : in front of all else ; God's glory in the sanctification of His name. This is the supreme end.

Second petition : coming immediately afterwards ; my own satisfaction in the kingdom of God. This is the end annexed.

Third petition : the will of God, marking out the way.

Fourth petition : God's bread, which comprises the means of sustenance of both soul and body. Here, then, we have had the end, the way, and the means.

Fifth petition : the removal of sin, which is the hindrance opposed to the end, and destructive of life.

Sixth petition : the removal of temptation, which is an obstacle that blocks the way, and hinders work.

Seventh petition : the removal of evils, which deprive me of the means of sustenance and work.

BOOK II

ORGANIZATION

(p. 41)

1. My obligations (p. 42).—Am I not bound to respect God's plan ?—Clearly, all my conduct must conform thereto.

But how is this to be done ?

(*a*) By considering God's glory in everything in the first place as the sole essential end of my life. By considering in creatures what serves the glory of God. To consider this in the first place is a primary obligation, an obligation of the mind.

(*b*) By loving God's glory above all else, by loving what glorifies God in creatures, not loving the creature for its own sake, nor for my own sake, but for God. To love this above all is the second obligation, an obligation of the heart, *i.e.*, of the will.

(*c*) By choosing and using all things in the measure, neither more nor less, in which they serve God's glory. Thus to employ and make use of all things is freedom of action : it is the third obligation, which binds my activity.

Seeing God and all things for Him, is truth ; loving God and all things for Him, is charity ; seeking God through all things, is freedom of action, which is liberated from the tyrannical fascination of being cheated by creatures.

2. The essence of piety (p. 46).—The union of these three obligations into one constitutes piety.

Piety is seeing, loving, and seeking God in all things, and all things in God.

An act of piety is made up of these three things : seeing, loving, and seeking God.

St. Paul defines piety : it is our increase in Jesus Christ by means of all creatures, by doing the truth in charity.

The increase and development of this life of piety proceeds through five main degrees, which I shall presently consider.

This increase makes use of all creatures, which serve as means for the purpose.

An act of this increase is that which does the truth in charity freely.

Truth in the mind, charity in the heart, freedom in action : such are the three elements of piety ; seeing. loving, and seeking God.

Piety is the resultant of these three things so united that it is the free putting into practice of the truth in charity.

The first question of the Catechism contains teaching as deep as that of St. Paul. Man, it says, is created to know, love, and serve God, and thus to merit eternal happiness. Here we have the whole of piety.

3. The virtue of piety (p. 50).—The virtue of piety is the habit of doing acts with facility and readiness.

Hence, I possess the virtue of piety when I have acquired facility and readiness in seeing, loving, and seeking God in all things and all things for God.

Piety is a kind of summing up and putting into practice of all the virtues. It is the great disposition, which results from the practice of all the virtues ; it is piety that produces unity in the soul, by concentrating into a single and general habit all the particular habits that are proper to the Christian virtues. It is the great duty which sums up all duties ; the great virtue which is the resultant of all the virtues ; it is life, it is the whole of man.

4. God's glory (p. 55).—I can now appreciate the meaning of these words : to glorify God. The glory of God means the divine perfections known, loved, exalted. All perfections, each in particular, or all together, are the object of glory ; every act of knowledge, love, and honour in isolation, and all such acts united together, are its form.

In the life of the Trinity, God possesses, knows, and loves all His own perfections ; this is His inward glory, as infinite as Himself.

As for me, I may and must know, love, and honour the divine perfections which are revealed to me ; this is the outward glory, in which my life ought to be employed.

5. Zeal (p. 58).—Hence, it is my piety that glorifies God. By dilating my life in piety, I shall increase God's glory, my soul will magnify the Lord. And I shall increase it not only in myself, but round about me. For God has done me the altogether divine honour of enabling me to be an author and propagator of life for Him and along with Him. Zeal for God's interests will then cause me to exercise around me all the vital influences belonging to my vocation. And thus I shall be bound to those I love by the very bonds of life, both in this world and in eternity.

6. Disorder. Adherence to creatures (p. 61).—Disorder consists in letting myself be deceived by pleasure in creatures, which, instead of helping me to pass quickly and readily through creatures to go to God, makes me adhere to them ; I get stuck fast, stop short, and rest outside God.

7. Disorder. Attachment to self (p. 64).—Stopping myself at creatures, I also stop them at myself ; I use them to entertain myself with pleasure. And thus I rob God, by appropriating to myself the use of the instruments and the life that ought to be directed towards Him.

And thus it is that the selfish spirit is formed, the spirit that makes me look at everything from the point of view of my own satisfaction ; self-love, which makes me like things for the pleasure they give me ; and self-interest, which makes me seek my own convenience in everything.

The evil does not lie in my satisfaction in itself, but in the displacement and subversion brought about by my taking as an end what ought to be merely a matter of instrumental facilitation.

8. **Disorder. Its effects (p. 66).**—There is the evil. There is no other evil but that, and what participates in it, leads to it, and comes of it.

It is the perversion of my life and the subversion of my entire being. It is falsehood in my mind, which disorder robs of the truth ; vanity in my heart, which it robs of charity ; slavery of my senses, which it deprives of liberty ; a wrong to creatures, which groan under its tyranny ; and, lastly, it is the wastage and destruction of my life, which gets spent and poured out far from God.

9. **Disorder. Its degrees (p. 71).**—There are three great stages of disorder. First, pleasure in creatures is inclined to be put on the same footing as God's glory, as an end ; the soul is divided, life is partitioned, God alone is not my sole end. This is *division*, the first stage.

Next, the fascination of pleasure gets the upper hand of God's honour, which drops back into the second place : then there is a subversion, and a preference of the human to the divine is set up. This is *dominance*, the second stage.

Lastly, evil pleasure goes to such extreme lengths as to exclude God's glory, to kill the divine life, and to separate man from God. This is *exclusion*, the third stage.

Hence, division, dominance, exclusion, here we have disorder in its fullest extent.

Piety has to regain possession of the soul in these depths, and to restore it to the heights of divine union.

First, it removes mortal sin which brings about exclusion, and restores God to the soul and the soul to God. This is the first stage.

Then, it destroys the dominance of the human, and restores its rights of precedence to the divine. This is the second stage, which comprises two degrees ; the avoidance of venial sin, and the avoidance of imperfection.

Lastly, it works for the re-establishment of unity, by doing away with mistaken division between pleasure and God. This is the third stage, and it, too, comprises two degrees : holiness, and fulfilment.

Hence, these three great stages include in all five degrees of ascent, which are now to be considered.

10. **Avoiding mortal sin : the first degree of piety (p. 74).**— The lowest degree of disorder is when I am seeking my own satisfaction in such a way as to break off with God altogether, separating from Him, and nullifying His glory. This is mortal sin, evil in all its horror.

Piety begins with the re-establishment of order in this matter; that is to say, in such circumstances as would lead me to break off with God altogether and to commit a mortal sin, my own satisfaction must be put below God's glory, and be immolated thereto, if necessary, rather than that I should commit this mortal sin. And even if I had to sacrifice all my own satisfactions, including life itself, I should do it. This is the absolute avoidance of mortal sin, the first degree of piety.

BOOK III

GROWTH

(p. 79)

1. Avoiding venial sin : the second degree of piety (p. 80).—Man still seeks for his own satisfaction before God's glory in things that hurt and vex God : this is venial sin : an offence, subversion, and dominance of the human, but in a lesser degree.

The correction of this disorder is the second degree of piety, which is the entire avoidance of venial sin.

This degree is attained, when the heart, mind, and senses are totally purified from voluntary venial sin, and when the soul can easily and readily make the *necessary* sacrifices, even that of life itself, rather than deliberately commit the slightest venial sin.

This second degree presupposes a virtue which is indeed rare, but which is still not perfection.

2. Imperfection : the dominance of the human (p. 82).—Imperfection is seeking self before God, yet doing this without any formal offence. It lies in two things : the dominance of the human ; the absence of sin.

The dominance of the human, known or unknown, intentional or unintentional, actual or habitual :—the soul is subject to certain natural instincts and tendencies, which lead it to prefer its own convenience to the perfect fulfilment of God's wishes. This is the first mark of imperfection.

3. Imperfection : the absence of formal offence (p. 85).—It has a second mark, inseparable from the first, which is that the dominance of the human never goes to the length of becoming a formal offence against God. Whether it be that, where something is formally forbidden, there is an acquittal from sinning because of want of advertence or consent, and the shortcoming is then only an imperfection : or else, because the soul, under the dominance of the human, is carried away so far as to infringe a counsel only.

When St. Peter testifies his love to our Lord by protesting against His passion, and the Saviour treats him as Satan for thus preferring the things of man to the things of God, the Gospel gives us a striking example of imperfection, and of the rebuke that it deserves.

4. Imperfection : its evil (p. 88).—In mortal sin, the perversion of my will separates me from God, and this is death. In venial sin, there is only a deviation, and this is a sickness. In imperfection, the slightness of the matter, the weakness of my will or mind, bring it about that the deviation is not complete enough, not deliberate and intentional enough on my part, to constitute a formal offence against God : and this is an uncivility. Such is the difference between them.

To know the extent of an imperfection, I must remember that life is almost entirely made up of good and indifferent acts Occasions of sin are relatively rare ; good and indifferent acts occur at every moment.

It is in these acts that imperfection is to be found ; and if it possess them all, one's whole life is a thing of disorder : a disorder, without being a sin.

Is not this an alarming thought ? I may avoid sin fairly regularly, and yet live in continual disorder, constantly subverting the plan of my creation by imperfection ! O God, what then must sin be ? . . .

5. **Perfection: the third degree of piety (p. 90).**—Perfection consists in making good the evil of imperfection, that is to say, in putting back in its place in the front rank God's glory in all our acts, good or indifferent, and in putting our own satisfaction in the second place and at His service.

Perfection is thus called, because it purifies my actions from all admixture of the evil of human preference ; it leaves no trace in them of the disorder of dominance of the human ; and my satisfaction is *never* again put before the glory of God. All is put right, and good is therefore *perfect* so far as this is concerned. This is the first kind of perfection, the perfection of ordinary ways.

6. **The state of perfection (p. 93).**—I shall reach this state, when my thoughts, affections, and actions have been all put right, in such a way that *in everything* I am quick and ready to see, love, and seek God's glory *before* my own satisfaction. *In everything :* it is this everything that is the mark of perfection.

How high is this state, since it affects everything in life ! . . . It sets everything straight !

This should be the characteristic state of Bishops, since they are bound, in virtue of their dignity, to be in the state of perfection.

It is the state that befits priests, since they participate to a large extent, by their priesthood, in the episcopal dignity.

And towards this state the religious is bound to tend by his vows, since a religious profession binds him to tend towards perfection.

7. **Perfection and sacrifice (p. 95).**—Perfection consists in setting straight, not in sacrifice : it requires me to subordinate my own satisfaction, not to immolate it.

Whether you eat or drink, or whatever you do, do all to the glory of God, says St. Paul.

Thus, perfection does not require me to deprive myself to any extraordinary extent in the use of food or drink, for instance, but only that, at least virtually, I should set the intention of God's glory before my feeling of hunger or thirst.

When I suppose that perfection consists in sacrifice, two evils arise : the first, I do not set about making the improvements in

SUMMARY

which perfection consists; the second, the sacrifices in which I think that perfection resides, are beyond my strength, and I get discouraged, and think perfection is impossible.

8. The state of my soul (p. 99).—And now, O my soul, let us make an examination of conscience ! . . . Let me fathom my mind . . . let me ask myself what place in my thoughts is given to the glory of God. . . . See now : I say of any season : it is a good, or a bad season. What guides me in making an estimate ? My own advantage, or pleasure. I say the same of my food, or animals, or flowers, or happenings, or men, or things. I call that good which is so for me ; that bad, which is bad for me. I fathom my judgements : God's glory often has no place in them.

Let me fathom my feelings. I love this person, and dislike that one, why ?—According to my liking . . . I avoid this person's company, and I seek the society of that other, I rejoice in a success, I am cast down by opposition, I want this occupation, and I dread that one, what someone says encourages me, some chance fills me with depression, some deed upsets me. . . . What is the principal motive of these impulses ?—My own interest. Where does God's glory come in ?

Let me examine my actions. What makes me act ?—My own interests. These are too generally the dominant purpose of what I do, and they determine my conduct. I try to find those actions whereof God's glory is really the dominant motive : are there many of them ?

What place is given to the glory of God in what is called piety ? —A prayer, a communion, a feast, a sermon, and any exercise whatever, are only good so far as I am pleased with them. It is my own satisfaction that is only too apt to provide me with a criterion, even in the things of the spirit.

I act for my own interest, I love for my own satisfaction, I think according to my own interests: such is the summing up of my life.

9. The general state (p. 103).—And this is just the position of society as a whole . . . *human* interest is now the universal motive. History, politics, science, industry, commerce, associations, families : in all and everywhere, human utility inspires people's judgements, determines their likings, and directs their actions. In practice, God has only a secondary place in society.

10. The state of the evil (p. 106).—That which is deepest in me, my thinking, is vitiated : it is just there that the evil is most to be dreaded.

What first demands cure is my thinking, my ideas, my judgements : there before all must the glory of God recover its place and ascendency.

11. Restoration (p. 108).—O my soul, let it be said squarely. I have to turn my life upside down, to transform my ideas, to renew my affections, to reverse my conduct.

Above all, there must be new thoughts . . . for all, new affections . . . in all, new conduct. . . . Everywhere God must take His proper place, the place which our own satisfaction has deprived Him of. What work there is to do !

BOOK IV

THE SUMMITS
(p. 113)

1. Holiness: the fourth degree of piety (p. 114).—When I can gain a hundred pounds, am I to be satisfied with fifty?—Certainly not. For my own interest I always try to get the best, and that seems reasonable.

And what about God's glory? . . . which is essential . . . am I to make less of it? Am I to be more unreasonable where God's glory is in question than where my own interest is concerned?

To seek the greater glory of God in all things is the proper and primary work of holiness.

In the three preceding degrees, the soul was busied in ordering its own satisfaction below the glory of God. Now that its satisfaction is so ordered, the soul no longer thinks of it, but forgets it. It becomes indifferent as to joy as well as grief, to sickness as well as health, to contempt as well as praise, all this does not take up its attention any longer. Forgetfulness of self, indifference as to pleasure in creatures, such is the second mark of holiness.

Hence, forgetfulness of and indifference about one's own satisfaction, and care for the greater glory of God, these constitute holiness.

The state of holiness is established in the soul, when it has acquired facility and readiness in forgetting itself in all things, and in seeing in all things the greatest glory of its Creator.

2. Mystical death (p. 117).—All that is *human* is mortal. My body is mortal, that is to say, it has to pass through dissolution, in order to rise again in glory.

In the same way, my thoughts, affections, actions, and *human* satisfactions are mortal, that is to say, they have to pass through forgetfulness and mystical death, in order to be transformed and to become divine.

In man and his actions, I call that "human" which is withdrawn from supernatural influence, and which comes from nature.

3. Transformation (p. 120).—Day by day the wall of separation gradually gives way, the human crumbles, and false satisfactions disappear. And in proportion as enjoyment ceases to be human, it becomes divine. Instead of taking my rest and happiness in creatures, I take them in God. Thus there is a continual transition from death to life.

The degrees of ascent of piety, in attaining perfection and fulfilment one after another, witness a gradual falling away of some portion of the falsities of the human before union with the divine. At the fourth degree, which is holiness, indifference and forgetfulness have reduced the human to a state of languor bordering upon death.

4. **Consummation: the fifth degree of piety** (p. 123).—When a soul has reached this point, what remains for it to do?—One thing only: to immolate the last remains of human satisfaction to the glory of God, in order that the latter, which is the only source of happiness, may triumph over the *débris* of creatures and of disorder.

This is the final but absolutely logical conclusion of the fundamental principle of my creation. I am made for God alone; His glory is my all. Therefore, the more God is left solely in Himself, the more does that which is apart from Him disappear, and the better do I attain my end. As long as I consider any satisfaction apart from God's glory, the latter is not wholly my end; there remains something apart from it, and this occupies some portion of my heart. But nothing must be left behind, my life must be no longer divided, and I must see, love, and seek nothing but God: He in me, and I in Him.

Hence, I must immolate and annihilate every satisfaction which is not included in God's glory.

The desire for immolation, the thirst for suffering, the love of the Cross, such are the marks of this state.

When the ascent of this degree is finished, unity is consummated: God only . . . . what a word is this! . . . When shall I understand it? . . .

5. **Purgatory** (p. 127).—None can enter into heaven until all the work of self-stripping and purification is over. One must possess absolute purity to appear before God. What has not been entirely purified in this world will be so in purgatory. Purgatory is the barest of purification, and does not increase merits: in this life I win merits while I am purifying myself. This is a great reason for raising myself as much as possible during my life on earth.

6. **A general view: unity** (p. 130).—When I seek my own selfish satisfaction, I am endlessly divided by the hosts of objects which attract my sight, love, and seeking.

This division is the cause of my weakness, falls, distractions, and interior indispositions. It is my great evil.

Piety tends towards unity, and works to concentrate everything on one thing only: God, and His glory for His own sake, and my happiness in Him. And its work is not done until unity is consummated: God only! . . .

7. **General view: peace** (p. 134).—This is why piety imparts to the soul: strength, from the unity of all its powers; freedom, through liberation from creatures; peace, through the re-establishment of order.

Piety cures all the evils of the soul, gives every kind of good, and is profitable to all things! . . . Glory to God, peace to man; piety gives all things.

8. For Priests (p. 137).—What is your weakness?—It is seeking self and seeking creatures. In your ministry, there is much self-seeking, and a too utilitarian anxiety as to creature interests. God is not in His place : He is not the sole end. Hence you are divided ; every one of your anxieties means division and rending ; each of them takes away a part of your soul. Thus partitioned, what strength have you ?

If you only knew how to keep God in view . . . , to seek God . . . , and Him alone . . . , in your prayers . . . , in your ministry . . . , do you understand ? Him alone ? . . . every one of your occupations, . . . whatever it might be . . . would become an act of piety. . . . Meditate upon this.

Prayer and work . . . all would bring you back to the sole centre ! . . . To him who seeks God alone . . . , everything becomes a devotional *exercise*. To him who seeks self, *nothing* can be so.

Conclusion (p. 142).—Such, then, is the development of the interior life. Starting from the fundamental principle of my creation, I am led successively to order, forget, and, lastly, to immolate my own satisfaction for the glory of God.

God's glory, growing through the work of inward cultivation, constantly dominates, and then absorbs and transforms my satisfaction.

At the outset, I enjoy contrary to God, and apart from God : at the end, I enjoy in God only.

At the outset, I live for self and not for God : at the end, I live for God, and not for self.

The interior life is that transformation whereby my whole being leaves its natural life and becomes a participator in the divine nature.

PART II

THE WAY
(p. 143)

The Will of God (p. 145).—To attain the end of God's glory, we must follow a way : we must not turn aside to the right or to the left, but go straight along the right road. What is this straight road ?—The road that shows the will of God.

It is the will of God which points out to me what creatures to make use of and what to avoid : for there are some that are useful, and others that are hurtful.

I cannot choose between them of my own accord ; first, because I do not know what is in the creature, and what its use, in every case, may be ; next, because the choice which I make of my own accord will be determined by my likings, and not by the glory of God.

None will enter into the kingdom of God unless he doeth the Father's will ; and entrance into the kingdom of heaven means the meeting of my soul with God in such wise that I give Him His glory and He gives me His happiness. God's glory, man's peace : therein is all the kingdom of God, begun in this world, continued in eternity. By what way, by what gate, does one enter therein ?—By the way of the will of God. The will of God is the only way leading to the glory of God.

One in itself, the will of God is twofold in the manner of its manifestation to me. God wishes to work Himself on the building up of my life, and this is His will of good pleasure. He next wills me to do the work which He signifies to me, and this is His will signified.

And since these two wills ought to be always united and in accord, I have three things now to consider : 1. the will signified ; 2. the will of good pleasure ; 3. the concurrence of the two wills. This is the ground and the subject of the three Books of this Part.

BOOK I

THE WILL SIGNIFIED

(p. 151)

1. Commandments and counsels (p. 152).—The will signified comprises God's commands and desires. His commands are contained in the commandments of God and in the commandments of the Church. His desires are expressed in the Evangelical Counsels. His commands bind under pain of sin, grave or light: His counsels bind under pain of the loss of good and progress.

2. The duties of one's state of life (p. 154).—The duties of one's vocation have the peculiar importance of making known the will of God in the particular state of life in which I find myself. They reveal to me: first, the way in which I have to keep the commandments; second, the part of the evangelical counsels I have to practise.

For priests, the duties of their state of life are laid down by ecclesiastical laws, and liturgical and disciplinary laws; for religious, by their Rule; for laymen, by their professional duties. Ecclesiastical laws for the priest, his Rule for the religious, his professional duty for the layman, these are the most immediate expression and the most practical embodiment of God's will signified.

3. The knowledge of duty. The general obligation (p. 158).— For the work of His glory and of my salvation, God, by His will signified, requires me to do my share of action; He wills me to do something, and lays down for me what I am to do. This is the active part of piety.

What I can do, and what I have to do, is to know, love, and fulfil. I must know my duty, love it, and fulfil it.

First, duties must be known. Knowing is the primary condition of all things. One cannot do well, if one knows badly.

I must know my duties, and all of them, just as they are, without alteration, or addition, or diminution; without allowing myself to be deceived by looking at my own satisfaction, which always tends to dim them, and to travesty and lessen them.

I must see in the obligation not merely the outward fact of its prescription, the letter of the law, but the will of God who commands it, and draws me to Himself in this particular way.

Oh! how much are ignorance and illusions to be feared: ignorance which cannot see, and illusions which see amiss! We are compounded of ignorance, and full of illusions!

4. The knowledge of duty. Special obligations (p. 161).—The main light of my way being the commandments of God, I shall be diligent to get to know them in the letter, and in the spirit; love of the light is needed in order to do the truth.

As a sheep that is true to the fold, I shall also love to hear the voice of the shepherd speaking to me by the commandments of the Church.

And I shall try not to be too much a stranger to the sublimity of the counsels, so that, getting some knowledge of the secrets of God's wishes, I may be able to approach more nearly to Him.

Lastly, I shall shun illusions and ignorance as to the duties of my vocation. Ignorance in such a matter is so harmful, and nowhere is illusion, which springs from self-love, so wide-spread and so fatal. Unfortunate duties of one's state of life! how are they twisted and mutilated, and moulded by every whim of self-interest! And thus misshapen and maimed, they only retain so much of God's will as to be insufficient to keep the conscience from being misled.

5. Love and practice (p. 164).—Let me love God's will before everything, attach myself thereto whenever I meet it in any obligation, and instead of dreading the law or my superiors, let me love them, because they are the organs and the signs of the will of God.

Let me execute this will as faithfully in little things as in great, in vexatious matters as in those that are pleasing, because it is everywhere the same, everywhere equally holy and perfect and amiable.

6. The piety of the priest (p. 167).—If the priest desires to know his duties, let him study them: in the liturgy, where his relations with God are formulated; and in the discipline which determines his duties towards himself and creatures. The denudation of self and the seeking of God have their priestly character therein.

The piety of the priest is composed above all of meditation on, and observance of, the liturgy and ecclesiastical law.

7. The piety of the religious (p. 170).—Its form is to be found in his Rule. Further, the Rule contains in its two parts the manner in which it is proper for the religious to strip himself of self, and to go to God. If only the religious had the spirit of his Rule, and knew how to live by it, if he could only be satisfied therewith, and get transformed by it! How real, strong, simple, right, and divine his piety would be!

8. The spirit of piety (p. 173).—That which has to be seen, loved, and fulfilled is the will of God; the law or the superior is only a sign, a veil, a letter. The sign, veil, and letter are only dead things in themselves; if I stop therein, I find no life. But behind the sign, veil, and letter, there is the will of God, that is to say, God Himself; and God is life. There I find Him in His will, and there only is He to be found.

Oh! if I only knew how to look for God where He is! Often, I fail to find Him, because I look for Him where He is not.

God is no more in prayer than in work, no more in contemplation than in action; He is where His will is. Prayer and action do not help me to find God, unless I see His will in them: but as soon as I see the divine will, I find God in work as well as in prayer.

The way in which we find God is the will of God.

BOOK II

THE WILL OF GOOD PLEASURE
(p. 177)

1. Divine action (p. 178).—Here, it is God who acts within me: it is no longer my action, but God's. How does He act?

He uses everything to work for the good of those whom His will calls unto holiness, everything, even to the falling of a hair. All that takes place within me, around me, for me, against me, all is ordered, calculated, and interwoven with infinite art by Providence for my advance in the way of holiness.

Nothing happens by chance; even the most insignificant details of life are all combined for only one purpose, the glorification of God by the holy soul.

It will be one of the wonders of eternity to see how all, absolutely everything, works together for the good of the elect.

2. The purpose of the divine operations (p. 182).—God laid down the plan of my life before He created me; and He alone knows it in its entirety. His will is to realize this plan, and He never loses sight of it. All His operations, so far as they concern me, are directed to carry it out. And each particular operation works to set, at the right moment, a stone in the building in the place shown on the plan.

Hence, every event in my life, small or great, inward or outward, embodies a thought, a desire, an action of God. His action, aroused by His desire, works towards the realization of His thought.

3. The two modes of God's operation (p. 185).—The divine operations, which work to raise me from evil towards the good, realize this twofold result by trials and consolations.

The purpose of trials is not to torment me, but to liberate me from what is low: consolations are not intended to entertain me, but to raise me towards the heights.

And in fact, when they operate according to God's design, how powerful are trials to create detachment by effecting a spirit of sacrifice, patience, self-denial, heroism, and the like! How efficacious are consolations in uplifting, and in imparting life and enthusiasm! How well will it be, when I can understand all the love of God in consolation, and still more in trial!

4. The progress of the divine work (p. 188).—This is the usual order in which the operations of God strip a man of self and lead him to God.

First of all come sensible consolations to detach the senses from creatures and to attach them to God. When the work of consolations is done, they give way to dryness.

SUMMARY

Next comes the great light of the faith to detach the mind from creatures, and to fix it upon God. When this is done, the light vanishes in darkness.

Lastly comes the burning ardour of zeal to detach the will from all creatures and to turn it towards God. When its mission is accomplished, the ardour dies out in distaste. Thus is external denudation fulfilled.

Next the soul itself must be stripped. Temptations come to subvert the senses, darkness to try the mind, the loss of active virtue, which is the power of acting, and then of passive virtue, which is the power of suffering, to annihilate all *human* activity of the will; and the inner denudation is completed in mystical death, followed by the marriage of the soul with God.

5. **Passive piety (p. 193).**—What have I to do to answer to these operations of the sovereign good pleasure?—I have only to give myself up, to abandon myself, to let be. To accept God's action, the whole of it, without reservation, without curiosity, without uneasiness, here is all my duty, the duty of being a little child in the arms of God.

There must be no reservation. God may bear me where He will, send me where He will, give me what He will; I accept everything, because I know He is only working to make me live.

There must be no curiosity. What is the use of my knowing why God deals with me thus? Why does He do this or that? I shall not insult God by desiring to check His action, or by doubting His intentions.

There must be no uneasiness. What danger do I run when I am in the arms of God? Whether He bears me through fire or over precipices, does not much matter: I close my eyes and fall asleep in His arms.

What the action of God's good pleasure requires of me is my acceptance. And it is because acceptance is the direct reply to make and the first way in which to correspond with God's operations, that this part of piety is called passive piety.

To accept means to acknowledge, welcome, and submit to God's operation in every event.

6. **Waiting for God (p. 197).**—In fine, I ought to expect God, to lay myself open to Him, to receive His action. It is He who is my life. I ought neither to stir and bustle apart from Him, nor to rest far away from Him, but to act by Him. And He must enter into me, if I am to act by Him; and He enters into me, if my soul lies open to Him with docility, with sincerity of attention, and with simple submission, in expectation of the operations of His good pleasure. And if I am uncertain about these operations, it is the divine mission of my spiritual director to explain them to me.

7. **Joys and sufferings (p. 202).**—Above all, I must know how rightly to accept consolation and suffering at God's hand. Both come from Him, and both have the same purpose, to unite me to Him

Consolation is easy to accept, and difficult to accept rightly. It is so dangerous to accept consolation for its own sake, to *stay* in it, and to be satisfied with it, forgetting that it is only a means of God's action.

Further, St. John of the Cross incessantly advises its rejection and avoidance, in order to preserve in all its purity the spiritual effect it produces in the soul. Such procedure presupposes great energy of will and entire detachment.

Other saints advise the acceptance of consolation with very great simplicity, seeking thereby to become more closely attached to God. This presupposes more humility, for humility alone can avoid the snare of self-seeking in consolation.

The great danger in suffering is that of getting discouraged or embittered. If I am given to seeking my own satisfaction, I inevitably fall into one or other of these abysses.

Here, true wisdom consists in conforming with God, following the advice of St. Francis of Sales : "Ask for nothing, and refuse nothing."

8. "I thank Thee" (p. 205).—How is suffering to be accepted? —As one accepts the present of a friend, by saying "Thank you."

This "I thank Thee" must come from the heart : it must be a simple, generous, and rapid exclamation. "O God ! I thank Thee !" That is all. There is no need to be constantly reiterating it, nor to linger much over it.

God hears this "Thank Thee," and it tells Him that His love is appreciated. And what wonderful effects does this little exclamation bring about ! It opens up in the depths of the soul a spring of incomparable joy. He alone who has experienced it, knows what it is like. What treasures does this little utterance reveal in suffering ! it is the key of the divine store-house.

And how easy it is to utter ! It is more difficult to suffer patiently than to make this one brief exclamation.

9. The aloes (p. 208).—A youth who had had some powdered aloes put in his mouth by mischievous companions, forced himself to masticate aloes for a week in order to harden himself and to prevent any future unpleasantness from practical joking.

What an excellent remedy it is to harden oneself to suffering ! And how is it to be done ?—By looking calmly on the bitterest side of any trial that may threaten me, until I can accept it without flinching. So too, I may choose for myself what is painful, leaving to others what is pleasant. Or else, I may feed upon some actual trouble without grimacing, as long as it pleases God to inflict it upon me.

This is the way to masticate one's aloes. The soul which tempers itself thus soon grows strong.

BOOK III

THE CONCURRENCE OF THE TWO WILLS
(p. 213)

1. The necessity of concurrence (p. 214).—On the one hand, I know what I must do, and on the other, what God does : on the one hand, passive piety ; and on the other, active piety. Can they be separated ?—By no means ; for, if separated, neither the one nor the other would belong to piety, because they would both be dead. They must be so united as to make a single life.

It is God who, through His good pleasure, worketh in us both to will and to do, says St. Paul. God's action precedes and determines, accompanies and gives the measure of mine. I cannot begin and finish the acts of active piety without the prevenient and sustaining action of God.

2. The nature of the concurrence (p. 217).—In what manner do the meeting and union of these two activities take place ?

God's is the principal one, and mine is secondary ; God's comes first, and mine comes afterwards ; God's governs, and mine submits. And in this manner.

God begins with an act of His good pleasure with regard to me, and I accept it ; this is passive piety. Having accepted it, the divine action enters into me, sets me in motion, and I am thus enlightened, urged, and strengthened for the performance of my duty. I act thus under God's impulse, and this is active piety. Such is their union.

3. The divine alliance (p. 222).—This union is, as it were, the marriage of my will and activity with God's. He first invites me, and I consent ; He enters, and I unite with Him ; next, I act with Him, and from our union arise complete and living acts of Christian piety, which are the offspring of my will united with God's.

At the outset this union is but partial ; my faculties only yield to God slowly, by degrees, one after the other. As the union advances, the divine marriage becomes more fruitful, until entire union takes place in mystical marriage.

4. God's action and man's action (p. 227).—Without this union, my life is unfruitful. For my action, my ideas, impulses, efforts, and all that is mine is mortal, is death. God's action is living and life-giving.

Therefore I must cease to be merely man, and forsake my own thoughts, and all my human determinations and acts ; and all that is myself must lose its *human* designation and character, to take upon itself the name and character of the divine. Thus it is that I shall live, and do living acts.

To allow myself to be led by God to do the duties of my vocation, this is the whole movement of piety.

5. **Divine guidance** (p. 229).—When I unite with God, I am led by Him to see, love, and perform that part of the duties of my state of life which is actually necessary and which is possible in practice. It is God's guidance that determines what is actually needed and gives the measure of what is practically possible. It determines it so aptly and gives the measure of it to such a nicety! How wise is it to allow myself to be led by God!

6. **Human resolutions: their sterility** (p. 233).—Hitherto, why have there been so many sterile resolutons in my career?—They were not born of God, and they did not rely upon Him. Born of self, relying on self, they possessed a twofold weakness which deprived them of life. What a deplorable illusion it is to think one can live without God!

7. **Human resolutions: their folly** (p. 236).—Why do I want, like St. Peter, to remonstrate with the Master who knows so well what I need, whereas I know so little? No, I must not want to anticipate Him, nor must I hang back far behind Him in carelessness; I must follow Him.

8. **Christian resolutions** (p. 238).—How good it is to rely upon God, to take His yoke upon one, and to shoulder His burden! Then it is that resolutions are living, work easy, and labour fruitful. If I could only trust in God, and make a few and fitting resolutions, such as are really necessary and profitable!

9. **The fundamental resolution** (p. 242).—Hence, let there be above all a single primary and governing resolution, from which there will arise, at the proper time, and on which there shall always be based, all particular resolutions that may become necessary according to the progress of the inner life.

This single resolution is that of trusting in God. The resolutions that spring from it will be radically living and will bear fruit. God's action is sufficient both for the present and for the future.

10. **Concurrence restored** (p. 245).—But what if I am not faithful to divine union, and resist God's action?—This is a fault.—How is it to be made good?—Very simply.

My fault immediately entails certain penal consequences. The fault is my own action; the avenging consequences of it are God's action; they are His action which is intended to avenge and repair mine. Thus it is that God shows His detestation of my sin, and works for its reparation.

What then must I do to detest my sin myself, and to make reparation for it?—I have only to accept its avenging consequences; by accepting them, I cause God's vindicatory and reparatory action to enter into me; and thus it is God Himself who detests and repairs my sin within me. This is a truly divine contrition.

In my *human* contrition, I have a strong detestation of the consequences, and rather a feeble detestation of my sin in itself. That is to say, I detest God's action, and continue to be attached to my own. A strange subversion!

PART III

THE MEANS

(p. 249)

Two sorts of means (p. 251).—I know the end, and the way: what more do I want?—The means to walk in this way towards this end.

There are two kinds of means, God's and man's. God's means is His grace: man's means are the practices of penance and the exercises of piety.

In Part I, I saw that for me there were two ends: one essential, which is God's glory; the other secondary, which is my satisfaction. In Part II, that on the way there are two operations that work together; that whereby God acts, and that whereby I act according to the will of God. Here again, I find these two parts: God's means, and my means united with God's.

In all three things, God is the essential, I the secondary; in all three things, God increases and I decrease, until His glory swallows up and transforms my satisfaction, His will swallows up, transforms, and unites with my will; His grace swallows up, transforms, and unites with my exercises. At last, God remains alone, dominant, and ruling; I have no satisfaction apart from His glory, will apart from His will, means apart from His grace: death is swallowed up in victory. This is the work of life.

In Part III, I shall consider: 1. the practices of penance which strip me of the human; 2. the exercises of piety which clothe me with the divine; 3. grace, which is the divine within me.

BOOK I

THE PRACTICES OF PENANCE

(p. 255)

1. Penance (p. 256).—As a sinner, I have to satisfy outraged justice and to undergo a penance. But I may also correspond with saving mercy, and I do this in accepting expiation voluntarily.

My Redeemer came to make expiation for me, and by His expiation to provide me with a means of making reparation for everything. Happy am I, if I am able to unite with His sufferings. I unite therewith by corporal mortification, self-denial of heart, and humility of mind : such are the three main kinds of penance.

2. Mortification and its function (p. 259).—So far as the body is concerned, it is the mission of mortification, as its name indicates, to put to death.—To put what to death ?—Not my members, nor their vigour, which it has to respect and help whenever no higher necessity requires me to sacrifice my health, or members, or life. What it must specially put to death and annihilate is the tyranny of pleasure, which deprives my senses of all outward fitness and inward vigour.

Satan always would urge the killing of the sinner and not of his sin ; God, the Church, and the saints know how to save the sinner and to destroy his sin.

3. General rules for mortification (p. 264).—Mortification must be practised rightly, reasonably, and according to the capacity of the body, the healing of which is to be desired ; therefore, avoiding with equal care the shrinking of the sensitive element as well as the cruelty of practices which are really degrading. Jesus says we must hate our souls if we would save them.

4. Special rules for mortification (p. 268).—There are three kinds of mortifications : official, providential, and voluntary.

I term official the mortifications of duty : first, those which it imposes directly, for there are forbidden pleasures, and penalties imposed by divine laws and human laws : next, those to which it gives rise, for duty is hardly fully carried out without subjection, self-restraint, suffering, loss and other inconveniences, which we must learn to submit to generously. The mortifications of duty are those which are most necessary.

Providential mortifications, which arise from events, until and including death, which is the last event in life, require generous, bold, and glad acceptance. How they liberate the senses which are skilled in yielding to them !

SUMMARY

Lastly, voluntary mortifications, for oneself and others, the favourite food of sacrificial souls, who are docile to divine inspirations and the suggestions of their spiritual directors.

5. The function of self-denial (p. 272).—Its function is to free the soul from the deceitfulness of an independence that keeps one away from God and from affection that attaches one to creatures, and to restore to it the full energy of its vigour and the true zeal of charity. Hence, it has to contain, without compressing or stifling, the power of impulse; and to detach, without breaking, the power of affection. It has to restore to their normal play the spontaneity of energy and the strength of affection—a difficult problem.

6. The practice of self-denial (p. 274).—The deviations of spurious independence are contained by the love of duty, faithfulness to the rule, and by the habit of living according to a fixed scheme of one's own.

Misplaced affection so far as material things are concerned is corrected by the vow of poverty and by alms-giving; so far as persons are concerned, by more or less complete separation from one's family, or by duties of maintenance, kind attention, rendering service, etc.; so far as self is concerned, by failures, vexations, and a host of other things that have to be put up with calmly and cheerfully.

7. The practice of humility (p. 276).—To know that I have nothing of myself, neither existence nor any of the gifts of existence, to be satisfied with everything that teaches and reiterates the lesson of my nothingness; and at the same time, to recognize the gifts God has given me, to deny none of them, the better to use them all; to turn them to good account, not to glorify myself or to get honour or profit by doing so, but to refer all to God, to whom alone are honour and glory,—this is humility.

8. The greatness of humility (p. 279).—If only once all my life were in the grace of God, all my activity in His will, all my being in His glory, I should be fully humble, since I should then have nothing for myself, nothing according to self, nothing by myself; all would be God's, all with God, all in God.

Humility does not consist in having nothing, but in keeping nothing for self. Receiving everything from God and referring everything to God, that is humility. Therefore, the greatest saint is the humblest; and she of all creatures who received the most was necessarily the most humble.

Oh! how good it is to be annihilated for the glory of God, in the will of God, by the grace of God!

BOOK II

EXERCISES OF PIETY
(p. 283)

1. **The purpose of exercises of piety** (p. 285).—Exercises of piety are not piety, which consists in the supreme end, seen, loved, and sought. Nor are they the way, which is the will of God. They are only the means of piety.

They are my means, since it is I who use them. They are means in two ways; first, as channels of grace, next, as instruments for the cultivation and increase within me of the one essential disposition: seeing, loving, and seeking God.

They are means, and the only value they possess is that of being means; and this value is relative and variable according to the state of the soul. An instrument is of no use except for the work to which it is adapted, and so far as it is good for doing it, and while it can be used for it. Thus, I must select only such exercises as are good for my supreme end, and continue to use them while they are profitable, and leave them off when they serve no longer.

2. **Pharisaic regularity** (p. 288).—If I understand this function of devotional exercises, I avoid three mistakes.

The first is pharisaic regularity. He who thinks that an exercise of piety is piety gets attached to the exercise for its own sake; he becomes bound to the mechanical, external, and material side of the exercise, and sees that only; his piety lies in fidelity to the letter. When that fails him, and it often does fail, he fails in everything; a mere external irregularity breaks the whole chain of his piety; and he is constantly upset. If however he hold on, he gets imprisoned in the letter that killeth.

If my piety is inward, if it lies in seeking God, since exercises are only a means, a passing irregularity does not destroy anything, and I ride safely at anchor. I do not fear a gust of wind, and I am not confined to the point of being stifled, in order to escape the storm. I live in God's open air.

3. **Isolation: general effects** (p. 291).—The second mistake is isolation. What a ruinous plan it is to divide up the day into compartments, as cut off from each other as the different drawers in a piece of furniture! One exercise is like one drawer, and another like another. At various times each one is drawn out, then closed, and it is done with. Life is split up, dead, and without any unity; it has neither connexion, nor direction, nor animation.

Each exercise has its own little corner; it is confined to one thing; it neither has any life, nor does it give any. The sap of the exercises ought to circulate throughout the whole structure of the day, otherwise it will dry up from lack of circulation. Later on, I shall see how the examination of my conscience should ensure this circulation.

4. Isolation: particular effects (p. 294).—Isolation is the great source of distractions, because of the want of communication and of unity which it entails between work and prayer. It is the principal destroyer of mental prayer, which, through being partitioned off, ceases to be the heart of the day's exercises.

When shall I be able to work and to pray, to pass from work to prayer and from prayer to work like the saints, and in the manner shown by the Psalms?

5. Inconstancy (p. 298).—The third mistake is inconstancy. When I seek my own satisfaction in spiritual exercises, they are apt to vary according to my whims. I take up one and leave off another, I keep to this and never touch that, I fly from one to another in agitation, as aimlessly and emptily as a wasp.

If I try to get the honey of divine glory and the wax of supernatural profit like a bee, I settle on the sweetest flowers, and only leave them after I have extracted their sweetness.

6. Examination of conscience (p. 302).—Exercises ought to produce unity in the soul. For this, they must be one; and how can they be this, unless *one* exercise bind them all together?

Exercises ought to destroy all self-seeking in me; and how can they do this, if I am self-seeking even in my exercises? Hence, there must be one in which I do not seek self, and which directs all the rest.

Exercises should form within me the vision of God, and how can they do this if there be not one which shows me where God is, where I am myself, and which thus sheds light on all the others?

This *one* exercise, which binds together and directs and throws light upon the rest, what is it?—Examination of conscience, an examination of conscience which is well made.—How is it to be made?—By a glance?—Where?—Directed to the centre of my heart. To discover what?—One thing only, its dominant disposition.—And what is this dominant disposition?—The feeling that sets the heart in motion. For I do nothing unless my heart is urged to do it by some determinant thought or feeling. When I ask anyone: Why do you do that?—He answers: This is the reason. This reason is the thought that makes me act; and this thought is the dominant disposition of his heart at the moment.

Well, it is this disposition, feeling, thought, that examination of conscience has to lay hold of. Why?—Because it is this that sets my heart in motion and determines my conduct. When I have laid hold of it, I know how I stand, and where I am going. If I am going straight, that is to say, to God, all is in order, and I have only to go right on my way. If I am going crooked, that is to say, to my own satisfaction, I correct my intention.

7. **The glance** (p. 307).—But is it easy to lay hold of this feeling, this dominant disposition ?—Very easy ; it only costs a glance. *Where is my heart ?* I look, and I see. I see clearly whether it is going on right or not, and why it is going right or not ; it is quite plain. if I am willing to look with my eyes wide open.

And is this all there is in an examination of conscience ?— Yes : at least all that is essential. As long as that is not done, there is no serious examination of conscience ; when that is done, the examination is all right.

8. **The examination into details** (p. 310).—But what about other thoughts and feelings ? . . . and acts ?—Well, it is like this. . . . Thoughts and feelings which do not dominate are not dangerous. They are only of serious importance when they dominate and direct the heart. But when they reach this point, they in turn must be laid hold of by the glance.

And when, one after the other, I have got hold of the good and bad (for both sorts must be grasped) feelings which set my heart in motion, how deeply I know my soul ! I know all the mainsprings of the mechanism ; and knowing this, it is easy to govern them.

As to acts, the knowledge of their number is only important so far as mortal sins are concerned, in order to confess them ; the knowledge of the rest is only of importance to guide me to a knowledge of my dominant disposition.

Is, then, examination of conscience such an easy thing ?— Nothing can be easier, a simple glance. And I can do it in a moment, and as often as I like.

9. **Contrition and firm purpose** (p. 314).—But what about contrition and firm purpose ?—When one knows how to use it, the glance contains all that. I see, I repent. I correct. It is just like piety, of which it is the eye. Piety is at one and the same time, sight, love, and search ; the glance of self-examination is the same thing ; sight, love, search ; look, contrition, firm purpose.

10. **The different kinds of self-examination** (p. 317).—In the evening, when I cast a glance over the whole of the past day, I prolong and separate the three parts of this one action ; glance, contrition, and firm purpose, and I assign to each enough time to satisfy and enlighten my piety. Such is the general examination of conscience.

In the morning, a glance as to the deeper bearings of my soul, and then my day has its course set aright. This is the preliminary examination.

During the day, a single glance shows my dominant feeling in the light of God ; there you have the particular examen.

Thus, the glance is the vital centre of all kinds of self-examination, at whatever time and in whatever way I may make them.

11. **The unity of the exercises** (p. 321).—This glance is simplicity in itself : no useless and tiresome hunting after details. It is

also efficacy : I get to the very bottom of my soul. It is the guide of my life : for I set straight all my conduct ; all my acts are reached, since I get at their cause. It is the eye of all the exercises : for it prevents them from going astray in self-seeking, and brings them face to face with God. Lastly, it is the unity of my life : by using it in my prayers, in my work, in whatever dealings I undertake, and when I am alone, it makes me see, love, and seek God in all things.

It is the bond of everything, the guide of everything, the light of everything. It is the great instrument of piety.

And what shall I say of the other exercises ?

Those that are instruments meant to form piety will soon be perfected by the glance of self-examination, if I am faithful to it.

There is no need to speak of the importance of those which are channels of grace ; I am about to consider the importance of grace.

BOOK III

GRACE
(p. 327)

1. The nature of grace (p. 328).—Grace is a kind of supernatural outpouring of the virtue of God, which raises me above myself, and fits my being and powers for direct union with God.

It is of two kinds : the one, actual grace, is a momentary help to enlighten the mind, animate the heart, and strengthen one's powers for the performance of duty : the other, habitual grace, is the outpouring of divine Goodness on my soul, which is thereby transformed, purified, sanctified, and made like God and pleasing to Him, and deserving of eternal life.

These two sorts of grace join in the supernatural upbuilding of my life, the one organizing the materials gathered by the other.

2. The source of grace (p. 332).—Jesus Christ's merits are what have purchased for me the grace of action and the grace of union : the grace of action which sets me in motion, and the grace of union which sanctifies me. This grace is to be found in all the instruments of divine action, but it is especially accumulated in the two great reservoirs of prayer and the sacraments.

Further, acts done in a state of grace have power to merit it.

3. The necessity of grace (p. 334).—"Without Me, ye can do nothing," says our Lord : hence, absolute impotence of action.

Neither willing nor doing is of any use, says St. Paul, it is God who worketh in us to will and to do : hence, entire impotence of will.

We are not even sufficient to think anything, says the same Apostle : hence, a radical impotence of knowing.

I can neither understand, nor will, nor act supernaturally : seeing, loving, seeking God, that is to say, piety, is therefore impossible to me by myself.

This life is a divine creation within me ; I am created for the life of piety, just as I am created for natural life : I can no more give myself the one than the other.

My body gets life only from the soul, and my soul gets its life only from God. Just as the soul makes use of the bodily powers for natural life, so does grace make use of the soul's faculties for supernatural life. The principal agent of the natural life is the soul ; of the supernatural life, grace.

Grace, then, must be the vital principle of my thoughts, affections, and actions. Every thought, affection, and action which does not come from grace forms no part of Christian piety.

SUMMARY

Everything I think, love, and do from a purely natural impulse is destitute of the life of piety, and supernaturally dead.

4. My weakness (p. 338).—What are the thoughts and actions to which grace in me gives rise ?—How much is withdrawn from any practical influence of grace ! And hence, how much death !

All my strength, all my life, lies in grace : in myself I am weakness and death. Whenever I rely on self, and reckon on my own strength, I fall. Confidence in self is the secret of my weakness and falling. Confidence in grace is the secret of my strength and life.

5. Remedies for weakness (p. 340).—Let me not be astonished in mind at the fact of my weakness, nor uneasy in heart from its consequences, nor discouraged in action by its results. And therefore, let me rely on God in all simplicity, since His strength will suffice to anticipate or to repair any new falls, and to heal my infirmities.

6. Prayer (p. 343).—It is both a means of drawing near to God and a channel of grace. It is the sovereign, universal, infallible means. Prayer is the soul's breath, which is exhaled in God, and inhales God. This process of divine breathing must always go on unceasingly.

And this function of breathing inevitably inhales the air of grace, because our Lord has undertaken to give this divine air to those who breathe. Why should I wonder if God makes me pray to Him, and pray so much, since thus He obliges me to draw in the air of eternity ?

7. The sacraments (p. 347).—These are great reservoirs and channels, set up by Jesus Christ, to minister to the necessities of my divine life. They are sensible signs which bring down to me and place within my reach sanctifying grace and infused virtues, permanent rights and sacramental graces, and the endlessly renewable treasures of actual grace. What wealth, if I only knew how to have recourse to it !

8. The Blessed Virgin (p. 350).—Being established by the privilege of her immaculate conception in the perfect state of consummated unity, Mary, full of grace, raised to the honour of divine maternity and human maternity, from the first moment of her mortal existence referred everything to the sole glory of her Creator. She only glorified her Lord, and rejoiced only in God her Saviour. What a life, what greatness, and what humility !

And for myself, what a model and what hope ! She has all graces of sanctity to communicate to me, all perfections to teach me. I find in her everything, both an example and strength.

9. Jesus Christ (p. 354).—Jesus Christ is perfect God and perfect man, God and man joined together in one Person. Three things combine to make Jesus Christ : the divine nature, the human nature, and the union of the two.

And these three same things combine to make the Christian, in the proportion and in the conditions which are proper to him, and these three things sum up this whole work. Divine glory, human deliverance, the unity of man in God, such is the foundation of the interior life. O Jesus, grant me to know by every means how to increase in Thee who art the Head of the body whereof I am called to be a member. Make me live on Thee, through Thee, and in Thee. Amen.

10. **General résumé** (p. 358).—To seek the glory of God in the will of God by the glance of self-examination, such is the centre of all my devotional activity. Therein I find the full and living unity of my being, and the sovereign and sole life in God, by God, for God.

Printed in Great Britain
by Amazon.co.uk, Ltd.,
Marston Gate.